PEARSON CUSTOM LIBRARY

ENGLISH
MERCURY READER

ENGL 401
First Year Writing

Custom Edition for
University of New Hampshire

PEARSON

Cover Art: Thomson Hall UNH: Courtesy of University of New Hampshire

Copyright © 2013 by Pearson Learning Solutions

Printed in the United States of America.
V3NL
Please visit our website at *www.pearsonlearningsolutions.com.*

Attention bookstores: For permission to return any unsold stock, contact us at *pe-uscustomreturns@pearson.com.*

Pearson Learning Solutions, 501 Boylston Street, Suite 900, Boston, MA 02116
A Pearson Education Company
www.pearsoned.com

ISBN 10: 1-269-26008-1
ISBN 13: 978-1-269-26008-4

General Editors

Janice Neuleib
Illinois State University

Kathleen Shine Cain
Merrimack College

Stephen Ruffus
Salt Lake Community College

Table of Contents

1. The First Week
Bruce Ballenger
1

2. The Second Week
Bruce Ballenger
29

3. The Third Week
Bruce Ballenger
79

4. The Fourth Week
Bruce Ballenger
121

5. The Fifth Week
Bruce Ballenger
163

6. Writing a Personal Essay
Bruce Ballenger
199

Appendix: Guide to MLA Styles
Bruce Ballenger
241

Appendix: Guide to APA Style
Bruce Ballenger
307

Appendix: Understanding Research Assignments
Bruce Ballenger
351

Handbook
Bruce Ballenger
359

Index
441

The First Week

The Importance of Getting Curious

Despite what they say, curiosity is not dead. You know the obituary: At some point around the age of (fill in the blank), we stop wondering about things. We lose that childlike sense that the world is something to explore. Actually, we never stop being curious, especially if we feel like there's a good reason for it. More than ever, we live in an information-rich environment, and the Internet makes information more accessible than ever before. Say you're having a conversation with a friend about deodorant. "I wonder what the first deodorant was?" asks she. "That's the kind of question that the Internet was made for," says you. And within a minute, you report that the first commercial deodorant was a product called "Mum," invented in the 1880s, though noncommercial deodorants were in use 5000 years ago. This kind of short-term curiosity—sometimes called "situational curiosity"—is incredibly common in this Internet age.

On the other hand, genuine research relies on a sustained interest in something. It can begin with situational curiosity. For example, I once wrote an entire books on lobsters, an interest that was initially triggered by childhood memories of eating them during the holidays with my family and, many years later, reading a newspaper article that reported the lobster catch was down 30 percent and some believed the lobster fishery was on the verge of collapse. I wondered, will lobster go the way of caviar and become too expensive for people like me?

That was the question that triggered my research, and it soon led to more questions. What kept me going was my own curiosity. If your research assignment is going to be successful, you need to get curious, too. If you're bored by your research topic, your paper will almost certainly be boring as well, and you'll end up hating writing research papers as much as ever.

Seeing the World with Wonder

Your curiosity must be the driving force behind your research paper. It's the most essential ingredient. The important thing, then, is this: *Choose your research topic carefully. If you lose interest in it, change your topic to one that does interest you, or find a different angle.*

In most cases, instructors give students great latitude in choosing their research topics. (Some instructors narrow the field, asking students to find a focus within some broad, assigned subject. When the subject has been assigned, it may be harder for you to discover what you are curious about, but it won't be impossible, as you'll see.) Some of the best research topics grow out of your own experience (though they certainly don't have to), as mine did when writing about lobster overfishing. Scholars tell us that a good way to sustain your curiosity in a topic is to find something to research that has some personal relevance. Begin searching for a topic by asking yourself this question: *What have I seen or experienced that raises questions that research can help answer?*

Getting the Pot Boiling

A subject might bubble up immediately. For example, I had a student who was having a terrible time adjusting to her parents' divorce. Janabeth started out wanting to know about the impact of divorce on children and later focused her paper on how divorce affects father-daughter relationships.

Kim remembered spending a rainy week on Cape Cod with her father, wandering through old graveyards, looking for the family's ancestors. She noticed patterns on the stones and wondered what they meant. She found her ancestors as well as a great research topic.

Manuel was a divorced father of two, and both of his sons had recently been diagnosed with attention deficit disorder (ADD). The boys' teachers strongly urged Manuel and his ex-wife to arrange drug therapy for their sons, but they wondered whether there might be any alternatives. Manuel wrote a moving and informative research essay about his gradual acceptance of drug treatment as the best solution for his sons.

For years, Wendy loved J. D. Salinger's work but never had the chance to read some of his short stories. She jumped at the opportunity to spend five weeks reading and thinking about her favorite author. She later decided to focus her research paper on Salinger's notion of the misfit hero.

Accidental topics, ideas that you seem to stumble on when you aren't looking, are often successful topics. My research on Maine lobsters was one of those. Sometimes one topic triggers another. Chris, ambling by Thompson Hall, one of the oldest buildings on his school's campus, wondered about its history. After a little initial digging, he found some 1970s news clips from the student newspaper describing a student strike that paralyzed the school. The controversy fascinated him more than the building did, and he pursued the topic. He wrote a great paper.

If you're still drawing a blank, try the following exercise in your notebook.

EXERCISE 1

Building an Interest Inventory

STEP 1: From time to time I'll hear a student say, "I'm just not interested in *anything* enough to write a paper about it." I don't believe it. Not for a second. The real problem is that the student simply hasn't taken the time to think about everything he knows and everything he might want to know. Try coaxing those things out of your head and onto paper by creating an "interest inventory."

Start with a blank journal page or word processing document. Define three columns per page with the words below:

PLACES, TRENDS, THINGS, TECHNOLOGIES,
PEOPLE, CONTROVERSIES, HISTORY,
JOBS, HABITS, HOBBIES

Under each title, brainstorm a list of words (or phrases) that come to mind when you think about *what you know and what you might want to know* about the category. For example, for TRENDS, you might be aware of the use of magnets for healing sore muscles, or you might know a lot about extreme sports. Put both down on the list. Don't censor yourself. Just write down whatever comes to mind, even if it makes sense only to you. This list is for your use only. You'll probably find that ideas come to you in waves—you'll jot down a few things and then draw a blank. Wait for the next wave to come and ride it. But if you're seriously becalmed, start a new column with a new word from the list above and brainstorm ideas in that category. Do this at least four times with different words. Feel free to return to any column to add new ideas as they come to you, and don't worry about repeated items. Some things simply straddle more than one category. For an idea of what this might look like, see what Amanda, one of my students, did with this exercise (Figure 1).

CONTROVERSIES

Guantanamo Bay
Iraq War
Palestine vs. Israel
Beijing Olympics
Steroids in baseball
Racism/sexism in politics
Gender identity
Homosexual marriage
Death penalty
When is a person created?
Right to euthanasia
Vegetative states
Drinking bottled water
Is organic stuff better?
Does the glass ceiling still exist?
Why are people poor?
Religion in the U.S. government
Sex lives of elected officials
What makes people fat?
Evolution in the school system
Gas vs. ethanol
Sales tax on groceries

TRENDS

Bluetooth headsets
Ipods
Drinking coffee
Crocs shoes
Giant purses
Designer everything
Organic products
Green/eco consciousness
"Some disease" awareness
Celebrity spokespeople
Internet television
Pets as children
Going to prison
Adult-oriented cartoons
Model/actress/singer combo
High-stakes kindergarten
Myspace
Blogs
Cohabiting
White teeth
Specialized TV channels
Hardwood floors
Locavores
Wikipedia
Pink shirts for men
Heated car seats
Splenda
Energy drinks

JOBS

Prison guard
Garbage man
Sewer cleaners
Undertakers
TV anchor
Hotel housekeepers
Rap stars
Child stars
Interior decorators
Manicurists
Tailors
Cobblers
Tour guides

HISTORY

The Holocaust
The Vietnam War
Ancient China
Who built the
   pyramids?
Why did the Aztecs
   die?
When did humans
   leave Africa?
What was President
   Washington like?
The Underground
   Railroad
Feudal Japan
Human sacrifices
Spanish Inquisition
Napoleonic wars
Stonecutter's guilds
Nostradamus
The Gold Rush
Immigrants to the
   U.S. in the 1900s
The Triangle
   Shirtwaist fire
The importance of the
   printing press
Hygiene habits in
   ancient Greece
Gender roles in
   ancient Egypt
Torture chambers
Foot binding
Pre-Christian religions
Canada's freedom from
   Europe

HABITS

Using a toothpick
Fingernail biting
Bouncing a leg
Verbal ticks: "so
   anyway…"
Wringing hands
Eating with mouth open
Chewing gum loudly
Laughing to oneself
Checking locks
Leaving cell phone on
Talking too loud
Nose picking
Hair twirling
Habits vs. superstitions
"God bless you"

FIGURE 1   **Amanda's Interest Inventory**

Allot a total of 20 minutes to do this step: 10 minutes to generate lists in four or more categories, a few minutes to walk away from it and think about something else, and the remaining time to return and add items to any column as they occur to you. (The exercise will also work well if you work on it over several days. You'll be amazed at how much information you can generate.)

STEP 2: Review your lists. Look for a single item in any column that seems promising. Ask yourself these questions: Is this something that raises questions that research can help answer? Are they potentially interesting questions? Does this item get at something I've always wondered about? Might it open doors to knowledge I think is important, fascinating, or relevant to my life?

Circle the item.

STEP 3: For the item you circled, generate a list of questions—as many as you can—that you'd love to explore about the subject. Here's what Amanda did with her topic on teeth whitening:

Are tooth whiteners safe?

What makes teeth turn browner over time?

How has society's definition of a perfect smile changed over time?

Are whiter teeth necessarily healthier than darker teeth?

Is it true that drinking coffee stains your teeth?

How much money is spent on advertising tooth whitening products each year?

What percentage of Americans feels bad about the shade of their teeth?

Do dentists ever recommend that people whiten their teeth?

Is there any way to keep your teeth from getting darker over time?

Can teeth get too white?

Why do I feel bad that my teeth aren't perfect?

Do other cultures have the same emphasis on perfectly white teeth as Americans do?

Are there the same standards for men's teeth and women's teeth?

What judgments do we make about people based simply on the color of their teeth?

How does America's dental hygiene compare with that of other countries? Is the "Austin Powers" myth really true?

The kinds of questions she came up with on her tentative topic seem encouraging. Several already seem "researchable." What about you? Do any of your questions give you a hunger to learn more?

Other Ways to Find a Topic

If you're still stumped about a tentative topic for your paper, consider the following:

■ *Surf the Net.* The Internet is like a crowded fair on the medieval village commons. It's filled with a range of characters—from the carnivalesque to the scholarly—all participating in a democratic exchange of ideas and information. There are promising research topics everywhere.

■ *Search a research database.* Visit your library's Web site and check a database in a subject area that interests you. For example, suppose you're a psychology major and would like to find a topic in the field. Try searching PsycINFO, a popular database of psychology articles. Most databases can be searched by author, subject, keyword, and so on. Think of a general area you're interested in—say, bipolar disorder—and do a subject or keyword search. That will produce a long list of articles, some of which may have abstracts or summaries that will pique your interest. Notice the "related subjects" button? Click that and see a long list of other areas in which you might branch off and find a great topic.

■ *Browse Wikipedia.* While the online "free content" encyclopedia isn't a great source for an academic paper, Wikipedia is a warehouse of potential research topic ideas. Start with the main page, and take a look at the featured or newest articles. You can also browse articles by subject or category.

■ *Consider essays you've already written.* Could the topics of any of these essays be further developed as research topics? For example, Diane wrote a personal essay about how she found the funeral of a classmate alienating—especially the wake. Her essay asked what purpose such a ritual could serve—a question, she decided, that would best be answered by research. Other students wrote essays on topics like the difficulty of living with a depressed brother and an alcoholic parent, which yielded wonderful research papers. A class assignment to read Ken Kesey's *One Flew Over the Cuckoo's Nest* inspired Li to research the author.

■ *Pay attention to what you've read recently.* What newspaper articles have sparked your curiosity and raised interesting questions? Rob, a hunter, encountered an article that reported the number of hunters was steadily declining in the United States. He wondered why. Karen read an account of a particularly violent professional hockey game. She decided to research the Boston Bruins, a team with a history of violent play, and examine how violence has affected the sport. Don't limit yourself to the newspaper. What else have you read recently—perhaps magazines or books—or seen on TV that has made you wonder?

■ *Consider practical topics.* Perhaps some questions about your career choice might lead to a promising topic. Maybe you're thinking about teaching but wonder about current trends in teachers' salaries. One student, Anthony, was being recruited by a college to play basketball and researched the tactics coaches use to lure players. What he learned helped prepare him to make a good choice.

■ *Think about issues, ideas, or materials you've encountered in other classes.* Have you come across anything that intrigued you, that you'd like to learn more about?

■ *Look close to home.* An interesting research topic may be right under your nose. Does your hometown (or your campus community) suffer from a particular problem or have an intriguing history that would be worth exploring? Jackson, tired of dragging himself from his dorm room at 3:00 A.M. for fire alarms that always proved false, researched the readiness of the local fire department to respond to such calls. Ellen, whose grandfather worked in the aging woolen mills in her hometown, researched a crippling strike that took place there 60 years ago. Her grandfather was an obvious source for an interview.

■ *Collaborate.* Work together in groups to come up with interesting topics. Try this idea with your instructor's help: Organize the class into small groups of five. Give each group ten minutes to come up with specific questions about one general subject—for example, American families, recreation, media, race or gender, health, food, history of the local area, environment of the local area, education, and so forth. Post these questions on newsprint as each group comes up with them. Then rotate the groups so that each has a shot at generating questions for every subject. At the end of 40 minutes, the class will have generated perhaps 100 questions, some uninspired and some really interesting.

What Is a Good Topic?

A few minutes browsing the Internet convinces most of my students that the universe of good research topics is pretty limited: global warming, abortion rights, legalization of pot, same-sex marriage, and the like. These are usually the topics of the papers you can buy with your Visa card at sites like freeessays.com (yeah, right). These are also often topics with the potential to bore both reader and writer to death because they inspire essays that are so predictable.

But beginning with a good question, rather than a preconceived answer, changes everything. Suddenly subjects are everywhere: What is with our cultural obsession about good teeth? Is it true that lawnmowers are among the most polluting engines around? What's the deal with the devastation of banana crops, and how will that affect prices at Albertson's down the street? Are "green" automobiles really green? Even the old tired topics get new life when you find the right question to ask. For example, what impact will the availability of medical marijuana vending machines in California have on the legal debate in that state?

What's a good topic? Initially, it's all about finding the right question and especially one that you are really interested in (see box below). Later, the challenge will be limiting the number of questions your paper tries to answer. For now, look for a topic that makes you at least a little hungry to learn more.

Where's Waldo and the Organizing Power of Questions

For a long time, I thought school writing assignments were exclusively exercises in deduction. You start by coming up with

What Makes a Question "Researchable"?

- It's not too big or too small.
- It focuses on some aspect of a topic about which something has been said.
- It interests the researcher.
- Some people have a stake in the answer. It has something to do with how we live or might live, what we care about, or what might be important for people to know.
- It implies an approach or various means of answering it.
- It raises more questions. The answer might not be simple.

a thesis and then try to find examples to support it. This kind of writing starts with an idea and supports it with evidence, moving from the general to the specific. There's nothing wrong with this. In a lot of writing situations—say, the essay exam or SAT writing test—this approach makes a great deal of sense. But much academic research, at least initially, works inductively. You look for patterns in information that raise interesting questions, and it is these questions that redirect the researchers' gaze back to the information, this time more selectively and purposefully.

In other words, you start with a lot of data, form a question or hypothesis about the patterns in what you see, and then return to the data again, this time focusing on what is relevant. In this way, you get control of the information by looking at less of it.

The visual puzzles in the *Where's Waldo?* series of children's books is a great example of the power of good questions to manage information. As you know, Waldo, with his red-and-white-striped stocking cap and jersey, is hidden in a picture among hundreds of other people, many of whom look a lot like him. The challenge, quite simply, is to find Waldo in all of this data. Imagine, though, if the game didn't ask "Where's Waldo?" but "Where are the men?" or "Where are the women?" in the picture. Suddenly, much more information is relevant and the search isn't nearly as focused. A better question might be, "Where are the people wearing yellow?" That eliminates some of the data but still leaves a lot to work with. Obviously, "Where's Waldo?" is the best question because you know what you're looking for and what you can ignore.

Similarly, a good inquiry question will focus your investigation of any topic. Starting with an answer—a thesis or main point—before you do any research is efficient; it sets you on a steady march to a destination you already know. But beginning with questions, while sometimes a messier process, is a much more powerful way to see what you don't expect to see. Try the following exercise, and you'll see what I mean.

EXERCISE 2

The Myth of the Boring Topic

This exercise requires in-class collaboration. Your instructor will organize you into four or five small groups and give each group a commonplace object; it might be something as simple as a nail, an orange, a pencil, a can of dog food, or a piece of plywood. Whatever the object, it will not strike you as particularly interesting—at least not at first.

STEP 1: Each group's first task is to brainstorm a list of potentially interesting questions about its commonplace object. Choose a recorder who will post the questions as you think of them on a large piece of newsprint taped to the wall. Inevitably, some of these questions will be pretty goofy ("Is it true that no word rhymes with orange?"), but work toward questions that might address the *history* of the object, its *uses,* its possible *impact on people,* or *the processes* that led to its creation in the form in which you now see it.

STEP 2: After 20 minutes, each group will shift to the adjacent group's newsprint and study the object that inspired that group's questions. Spend 5 minutes thinking up more interesting questions about the object that didn't occur to the group before you. Add these to the list on the wall.

STEP 3: Stay where you are or return to your group's original object and questions. Review the list of questions, and choose *one* you find both interesting and most "researchable" (see the box "What Makes a Question 'Researchable'?"). In other words, if you were an editorial team assigned to propose a researched article for a general interest magazine that focuses on this object, what might be the starting question for the investigation? The most interesting question and the most researchable question may or may not be the same.

In Idaho where I live, there are stones called geodes. These are remarkably plain-looking rocks on the outside, but with the rap of a hammer they easily break open to reveal glittering crystals in white and purple hues. The most commonplace subjects and objects are easy to ignore because we suspect there is nothing new to see or know about them. Sometimes it takes the sharp rap of a really good question to crack open even the most familiar subjects, and then suddenly we see that subject in a new light. What I'm saying is this: A good question is the tool that makes the world yield to wonder, and knowing this is the key to being a curious researcher. Any research topic—even if the instructor assigns it—can glitter for you if you discover the questions that make you wonder.

Making the Most of an Assigned Topic

Frequently, you'll be encouraged to choose your own topic for a research essay. But if your instructor either assigns a topic or asks you to choose one within a limited subject, there's still hope. Exercise 2, "The Myth of the Boring Topic," suggests that writers can write about nearly any topic—assigned or not—if they can discover good questions. But if all else fails, examine your assigned topic through the following "lenses." One might give you a view of your topic that seems interesting.

■ *People.* Who has been influential in shaping the ideas in your topic area? Is there anyone who has views that are particularly intriguing to you? Could you profile that person and her contributions?

■ *Trends.* What are the recent developments in this topic? Are any significant? Why?

■ *Controversies.* What do experts in the field argue about? What aspect of the topic seems to generate the most heat? Which is most interesting to you? Why?

■ *Places.* Can you ground a larger topic in the particulars of a specific location that is impacted by the issue? For example, controversies over wolf management in the West can find a focus in how the debate plays out in Challis, Idaho, where some of the stakeholders live.

■ *Impact.* What about your topic currently has the most effect on the most people? What may have the most effect in the future? How? Why?

■ *Relationships.* Can you put one thing in relationship to another? If the required subject is Renaissance art, might you ask, "What is the relationship between Renaissance art and the plague?"

Admittedly, it is harder to make an assigned topic your own. But you can still get curious if you approach the topic openly, willing to see the possibilities by finding the questions that bring it to life for you.

Developing a Working Knowledge

If you have a tentative topic that makes you curious, then you're ready to do some preliminary research. At this stage in the process, it's fine to change your mind. As you begin to gently probe your subject, you may discover that there's another topic that interests you more—or perhaps there's a question that hadn't occurred to you. One of the advantages of developing a "working knowledge" of your topic at this stage is that these other possibilities may present themselves.

What's a working knowledge? William Badke, in his great book *Research Strategies*, calls a "working knowledge" of a topic the ability "to talk about it for one minute without repeating yourself." The advantage of developing a working knowledge of your tentative topic at this point is that it will help you find a focus. Aside from giving you something new to talk about when conversation lags at Thanksgiving dinner, a working knowledge helps you to see what *part* of the landscape of your topic you might want to venture into. Here's an example:

Case Study on Developing Working Knowledge: Theories of Dog Training

A few years ago, we took our lab puppy, Stella, to eight weeks of dog training. We thought things went well: She learned a "down stay," she would come when we called, and she wouldn't pull on her leash. Recently, we took our new golden retriever, Ada, to a different trainer and the first thing he said is that the method we used with Stella "simply wouldn't work" with Ada. It was clear that he disapproved of our first trainer's approach. "I don't know how she stays in business," he said. The experience confirmed the feeling I already had that despite advances in the study of animal behavior, there is little agreement on the best way to make Fido sit on command. Dog trainers are a particularly contentious lot.

If I develop a working knowledge on theories of dog training, what might I discover?

1. *Definitions.* I quickly discover that there are competing definitions about things I thought were settled. What, for example, is a "well-behaved" dog? What do trainers mean when they use the term "correction"? What's the difference between "operant" and "classical" conditioning?
2. *Debates.* After just ten minutes of searching online it's obvious that there are fundamental disagreements among dog trainers on a whole range of issues. Should you reward dogs with food or simply with praise? Should disobedient dogs be punished with pain—say, a yank on a prong collar or a jolt from a shock collar—or with removing something they want—a treat or a ball? Should theories of dog training be based on the behavior of wild canines like wolves or based on the belief that there are fundamental differences between them?

3. *People.* It doesn't take much searching on this subject to begin to recognize certain experts or advocates whose names come up again and again in the debates. There is, for example, the "Dog Whisperer" on cable TV, Cesar Milan, who applies some of the principles of the wolf pack to dog training. Then there are behaviorists like Patricia McConnell and Victoria Stilwell, who advocate positive reinforcement.
4. *Contexts.* Before long, I realize that you can understand dog training in more than just the context of debates among trainers. This is a topic that leashes together a whole range of disciplines: animal behavior, social psychology, wildlife biology, and anthropology.

Research Strategies for Developing Working Knowledge

There are many ways to develop a working knowledge of your topic, but generally the research strategy is like many others: Work from more general information to more specialized information. Try these steps:

1. *Begin with a Google search.* Enter as many search terms as you can at one time to narrow the results, with the most important terms first. Save the relevant results.
2. *Search general and subject encyclopedias.* I know that Wikipedia is the first thing that comes to mind, but there are other, better encyclopedias. You'll find bound versions of the venerable *Encyclopaedia Britannica* in your library; your library might also provide free online access. There are online encyclopedias galore, including the *Columbia Encyclopedia* and *Encyclopedia. com.* Subject encyclopedias are more focused references, and they are sadly underused by students. There are subject encyclopedias on hundreds of subjects: art history, war, African American literature, nutrition—you name it. (My favorite is the *Encyclopedia of Hell.*) You can find these online at your university library as well as at the Internet Public Library (http://www.ipl.org).
3. *Use the Internet Public Library.* The merger of the Internet Public Library and Librarians' Internet Index created a super site that is a boon to online researchers. This is currently the most successful effort on the Web to bring some order to the chaos that is the Internet. Here you will find specialized encyclopedias, a search portal for finding more reliable sources on your topic, and even special collections.

SUBJECT ENCYCLOPEDIAS

HUMANITIES	SOCIAL SCIENCES
Dictionary of Art	*African-American Encyclopedia*
International Dictionary	*Dictionary of Psychology*
of Films and Filmmakers	*Encyclopedia of Marriage*
Encyclopedia of World Art	*and the Family*
Encyclopedia of Religion	*Encyclopedia of Psychology*
Encyclopedia of Philosophy	*The Blackwell Encyclopedia*
Encyclopedia of African American	*of Social Psychology*
Culture and History	*Encyclopedia of Educational*
Encyclopedia of America	*Research*
Encyclopedia of Sociology	*Encyclopedia of Social Work*
Social History	*Encyclopedia of World Cultures*
	Encyclopedia of the Third World
	Encyclopedia of Democracy
	Guide to American Law:
	Everyone's Legal Encyclopedia

SCIENCE	OTHER
Dictionary of the History	*Encyclopedia of the Modern*
of Science	*Islamic World*
Dictionary of the History	*The Baseball Encyclopedia*
of Medicine	*Encyclopedia of Women*
Encyclopedia of the Environment	*and Sports*
Concise Encyclopedia of Biology	*Encyclopedia of World Sport*
Encyclopedia of Bioethics	*The World Encyclopedia*
Encyclopedia of Science	*of Soccer*
and Technology	*Worldmark Encyclopedia*
Macmillan Encyclopedias	*of the Nations*
of Chemistry and Physics	
Food and Nutrition Encyclopedia	

4. *Try Google Scholar.* Regular Google searches will turn up all kinds of results—mostly commercial sites—but Google Scholar will get you the kind of information that you know you can count on as reliable and authoritative—journal articles and scholarly books. These publications are often "peer-reviewed," so everything that sees print, online or off, passes academic muster.

5. *Start building a bibliography.* Finally, conclude your working knowledge search by collecting the basic bibliographic information on the most useful sources you found. A convenient way to do this is to use a "citation machine," a Web-based program that

automatically prompts you for the bibliographic information and then magically turns it into citations in whatever citation format you want. Don't trust one of these to generate references for your final essay—they can make mistakes—but they're great as a preliminary method for collecting a list of citations. Visit Citation Machine (http://citationmachine.net), bibme (http://www.bibme.org), or another site and enter information about your best sources, choosing APA or MLA format.

Using Zotero to Manage Your Research

It's not hard to quickly accumulate quite a few helpful search results. You can organize these, of course, by using the bookmarking feature in your browser, downloading files to a folder on your computer, or printing them out. But if you use the Firefox browser (available free), consider Zotero as a tool to manage your online research.

Zotero (http://www.zotero.org) is a free application developed by researchers at George Mason University that is integrated into Firefox, and it can save and organize all kinds of Web resources in folders you create that are accessible wherever you have an Internet connection. The program can actually "sense" what kind of online document or image you're looking at and organize the citation information automatically. Not only that: Zotero offers a Word (or Open Office) plug-in that will allow you—while you're writing your paper—to automatically build a bibliography in the right format whenever you cite a source in your text.

Once installed, Zotero will appear as an icon on your browser. Click on it, and your Zotero library will open at the bottom of the browser page. You'll see three columns (see Figure 2). On the left will be your library of saved research materials. The middle column will be the open document on your browser, and the right column will be citation information.

The Reference Librarian: A Living Source

There are compelling reasons to visit the library, even at this early stage in your research. First and foremost is that the reference desk is where reference librarians hang out, and these are people you should get to know. They can save you time by guiding you to the very best sources on your topic, and they often give great advice on how to narrow your research question. Reference specialists are invaluable to college researchers; without a doubt, they're the most important resource in the library.

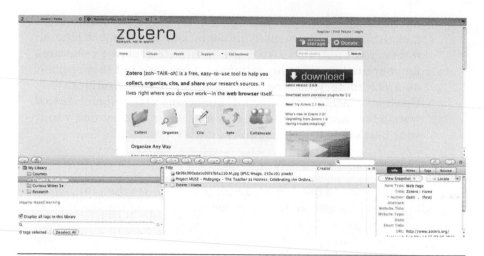

FIGURE 2   Zotero

Narrowing the Subject

It never occurred to me that photography and writing had anything in common until I found myself wandering around a lonely beach one March afternoon with a camera around my neck. I had a fresh roll of film (it was that long ago) and, full of ambition, I set out to take beautiful pictures. Three hours later, I had taken only three shots, and I was definitely not having fun. Before quitting in disgust, I spent 20 minutes trying to take a single picture of a lighthouse. I stood there, feet planted in the sand, repeatedly bringing the camera to my face; but each time I looked through the viewfinder, I saw a picture I was sure I'd seen before, immortalized on a postcard in the gift shop down the road. Suddenly, photography lost its appeal.

A few months later, a student sat in my office complaining that he didn't have anything to write about. "I thought about writing an essay on what it was like going home for the first time last weekend," he said. "But I thought that everyone probably writes about that in freshman English." I looked at him and thought about lighthouse pictures.

Circling the Lighthouse

Almost every subject you will choose to write about for this class and for this research paper has been written about before. The challenge is not to find a unique topic (save that for your doctoral dissertation) but to find an angle on a familiar topic that helps readers to see what they probably haven't noticed before. For example, once in a research essay titled "The Bothersome Beauty of Pigeons," I wrote about the most common of subjects—the urban pigeon—and took a close look at its habits and behaviors, finding in them an explanation for my conflicted feelings about "pests" that are inconveniently attractive.

I now know that it was a mistake to give up on the lighthouse. The problem with my lighthouse picture, as well as with my student's proposed essay on going home, was not the subject. It was that neither of us had yet found our own angle. I needed to keep looking, walking around the lighthouse, taking lots of shots until I found one that surprised me, that helped me see the lighthouse in a new way, in *my* way. Instead, I stayed put, stuck on the long shot and the belief that I couldn't do better than a postcard photograph.

It is generally true that when we first look at something, we mostly see its obvious features. That became apparent when I asked my freshman English class one year to go out and take pictures of anything they wanted. Several students came back with single photographs of Thompson Hall, a beautiful brick building on campus. Coincidentally, all were taken from the same angle and distance—straight on and across the street—which is the same shot that appears in the college recruiting catalog. For the next assignment, I asked my students to take multiple shots of a single subject, varying angle and distance. Several students went back to Thompson Hall and discovered a building they'd never seen before, though they walked by it every day. Students took abstract shots of the pattern of brickwork, unsettling shots of the clock tower looming above, and arresting shots of wrought iron fire escapes, clinging in a tangle to the wall.

The closer students got to their subjects, the more they began to see what they had never noticed before. The same is true in writing. As you move in for a closer look at some aspect of a larger subject, you will begin to uncover information that you—and ultimately your readers—are likely to find less familiar and more interesting. One writing phrase for this is *narrowing your subject*. (The photographic equivalent would be *varying distance from the subject*.)

From Landscape Shots to Close-ups

The research reports many of us wrote in high school typically mimicked landscape photography. We tried to cram into one picture as much information as we could. A research report is a long shot. The college research essay is much more of a close-up, which calls for narrowing the boundaries of a topic as much as you can, always working for a more detailed look at some smaller part of the landscape.

You are probably not a photographer, and finding a narrow focus and fresh angle on your research topic is not nearly as simple as it might be if this were a photography exercise. But the idea is the same. You need to see your topic in as many ways as you can, hunting for the angle that most interests you; then go in for a closer look. One way to find your *focus* is to find your *questions*.

Other Ways to Narrow Your Subject

1. **Time.** Limit the time frame of your project. Instead of researching the entire Civil War, limit your search to the month or year when the most decisive battles occurred.
2. **Place.** Anchor a larger subject to a particular location. Instead of exploring "senioritis" at American high schools, research the phenomenon at the local high school.
3. **Person.** Use the particulars of a person to reveal generalities about the group. Instead of writing about the homeless problem, write about a homeless man.
4. **Story.** Ground a larger story in the specifics of a "smaller" one. Don't write about dream interpretation, write about a dream *you* had and use the theories to analyze it.

EXERCISE 3

Finding the Questions

Although you can do this exercise on your own, your instructor will likely ask that you do it in class this week. That way, students can help one another. (If you do try this on your own, only do Steps 3 and 4 in your research notebook.)

STEP 1: Post a large piece of paper or newsprint on the wall. (In a classroom with computers you can do this exercise in an open Word document.) At the very top of the paper, write the title of your tentative topic (e.g., "Plastics in the Ocean").

STEP 2: Take a few minutes to briefly describe why you chose the topic.

STEP 3: Spend five minutes or so briefly listing what you know about your topic already. This is information you harvested this week from your effort to develop working knowledge on your proposed topic. You might list any surprising facts or statistics, the extent of the problem, important people or institutions involved, key schools of thought, common misconceptions, observations you've made, important trends, major controversies, and so on.

STEP 4: Now spend 15 or 20 minutes brainstorming a list of questions *about your topic* that you'd like to answer through your research. Make this list as long as you can; try to see your topic in as many ways as possible. Push yourself on this; it's the most important step.

STEP 5: As you look around the room, you'll see a gallery of topics and questions on the walls. At this point in the research process, almost everyone will be struggling to find a focus. You can help one another. Move around the room, reviewing the topics and questions other students have generated. For each topic posted on the wall, do two things: Add a question *you* would like answered about that topic that's not on the list, and check the *one* question on the list you find most interesting. (It may or may not be the one you added.)

If you do this exercise in class, note the question about your topic that garnered the most interest. This may not be the one that interests you the most, and you may choose to ignore it altogether. But it is helpful to get some idea of what typical readers might want most to know about your topic.

You also might be surprised by the rich variety of topics other students have tentatively chosen for their research projects. The last time I did this exercise, I had students propose papers on controversial issues such as the use of dolphins in warfare, homelessness, the controversy over abolishment of fraternities, legalization of marijuana, and censorship of music. Other students proposed somewhat more personal issues, such as growing up with an alcoholic father, date rape, women in abusive relationships, and the effects of divorce on children. Still other students wanted to learn about historical subjects, including the role of Emperor Hirohito in World War II, the student movement in the 1960s, and the Lizzie Borden murder case. A few students chose topics that were local. For example, one student recently researched the plight of nineteenth-century

Chinese miners digging for gold in the mountains just outside of Boise. Another did an investigation of skateboard culture in town, a project that involved field observation, interviews, as well as library research.

Crafting Your Opening Inquiry Question

What do you do with the gazillion questions you've generated on your research topic? Throw most of them away. But not yet! If you look carefully at the list of questions you (and your peers) generated in Exercise 3, you will likely see patterns. Some of your questions will clump together in more general categories. Perhaps a group of questions is related to the history of your topic, trends, processes, local relevance, and so on. Look for these patterns, and especially questions that might be combined or that inspire new questions.

Your work this week will culminate in the crafting of a tentative inquiry question that will guide your research and writing. This question will constantly evolve as you learn more; but for now, create the one question around which you will launch your project. Among the most common types of inquiry questions are sense-making questions, hypothesis-testing questions, and relationship-analyzing questions (see Table 1). Don't worry too much about the distinctions between question types; for one thing, they overlap quite a bit. But these categories should help you see some of the kinds of questions you might ask about your topic.

As the name implies, *sense-making questions* arise when we are searching for an explanation (think CSI or Sherlock Holmes). Why

TABLE 1 Types of Inquiry Questions

Sense-Making	Hypothesis-Testing	Relationship-Analyzing
Why might this be true or not true?	Is this evidence for or against the idea of _____?	What is the relationship between _____ and _____?
What might explain _____?	Is my assumption about _____ true?	Does _____ cause _____?
	Is it true that _____?	Is _____ similar to _____?

does one dog trainer see "correction" in a way that conflicts with the way another dog trainer sees it?

Frequently, we have hunches about what might be true. *Hypothesis-testing questions* test these assumptions. These are ideas that often emerge when we ask a bunch of sense-making questions; for instance, some preliminary research on the conflicts between dog trainers on the issue of correction suggests that the debate is related to assumptions about whether domestic dogs respond like wild canines—wolves, coyotes, and the like. A hypothesis-testing question might be something like this: Is it true that the often-bitter debates between dog trainers about the best approach to correction is based on assumptions about the links between wild dogs and domestic ones?

Finally, *relationship-analyzing questions* are among the most common types of inquiry questions. Most questions researchers explore have to do with trying to figure out whether one thing causes another thing or whether one thing is like or unlike something else. For example, does painful correction destroy the bond between a dog and its owner?

EXERCISE 4

Finding the Inquiry Question

Review the questions you or your class generated in Exercise 3, steps 4 and 5, and ask yourself, Which questions on the list am I most interested in that could be the focus of my paper? Remember, you're not committing yourself yet.

Using one or more of the templates suggested in Table 1, craft several research questions that seem to capture what most interests you in the topic. For example,

- What might explain the rise of recruiting violations in the NCAA?
- What is the connection between having anorexia and the anorexic's relationship with her father?
- Is it true that the major climate change denial organizations are funded by special interests that oppose cap-and-trade legislation?
- Is risk-based behavior in extreme sports caused by a certain personality type?

Methods for Focusing Your Paper: An Example

A clear, narrow research question is the one thing that will give you the most traction when trying to get your research project moving. It's also one of the hardest steps in the process. Like gulping air after a dive into the deep end of a pool, our natural instinct at the beginning of a research project is to inhale too much of our subject. We go after the big question— why is poverty a problem?—and quickly wonder why we are submerged in information, struggling to find a direction. That's why I've spent so much time on a range of methods to craft a workable research question.

Here's an example of how one student used some of these approaches to satisfy both her general curiosity about the origins of terrorism and her need to write an essay about it that would be interesting, specific, and manageable over a five-week period. Helen used the *time, person, place*, and *story* methods as a means of refining her research question (see "Other Ways to Narrow Your Subject"). Any one of these questions would be a good starting place for her inquiry into terrorism.

Topic: Terrorism

Opening Question—What is the cause of terrorism by Islamic extremists?

1. *Time as a Focusing Device—What might be the historical roots of Islamic extremism during the first jihad in the seventh century?*

2. *Person as a Focusing Device—Did President Jimmy Carter's policies in the Middle East contribute to the radicalization of some Islamic groups?*

3. *Place as a Focusing Device—Have Islamic religious schools in Pakistan contributed to the extremist thought and the radicalization of Muslim activists?*

4. *Story as a Focusing Device—What might the story of Shehzad Tanweer, one of the men who allegedly participated in the 2005 London bombings, reveal about how young men are radicalized?*

Possible Purposes for a Research Assignment

If you have a decent research question, you're off and running. But your next step should be to pause, look at your question, and think a bit about which of the following purposes are implied by the question you chose. Each of these purposes will profoundly influence the way you read your sources and how you approach writing the first draft. While any essay can use more than one purpose, which would you say is your *main* motive in writing your paper—at least at this moment?

1. *To explore.* You pose the question *because* you're unsure of the answer. This is what draws you to the topic. You're most interested in writing an essay, not a paper; that is, you want to write about what you found out in your research and what you've come to believe is the best or truest answer to the question you pose. Your essay will have a thesis, but it will probably surface toward the end of the paper rather than at the beginning. This is what I would call a *research essay* rather than a research paper, and it's the most open-ended form for academic inquiry. Exploratory essays often begin with sense-making or relationship-analyzing questions.

2. *To argue.* You know you have a lot to learn about your topic, but you have a very strong hunch about what the answer to your research question might be. In other words, you have a hypothesis you want to test by looking at the evidence. Inspired by a hypothesis question ("Is it true that…?"), you report on your investigation. However, you may quickly move from a hunch to a conviction; and then you move immediately into arguing your claim, trying to influence what your readers think and even how they behave. Your thesis is a statement—for example, *Muslim religious schools in Pakistan are not to blame for Islamic extremism*—that you can probably roughly articulate at the beginning of your project. It may very well change as you learn more, but when you write your paper, your purpose is to state a central claim and make it convincing. Frequently, that claim is stated near the beginning of the paper.

EXERCISE 5

Research Proposal

This is an important moment in the research process. How well you've crafted your research question will significantly influence the success of your project. You can change your mind later, but for now, jot down a brief proposal that outlines your research plan in your research notebook or to turn in to your instructor. It should include the following:

1. Inquiry question
2. Primary purpose
   - *Explore:* What are additional questions that most interest you and might help you discover the answers to your research question?
   - *Argue:* What theory or hypothesis about your topic are you testing? What is your tentative main claim or thesis?
3. What, if any, prior beliefs, assumptions, preconceptions, ideas, or prejudices do you bring to this project? What personal experiences may have shaped the way you feel? Before you began developing working knowledge on the topic, what were you thinking about it? What are you thinking about it now?

Reading for Research

For this assignment, and many others in your other college classes, you will have to read things that you find difficult. Maybe they seem really boring or full or jargon or hard to follow, or perhaps they seem to be all of those things. Aside from procrastinating, how do you deal with that?

Researchers who study reading say that the best readers are guided by a strong sense of purpose—they know why they are reading something and what they hope to get from it. They also have some knowledge of the *type* of text they're reading. They know where to look for what they need to know. More than anything, though, the strongest readers are those who already have some prior knowledge about the subject. Yet even in situations where you have little prior knowledge of the subject you're reading about, you can still read effectively if you read "rhetorically."

Reading Rhetorically

We all learned to read in school, but we probably never really learned how to read *rhetorically*. Reading rhetorically means selecting particular reading strategies that are most effective in certain situations and for certain purposes and applying them. Actually, you already do this with some texts you encounter every day. For example, there's this:

> u stupid girl, why ru upset & worried? i'm not in a mood or stressed so u shouldn't be + def don't b scared of me-i'm a softy! cu in a bit x

Of course you recognize this kind of text as a familiar genre—the text message—and though you didn't write the message or receive it, you know how to read it. You know the language. You know the social situations that give rise to this kind of message. And you know the writer's purpose.

The sentence that follows is from the first line of a scholarly article titled "The Architecture of the Personal Interactive Homepage: Constructing the Self Through MySpace."

> Structural symbolic interactionism understands the creation of self and identity to occur within existing social structures (Burke, 1980, 2004; Burke and Reitzes, 1981; Burke and Tully, 1977; Cast, 2003; Goffman, 1959; Stets and Burke, 2005; Stryker, 1980).

How are you to read something like this with its unfamiliar references to things like "structural symbolic interactionism" and the list of unfamiliar names in the citation? It's likely that your usual reading strategies will fail you here.

In high school, much of the writing about reading you may have done was in English class, writing critical essays about novels, poems, or short stories. In many ways, reading to write about a novel or a short story is quite different from reading to write research essays. For one thing, there are very basic differences between a literary text and a research article. In a short story, the author's purpose may be *implicit*; you have to "read into" the evidence provided in a narrative to make some interpretation about its meaning. An academic article, on the other hand, is *explicit*. The author states his or her conclusions rather than inviting the reader to make a reasoned interpretation. In addition, academic writing, like the previous example, uses specialized language and conventions—terms, references, evidence, and organizing principles that the people for whom the article was intended (usually other experts in the field) can understand. Stories have their own internal logic and language, but these are usually accessible to most readers even if the meaning is not.

Finally, we usually enjoy the *experience* of reading a story, or at least feel something in response to a good one, but we usually read articles with a much more practical purpose in mind: to acquire information.

Shouldn't the fundamental differences between these types of texts mean that the *way* we read them is also different? I think so. But we rarely think about our reading strategies, pretty much resorting to reading the way we always have in school. Maybe you never highlight, or maybe the pages you've read are fields plowed with yellow rows. Maybe you make marginal notes when you read, or maybe you never write a thing. Maybe you always read everything just once, or maybe you read a text many times to make sure you understand it. Maybe you always read every word, or maybe you skim like a flat rock on smooth water. Whatever your reading practices, becoming aware of them is a first step to reading strategically.

Reading Like an Outsider

Why spend precious time thinking about your reading process? For the same reason this course focuses on the writing process: By becoming aware of *how* you do things that have become habits, you exercise more control over them. In many ways, this book is about challenging old habits and assumptions about research, and this includes approaches to reading when you have to write a research essay. For example, consider what's unique about this situation:

■ In a general sense, you're just reading to collect information. But researchers use what they read in some particular ways: to provide support for their ideas, to create a context for the questions they're asking, and to complicate or extend their thinking.

■ College research often requires students to read the specialized discourses of fields with which they're not familiar. That means they must struggle with jargon and conventions that make reading particularly difficult.

■ Typically, the purpose of the research paper is not to report but to explore or argue. Information is in the service of the writer's own ideas about a topic.

■ In some classes (though probably not this one), the main audience for the research essay is an expert in the subject the writer is exploring.

In a way, the student researcher has to read like an outsider—or, as essayist Scott Russell Sanders put it, "an amateur's raid in a world of specialists." What does this suggest about your reading strategy? First, it makes sense to develop a working knowledge of your topic *before* you tackle the more scholarly stuff. As I noted earlier, research in reading suggests that knowledge of a subject makes a big difference in comprehension and retention of information. Second, your own purposes should firmly guide what you read and how you read it. Mentally juggle at least the three purposes I mentioned earlier—reading for example, for context, and for challenge. Third, anticipate your own resistance to the scholarly writing that seems "boring." It's boring because you're an outsider and haven't broken the code. The more you read in your subject area, the more you'll understand; the learning curve is steep. Fourth, in scholarly writing especially, quickly learn the organizing principles of the articles. For example, in the social sciences, articles often have *abstracts, introductions, methods*, and *discussion* sections. Each provides particular kinds of information that might be useful to you. It often isn't necessary to read an academic article from beginning to end. And, finally, the most important thing: Read with a pen in your hand. Write-to-learn activities such as fastwriting can help you take possession of information and help you write a stronger paper.

Reading Strategies for Research Writers

- First develop a working knowledge.
- Let your own purposes guide: example, context, challenge.
- Anticipate your own resistance.
- Learn the organizing principles of articles.
- Read with a pen in your hand.

The Second Week

Developing a Research Strategy

A few years ago, I wanted a pair of good birding binoculars for my birthday. I thought of the local store that seemed to carry the largest selection of binoculars and went there; within 20 minutes or so I had spent about $300 on some Swift binoculars, a brand that is highly regarded by wildlife watchers. Did you ever notice that is often *after* your purchase when you're most motivated to seek out information that reinforces your decision to buy something? Within days of buying the Swifts, I searched the Internet just to make certain that the model I bought was the one recommended by most birders. Sure enough, that seemed to be the case. Then I casually checked the prices on the binoculars, quite certain that I made a fairly good deal on them. To my horror I discovered that I had paid about $100 more than I had to.

Sometimes having no research strategy costs more than time.

A research essay is time consuming, and although you aren't risking money, the quality of your paper will make a big difference in your final grade. Your time and your grade are two reasons that it pays to be thoughtful about *how* you approach gathering and using information. A typical "strategy" is something like this: (1) get the assignment, (2) choose a topic, (3) wait until a few days before the paper is due, (4) madly search the Internet, (5) write the paper the night before you have to hand it in, (6) pray.

This time, you've already approached the paper more strategically than outlined in the typical strategy. In the last chapter, you spent time exploring possible topics, narrowing your focus, and developing research questions that will help guide your search for information. This will make a big difference in the efficiency of your research in the library and on the Web. But what do experienced researchers know that will help you find what you're looking for fast and use what you find effectively? Here's what you will learn this week:

1. How to create a chronology for the searches
2. How to control the language of your searches to get the best results
3. How to perform advanced searches at the library and on the Web, and how to use other sources of information, including surveys and interviews
4. How to evaluate what you find
5. How to take notes that will help you to begin writing your essay even before you begin the draft

Google vs. the Library

Despite all the fat, the carbs, and the empty calories, the convenience of a Big Mac is hard to ignore. Similarly, a few minutes feasting on the information served up by Google is far more convenient than searching an online database at the university library. As one analyst put it recently, "Googling has become synonymous with research." Another called the relentless feast of online information "infobesity."

Should we be wringing our hands about this? The answer is *yes* and *no*. The power and accessibility of Google and other Internet search tools have turned virtually everyone into a researcher. No question is too arcane and no quest is completely hopeless when typing a few words into a search window allows you to lurch through millions of documents in a second. It's really hard to understate the wonder of this. Along with the junk, the results of Internet searches often turn up something useful, even for an academic paper. In fact, at least one study* suggests that when Google searches are matched with searches on library databases, the popular search engine doesn't do too badly. When researchers looked for relevant documents on four test topics, they found a total of 723 sources. Google produced 237 of these, and the library databases turned up 163. Predictably, however, the documents from the library were generally of a much higher quality—they tended to be from more qualified sources: more up-to-date, more balanced, and more accurate. Still, while Google produced more stinkers, researchers concluded that 52 percent of its results were actually pretty good.

Undoubtedly, it's Google's accessibility that makes it so irresistible. In addition to avoiding a hike to the library or sorting through academic

*Brophy, Jan, and David Bawden. "Is Google Enough? Comparison of an Internet Search Engine with Academic Library Sources." *Aslib Proceedings: New Information Perspectives* 57 (2005): 498–512. Print.

databases online, Google gives you results you can often find and use immediately. In the Google matchup with the library, 90 percent of the documents produced by the popular search engine were instantly accessible, full-text articles, while the library fared less well—only 65 percent of those results were full text. In some cases, getting an article on a library database required interlibrary loan or a microfilm search.

Yet for all Google's appeal, in academic writing *quality matters*. A lot. You must always try to use accurate sources that are written by people who know what they're talking about. For those kinds of sources, your library is indispensable. The dilemma here is this: Do you value the accessibility of an Internet search above the quality of the library sources? At first, not many of my students struggle with this. Google wins, hands down. But savvy researchers know that's like juggling with one hand—you're making it much harder than it needs to be. In academic research, you need as much relevant, accurate information as you can get. The answer, obviously, is to learn how you can *complement* your Google searches with library searches.

A Complementary Research Strategy

Writers are always better off when they work from abundance. It is far better to have more information than you can use because this allows you to understand your subject more deeply and focus your investigation more narrowly. Attack your research question on multiple fronts—the Internet, the library, and interviews or surveys—and you're much more likely to succeed in finding out what you want to know (see Figure 1). This inclusive approach will help you accomplish the three things that make up a sound search strategy:

1. Find *enough* information to fully explore a narrowly focused topic.
2. Find *varied* sources.
3. Find *quality* information.

Find Enough Information by Using the Best Search Terms

Around my house a few years back, the Harry Potter phenomenon had everyone muttering magic words. "Flipendo," said Julia, trying to turn the dog into a gerbil. "Wingardium leviosa," said Becca, who was determined to elevate her little sister six feet off the ground. Chopsticks substituted for magic wands. I knew this because we

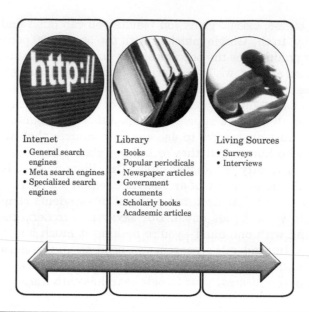

FIGURE 1   Maximize coverage of quality sources by investigating on three fronts.

suddenly had too few when the take-out Chinese meal arrived; that was the only part of this magical revival that swept the household that I didn't much like.

Some writers foolishly think that there's magic involved in getting good words to the page when it's really much more simple and not at all mysterious: You have to have your seat in the chair and your fingers on the keyboard or curled around a pen. But there is a kind of magic you can perform as a researcher, and it also involves the right words uttered in the right order. *How* you phrase your search of a library database or the World Wide Web makes an enormous difference in the results. I've come to believe that this ability, almost more than any other, is the researcher's most important skill.

You can harvest more and better results by understanding and effectively using three search tactics:

- *Index searches* deploy the language that librarians use to catalog books and other materials in university libraries.
- *Keyword searches* in library databases use relevant terms with "connectors" like AND, OR, or NOT to produce better results.
- *Keyword searches* on the Web combine a string of terms, along with exact phrases to generate more relevant hits.

Index Searches Using the Library of Congress Subject Headings

An advantage that libraries have over the Web is that information in libraries is more organized. That's the good news. The bad news is that there is so much information to organize that librarians had to develop a special language for searching it. It's not alien language—the words are familiar—but it is a language that requires that certain words be used to reflect the way librarians organize information. These searches, called *index searches,* may therefore initially seem less straightforward than the more familiar *keyword searches.*

More specifically, reference librarians use something called the *Library of Congress Subject Headings (LCSH),* which divides all knowledge into areas. These divisions are the *index terms* that you can use for index searches, which will almost always help you to find more relevant books on your topic. How do you find out these index terms? A couple ways: There is a four-volume book in your library's reference room—sometimes called the "Red Book." These volumes are the standard reference to index terms. You can also go online to search the *LCSH* (http://authorities.loc.gov/). There you can search by subject, name, or title, and the software will tell you what subject headings to use when searching for books in the library. But the easiest method to know what Library of Congress (LOC) terms to use is to go to your library's online book database and do an initial search with terms you *think* might work. When you find relevant books, you'll likely see the relevant LOC terms in your results. For example, I did a keyword search using the term *cyberterrorism* in my library's book database and found a great book: *Cyberterrorism: The Use of the Internet for Terrorist Purposes.* The results page suggested the following index terms as active links that would help me narrow my search:

Cyberterrorism—Prevention

Computer networks—Security measures

Computer security—Law and legislation

Knowing these index terms is a huge help, particularly in the early stages of a research project. Just enter the suggested terms in your library online book index, and you'll be surprised by the quality of the results.

Keyword Searches in Library Databases

Compared to a Google search, library database searches rely much more on coming up with keywords and trying them in different combinations. For example, searching for books using the word "Wildfires" will produce an avalanche that will quickly bury you. Efficient research requires that you maximize the number of relevant results and minimize the number of irrelevant ones. That's where searches that use careful combinations of keywords are so important. Many libraries and Internet search engines use something called "Boolean" connectors to help you when you search databases. (These connectors were invented by George Boole, a British logician, more than 100 years ago.)

The system essentially requires the use of the words AND, OR, and NOT between the search terms or keywords. The word AND, say, between "Animal" and "Rights" will search a database for documents that include *both* of those terms. Just keying in *animal rights* without the AND connector will often get the same results because the AND is implied. If you want to search for *animal rights* as an exact phrase, most library databases ask you to put the phrase in parentheses rather than quotation marks.

The use of the connector OR between search terms, obviously, will produce a list of documents that contain either of the terms. That can be a lot of results. In the early stages of your project, you might want to browse a heap of results; that way you can explore different angles on your topic, see the more common treatments, and discover some alternative search terms. The NOT connector is less frequently used but really can be quite helpful if you want to *exclude* certain documents. Suppose, for example, you were interested in researching the problem of homelessness in Washington State, where you live. To avoid getting information on Washington D.C., where it's also a problem, use the connector NOT.

Homeless AND Washington NOT D.C.

As you can see from the example above, it's possible to use the connectors between a number of terms—not just two. In fact, the art of creating keyword searches is using both the right words (those used by librarians) and using them in the right combinations (those that in combination sufficiently narrow your search and give you the best results).

One final search technique that can be very useful, especially in library database searches, is something called "nesting." This involves the use of parentheses around two or more terms in a phrase. This prompts the computer to look for those terms first. For example, suppose you were searching for articles on the ethics of animal rights, but you were particularly interested in information in two states, Idaho and Montana. You might construct a search phrase like this one:

> ## (Montana OR Idaho) AND animal AND rights AND ethics

Putting the two states in parentheses tells the software to prioritize Montana or Idaho in the results, generating a much more focused list of sources related to animal rights and ethics.

Keyword Searches on the World Wide Web

You did a subject search on the Web, using popular sites, such as the Internet Public Library (http://ipl.org), that specialize in those kinds of searches. Far more common are searches that use so-called search engines, such as Google. As you probably know, these are remarkable software programs that in a split second "crawl" the Web, searching for documents that contain the keywords you type in. Lately, the magic of these search engines has been tarnished a bit by commercialism, allowing advertisers to purchase priority listings in search engine results and not always making that fact obvious to the searcher. But these search engines are still essential and getting better all the time.

Keyword searches are the most common method of searching the Web, used much than subject searches. Unfortunately, there isn't consistency in search languages. Some permit Boolean searching. Some use a variation on Boolean that involves symbols rather than words.

> ## What Studies Say About How Students Research Online
>
> - Most use a trial-and-error approach to searching.
> - They rarely use anything more than basic searches, avoiding advanced searching features.
> - Typically, they use only two search terms every session, and these search sessions last an average of 15–19 minutes.
> - Only 8 percent use Boolean operators.
> - 60 percent admit that they are overwhelmed by the amount of information available to them.
> - Nearly three-quarters use the Internet rather than the library.

But Google, the giant of search engines, has made all of this a bit simpler through the search form provided by its Advanced Search option. You can find this on Google's search page. Once in Advanced Search, you can use the boxes provided to perform all the usual Boolean tricks but without having to use the "connector" words like AND, OR, or NOT.

Because of the mind-boggling amount of information on the Web, careful keyword searches are critical. Researchers waste more online time either not finding what they wanted or sifting through layers and layers of irrelevant documents because of thoughtless keyword searches. For example, notice in Figure 2 how the search on the relationship between social networks and friendship can be dramatically changed by adding terms. An initial search on Google simply using the keywords *social* and *network* produced a mind-boggling 334 million documents. Just adding *one more* keyword cut the number of hits by 6,000 percent! Finally, when combined with a phrase ("intimacy of friendship"), a search with the two terms *social* and *network* yielded significantly fewer and more focused results.

Find Varied Sources

One of the first things I notice when I'm reading research essay drafts is whether the writer leans too heavily on a single source. Does an author or article reappear again and again on page after page, like a pigeon at a favorite roost? This is not good. It typically means that the writer has too few sources and must keep turning to these few, or one source is especially relevant to the

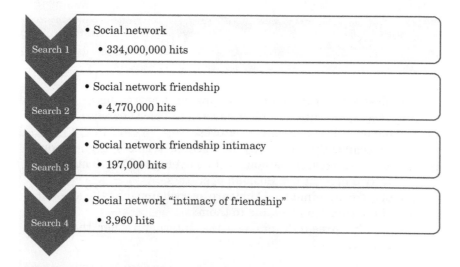

Search 1	• Social network • 334,000,000 hits
Search 2	• Social network friendship • 4,770,000 hits
Search 3	• Social network friendship intimacy • 197,000 hits
Search 4	• Social network "intimacy of friendship" • 3,960 hits

FIGURE 2   **How Multiple Search Terms Narrow Results**

topic, and the writer can't resist repeatedly inviting the author to reappear.

Vary your sources. This not only means using a sufficient number so that your essay is informative but also using different *kinds* of sources whenever you can. In part, the kinds of sources you rely on in preparing your paper depend on your topic. Remember my research question on competing theories of dog training? That's a current topic. There's an ongoing debate online and on cable TV about which approach is best. In addition, the topic has a history in the published literature. I'll be checking both newspapers and magazines, along with Web sites, but I'll also search the journals and books at the library. If you're writing about whether the release of secret documents by WikiLeaks endangers U.S. service members in Afghanistan, then much of your information will come from current sources; you're less likely to find books.

There are several ways to think about how sources can be distinguished from each other:

- Are they primary or secondary sources?
- Are they objective or subjective?
- Are they stable or unstable?

Primary vs. Secondary Sources

One way of looking at information is to determine whether it's a *primary* or a *secondary* source. A primary source presents the original words of a writer—his speech, poem, eyewitness account, letter, interview, or autobiography. A secondary source analyzes somebody else's work. Whenever possible, choose a primary source over a secondary one, because the primary source is likely to be more accurate and authoritative.

The subject you research will determine the kinds of primary sources you encounter. For example, if you're writing a paper on a novelist, then his novels, stories, letters, and interviews are primary sources. Research on the engineering of the Chicago River in 1900, a partly historical subject, might lead to a government report on the project or a firsthand account of its construction in a Chicago newspaper. Primary sources for a paper in the sciences might be findings from an experiment or observations. For a paper in business, marketing information or technical studies might be primary sources. A videotape of a theatrical performance is a primary source, while the reviews in the local newspaper are secondary sources.

Objective vs. Subjective

For now, I'm going to sidestep the debate over whether *any* source can be fully objective and simply point out that, generally speaking, we can divide all sources into those that attempt to report facts that have been gathered systematically, minimizing author bias, and those that don't pretend to be anything more than the author's opinion, perhaps supported by evidence gleaned from objective sources. You can probably guess some examples of objective sources: experiments, survey results, carefully designed studies of many kinds. The best of these are "peer reviewed" to double-check their accuracy. As you know, many academics prize these objective sources as the best evidence. Subjective sources are all over the map, from government propaganda to blogs to op-ed essays in the local newspaper. Of course, just because someone is pushing a point of view doesn't make a source useless. It just means that you need to consider how that point of view colors the source and read it more critically.

Stable or Unstable?

When information went digital, a new phenomenon emerged; sometimes information simply disappears. That Web page you cited in your draft, with the great statistics on scooter fatalities, is there one day and gone the next. One of the reasons you cite sources in academic writing is so readers can consult them, making a missing Web page a serious problem. Disappearing Web pages, of course, are hard to predict, but you can make some judgments about the stability of an online source. Has it been around for a long time? Is it routinely updated? Are print versions of an online document available? Is the site associated with a reputable institution? Unstable sources are a shaky foundation for any academic essay. It's best to avoid them.

Find Quality Sources

The aim of your research strategy is not only to find interesting information on your topic but also to find it in *authoritative* sources. What are these? The highest-quality sources are those types found on the bottom of the upside-down pyramid in Figure 3. These are works that are most likely to be written by and then reviewed by experts in their field (see "What Does 'Peer Reviewed' Mean?"). You find these "peer-reviewed" articles in scholarly journals, some of which are now available online as well as in the library. The downside of dealing with sources at the bottom of the authoritative pyramid is that they may be written in the *discourse* of the field; to you that may make the writing seem jargon-filled and hard to follow. Of course, as a nonspecialist you aren't the intended audience for the work. But the effort to make sense of an academic article really pays off. Your readers know that you're relying on the best information available; beyond that,

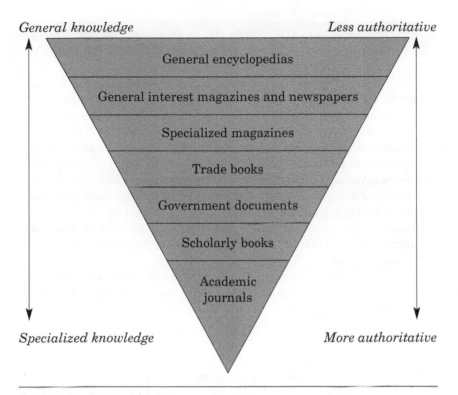

General knowledge · Less authoritative

General encyclopedias

General interest magazines and newspapers

Specialized magazines

Trade books

Government documents

Scholarly books

Academic journals

Specialized knowledge · More authoritative

FIGURE 3 **Pyramid of Library Sources**

you're more credible because it's clear that you're willing to dig deeply to explore your research question.

When Was It Published?

If you're researching the treatment of slaves in nineteenth-century New Orleans, then currency is obviously less of an issue than it might be if your project were to explore the impact of the Toyota Prius on marketing practices for hybrid vehicles. Generally, in any project related to the social sciences, a recent publication date carries more weight, which is one reason APA citations emphasize date of publication. The currency of Web pages and online documents can also be important. A site that is regularly updated is obviously more likely to have the latest information on the topic.

Why Journal Articles Are Better Than Magazine Articles

If your topic has been covered by academic journal articles, rely heavily on these sources if you can. An article on, say, suicide

What Does "Peer Reviewed" Mean?

Broadly speaking, periodicals, books, Web sites, and magazines are one of two types: scholarly or popular. Popular publications include magazines like *Newsweek* or online sites like *Slate,* which are staff written, usually by nonexperts for a more general audience. Scholarly publications are written and edited by experts for others in their fields, and the best of these are "peer reviewed." This means that before an article is published online or in print, a group of fellow experts read and comment on its validity, argument, factual accuracy, and so on. The article doesn't appear in print until this review is completed and the journal editor is satisfied that the other scholars think the work is respectable.

What does this mean to you? It means that you can count on the authoritative muscle of a peer-reviewed source to help you make a strong point in your paper.

among college students in a magazine like *Time* is less valuable than one in the *American Journal of Psychology.* Granted, the latter may be harder to read, but you're much more likely to learn something from a journal article because it's written by an expert and is usually narrowly focused. Also, because academic articles are carefully documented, you may be able to mine bibliographies for additional sources. And, finally, scholarly work, such as that published in academic journals and books (usually published by university presses), is especially authoritative because it's often subject to peer review. Other authorities in the field have scrutinized the author's evidence, methods, and arguments; the published work has truly passed muster.

Look for Often-Cited Authors

As you make your way through information on your topic, pay attention to names of authors whose works you often encounter or who are frequently mentioned in bibliographies. These individuals are often the best scholars in the field, and it will be useful to become familiar with their work and use it, if possible, in your paper. If an author's name keeps turning up, use it as another term for searching the library databases or Google Scholar. Doing so might yield new sources you wouldn't necessarily encounter in other ways.

Not All Books Are Alike

When writing my high school research reports, I thought that books were always the best sources because, well, books are thick, and anyone who could write that much on any one subject probably knows what she's talking about. Naive, I know.

One of the things college teaches is *critical thinking*—the instinct to pause and consider before rushing to judgment. I've learned not to automatically believe in the validity of what an author is saying (as you shouldn't for me), even if she did write a thick book about it.

If your topic lends itself to using books as sources, then evaluate the authority of each before deciding to use it in your paper. This is especially important if your paper relies heavily on one or two books. Consider the following:

- Is the book written for a general audience or more knowledgeable readers?
- Is the author an acknowledged expert in the field?
- Is there a bibliography? Is the information carefully documented?
- How was the book received by critics? To find out quickly, search the Web using the author's name and title of the book as search terms.

Evaluating Online Sources

Librarians help maintain the order, stability, and quality of information in the library. By comparison, the Internet is anarchy. Everyone knows that you have to be vigilant about trusting the accuracy, balance, and reliability of Web documents. Unfortunately, there's continuing evidence that student researchers still have a hard time assessing the quality of online sources. While the criteria for evaluating sources just mentioned apply to Web documents, Web documents also deserve special attention.

Here are some general guidelines to follow:

- *Always keep your purpose in mind.* For example, if you're exploring the lobbying methods of the National Rifle Association, then you will want to hear, and see, what this organization has to say on its Web site. In looking at the NRA Web pages, you'll know full well that they are not unbiased; however, for your purpose, they are both relevant and authoritative. After all, who knows more about the NRA than the NRA?

- *Favor governmental and educational sources over commercial ones.* There are plenty of exceptions to this, but in general you're wise to rely more heavily on material sponsored by groups without a commercial stake in your topic. How can you tell the institutional affiliation of sources? Sometimes it's obvious. They tell you. But when it's not obvious, the *domain name* provides a clue. The *.com* that follows a server name signifies a commercial site, while *.edu, .org,* or *.gov* usually signals an educational, nonprofit, or governmental entity. The absence of ads also implies a site is noncommercial.

■ *Favor authored documents over those without authors.* There's a simple reason for this: You can check the credentials of an author. You can do this by sending an e-mail message to him or her, a convenience often available as a link on a Web page, or you can do a quick search to see if that author has published other books or articles on your topic. If writers are willing to put their names on a document, they might be more careful about the accuracy and fairness of what they say.

■ *Favor Web pages that have been recently updated over those that haven't been changed in a year or more.* Frequently, at the bottom of a Web page there is a line indicating when the information was posted to the Internet and/or when it was last updated. Look for it.

■ *Favor Web sources that document their claims over those that don't.* Most Web documents won't feature a bibliography. That doesn't mean that they're useless to you, but be suspicious of a Web author who makes factual assertions without supporting evidence.

A Key to Evaluating Internet Sources. As an undergraduate, I was a botany major. Among other things, I was drawn to plant taxonomy because the step-by-step taxonomic keys for discovering the names of unfamiliar plants gave the vegetative chaos of a Wisconsin meadow or upland forest a beautiful kind of logic and order. The key that follows is modeled after the ones I used in field taxonomy. This one is a modest attempt to make some sense of the chaos on the Web for the academic researcher, particularly when the usual approaches for establishing the authority of traditional scholarship and publications fail—for example, when documents are anonymous, their dates of publication aren't clear, or their authors' affiliations or credentials are not apparent.

If you're not sure whether a particular Web document will give your essay credibility, see Figure 4 and work through the following steps:

1. Does the document have an author or authors? If *yes,* go to Step 2. If *no,* go to Step 7.

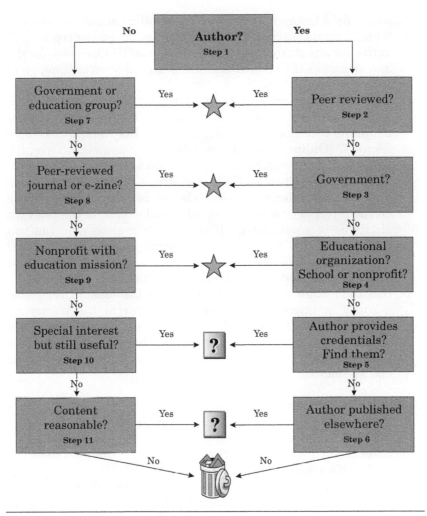

FIGURE 4   Follow the flowchart for a rigorous review of a Web document or page, beginning with whether the author is obvious or not. Sites that earn stars are generally more trustworthy. Those with question marks still may be useful, depending on the situation. Be particularly wary of information on commercial or special interest sites.

Authored Documents

2. Does the document appear in an online journal or magazine that is "refereed"? In other words, is there any indication that every article submitted must be reviewed by other scholars

in the field before it is accepted for publication? If *yes*, you've found a good source. If *no* (or you're unsure), go to Step 3.

3. Is the document from a government source? (Online, look for the .gov domain.) If *yes,* then it is likely a good source. If *no*, go to Step 4.

4. Does the document appear in an online publication affiliated with a reputable educational institution (e.g., a university) or nonprofit educational organization (e.g., the American Cancer Society)? (Online, look for the .edu or .org domain.) If *yes*, it's likely to be trustworthy. If *no*, go to Step 5.

5. If the author isn't clearly affiliated with a reputable institution, does he or she offer any credentials that help establish expertise on the topic? (For example, an advanced degree in the relevant discipline is encouraging.) If credentials are missing, can you find an author's credentials by Googling the author's name? Is there an e-mail link to the author so you can inquire about affiliations or credentials? If *no*, go to Step 6.

6. Has the author published elsewhere on the topic in reputable journals or other publications? Check this at the library by searching under the author's name in the catalog or appropriate databases. If *no*, reconsider the value of the source. You could be dealing with a lone ranger who has no expertise on your topic and no relevant affiliations.

Unauthored Documents

7. If the online document has no author, is it from an institutional source like a university (.edu) or the state or federal government (.gov)? If *yes*, then chances are the document is useful. If *no*, go to Step 8.

8. Is the anonymous document published in an online journal or magazine? Is it refereed? (See Step 2.) If *yes*, it's likely a good source. If *no*, go to Step 9.

9. Is the document part of a publication or Web page from a nongovernment source whose mission is described in the document, and does it suggest that the organization's goals include research and education? Is there a board of directors, and does it include professionals and academics who are respected in the field? If *no*, go to Step 10.

10. Even if the organization offering the information represents a special interest group or business with an axe to grind, the information may be useful as a means of presenting its point of view. Make sure, if you use it, that the information is qualified to make that obvious.

11. Does the site seem reasonable? Try to apply the usual criteria for evaluating a source to this anonymous document. Does it

have a citations page, and do the citations check out? Was it published on the Internet recently? Does the argument the writer is making seem sound? Do the facts check out? If the answer is *no* to all of the above, then don't trust the document. If you can answer *yes* to more than one of these questions, the material might have some marginal value in a college paper.

A good researcher always takes a skeptical view of claims made in print; she should be even more wary of claims made in Internet documents. And while these approaches for evaluating online sources should help, it still can be pretty tricky deciding whom to take seriously in cyberspace. So to sort it all out, always ask yourself these questions: How important is this Internet document to my research? Do I really need it? Might there be a more reliable print version? For an example, see Figure 5.

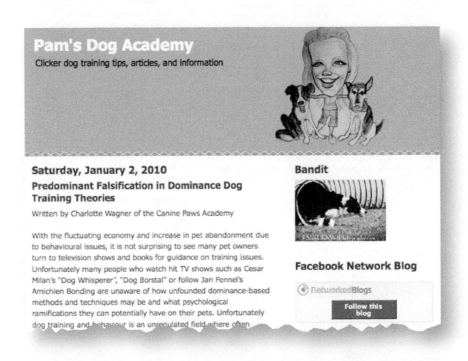

FIGURE 5   Evaluating a Web Site: A Case Study. I'm writing about the debates between dog trainers, and I encountered this site. "Pam's Dog Academy" is a blog, and it's got some really interesting information. Overall, how would you evaluate this site as a source for my essay? What exactly do you see that influences your judgment about that? Is there anything about the site that you might want to know? How would you find it?

b ee⸱e⸱ , v⸱⸱⸱⸱⸱arians, gro⸱⸱⸱⸱⸱ ⸱nd a⸱⸱ ⸱⸱eu⸱ ⸱aine⸱⸱ without second thought to the validity of the information being provided to the reader.

Behaviourist James O'Heare (2003) claims that: "Dominance theory is probably the most misunderstood commonly used ethological theory in the dog behaviour field." There are a variety of views on dominance, including those advocating dominance as a personality flaw where the dog is trying to take over the owner: "When a dog growls at the wife or kids in the family, it sees itself as a higher rank than family members." (Frawley, 2009) and modern establishments opposing the use of dominance-oriented intimidation techniques: "Sadly, many techniques used to teach a dog that his owner is leader of the pack is counter-productive; you won't get a better behaved dog, but you will either end up with a dog so fearful it has structure and communication regarding appropriate behaviours, and one in which their need for mental and physical stimulation is addressed." B. F. Skinner's operant principles of positive reinforcement and negative punishment can easily aid in the increase of desired behaviours and the extinction of undesired traits with the use of motivation rather than intimidation and suppression through aversion. There are many associations certifying trainers and behaviourists which promote the use of learning theory and scientific methods of understanding and modifying behaviour. Many of these respected bodies require professionals to either: have a degree relevant to animal behaviour, further education in training, or extensive experience with another qualified professional before accepting applicants to become members. These association include but are not limited to the: Association of Pet Dog Trainers (APDT), International Association of Animal Behaviour Consultants (IAABC), Association of Pet Behaviour Consultants (APBC), Certified Council for Professional Dog Trainers (CCPDT) and International Positive Dog Training Association (IPDTA) to name a few.

Written by Charlotte Wagner of the Canine Paws Academy
1 January 2010

RESOURCES

Association of Pet Dog Trainers. (2009) Dominance and Dog Training: Association of Pet Dog Trainers position statement [www document]. http://www.apdt.com/about/ps/ dominance.aspx (Accessed 7 December 2009)

Coppinger, L. and Coppinger, R. (2004) Dogs: A new understanding of canine origin, behaviour and evolution. Romford, Essex: Crosskeys Select.

Dennison, P. (2005) How to Right a Dog Gone Wrong. Loveland: Alpine.

Donaldson, J. (1996) The Culture Clash. Berkeley: James and Kenneth.

Fennel, J. (2006) The Practical Dog Listener. London: HarperCollins.

Frawey, E. (2009) Dealing with the Dominant Dog [www document] http://leerburg.com/ pdf/dealingwithdominantdog.pdf (Accessed 10 December 2009)

Millan, C. and Peltier, M. J. (2006) Cesar's Way. New York: Crown.

O'Heare, J. (2003) Dominance Theory and Dogs. Ottawa: DogPsych.

Science Daily (2009) Using 'Dominance' to Explain Dog Behaviour is Old Hat [www document] http://www.sciencedaily.com/releases /2009/05/090521⸱⸱271⸱.htm (Accessed 7 December 2009)

▶ June (1)

▶ May (3)

▶ April (3)

▶ March (1)

▶ February (5)

▼ January (8)

   Both Ends of the Leash: Fear Reduction

   Bandit's Puppy Picture Photo Contest...

   Training your dog to come when called, reliability...

   Clicker Mechanics

   Why Not Punishment?

   Debunking the Dominance Myth - Dog Public

   Pet dogs rival humans for emotional satisfaction

   Predominant Falsification in Dominance Dog Trainin...

▶ 2009 (67)

About Me

Pam's Dog Academy
San Diego, CA, United States

I have been training for over 5 years. I opened my dog training business in 2007. I only train using clicker training and Positive Reinforcement.

View my complete profile

Here are some awesome blogs...

🅱 DOGMANTICS
1 week ago

FIGURE 5 (Continued)

Developing Focused Knowledge

If working knowledge equips you to sustain a 1-minute dinner conversation on your topic, then focused knowledge is enough for you to make a 15- or 20-minute presentation to the rest of the class (for more on presentations, see the box "Working Together: In-Class News Conference"). You'll probably be able to answer all of your classmates' questions. You'll hardly be an expert, but you'll probably know a lot more about your topic than any of your peers.

Focused knowledge is the product of smart research this week and the next, refining your search terms, knowing where to look for the most useful information, and using your time efficiently. As you'll see later in this section, focused knowledge also depends on what you *do* with what you find. Most important, especially at this point, are these two questions:

1. Is this information relevant to my inquiry question?
2. Does it *change* my question?

At its most basic, relevance is simply deciding whether that article or book you found is on topic. Say you're researching the disappearance of the world's frogs, and you find a *Scientific American* article called "Extinction Countdown: World's Frogs Are Disappearing." It obviously couldn't be more relevant. But, as you develop more focused knowledge, you can make more focused judgments. *How* is a source relevant? With some traditional research papers, this question may simply mean, how does it support my point? But genuine academic inquiry is about discovery, and because it begins with questions, information isn't just used to line up ducks in the service of a preconceived point. The relevant sources you encounter online and in the library can help your project in many more ways:

■ *Refine the inquiry question.* Last week your question was, "Why are the world's frog's disappearing?" But you read some articles and browse some books and you realize that a more focused and interesting question is this: "How is climate change influencing the worldwide decline in amphibians?"

■ *Help the literature review.* A very common move in most academic research is establishing what has already been said about the question you're posing. Which scientists have published on frogs and climate change? What do they agree on? What are the disagreements? What don't they know?

Working Together: In-Class News Conference

By the end of this week, you should be ready to make a presentation to your class on your topic. Imagine that it's a press conference similar to the ones shown on television. You will give a 15-minute talk on your topic to your classmates, who will later, like veteran newspaper reporters, follow up with questions. Your presentation will be carefully timed. It shouldn't be any longer than the allotted time limit; any less than the allotted time suggests that you haven't yet developed a focused knowledge of your topic.

Plan your presentation with the following things in mind:

- *Rather than simply report everything you've learned about your topic, try to give your talk some emphasis.* For example, focus on what you've learned so far that most surprised you and why. Or present the most common misconceptions about your topic and why they miss the mark. Or provide some background about why the question you're exploring is important and share some of the answers you've discovered so far. If your topic has a personal dimension, tell the story, and share how your research has helped you understand your experience differently.

- *Don't read a speech.* It's fine to have notes with you—in fact, it's a good idea—but try to avoid reading them. Make your presentation as interesting as you can. After all, this is a chance to discover what other people think about your topic—what interests them about it and what doesn't. This talk is a great chance to try out some approaches to your topic that you may later use to make your essay more compelling.

- *Consider visuals.* PowerPoint or Prezi (see http://prezi.com) presentations are great because they help you organize the talk. Also think about photographs, graphs, charts, and other visual ways to present your information.

- *Begin by stating your focusing question.* Every presentation should start by establishing what question is driving your investigation. You might even put this on the board when you begin.

While you listen to your peers' presentations, think about what questions they raise that interest you. These might be questions of clarification, questions about an assertion the presenters or one of their sources made, or areas that the speakers didn't cover but that you wonder about. Imagine that you're a hard-nosed reporter anxious to get the story right.

■ *Reveal interesting patterns.* Scholars who study the differences between how experts and novices do research often notice this: Experienced researchers see patterns in data that novices don't notice. Experts *expect* patterns, and you should look for them, too. Does the information you find seem to tell a story? Does the most persuasive information suggest a particular answer to your research question? Are there relationships between facts, theories, or claims that surprise you? Are there any unexpected contradictions, causes, or connections? For example, in Figure 6, I've created a "word

FIGURE 6   Looking for Patterns

cloud" of the last 320 words you just read. A "word cloud" takes some text and creates an image that represents word frequency in the text. The visually bigger words are repeated more than the smaller ones. Note the pattern of emphasis on certain subjects and relationships—questions and information, relevance and research, change and focus. In a sense, when you develop focused knowledge on your topic, you gather a cloud of information much like this one, except richer and more complicated. Constantly analyze the relationships in what you're finding—what are the most frequent arguments, which ideas seem connected, what facts stick out?

What About a Thesis?

Ultimately, you must have a thesis, something you are saying about your research question. But when should you know what that is?

Are You Suspending Judgment?

Should you have a thesis at this point? That depends on the purpose of your project. If it's exploratory, if your motive is to discover what you think, then it's too early to make any bold statements that answer the question you're researching. It might even be counterproductive. Inquiry-based investigations depend on your willingness to *suspend judgment* long enough to discover what you think.

Are You Testing Assumptions?

If, however, you feel that you have developed some ideas about what you want to say, now might be an excellent time to make a list of your theories, assumptions, or beliefs about your topic. They will be invaluable guides for your research this week because you can examine these beliefs against the evidence and potentially break through to new understandings about your research question.

What Are You Arguing?

In some cases, you know what you think is the best answer to your research question even before you've done much investigation of the topic, and your motive is to build a convincing argument around that claim. For example, consider this claim: *Lawn mowers make a significant contribution to CO_2 emissions in the United States.* Maybe this is something you heard or read somewhere from a reputable source, and it's something you strongly suspect is true. Maybe your instructor asked you to make that argument, or you're writing an opinion piece for an assignment. Conventional research papers are frequently organized from the beginning around a thesis or claim. If that's the kind of project you're working on, now would be a good time to craft a sentence that states your most important assertion or main idea. This may well be refined or even discarded later on as you learn more, but it will help with your research this week.

To generate a *tentative* thesis statement at this point, try finishing one of the following sentences:

1. While most people think _____ about _____, I think _____.
2. The most convincing answer to my research question is _____.
3. The main reason that _____ is a problem is _____, and the best solution is _____.
4. Among the causes of _____, the least understood is _____.
5. Though much has been said about _____, very little attention has been paid to _____.
6. All of the evidence so far about _____ points to _____ as a significant cause/solution/effect/problem/interpretation/factor.

You'll be implementing your research strategy this week and next, looking at sources in the library and on the Web. The exercises that follow will help guide these searches, making sure that you don't overlook some key source or reference. Your instructor may ask you to hand in a photocopy of the exercise as a record of your journey.

Keeping Track of What You Find: Developing a Bibliography

For the next two weeks, you're going to collect a lot of material on your research question: PDF copies of articles, books, bookmarked Web pages, images, and perhaps even audio and video files. You will make your life easier if you don't just collect but *record* what you find. Your options include the following:

■ *Basic bibliography.* This is the minimalist approach. You simply keep a running list, using the appropriate citation method, of information on each source you think you'll use in your essay. If you're using MLA, for example, this will become your Works Cited page. An online citation machine, like bibme (http://www.bibme.org) can help you build it. You can, of course, wait until the last minute to do this but, trust me, you will regret it.

▪ *Working bibliography.* This is one step up from the basic bibliography (see Figure 7) and is the simplest form of what's called an "annotated bibliography." A working bibliography provides a brief

---

Topic: Theories of Dog Training
Focusing Question: Should dogs be trained using positive reinforcement exclusively?

1. Katz, Jon. "Why Dog Training Fails." *Slate Magazine.*
   N.p. 14 Jan. 2005. Web. 22 Dec. 2010. Web.

   Katz argues that most theories of dog training fail to take into account the realities of raising an animal in a "split-level," not a training compound. He calls his own method the "Rational Theory," which he describes as an "amalgam" of techniques that takes into account the actual situation of both dog and owner.
2. Schilder, Matthijs B. H., and Joanne A.M. van der Borg. "Training Dogs with the Help of the Shock Collar: Short and Long Term Behavioural Effects." *Applied Animal Behaviour Science* 85 (2004): 319–334. Medline. Web. 23 Dec. 2010.

   Researchers had two groups of German shepherds, one training with shock collars and the other training without them. They then studied both "direct reactions" of dogs to the shock and their later behavior. Study found that dogs trained with shock collars consistently showed more signs of stress during and after training, including "lower ear positions." Finding "suggests that the welfare of these shocked dogs is at stake, at least in the presence of their owner."
3. Shore, Elise, Charles Burdsal, and Deanna Douglas. "Pet Owners' Views of Pet Behavior Problems and Willingness to Consult Experts for Assistance." *Journal of Applied Animal Welfare Science.* 11.1 (2008): 63–73. Print.

   Study notes that 30 percent of dogs that are given to shelters are there because owners complained of behavior problems; yet only 24 percent of owners surveyed enrolled in obedience classes. Researchers surveyed 170 dog and cat owners and determined that the highest concern was about animals who threatened people, and those owners were most likely to ask for assistance and they mostly turned to the Web unless there was a charge.

FIGURE 7   **Working Bibliography: An Example**

summary of what the source says: what topics it covers and what the basic argument or main ideas are. If you're using a double-entry journal, then you can find the material you need for your summary there. Your annotation may be a brief paragraph or more, depending on the source.

■ *Evaluative bibliography.* In some ways, this is the most useful annotated bibliography of all because it challenges you to not only "say back" what you understand sources to be saying but also to offer some judgments about whether you find them persuasive or relevant. You might comment on what you consider the strengths of the source or its weaknesses. Is writing an evaluative bibliography more work? You bet. But ultimately you are writing your paper as you go because much of the material you generate for the bibliography can be exported right into your essay. Your double-entry journal provides the raw material for these annotations.

Your instructor will tell you what kind of bibliography you should build for this project, but at the very least you should consider maintaining a basic bibliography as you go. Put it on a "cloud," like Google Docs or Evernote, that will store your draft bibliography on the Web and always be available wherever you find a new source—in the library, at home, or in the campus computer lab.

Searching Library Databases for Books and Articles

Despite the appeal of the Web, the campus library remains your most important source of information for academic research. Sure, it can be aggravating. There's that missing book that was supposed to be there or that article that isn't available in full text. You needed that article. Most of all, there's the sense of helplessness you might feel as a relative novice using a large, complicated, and unfamiliar reference system.

In this chapter, you were introduced to basic library search strategies, knowledge that will help give you some mastery over the university library. Now you'll expand on that knowledge, and at the same time you'll move from a working knowledge of your topic to a deeper understanding, one that will crystallize by reading and writing about what you find.

It's hard for newcomers to the university to fully appreciate the revolution the last decade brought to how we do college research. All you need to know, really, is that finding sources is infinitely easier. And with the growing availability of full-text PDFs of articles, you can end a session of searching with not just a citation but also the printout of the article.

You can't click a mouse and get a digital copy of a book—yet—but with one search you can scour the world, rather just your library, for books on your topic. If the book you want is in a library across the country, you can spend 60 seconds filling out an interlibrary loan form online (see "Interlibrary Loan") and get the book you want—often in just a few days.

Find the book you want in your university library the old fashioned way: Journey into the "stacks," which at big schools can be cavernous floor-to-ceiling aisles of books. The trip is well worth it because even if you discover that the book you want isn't right for your project, that book is surrounded by 100 others on your topic or related ones. Browse like you do on Amazon.

You will save time if you know *where* to look for the book you want, and so you must be familiar with how librarians organize books.

Finding Books

There are two systems for classifying books: the Dewey Decimal and the Library of Congress systems. They are quite different. The Dewey system, reportedly conceived in 1873 by an Amherst College undergraduate while daydreaming in church, is numerical, dividing all knowledge into 10 broad areas and further subdividing each of these into 100 additional classifications. Adding decimal points allows librarians to subdivide things even further. Just knowing the *call number* of a book will tell you its subject.

The Library of Congress system, which uses both letters and numbers, is much more common in college libraries. This is the system with which you should become most familiar. Each call number begins with one or two letters, signifying a category of knowledge, which is followed by a whole number between 1 and 9,999. A decimal and one or more Cutter numbers sometimes follow. The Library of Congress system is pretty complex, but it's not hard to use. As you get deeper in your research, you'll begin to recognize call numbers that consistently yield useful books. It is sometimes helpful to simply browse those shelves for other possibilities.

Understanding Call Numbers

The call number, that strange code on the spine of a library book, is something most of us want to understand just well enough to find that book on the shelf. How much do you need to know? First, you should know that there is more than just the alphabet at work in arranging books by their call numbers, and the call numbers tell you more than merely where books are shelved. For example, here's the call number for *The Curious Researcher*:

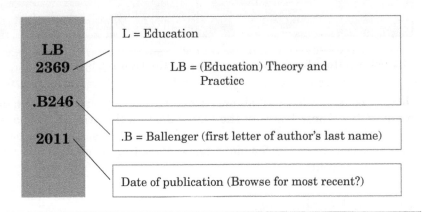

FIGURE 8 **Deciphering the Call Number Code**

The call number shown in Figure 8 tells you the subject area of the book, a little something about its author, and when the book was published. This is useful to know not only because it will help you find the book, but it also might prompt you to find other, possibly more recent, books on the same subject on a nearby shelf. In Figure 9, you can see how Library of Congress call numbers determine the arrangement of books on the shelf.

Coming Up Empty Handed?

In the unlikely event that you can't find any books by searching directly using the online catalog, there's another reference you can check that will help locate relevant articles and essays that are *a part* of a book whose title may otherwise seem unpromising. Check to see if your library has a database called the Essay and General Literature Index. Search that database with your keywords or subject and see if it produces something useful. List the relevant results as instructed previously. In addition, Google Book Search

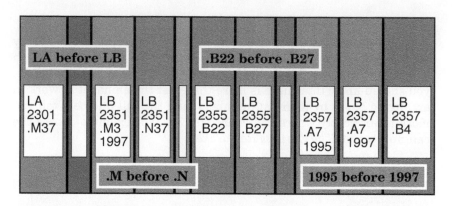

FIGURE 9 **How Books Are Arranged on the Library Shelf**

(http://books.google.com) allows users to do full-text searches of many titles. Those books in the public domain (i.e., the rights have lapsed) are available to any user in digital versions. This is a particularly rich resource for older texts, including some dating back hundreds of years.

Checking Bibliographies

One tactic that might lead to a mother lode of sources for your essay is to look at the bibliographies at the back of (mostly) scholarly books (and articles). Don't ever set aside a promising book until you've checked the bibliography! Jot down complete bibliographic information from citations you want to check out later. Keep a running list of these in your research notebook.

Interlibrary Loan

If your library doesn't have the book (or article) you really want, don't despair. Most college libraries have a wonderful low- or no-cost service to students called interlibrary loan. The library will search the collections of other libraries to find what you're looking for and have it sent, sometimes within a week or less. Use the service by checking with the reference desk or your library's Web site.

Article Databases

There are two kinds of article databases at your library: general subject databases that cover multiple disciplines and specialized databases that are discipline specific. Of course, I don't know which of these general databases you have at your library, but here are some of the most common:

GENERAL SUBJECT DATABASES

Academic OneFile

Academic Search

Academic Search Premier

ArticleFirst

IngentaConnect

JSTOR

ProQuest Central

Web of Science

Many of these multidisciplinary databases index popular magazines and some newspapers, and even some scholarly journals, which makes them very useful. For example, Academic Search Premier indexes nearly 8,000 magazines and journals. Increasingly, these databases include full-text articles, an extraordinary convenience for students working from home.

Specialized databases are subject specific. These are usually listed by discipline on your library's Web pages. The advantage of using these databases is that they will produce many more scholarly articles that might be relevant to your research question, though they may not all be full text. For a list of some of these, see the following table.

COMMON SPECIALIZED DATABASES

HUMANITIES	SCIENCE AND TECHNOLOGY	SOCIAL SCIENCES
America, History and Life	AGRICOLA (Agriculture)	Anthropological Index
Arts and Humanities Citation Index	Applied Science & Technology Index	ComAbstracts (Communication)
Historical Abstracts	Biological Abstracts	Contemporary Women's Issues
Humanities Index	CINAHL (Nursing)	Criminal Justice Abstracts
Literature Resource Center	Computer Literature Index	PAIS (Public Affairs)
MLA International Bibliography (Literature and composition)	GeoRef (Geology) Abstracts	PsycINFO
	Health Reference Center	Social Sciences Index
		Social Work
		Sociological Abstracts

(continued)

HUMANITIES	SCIENCE AND TECHNOLOGY	SOCIAL SCIENCES
Music Index	MathSciNet	Worldwide Political
Project Muse	Medline (Medicine)	Science Abstracts
Religion and	Web of Science	
Philosophical		
Collection		

BUSINESS	EDUCATION
ABI/Inform	Education Full Text
Business Source Elite	Education Index
FreeEDGAR	ERIC

Finally, certain article databases are focused on certain *types* of publications. The most important of these are indexes to newspapers (see following list, "Newspaper Databases"). They don't index the small-town papers, but they do provide citations to the so-called national newspapers such as the *New York Times,* the *Washington Post,* the *Los Angeles Times,* the *Wall Street Journal,* and the *Christian Science Monitor.* What's good about the national newspapers is that they're among the most authoritative journalistic sources; in other words, because of their large and experienced staffs, the information they provide is more trustworthy than smaller newspapers and online news outlets.

If you're looking for state or local newspapers you have a couple of options. The larger papers (and many magazines, for that matter) also have their own Web sites where you may be able to search their archives and retrieve full-text articles. Some sites charge for this service, though you can usually request them from your campus library for free. A convenient method for searching some of these sites is to use a news search engine that will consult thousands of papers in a few seconds. Two of the best of these search engines are Google News (http://news.google.com) and Yahoo News (http://news.yahoo.com).

Occasionally, the local papers are also indexed online by the university library, and copies are available on microfilm. More and more frequently, however, local papers, like their larger counterparts in major cities, have their own Web sites where you can use keyword searches to scour their archives.

NEWSPAPER DATABASES

Alternative Press Index

Ethnic Newswatch

LexisNexis Academic

National Newspaper Index

National Newspapers
Newspaper Source
ProQuest Central

Saving Search Results

Most online book indexes and article databases allow you to save your search results. Some of these databases allow you to mark the relevant results and then print them out. Some databases and most university libraries also allow you to create an account and a file for your search results. Through the Web page at my library, I can save searches, build a list of books I want to check out, and even publish my bibliographies so others can see them (and I can see theirs). Finally, you can always e-mail your search results page to yourself and organize a bibliography on your own computer.

EXERCISE 1

Search Book and Article Databases

Develop your focused knowledge by doing a thorough search using your library's book index and article databases. Unlike in Web and database searches, in book searches it often pays off to begin with broad subject terms. I got better results, for example, when I searched for books on theories of dog training with *animal behavior-canine* than I did with *dog training theories*. Searches that begin broadly might lead you to a relevant chapter in an otherwise irrelevant book.

Choose one of the bibliographies as a way of collecting relevant results. Your instructor may ask you to hand these in to gauge your progress. Remember that online citation machines like bibme.org can help you compile these results in the appropriate format (MLA or APA).

Advanced Internet Research Techniques

I love the word "portal." It summons images of a little window on some vast spaceship that frames the face of an open-mouthed observer looking in wonder at the vast reaches of the universe beyond. Researching on the Internet is a lot like peeping out of that window. There is just so much out there: billions of documents, gazillions of words, each a fragment of electronic data floating in cyberspace, like dust motes in some vast sunbeam. There's useful knowledge for academic writing out there, but it's hard to find and it's easy to get lost.

You're no stranger to the Web, of course, but now, more than ever, your research on the Internet needs to be *efficient*. You need fewer, more focused results and better-quality results. To get these, you need to amp up your Internet search skills by understanding the differences among search engines and what each can do to maximize your penetration of information on the Web.

Types of Search Engines

The most popular search engine is Google, a search engine with an enormous database that is relatively simple to use. It's easy to forget sometimes that Google is in good company; there are plenty of powerful alternatives that may generate some different results. In fact, a recent study showed that each search engine produced unique results *more than 80 percent* of the time.* It obviously pays off for researchers to use more than one.

Here's a partial list of the best of these general research engines.

POPULAR GENERAL SEARCH ENGINES

AltaVista (http://www.altavista.com)

Ask.com (http://www.ask.com)

Bing (http://www.bing.com)

Google (http://www.google.com)

Hotbot (http://www.hotbot.com)

Lycos (http://www.lycos.com)

Yahoo! Search (http://search.yahoo.com)

Google and the others are really quite amazing, but they do have limitations. For one thing, they only index pages on the Web that have hyperlinks pointing to them elsewhere or whose creators have requested they be indexed by a particular search tool. In addition, these databases may not be current.

There are so-called metasearch tools such as Dogpile (http://www.dogpile.com/) that are able to deploy multiple general search engines in the service of a single search (see the following list). These are very useful, particularly at the beginning of an Internet

*"Different Engines, Different Results." *Dogpile.com*. Dogpile. Apr. 2007. Web. 1–26. 4 Jan. 2011.

search on your topic. However, metasearch engines aren't quite as good as they sound because they skim off the top results from each individual search tool so you won't see the range of results you would get if you focus on one of the search engines with its own large database.

METASEARCH ENGINES

Dogpile (http://www.dogpile.com)

Mamma (http://www.mamma.com)

Search.com (http://www.search.com)

SurfWax (http://www.surfwax.com)

Yippy (http://yippy.com)

Finally, there are also specialized search engines (sometimes called "vertical" search engines) that focus on particular subjects such as education, politics, and psychology, as well as search engines that specialize in searching certain *kinds* of content, like finding people, images, blogs, and so on. You probably already use a specialized search engine (and might not know it) when you use a site like Pricegrabber (http://www.pricegrabber.com) to comparison shop online. You were also introduced to Google Scholar, another example of a search portal that focuses on specialized content, in this case journal articles. There are so many of these that a list—even if it's selective—wouldn't do justice to these focused Web crawlers. One place to visit online to help you find a relevant specialized search engine for your project is Noodletools (http://www.noodletools.com/).

What are the keys to maximizing the efficiency of your Internet research? In the exercise that follows, you'll learn to do the following:

1. Increase your coverage by using multiple search engines, not just your favorite one.
2. If possible, exploit subject directories that allow you to drill down from general to more specific topic categories. These are often put together by people—not software—who are concerned with quality content.
3. Be thoughtful about what and how many keywords you use to search. Generally, the more words—and especially phrases—you use, the more likely you are to generate relevant hits. This contrasts with searching library databases, which respond better to more focused keywords and phrases.

EXERCISE 2

Academic Research on the Internet

STEP 1: You already searched on your topic on a general search engine—probably Google—and in the last chapter you tried Google Scholar. Now, using some of the keyword combinations you developed for your topic, try at least two more general search engines from the list. Remember to play around with keywords, and don't forget the search language you learned earlier in this chapter. The Help button on whatever metasearch tool you use will give you the specifics on what connectors—Boolean or others—it accepts.

STEP 2: Launch a search on one or more of the metasearch engines listed. Save your relevant results.

STEP 3: Finally, visit Noodletools (http://www.noodletools.com/) and find the link for "Choose the Best Search." Scroll down and find a search engine, perhaps a specialized one, that you haven't tried yet. As before, save relevant results.

STEP 4: Add to your bibliography (see "Keeping Track of What You Find") by including Web pages that seem promising, and print copies of them for notetaking. A Web-based citation machine like bibme.org can help you with this.

Living Sources: Interviews and Surveys

Arranging Interviews

A few years ago, I researched a local turn-of-the-century writer named Sarah Orne Jewett for a magazine article. I dutifully read much of her work, studied critical articles and books on her writing, and visited her childhood home, which is open to the public in South Berwick, Maine. My research was going fairly well, but when I sat down to begin writing the draft, the material seemed flat and lifeless. A few days later, the curator of the Jewett house mentioned that there was an 88-year-old local woman, Elizabeth Goodwin, who had known the writer when she was alive. "As far as I know, she's the last living person who knew Sarah Orne Jewett," the curator told me. "And she lives just down the street."

The next week, I spent three hours with Elizabeth Goodwin, who told me of coming for breakfast with the famous author and eating strawberry jam and muffins. Elizabeth told me that many years after Jewett's death, the house seemed haunted by her friendly presence. One time, when Elizabeth lived in the Jewett house as a curator, some unseen hands pulled her back as she teetered at the top of the steep staircase in the back of the house. She likes to believe it was the author's ghost.

This interview transformed the piece by bringing the subject to life—first for me as the writer, and later for my readers. Ultimately, what makes almost any topic compelling is discovering why it matters to *people*—how it affects their lives. Doing interviews with people close to the subject, both experts and nonexperts, is often the best way to find that out.

If you'd like to do some interviews, now is the time to begin arranging them.

Finding Experts

You may be hesitant to consider finding authorities on your topic to talk to because, after all, you're just a lowly student who knows next to nothing. How could you possibly impose on that sociology professor who published the book on anti-Semitism you found in the library? If that's how you feel, keep this in mind: *Most people, no matter who they are, love the attention of an interviewer, no matter who she is, particularly if what's being discussed fascinates them both.* Time and again, I've found my own shyness creep up on me when I pick up the telephone to arrange an interview. But almost invariably, when I start talking with my interview subject, the experience is great for us both.

How do you find experts to interview?

■ *Check your sources.* As you begin to collect books, articles, and Internet documents, note their authors and affiliations. I get calls from time to time from writers who come across my book on lobsters in the course of their research and discover that I am at Boise State University. Sometimes the caller will arrange a phone interview or, if he lives within driving distance, a personal interview.

■ *Check the phone book.* The familiar Yellow Pages can be a gold mine. Carin, who was writing a paper on solar energy, merely looked under that heading and found a local dealer who sold solar systems to homeowners. Mark, who was investigating the effects of sexual abuse on children, found a counselor who specialized in treating abuse victims.

■ *Ask your friends and your instructors.* Your roommate's boyfriend's father may be a criminal attorney who has lots to say about the insanity defense for your paper on that topic. Your best friend may be taking a photography course with a professor who would be a great interview for your paper on the work of Edward Weston. One of your instructors may know other faculty working in your subject area who would do an interview.

■ *Check the faculty directory.* Many universities publish an annual directory of faculty and their research interests. On my campus, it's called the *Directory of Research and Scholarly Activities.* From it, I know, for example, that two professors at my university have expertise in eating disorders, a popular topic with student researchers.

■ *Check the* Encyclopedia of Associations. This is a wonderful reference book that lists organizations with interests ranging from promoting tofu to preventing acid rain. Each listing includes the name of the group, its address and phone number, a list of its publications, and a short description of its purpose. Sometimes such organizations can direct you to experts in your area who are available for live interviews or to spokespeople who are happy to provide phone interviews.

■ *Check the Internet.* You can find the e-mail addresses and phone numbers of many scholars and researchers on the Internet, including those affiliated with your own university and ones nearby. Often, these experts are listed in online directories for their colleges or universities. Sometimes you can find knowledgeable people by subscribing to a listserv or Internet discussion group on your topic. Often an expert will have her own Web page, and her e-mail address will provide a hypertext link. (For more details, see "Finding People on the Internet," later in this chapter.)

Finding Nonexperts Affected by Your Topic

The distinction between *expert* and *nonexpert* is tricky. For example, someone who lived through 12 months of combat in Vietnam certainly has direct knowledge of the subject, though probably hasn't published an article about the war in *Foreign Affairs.* Similarly, a friend who experienced an abusive relationship with her boyfriend or overcame a drug addiction is, at least in a sense, an authority on abuse or addiction. Both individuals would likely provide invaluable interviews for papers on those topics. The voices and the stories of people who are affected by the topic you're writing about can do more than anything else to make the information come to life, even if they don't have PhDs.

You may already know people you can interview about your topic. Last semester, Amanda researched how mother-daughter relationships change when a daughter goes to college. She had no problem finding other women anxious to talk about how they get along with their mothers. A few years ago, Dan researched steroid use by student athletes. He discreetly asked his friends if they knew anyone who had taken the drugs. It turned out that an acquaintance of Dan's had used the drugs regularly and was happy to talk about his experience.

If you don't know people to interview, try posting notices on campus kiosks or bulletin boards. For example, "I'm doing a research project and interested in talking to people who grew up in single-parent households. Please call 555-9000." Also, poll other students in your class for ideas about people you might interview for your paper. Help each other out.

Making Contact

By the end of this week, you should have some people to contact for interviews. First, consider whether to ask for a face-to face, telephone, or e-mail interview. Though I've never tried it for this purpose, Skype, the free online software that allows users to make a video call anywhere in the world, might be a great interview tool. The personal interview is almost always preferable; you not only can listen, but you can watch, observing your subject's gestures and the setting, both of which can be revealing. When I'm interviewing someone in her office or home, for example, one of the first things I may jot down are the titles of books on the bookshelf. Sometimes, details about gestures and settings can be worked into your paper. Most of all, the personal interview is preferable because it's more natural, more like a conversation.

Be prepared. You may have no choice in the type of interview. If your subject is off campus or out of state, your only options may be the telephone, e-mail, or regular mail.

When contacting a subject for an interview, first state your name and then briefly explain your research project. If you were referred to the subject by someone she may know, mention that. A comment like "I think you could be extremely helpful to me," or "I'm familiar with your work, and I'm anxious to talk to you about it," works well. When thinking about when to propose the interview with an expert on your topic, consider arranging it *after* you've done some research. You will not only be more informed, but you will also have a clearer sense of what you want to know and what questions to ask.

Conducting Interviews

You've already thought about whether interviews might contribute to your paper. If there's a chance that they will, build a list of possible interview subjects and contact several of them. By the end of this week, you should begin interviewing.

I know. You wouldn't mind putting it off. But once you start, it will get easier and easier. I used to dread interviewing strangers, but after making the first phone call, I got some momentum going, and I began to enjoy it. It's decidedly easier to interview friends, family, and acquaintances, but that's the wrong reason to limit yourself to people you know.

Whom to Interview? Interview people who can provide you with what you want to know. That may change as your research develops. In your reading, you might have encountered the names of experts you'd like to contact, or you may have decided that what you really need is some anecdotal material from someone with experience in your topic. It's still not too late to contact interview subjects who didn't occur to you earlier, but do so immediately.

What Questions to Ask? The first step in preparing for an interview is to ask yourself, What's the purpose of this interview? In your research notebook, make a list of *specific questions* for each person you're going to interview. Often, these questions are raised by your reading or other interviews. What theories or ideas encountered in your reading would you like to ask your subject about? What specific facts have you been unable to uncover that your interview subject may provide? What don't you understand that he could explain? Would you like to test one of your own impressions or ideas on your subject? What about the subject's work or experience would you like to learn? Interviews are wonderful tools for clearing up your own confusion and getting specific information that is unavailable anywhere else.

Now make a list of more *open-ended questions* you might ask some or all of the people you're going to talk to. Frankly, these questions are a lot more fun to ask because you're likely to be surprised by some of the answers. For example:

- In all your experience with _____, what has most surprised you?
- What has been the most difficult aspect of your work?
- If you had the chance to change something about how you approached _____, what would it be?
- Can you remember a significant moment in your work on _____? Is there an experience with _____ that stands out in your mind?
- What do you think is the most common misconception about _____? Why?
- What are significant current trends in _____?
- Who or what has most influenced you? Who are your heroes?

- If you had to summarize the most important thing you've learned about _____, what would it be?
- What is the most important thing other people should know or understand?

As you develop both specific and open-ended questions, keep in mind what you know about each person—his work in the field and personal experience with your topic. You may end up asking a lot of the same questions of everybody you interview, but try to familiarize yourself with any special qualifications a subject may have or experiences he may have had. That knowledge might come from your reading, from what other people tell you about your subject, or from your initial telephone call to set up the interview.

Also keep in mind the *kinds* of information an interview can provide better than other sources: anecdotes, strong quotes, and sometimes descriptive material. If you ask the right questions, a live subject can paint a picture of his experience with your topic, and you can capture that picture in your paper.

During the Interview. Once you've built a list of questions, be prepared to ignore it. Interviews are conversations, not surveys. They are about human interaction between two people who are both interested in the same thing.

I remember interviewing a lobsterman, Edward Heaphy, on his boat. I had a long list of questions in my notebook, which I dutifully asked, one after the other. My questions were mechanical and so were his answers. I finally stopped, put my notebook down, and talked informally with Edward for a few minutes. Offhandedly, I asked, "Would you want your sons or daughter to get in the business?" It was a totally unplanned question. Edward was silent for a moment, staring at his hands. I knew he was about to say something important because, for the first time, I was attentive to him, not my notepad. "Too much work for what they get out of it," he said quietly. It was a surprising remark after hearing for the last hour how much Edward loved lobstering. What's more, I felt I had broken through. The rest of the interview went much better.

Much of how to conduct an interview is common sense. At the outset, clarify the nature of your project—what your paper is on and where you're at with it. Briefly explain again why you thought this individual would be the perfect person to talk to about it. I find it often helps to begin with a specific question that I'm pretty sure my subject can help with. But there's no formula. Simply be a good conversationalist: Listen attentively, ask questions that your subject seems to find interesting, and enjoy sharing an interest with your subject. Also, don't be afraid to ask what you fear are obvious questions. Demonstrate to the subject that you *really* want to understand.

Always end an interview by making sure you have accurate background information on your subject: name (spelled correctly), position, affiliation, age (if applicable), phone number. Ask if you can call him with follow-up questions, should you have any. And always ask your subject if he can recommend any additional reading or other people you should talk to. Of course, mention that you're appreciative of the time he has spent with you.

Notetaking. There are basically three ways to take notes during an interview: Use a digital recorder, a notepad, or both. I adhere to the third method, but it's a very individual choice. I like digital recorders because I don't panic during an interview that I'm losing information or quoting inaccurately. I don't want to spend hours transcribing interviews, so I also take notes on the information I think I want to use. If I miss anything, I consult the recording later. It's a backup. Sometimes, I find that there is no recording—the machine decided not to participate in the interview—and at least I have my notes. Again, a backup.

Get some practice developing your own notetaking technique by interviewing your roommate or taking notes on the television news. Devise ways to shorten often-used words (e.g., *t* for *the, imp* for *important,* and *w/o* for *without*).

The E-mail Interview

The Internet opens up new possibilities for interviews; increasingly, experts (as well as nonexperts interested in certain subjects) are accessible through e-mail and even Facebook. While electronic communication doesn't quite approach the conversational quality of the conventional face-to-face interview, the spontaneous nature of e-mail exchanges can come pretty close. It's possible to send a message, get a response, respond to the response, and get a further response—all in a single day. And for shy interviewers and interviewees, an e-mail conversation is an attractive alternative.

Finding People on the Internet. Finding people on the Internet doesn't have to involve a needle and hay if you have some information on the person for whom you're looking. If you know an expert's name and his organizational affiliation, several search tools may help you track down his e-mail address. You can, of course, Google the person. But there are other methods, too.

For example, an easy way to use the Internet to find someone to interview is through a Web document on your topic. These often include e-mail links to people associated with the site or document. You can also find academics by visiting the Web sites of the universities or colleges where they teach and use the online faculty/staff directories to find their addresses. If you don't know the institutions with which an academic is affiliated, you can often find these listed in their articles, books, or Web page. To find the home pages of hundreds of American universities and colleges, visit the following site: The Yahoo Education Directory (http://dir.yahoo.com/Education/). This search page allows you to find the home pages of universities in the United States. It includes links to a number of sites that also index colleges and universities, as well as their various programs.

Making Contact by E-mail. Once you find the e-mail address of someone who seems a likely interview subject, proceed courteously and cautiously. One of the Internet's haunting issues is its potential to violate privacy. Be especially careful if you've gone to great lengths in hunting down the e-mail address of someone involved with your research topic; she may not be keen on receiving unsolicited e-mail messages from strangers. It would be courteous to approach any potential interview subject with a short message that asks permission for an online interview. To do so, briefly describe your project and why you think this individual might be a good source for you. As always, you will be much more likely to get an enthusiastic response from someone if you can demonstrate your knowledge of her work on or experience with your topic.

Let's assume your initial contact has been successful and your subject has agreed to answer your questions. Your follow-up message should ask a *limited* number of questions—say, four or five—that are thoughtful and, if possible, specific. Keep in mind that while the e-mail interview is conducted in writing rather than through talking, many of the methods for handling conventional interviews still apply.

The Discussion Board and Listserv Interview. Discussion or message boards can be good places to find people—and sometimes experts—who are passionately interested in your research topic or question. How do you find one that might be relevant to your project? Try visiting one of the following directories that list these sites by subject.

SEARCH ENGINES FOR DISCUSSION GROUPS
BoardReader (http://boardreader.com)
BoardTracker (http://www.boardtracker.com)
Google Groups (http://groups.google.com)
Yahoo! Groups (http://groups.yahoo.com)

A way to get some help with knowing what to ask—and what not to—is to spend some time following the discussion of list participants before you jump in yourself. You might find, for example, that it would be far better to interview one participant with interesting views than to post questions to the whole list.

But if you do want to query the discussion board, avoid posting a question that may have already received substantial attention from participants. You can find out what's been covered by consulting the list's FAQs (frequently asked questions). The issue you're interested in may be there, along with a range of responses from list participants, which will spare you the need to ask the question at all.

Planning Informal Surveys

Christine was interested in dream interpretation, especially exploring the significance of symbols or images that recur in many people's dreams. She could have simply examined her own dreams, but she thought it might be more interesting to survey a group of fellow students, asking how often they dream and what they remember. An informal survey, in which she would ask each person several standard questions, seemed worth trying.

You might consider it, too, if the responses of a group of people to some aspect of your topic could reveal a pattern of behavior, attitudes, or experiences worth analyzing. Informal surveys are decidedly unscientific. You probably won't get a large enough sample size, nor do you likely have the skills to design a poll that would produce statistically reliable results. But you probably won't actually base your paper on the survey results, anyway. Rather, you'll present specific, concrete information about some patterns in your survey group or, perhaps, use some of your findings to help support your assertions.

Defining Goals and Audience

Begin planning your informal survey by defining what you want to know and whom you want to know it from. Christine suspected that many students have dreams related to stress. She wondered if there were any similarities among students' dreams. She was also curious about how many people remember their dreams and how often and whether this might be related to gender. Finally, Christine wanted to find out whether people have recurring dreams and, if so, what those were about. There were other things she wanted to know, but she knew she had to keep the survey short.

If you're considering a survey, make a list in your research notebook of things you might want to find out and specify the group of people you plan to talk to. College students? Female college students? Attorneys? Guidance counselors? Be as specific as you can about your target group.

Types of Questions

Next, consider what approach you will take. Will you ask *open-ended questions,* which give respondents plenty of room to invent their own answers? For example, Christine might ask, *Describe any dreams that seemed related to stress.* The payoff for open-ended questions is that sometimes you get surprising answers. The danger, which seems real with Christine's question, is that you'll get no answer at all. A more *directed question* might be, *Have you ever dreamed that you showed up for class and didn't know that there was a major exam that day?* Christine will get an answer to this question—yes or no—but it doesn't promise much information. A third possibility is the *multiple-choice question.* It ensures an answer and is likely to produce useful information. For example:

Have you ever had any dreams similar to these?

A. You showed up for a class and didn't know there was a major exam.
B. You're late for a class or an exam but can't seem to move fast enough to get there on time.
C. You were to give a presentation but forgot all about it.

Ultimately, Christine decided to combine the open-ended question about stress and the multiple-choice approach, hoping that if one didn't produce interesting information, the other would (see Figure 10). She also wisely decided to avoid asking more than seven questions, allowing her subjects to respond to her survey in minutes.

Survey Design

A survey shouldn't be too long (probably no more than six or seven questions), it shouldn't be biased (questions asked shouldn't skew the answers), it should be easy to score (especially if you hope to survey a relatively large number of people), it should ask clear questions, and it should give clear instructions for how to answer.

As a rule, informal surveys should begin (or end) as polls often do: by getting vital information about the respondent. Christine's survey began with questions about the gender, age, and major of the respondent (see Figure 10). Depending on the purpose of your survey, you might also want to know whether respondents are registered to vote, whether they have political affiliations, what year of school

The following survey contains questions about dreaming and dream content. The findings gathered from this survey will be incorporated into a research paper on the function of dreaming and what, if anything, we can learn from it. I'd appreciate your honest answers to the questions. Thank you for your time!

General Subject Information

Gender:　　☐ Male　　☐ Female

Age: _____

Major: _____

Survey Questions
(Circle all letters that apply.)

1. How often do you remember your dreams?
   A. Almost every night
   B. About once a week
   C. Every few weeks
   D. Practically never
2. Have you ever dreamt that you were:
   A. Falling?
   B. Flying?
3. Have you ever dreamt of:
   A. Your death?
   B. The death of someone close to you?
4. Have you ever had a recurring dream?
   A. Yes
   B. No
   If yes,　　How often? _____
   　　　　　What period of your life? _____
   　　　　　Do you still have it? _____
5. Have you ever had any dreams similar to these?
   A. You showed up for a class and didn't know there was a major exam.
   B. You're late for a class or an exam but can't seem to move fast enough to get there.
   C. You were to give a presentation but forgot all about it.
6. Do you feel your dreams:
   A. Hold some deep, hidden meanings about yourself or your life?
   B. Are meaningless?
7. Please briefly describe the dream you best remember or one that sticks out in your mind. (Use the back of this survey.)

FIGURE 10　Sample Informal Survey

Source: Reprinted with permission of Christine Bergquist.

they're in, or any number of other factors. Ask for information that provides different ways of breaking down your target group.

Avoid Loaded Questions. Question design is tricky business. Biased questions should be avoided by altering language that is charged and presumptuous. Take, for example, the question *Do you think it's morally wrong to kill unborn babies through abortion?* This wording is charged and is also presumptuous (it is unlikely that all respondents believe that abortion is killing). One revision might be *Do you support or oppose providing women the option to abort a pregnancy during the first 20 weeks?* This is a direct and specific question, neutrally stated, that calls for a yes or no answer.

Controversial topics, like abortion, are most vulnerable to biased survey questions. If your topic is controversial, take great care to eliminate bias by avoiding charged language, especially if you have strong feelings yourself.

Avoid Vague Questions. Another trap is asking vague questions. One such question is *Do you support or oppose the university's alcohol policy?* This wording assumes that respondents know what the policy is, and it ignores the fact that the policy has many elements. A revised question might ask about one part of the policy: *The university recently established a policy that states that underage students caught drinking in campus dormitories are subject to eviction. Do you support or oppose this policy?* Other equally specific questions might ask about other parts of the policy.

Drawbacks of Open-Ended Questions. Open-ended questions often produce fascinating answers, but they can be difficult to tabulate. Christine's survey asked, *Please briefly describe the dream you best remember or one that sticks out in your mind.* She got a wide range of answers—or sometimes no answer at all—but it was hard to quantify the results. Almost everyone had different dreams, which made it difficult to discern much of a pattern. She was still able to use some of the material as anecdotes in her paper, so it turned out to be a question worth asking.

Designing Your Multiple-Choice Questions. As you've seen, the multiple-choice question is an alternative to the open-ended question, leaving room for a number of *limited* responses, which are easier to quantify.

The challenge in designing multiple-choice questions is to provide choices that will likely produce results. From her reading and talking to friends, Christine came up with what she thought were three stress-related dreams college students often experience (see question 5, Figure 10). The results were interesting (45 percent circled "B"). But Christine wasn't sure about their reliability because she hadn't given respondents a "none of the above" option. How many respondents felt forced to choose one of the dreams listed because there was no other choice? Design choices you think your audience will respond to, but give them room to say your choices weren't theirs.

Using Continuum Questions. Christine's question 6 has a similar problem in that it asks a direct either/or question: *Do you feel your dreams: (A) Hold some deep, hidden meanings about yourself or your life?* or *(B) Are meaningless?* Phrased this way, the question forces the respondent into one of two extreme positions. People are more likely to place themselves somewhere in between.

A variation on the multiple-choice question is the *continuum*, where respondents indicate how they feel by marking the appropriate place along a scale. Christine's question 6 could be presented as a continuum:

> How do you evaluate the significance of your dreams? Place an "X" on the continuum in the place that most closely reflects your view.

> My dreams always   My dreams are
> hold some meaning   meaningless

Though it is a bit more difficult to tabulate results of a continuum, this method often produces reliable answers if the instructions are clear.

Conducting Surveys

Once you have finalized your questions, using whatever combination of *open-ended, multiple choice,* and *directed* questions you found most appropriate for your purpose, you can make plans to distribute the survey to the target group you defined earlier. Surveys can be administered by phone, in person, or online.

Telephone Surveys. Surveys administered by telephone have some advantages. People are more likely to be direct and honest over the phone because they are relatively anonymous. Surveys are also more likely to be completed correctly because the answers are recorded by the survey giver. However, making multiple phone calls can be tedious and expensive, if your target group goes beyond the toll-free calling area. But you may have no choice, especially if the target group for your survey isn't exclusively on campus.

In-Person Surveys. One alternative to conducting a telephone survey is to distribute the survey yourself. The university community, where large numbers of people are available in a confined area, lends itself to administering surveys this way. A survey can be distributed in dormitories, dining halls, classes, or anywhere else the people you want to talk to gather. You can stand outside the student union and stop people as they come and go, or you can hand out your survey to groups of people and collect them when the participants have finished. Your instructor may be able to help distribute your survey to classes. I asked a number of my colleagues to distribute Christine's survey in their freshman English classes, a required course representing a relatively random sample of freshmen. Because the survey took only five minutes to fill out, other instructors were glad to help, and in one day Christine was able to sample more than 90 students.

Although an exclusively university audience won't always be relevant, for some research questions it is exactly what's needed. Anna, writing a paper on date rape, surveyed exclusively women on campus, many of whom she found in women's dormitories. For his paper on the future of the fraternity system, David surveyed local "Greeks" at their annual awards banquet.

How large a sample should you shoot for? Because yours won't be a scientific survey, don't bother worrying about statistical reliability; just try to survey as many people as you can. Certainly, a large (say, more than 100) and representative sample will lend more credence to your claims about any patterns observed in the results.

Internet Surveys. You can create an online survey easily using a program like SurveyMonkey (http://surveymonkey.com/). Such programs are remarkably easy to use, walking you through the process of designing questions, posting the survey, and even analyzing the results. For example, SurveyMonkey's free "basic" service will allow you to create a ten-question survey and collect up to 100 responses. You can then post the survey on your blog, send it out to an e-mail address list, or put a link to it on your Web site. The challenge, as usual, is reaching the people you'd like to survey and getting them to respond.

Listservs, discussion boards, and even real-time communication tools such as chat rooms all organize people with similar interests—and in some cases similar demographics. This makes cyberspace a potentially appealing place to conduct survey work. Consider, for example, posting three or four questions on your topic to a relevant discussion group or to a group that may reach an audience you'd like to survey. For example, Marty was working on an essay that explored the extent to which college students felt a generational identity. A search on Google Groups produced a Usenet group (alt.society.generation-x) that proved an ideal forum to respond to her questions.

Fieldwork: Research on What You See and Hear

My daughter Julia, a senior in high school, belonged to the school's theater group, performing in plays and taking theater classes. She enjoyed it. But she also claimed that certain qualities distinguished "theater kids" from other kinds. How did she come to these conclusions? By hanging out with the theater crowd. To use a more academic phrasing, Julia was a "participant-observer," though there was certainly no method involved. We all make judgments about social groups, inferences that come from experience. Usually there's nothing systematic about this process, and sometimes these judgments are unfair.

Yet the data that comes from observation, particularly if we take care to collect and document it, can be a rich vein to mine. This kind of data is also relevant to research in the social sciences and humanities and even relevant to research essays in composition courses. Suppose, for instance, that your research question focuses on comparing crowd behavior at college and high school football games. How can you research that essay *without* observing a few games? If your topic has anything do to with subcultures or social groups—say, international students on your campus or the snowboarding community—fieldwork can be invaluable.

Preparing for Fieldwork

The kind of fieldwork you're able to do for your essay simply won't be the more rigorous and methodologically sophisticated work that academic ethnographers, anthropologists, or sociologists do. For one thing, you don't have the time it requires. But you can collect some useful observations for your paper. There are three tools for this you might find useful:

1. *Notebook.* You can't do without this. For convenience, you might choose a pocket notebook rather than a full-size one.
2. *Digital camera.* Take pictures of the site you're observing and the people participating in an activity for later study. Also photograph

objects (ethnographers call these "artifacts") that have symbolic or practical significance to the people you're observing.

3. *Digital recorder.* Use it for interviews and other recording in the field. (Remember to ask permission to record interviewees.)

Where you go to conduct field observations of course depends on your topic. Typically you choose a physical space in which people in particular social or cultural groups meet to participate in meaningful (to them) activities. If your research is on the high school theater group as a subculture, you might go to rehearsals, auditions, or perhaps a cast party. A researcher interested in adult video gaming addiction might spend a few evenings watching gamers do their thing at someone's home. An essay on Kwanzaa, an African American holiday tradition, might observe some families participating in its rituals.

Notetaking Strategies

What do you look for and how do you document it? Well, that depends on your project. Generally, of course, the task is to watch what people do and listen to what they say. More specifically, though, consider the following:

■ *Look for evidence that confirms, contradicts, or qualifies the theories or assertions you've read about in your research.* Is it true that when they're not playing, adult video gamers can appear irritable and depressed? Do dogs that are punitively corrected during a training class demonstrate submissive behavior?

■ *Look and listen to what people say during moments with particular significance for participants.* How do fans behave when the referee doesn't call the foul? What does one gamer say to another when she beats him?

■ *Describe "artifacts"—things that people in the situation typically use.* A skater's skateboard. The objects in an actor's dressing room. The clothing traditionally worn by women celebrating Kwanzaa.

When you take notes, consider using the double-entry journal system that is discussed in detail in the next chapter. Use the left-facing page of your notebook to scribble your observations and the right-facing page to later freewrite about what strikes you about these observations. Make sure that you clearly indicate when you are quoting someone and when you are describing something.

Using What You See and Hear

Unless your research topic is an ethnography—an investigation that describes and interprets the activities of a cultural group in the field—it's likely that you will use your own fieldwork in your essay in a relatively limited way. Still, it can really be worth the effort. For example, fieldwork can be especially useful to:

■ *Give your topic a face.* Nothing makes a problem or idea more meaningful than *showing* how it affects people. Can you use your descriptions of individuals (perhaps along with your interviews) to show rather than simply explain why your topic is significant?

■ *Make a scene.* Observations in the field give you the ingredients of a scene: In a particular time and place, people are *doing something.* If what they are doing is significant and relevant to your research question, you can describe the place, the people, the action, and even the dialogue. Few techniques give writing more life.

■ *Incorporate images.* Depending on the nature of your project, the digital pictures you take in the field can be powerful illustrations of what you're writing about.

■ *Develop a multimodal research essay.* Using the digital recordings you made in the field, and free editing software like Audacity, you can create a podcast of your research essay, even incorporating music. You can use free software like Microsoft Photo Story to use images, text, and voice narration to present your findings.

The Third Week

Writing in the Middle

Tim's inquiry question explores the impact that an adult's addiction to video games has on family and friends. He spends a week collecting research, mostly printing out articles from library databases and Web sites. Tim skims things, underlining a line or a passage from time to time, but for the most part he's like a bear in a blueberry patch, voraciously collecting as much information as he can. This is all in preparation for the writing, which he'll postpone until right before the paper is due.

Sound familiar? This is certainly similar to the way I always did research.

Here's how I would rewrite this scene for Tim: Tim is still hungrily collecting information about video gaming addiction, *but as he does it, he's writing about what he's found.* Tim's notebook is open next to his laptop, and he's jotting down quotations and summaries and maybe an interesting fact or two. He's also marking up the electronic copy, highlighting passages of an article he might want to return to or cutting and pasting relevant passages into an open Word document. Then, when he's done reading the article, Tim writes furiously in his notebook for ten minutes or so, exploring his reaction to what he found.

I now believe that the writing that takes place in the *middle* of the research process—the notetaking stage—may be as important as, if not more important than, the writing that takes place at the end—composing the draft. Writing in the middle helps you take possession of your sources and establish your presence in the draft. It sharpens your thinking about your topic, and it is the best cure for unintentional plagiarism.

I realize I have a sales job to do on this. Writing in the middle, particularly if you've been weaned on notecards, feels like busywork. "It gets in the way of doing the research," one student told me. "I just want to collect as much stuff as I can, as quickly as I can. Notetaking slows me down." Though it may seem inefficient, writing as you read may actually make your research *more* efficient. Skeptical? Read on.

Becoming an Activist Notetaker

Notetaking can and probably should begin your process of writing your paper. Notetaking is not simply a mechanical process of vacuuming up as much information as you can and depositing it on notecards or in a notebook with little thought. Your notes from sources are your first chance to *make sense* of the information you encounter, to make it your own. You do need more time to take thoughtful notes, but the payoff is that you'll write a draft more quickly and produce a paper that reflects your point of view much more strongly.

Writing in the middle is basically something you should do every day: Have a conversation. In this case you're conversing with a stranger who shares your interest in something, and you're talking with texts. The exercise that follows is an opportunity to practice this new kind of dialogue.

EXERCISE 1

Getting into a Conversation with a Fact

Mostly, we just collect facts to deploy them in support of a point we're trying to make, conveniently assuming they are true, of course. But facts can ignite thought, if we let them. They can help us discover what we think, refine our point of view, and explore new avenues of thought. But for this to happen, you have to interact with information. Rather than a monologue—simply jotting down what an author is saying—you engage in a conversation—talking *with* an author: questioning, agreeing, speculating, wondering, connecting, arguing. You can do this in your head, but it's far more productive to have this dialogue through writing.

Let's try it.

I'm going to share with you two facts—one at a time—that together start to tell an interesting story about gender, beauty, and culture. Each fact will be a prompt for about five minutes of fast-writing in which you explore your thinking about the fact.

STEP 1: How do women see men's "attractiveness"? *Harper's Magazine* recently reported the following:

Portion of men whose attractiveness is judged by U.S. women to be "worse than average": 4/5

What do you make of this? Does it surprise you? Assuming it's true, how would you explain it? If you doubt it's true, why? Fastwrite your response for five minutes.

STEP 2: Now that you've done five minutes of "thinking through writing" about how women view men, consider how men view women's "attractiveness."

Portion of women whose attractiveness is judged by U.S. men to be "worse than average": 2/5

What do you make of men's more generous attitude toward women? Does this surprise you? How might you explain both "facts"? Together, what does this information say to you about gender and "attractiveness"? Fastwrite for five minutes, exploring these questions.

As you reread your two fastwrites, do you see any consistent line of thought developing? If someone asked you what you thought about these two facts, what would you say?

In a small way, you've just practiced a method of notetaking that can help you make sense of information you encounter when you read for your research project or read any other text you want to think about. Later in this chapter, I'll show you something called the "double-entry journal," which is a system for using this technique. But in this exercise, you have practiced the essence of writing in the middle: seeing information as the beginning of a conversation, not the end of one.

Exploring your reaction to what you read during an open-ended fastwrite is only part of using information to discover what you think. You must also *understand* what you're reading. Most *good* conversations make demands on both speakers. The most important of these is simply to listen carefully to what the other person is saying, even (and perhaps especially) if you don't agree. In couples therapy there's a method to help this along called "say back"—each partner has to listen first and then repeat what he or she heard the other say. Response or reaction comes later. Researchers entering into a conversation with their sources need to engage in the same practice: You need to listen or read carefully, first making an effort to understand a subject or an author's arguments or ideas and then exploring your response to them, as you did in the preceding exercise.

The academic equivalent of "say back" is paraphrasing or summarizing, something we'll look at in more detail later in this chapter. Both are undervalued skills, I think, that require practice. Try your hand at it in the following exercise.

EXERCISE 2

"Say Back" to a Source

The following passage is from an article by linguist Deborah Tannen on the complexity of communication within families.

> Through talk, we create and shape our relationships. Through talk, we are comforted; through talk we are hurt. We look to family members for come-as-you-are acceptance, but instead of an intimate ally, we sometimes find an intimate critic. A small remark can spark a big conflict because with the family, no utterance stands alone. Every remark draws meaning from innumerable conversations that came before.*

In your notebook, rewrite the passage in your own words in roughly the same length—a *paraphrase*. You'll find it's easier to do if you first focus on understanding what Tannen is trying to say and then on writing without looking much at the passage, if possible. If your instructor assigns this as an in-class exercise, exchange your rewrite with a partner. Then read the following sections on plagiarism.

Plagiarism: What It Is, Why It Matters, and How to Avoid It

Simply put, *plagiarism* is using others' ideas *or* words as if they were your own. The most egregious case is handing in someone else's work with your name on it. Some schools also consider using one paper to meet the requirements of two classes to be a grave offense. But most plagiarism is unintentional. I remember being guilty of plagiarism when writing a philosophy paper my freshman year in college. I committed the offense largely because I didn't know what plagiarism was, and I hadn't been adequately schooled in good scholarship (which is no excuse).

I Read What You Said and Borrowed It, Okay?

Here's another passage from the same article by Deborah Tannen as the passage in Exercise 2. In this excerpt she is talking

---

*Tannen, Deborah. "I Heard What You Didn't Say." *Washington Post* 13 May 2001: B1. Print.

about a situation with which we're all familiar. We're talking with a loved one and he or she makes a comment that seems innocuous: "I'll put the dishes in the dishwasher because I can pack more in." But we hear the comment as a larger criticism: "You're not good at house-work." There are what seem to be simple messages with equally simple motives, and then there are "metamessages" that we sometimes hear instead of the simple ones. Following the excerpt from Tannen's passage is what seems like a pretty good paraphrase:

> **Original passage:** Distinguishing the message from the meta-message (terms I have adopted from anthropologist Gregory Bateson) is necessary to ensure that family members work things out rather than working each other over. It's frustrating to have the same arguments again and again. But some arguments can be constructive—if family members use them to articulate and understand the metamessages they are intending and hearing.*

> **Paraphrase:** Sometimes family members can have the same argument over and over, not realizing what they're really argu-ing about. Linguist Deborah Tannen writes that it's important to try distinguishing the message from the metamessage. By articulating what was said and what was heard, arguments can be constructive rather than frustrating.

There are a couple of problems with this paraphrase, but they might, at first glance, be pretty subtle. Notice that the first sentence uses the phrase "have the same argument over and over," which, though worded slightly differently, copies the pattern of Tannen's original "have the same arguments again and again." That won't do.

Worse, the paraphrase fails to include quotation marks around the borrowed phrase "distinguishing the message from the metames-sage." It also lifts "constructive" and "frustrating" from the original without quotation marks and uses the word "articulating," which is uncomfortably close to Tannen's "articulate." But the bigger problem is not one I would expect you to notice yet. Even though the paraphrase uses an attribution tag—"Linguist Deborah Tannen writes…"—the paraphrase doesn't include a parenthetical citation, something like "(Tannen 2)," indicating the page of the original passage. *Whenever you quote, paraphrase, or summarize a source, it must always be fully cited, even if you mention the author's name.*

---

*Tannen, Deborah. "I Heard What You Didn't Say." *Washington Post* 13 May 2001: B2. Print.

What Is Plagiarism?

Each college or university has a statement in the student handbook that offers a local definition. But that statement probably includes most or all of the following forms of plagiarism:

1. Handing in someone else's work—a downloaded paper from the Internet or one borrowed from a friend—and claiming that it's your own.
2. Handing in the same paper for two different classes.
3. Using information or ideas that are not common knowledge from any source and failing to acknowledge that source.
4. Using the exact language or expressions of a source and not indicating through quotation marks and citation that the language is borrowed.
5. Rewriting a passage from a source, making minor word substitutions but retaining the same syntax and structure as the original.

Corrected paraphrase: To get beyond old family arguments and avoid hurting one another, linguist Deborah Tannen writes, it's important for family members to try **"distinguishing the message from the metamessage."** Even old family arguments can be **"constructive,"** says Tannen, if family members are careful to talk openly about the metamessages **(Tannen 2)**.

Here are some simple tactics for avoiding plagiarism:

- It's fine to borrow distinctive terms or phrases from a source, but signal that you've done so with quotation marks.
- Make a habit of using attribution tags, signaling to your reader who is the source of the idea, quotation, or fact. These tags include things such as "Tannen argues," "Tannen writes," "According to Tannen," and so on.
- *Always* cite borrowed material (more about how to do so in the next chapter).

As a follow-up to Exercise 2, return to your paraphrase of the Tannen passage on talk within families. Do you need to edit or alter the

The Common Knowledge Exception

While you always have to tell readers what information you have borrowed and where it came from, things that are "common knowledge" are excluded from this. Everyone knows, for example, that John Kennedy died in Dallas in November 1963. These and other widely known facts need not be cited. Neither do observations that anyone could make or common sayings, such as "home is where the heart is."

paraphrase you wrote to avoid possible plagiarism problems? If you're in class, your instructor may ask you to work in pairs on this. What are the common plagiarism mistakes—almost always unintentional—that students in the class made when they paraphrased the passage in Exercise 2? (Forms of plagiarism are summarized in the box "What Is Plagiarism?")

Why Plagiarism Matters

It may seem that concern over plagiarism is just a lot of fuss that reflects English teachers' obsession with enforcing rules. In reality, the saddest days I've ever had as a writing teacher have always been when I've talked with a student about a paper she downloaded from the Internet or borrowed from her roommate. Most instructors hate dealing with plagiarism.

Deliberate cheating is, of course, a moral issue, but the motive for carefully distinguishing between what is yours and what you've borrowed isn't just to "be good." It's really about making a gesture of gratitude. Research is always built on the work that came before it. As you read and write about your topic, I hope that you come to appreciate the thoughtful writing and thinking of people before you who may have given you a new way of seeing or thinking.

Knowledge is a living thing (see Figure 1), growing like a great tree in multiple directions, adding (and losing) branches that keep reaching higher toward new understandings and truths. As researchers we are tree climbers, ascending the branches in an effort to see better. It's only natural that as we make this climb, we feel grateful for the strength of the limbs supporting us. Citing and acknowledging sources is a way of expressing this gratitude.

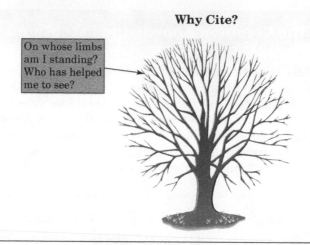

Why Cite?

FIGURE 1 Like a tree, knowledge in a discipline is a living thing, from time to time losing and adding branches, growing in new directions.

Making Information Your Own: Quotation, Paraphrase, and Summary

Taylor is writing a paper on plastics in the ocean, and from the European Environment Commission Web site, she cuts and pastes the following text into a Word document:

> Marine litter is a global concern, affecting all the oceans of the world. Every year, approximately 10 billion tons of litter end up in the ocean world wide, turning it into the world's biggest landfill and thus posing environmental, economic, health, and aesthetic problems. Sadly, the persistence of marine litter is the result from poor practices of solid waste management, lack of infrastructure, and a lack of awareness of the public at large about the consequences of their actions.*

She likes the passage—it succinctly states the problem of ocean pollution and even includes a powerful statistic: 10 billion tons of garbage end up in the world's oceans each year. Now what does she do with it? Consider her choices:

1. Do nothing. Set the passage aside and hope there will be a place in her paper where she can digitally dump the whole thing or part of it.
2. Rewrite all or part of it in her own words. Set the rewrite aside and hope to weave it into her paper later.

*From http://ec.europa.eu/environment/water/marine/pollution.htm. © European Union, 1995–2011. Reproduction is authorized.

Student writers often face this dilemma, and in the digital age, when it's easy to cut and paste text, choice #1 is the odds-on favorite. Just collect and dump. What this usually means in the draft research essay is a quotation. In some cases, this is justified. Perhaps the material *is* so well said that you want the voice of the source to speak for itself. But more often, a cut-and-paste quotation—particularly an extended one—looks like a sign of surrender: Instead of actively guiding a reader through information, the writer opts to take a nap.

What about choice #2? How might Taylor rewrite the passage to establish herself as a reliable guide?

> None of the world's oceans are spared from pollution, notes the European Environment Commission, which also reports that 10 billion tons of garbage are dumped in the world's oceans every year. They now represent "the world's biggest landfill" ("Marine Pollution Awareness").

In the rewrite, Taylor mines the original passage selectively, emphasizing what she thinks is important but without misrepresenting what was said. Here is a writer who is controlling information rather than being controlled by it.

The relationship between a source and a research writer is often complex, for various reasons. Consider how difficult it can be to read someone else's words, make an effort to understand what they mean, and then find your own words to restate the ideas. What's worse is that sometimes the authors are experts who use language you may not easily grasp or use reasoning in ways you can't easily follow. And then there are those authors who write so beautifully, you wonder how you could possibly say it better. Finally, you might fear that somehow you will goof and accidentally plagiarize the source's ideas or words.

One useful, if somewhat crude, way of describing how a writer might take possession of information she gathers is in terms of three approaches you've no doubt heard of before: paraphrase, summary, and quotation. These are useful to learn about, not only so that you know the rules for how to employ them, but, perhaps more important, so you can see each as a different way of interacting with what you read. Ultimately, they are tools that keep you in the game.

Paraphrasing

In Exercise 2, you practiced "say back," a technique that helps many married couples who may be headed for divorce. As I mentioned, *paraphrase* is the academic equivalent of this therapeutic method for

How Can I Use That? Four Motives for Using a Source

My daughter Julia wants a pug. This isn't good news because I don't think much of little dogs with sinus problems. I also heard a rumor that if a pug sneezes hard enough its eyes might pop and dangle by the optical nerve until the eyeball is greased and popped back into the eye socket. This posed a research question: *Are pugs typical of overbred dogs that tend to suffer from a range of physiological and psychological problems?*

Because this is a question that goes way beyond my personal experience, I naturally need to turn to outside sources to learn more. When most of us do research for an academic paper, we typically search for sources that exemplify or support a point we want to make. But, especially in an inquiry-based project, you'll want to find sources for reasons other than just supporting your points. For example:

1. *Sources can extend your thinking.* This is an essential motive for doing research, particularly early in the process. You want to learn more about your subject so that you can refine your research question and understand more fully what it is you're asking. For example, in an article in *The Economist* magazine, I learn that kennel clubs, which began in England in the second half of the nineteenth century, have played a key role in "genetic painting" of dog breeds, a euphemism for genetic manipulation (1).* The article goes on to argue that it is

*"It's a Dog's Life." *The Economist* 12 Dec. 2002: 1–5. *Academic Search Premier.* Web. 8 August 2005.

the demands of these associations for a kind of "racial purity" that have contributed to overbreeding (2). Perhaps I should revise my research question: *What role has the Pug Dog Club of America (PDCA) played in promoting or confronting the problem of inbreeding in the dog?*

2. *Sources can provide necessary background.* For a full understanding of your topic, there may be things you—and ultimately your readers—need to know. For example, the *Encyclopedia of Animals** tells me that pugs are one of the oldest breeds and live an average of eight years. The dog's genetic history is a long one, which may be a significant fact. The average life span of a pug means that Julia will go to college before the dog dies, which means her pug will become my pug.

3. *Sources can support or exemplify a point you want to make.* As I just mentioned, this is the motive we usually think of for research. We have a point, claim, or assertion we want to support with the information we've found. For instance, here's a quotation that seems to confirm the claim that kennel clubs have indeed contributed to medical problems in dogs:

The Kennel Club, the top canine body in Britain, working with breed-specific dog clubs has laid out the "right" looks—a narrow set of desirable characteristics that breeders try to match. "Judges judge against a standard, and it's rewarding and challenging for breeders to try to meet those standards," says Geoff Sampson, a geneticist who works for the Kennel Club. But that kind of judging has too often been unrewarding for the dog. In the quest to create the perfect pooch, close relatives will often be mated, sometimes even brother and sister or mother and son. The danger of this practice is that it increases the likelihood that puppies will inherit genetic diseases—some 400 have now been identified in dogs.†

4. *Sources can present opportunities for analysis and interpretation.* Sometimes you encounter information that raises

(*continued*)

*"Pug." *Encyclopedia of Animals* n.d. *EBSCO Animals.*Web. 8 August 2005.
†Gibson, Helen. "A Flawed Beauty." *Time Europe.* 8 Aug. 2001: 2–3. *MasterFile Premier.* Web. 8 Aug. 2005.

new questions, and when it does, you have a chance to offer your own analysis or interpretation of how that information or assertion might be understood. For example, one article asserted that the whole movement to promote purebred dogs for show, which originated with the British Kennel Clubs in the nineteenth century, might be part of a larger, social push toward racial purity in people. That dog breeding may have "racist" origins is an explosive and fascinating assertion. While I concede this might have been true, is it a relevant claim today? Isn't it faulty reasoning to infer that the motives of some people 150 years ago necessarily remain the motives of people today?

By the way, I could not find evidence that pugs blow out their eyeballs when they sneeze. Sadly, I can't use that as a reason for discouraging Julia about pug ownership unless I find some convincing evidence to support it. But I'll keep looking.

getting people to listen to each other. Try to say in your own words—and in about the same length as the author said it—what you understand the author to mean. This is hard, at first, because instead of just mindlessly quoting—a favorite alternative for many students—you have to *think*. Paraphrasing demands that you make your own sense of something. The time is well worth it. Why? Because not only are you lowering the risk of unintentional plagiarism and being fair to the source's ideas, *you are essentially writing a fragment of your draft*. Exercise 3 will help you develop these skills.

EXERCISE 3

Paraphrase Practice

At the heart of paraphrasing is this very simple idea: *Good writers find their own way of saying things*. That's your challenge here. Read each line or passage below until you think you thoroughly understand it, and then don't look at it again. Paraphrase the line or passage on a separate piece of paper, finding your own way of saying what you understand the original to mean. Finally, review your paraphrase to make sure that any borrowed words or phrases from the original are within quotation marks in your paraphrase.

The lines and passages get progressively harder to paraphrase.

1. For most of the last 500 years, imitation was the sincerest form of architectural flattery.*
2. According to the National Institutes of Health,
    - Percentage of U.S.-born Mexican Americans who have suffered from some psychological disorder: 48
    - Percentage of Mexican immigrants who have: 29
    - Percentage of Mexico City residents who have: 23
3. Houseflies not only defecate constantly but also do so in liquid form, which means they are in constant danger of dehydration.†
4. It should also be understood that the thought content of student recitation or writing need not be original or creative. It's highly unlikely that a freshman will come up with a truly original idea about psychology, economics, or chemistry. But an absolutely original sentence that relates a known fact or logical argument is about the best proof we have of understanding.‡

Exercise 3 returns me to my original argument: Thoughtful notetaking pays off in the long run because you're essentially writing your essay in the middle of the process. Imagine what an advantage you'll have over those who wait until the night before the paper is due. Rather than having pages of journal notes that are ripe for the picking, the night-before-it's-due clan is looking at bare branches. In a few pages, I'll suggest several notetaking methods that I think will give you the most to harvest. But first, let's review another listening technique useful for academic writers: summary.

Summarizing

In order to sell a movie to Hollywood, a screenwriter should be able to summarize what it's about in a sentence. "*Juno* is a film about a smart, single, pregnant teenager who finds unexpected humor in her situation but finally finds that her wit is not enough to help her navigate the emotional tsunami her pregnancy triggers in the lives of those around her." That statement hardly does justice to the

*Rybczynski, Witold. "When Architects Plagiarize It's Not Always Bad." *Slate.com*. Slate, 14 Sept. 2005. Web. 15 Sept. 2005.
†Conniff, Richard. "Why Did God Make Flies?" *Wonders*. New York: Owl, 1997. Print.
‡Leamnson, Robert. *Thinking About Teaching and Learning*. Sterling, VA: Stylus, 1999. Print.

film—which is about so much more than that—but I think it basically captures the story and its central theme.

Obviously, that's what a *summary* is: a reduction of longer material into a brief statement that captures a basic idea, argument, or theme from the original. Like paraphrasing, summarizing often requires careful thought. This is especially the case when you're trying to capture the essence of a whole movie, article, or chapter that's fairly complex. Many times, however, summarizing involves simply boiling down a passage—not the entire work—to its basic idea.

EXERCISE 4

Summary Practice

While a summary can never be purely objective, it needs to be fair. After all, each of us will understand a text differently, but at the same time we have to do our best to represent what a source is actually saying without prejudice. That's often a particular challenge when you have strong feelings about a topic. The passage that follows, an excerpt on the debate over gay marriage from the Pew Forum on Religion and Public Life, is itself a summary of sorts; it attempts to capture the sentiments of both sides of the debate.

Carefully read the passage, and write a brief (two to four sentences) summary of its main point. Make sure to summarize in your own words, and if you borrow any words or phrases from the original passage, don't forget those quotation marks.

Most supporters of same-sex marriage contend that gay and lesbian couples should be treated no differently than their heterosexual counterparts and that they should be able to marry like anyone else. Beyond wanting to uphold the legal principles of nondiscrimination and equal treatment, supporters say there are very practical reasons behind the fight for marriage equity. They point out, for instance, that homosexual couples who have been together for years often find themselves without the basic rights and privileges that are currently enjoyed by heterosexual couples who legally marry—from the sharing of health and pension benefits to hospital visitation rights.

Most social conservatives and others who oppose same-sex marriage argue that marriage between a man and a woman is the bedrock of a healthy society because it leads to stable families and, ultimately, to children who grow up to be productive adults. Allowing gay and lesbian couples to wed, they contend, will radically redefine marriage and further weaken it at a time when the institution is already in serious trouble due to high divorce rates and a significant number of out-of-wedlock births. Moreover, many predict that giving gay couples the right to marry will ultimately lead to granting people in polygamous and other nontraditional relationships the right to marry as well.*

Quoting

I'll never forget a scene from the documentary *Shoah,* an 11-hour film about the Holocaust, which presents an interview with the Polish engineer of one of the trains that took thousands of Jews to their deaths. As an old man still operating the same train, he was asked how he felt about his role in World War II. He said quietly, "If you could lick my heart, it would poison you."

It would be difficult to restate the Polish engineer's comment in your own words. But more important, it would be stupid even to try. Some of the pain and regret and horror of that time in history is embedded in that one man's words. You may not come across such a distinctive quote as you read your sources this week, but be alert to *how* authors (and those quoted by authors) say things. Is the prose unusual, surprising, or memorable? Does the writer make a point in an interesting way? If so, jot it down in your journal or cut and paste it into a digital file, making sure to signal the borrowed material with quotation marks.

There are several other reasons to quote a source as you're taking notes. Sometimes it's desirable to quote an expert on your topic who is widely recognized in the field. Used to support or develop your own assertions, the voice of an authority can lend credit to your argument and demonstrate your effort to bring recognized voices into the discussion. If your paper is on a literary topic—involving novels, stories, poems, and other works—then purposeful and selective quoting is especially important and appropriate. The texts and the actual language the writers use in them are often central to the argument you're making.

As a general rule, however, the college research paper should contain no more than 10 or 20 percent quoted material. This principle sometimes gets ignored because it's so easy to just copy a passage from a source and paste it into an essay. But keep in mind that a

*Excerpt from "A Contentious Debate: Same-Sex Marriage in the U.S.," *Pew Forum on Religion & Public Life*, http://pewforum.org/Gay-Marriage-and-Homosexuality/A-Contentious-Debate-Same-Sex-Marriage-in-the-US.aspx. © 2009 Pew Research Center. Reprinted by permission.

writer who quotes may not really need to think much about and take possession of the information, shaping it and allowing herself to be shaped by it. Still, you can retain a strong presence in your work even when using the words of others, if you remember to do the following:

1. *Quote selectively.* You need not use all of the passage. Mine phrases or sentences that are particularly distinctive and embed them in your own prose.
2. *Provide a context.* The worst way to use a quote is to just drop it into a paragraph without attribution or comment. If you're going to bring someone else's voice into your work, you should, at the very least, say who the source is and perhaps why what this person says is particularly relevant to what you're saying.
3. *Follow up.* In addition to establishing a context for a quotation, seize the chance to analyze, argue with, amplify, explain, or highlight what is in a quotation.

As an example of effective use of quotation, consider the following excerpt from Bill Bryson's book *At Home: A Short History of Private Life*. Bryson is especially talented at telling compelling nonfiction stories using research, and here he explains the fears of people in the nineteenth century about being buried alive. In this case, Bryson incorporates a "block quotation"—that is, the passage he quotes is set off and indented, as is required in MLA style for passages of four or more lines.

> According to one report, of twelve hundred bodies exhumed in New York City for one reason or another between 1860 and 1880, six showed signs of thrashing or other postinternment distress. In London, when the naturalist Frank Buckland went looking for the coffin of the anatomist John Hunter at St. Martin-in-the-Fields Church, he reported coming upon three coffins that showed clear evidence of internal agitation (or so he was convinced).... A correspondent to the British journal *Notes and Queries* offered this contribution in 1858:
>
> > A rich manufacturer named Oppelt died about fifteen years since at Reichenberg, in Austria, and a vault was built in the cemetery for the reception of the body by his widow and children. The widow died about a month ago and was taken to the same tomb; but, when it was opened for the purpose, the coffin of her husband was found open and empty, and the skeleton discovered in the corner of the vault in a sitting posture.

For at least a generation such stories became routine in even serious periodicals. So many people became morbidly obsessed with the fear of being interred before their time that a word was coined for it: *taphephobia*.

Notice that Bryson provides a context for his quotation—the name of the source as well as mention of its stature as a "serious publication"—and then follows up the quoted passage by noting that the story it tells is typical of nineteenth-century fears of being buried alive. He also notes that the anecdote is an illustration of what was then called taphephobia. Bryson's book is not an academic work, so you don't see citations, something that you will incorporate into your own essay, but you can see how a powerful quotation can bring the work to life, especially when it's sandwiched within the commentary of the writer who chooses to allow another voice to speak.

Notetaking

There's the skills part of notetaking—knowing how to cite, summarize, paraphrase, and quote correctly—and then there's the more interesting, harder part—making *use* of what you're reading to discover what you think. So far, we've talked about this latter process using the metaphor of conversation. In Exercise 1, you tried out this idea, responding in writing to facts about gender and notions of "attractiveness." This conversation metaphor doesn't originate with me. Lots of people use it to describe how all knowledge is made. One theorist, Kenneth Burke, famously explained that we might imagine that all scholarship on nearly any subject is much like a parlor conversation between people in the know (see the box "The Unending Conversation"). These are the experts who, over time, have contributed to the discussions about what might be true and who constantly ask questions to keep the conversation going.

As newcomers to this conversation, we don't really have much to contribute. It's important that we listen in so that we begin to understand what has already been said and who has said it. But at some point, even novices like us are expected to speak up. We're not there to simply record what we hear. We're writers. We're supposed to discover something to say.

Fortunately, we rarely enter the parlor empty handed. We have experiences and other prior knowledge that is relevant to the conversation we're listening in on. For example, you certainly know something about the subject of Thomas Lord's essay, "What? I Failed? But I Paid

---

The Unending Conversation

Imagine that you enter a parlor. You come late. When you arrive, others have long preceded you, and they are engaged in a heated discussion, a discussion too heated for them to pause and tell you exactly what it is about. In fact, the discussion had already begun long before any of them got there, so that no one present is qualified to retrace for you all the steps that had gone before. You listen for a while, until you decide that you have caught the tenor of the argument; then you put in your oar. Someone answers; you answer him; another comes to your defense; another aligns himself against you, to either the embarrassment or gratification of your opponent, depending upon the quality of your ally's assistance. However, the discussion is interminable. The hour grows late, you must depart. And you do depart, with the discussion still vigorously in progress.

Kenneth Burke

---

for Those Credits! Problems of Students Evaluating Faculty." After all, you've probably filled out an evaluation or two for a course you've taken. But clearly, Lord, as a science educator, has spent considerably more time than you considering whether these evaluations are useful for judging the quality of teaching. Yet college writers, even if they have limited expertise, are expected to speak up on a topic they're writing about, entering the conversation by raising questions, analyzing arguments, speculating, and emphasizing what they think is important.

EXERCISE 5

Dialogic Notetaking: Listening In, Speaking Up

Drop into the conversation that Thomas Lord has going in his essay, and, drawing on what you've learned so far, use your journal writing to listen in and speak up.

STEP 1:

1. Begin by listening in. Read Thomas Lord's essay once straight through. Underline and mark passages that you think are:
   a. important to your understanding of the article,
   b. puzzling in some way,

c. surprising, or

d. connected with your own initial ideas and experiences.

2. Reread the opening paragraph, the last few paragraphs, and all of your marked passages; then, without looking at the article, compose a two- or three-sentence summary of what you understand to be the most important thing the article is saying. Write this down on the left page of your notebook.

3. Find two passages in the article that you think are good examples of what you state in your summary. Copy these on the left page of your notebook, too. Or if you're doing this on your computer, use the Table function to create two columns, and use the left one.

STEP 2: Now speak up. Use the right side of your notebook to explore your thinking about what Lord is saying. Look on the opposing left pages to remind yourself of some of his ideas and assertions. This is an open-ended fastwrite, but here are some prompts to get you writing and thinking:

- Tell the story of your thinking:
  - *Before I read about this topic, I thought _____, and then I thought _____, and then _____, and then … but now I think _____.*
- Consider ways you've begun to think differently:
  - *I used to think _____, but now I'm starting to think _____.*
- Try both believing and doubting:
  - *The most convincing points Lord makes in his essay are _____. or Though I don't necessarily agree with Lord, I can understand why he would think that _____.*
  - And then: *The thing that Lord ignores or fails to understand is _____. or The least convincing claim he makes is _____ because _____.*
- Consider questions:
  - *The most important question Lord raises is _____.*
  - *The question that he fails to ask is _____.*

Discuss in class how this notetaking exercise worked. What went well? What was difficult? How did your initial thoughts influence your reading of the article? Did your thinking change? Which of these techniques will you continue to use in your notetaking?

What? I Failed? But I Paid for Those Credits! Problems of Students Evaluating Faculty*

by Thomas Lord

Late one afternoon several days ago, I was startled by a loud rap on my office door. When I opened it, I immediately recognized a student from the previous semester clutching the grade slip he had just received in the mail. Sensing his anger and frustration, I invited him in to discuss his scores. I was surprised that he had not anticipated the failing grade because his exam scores were abysmal, his class work was marginal, and his attendance was sporadic. When I scooted my chair over to my computer to open the course's spreadsheet to review his grade, he told me he didn't have an argument with the test, class, and attendance records. His reason for coming to see me was to ask how he could get his refund. He had, after all, paid for the credits, right? I was astonished. In all my years in higher education, this was the first time I had been asked for a refund.

A day later over lunch, a colleague remarked that with the nation's troublesome economy, many universities have turned to the business model of running the institution. "The business model," he acknowledged, "focuses on financial efficiency while maintaining a quality product."

"Perhaps so," another colleague responded, "but the principal foundation of the business model is the notion of satisfying the customer. Because the products of a college are its graduates, it requires the college to meet their expectations for both a quality education and a gratifying experience. This is nearly impossible if the college wants to retain its integrity and high standards."

Furthermore, what students expect from their college experience varies greatly. A quality, highly respected education is, of course, always desirable, but that's about as common as the expectations get. Some college students relish the liberal challenges universities can provide, some look for a cultural experience, and others simply want to be trained for a career. A large number of undergraduates seek strong intercollegiate athletic or theater programs, and some students are most interested in an exciting social life. This diversity is where the difficulty lies. With such an assortment of demands and expectations, it's simply not possible for any institution to provide it all and maintain a student-as-consumer philosophy. Many universities have tried, and in so doing, have undercut their reputation. Several decades ago, education theorist David Reisman (1981) wrote, "This shift from academic merit to student consumerism is one of the two greatest reversals of direction in all the history of American Higher Education; the other being the replacement of the classical college by the modern university a century ago."

Despite Reisman's statement, the student-as-consumer philosophy has become more widely spread in academic institutions over the last two decades, and with it has come a tendency for students to have a stronger voice in higher education (d'Apollonia and Abrami 1997). It is common nowadays for student representatives to serve on university committees. Students are often consulted on ventures that include curriculum, discipline, regulation, and campus construction. In many schools, segments of the institution's governance are shared with students. My institution, for example, retains two students on the University Executive Board.

But by far the greatest number of student voices impacting the institution is in the evaluation of the instructors. The practice was first implemented at Purdue University in 1927, when surveys were distributed to students in a sociology class to solicit their opinions of the course (Remmers 1927). The surveys were not shared with the administration, but were retained by the professors as feedback for self-improvement. Two years later, Remmers revised the surveys to include "student ratings of their instructor's teaching and what they have learned in the course." The researcher reported his finding at a national professional meeting, and soon other universities began soliciting instructor ratings on their campuses. Course and instructor evaluations remained benign until the 1960s, when students discovered the power their united voices could make in higher education. During this time, students began vocalizing their resistance to the war in Vietnam, the ills of the environment, and the materialism of society. It was a time of student free speech about ethical, cultural, and racial issues. Suddenly, evaluations of instructors and courses became more about student satisfaction than about a professor's instructional effectiveness.

. . . .

When the driving mechanism for faculty evaluations shifts from educating to pleasing, many problems occur. "Student evaluations of their professors are impacted heavily by student perception," states Professor Stanley Fish, dean emeritus at the University of Illinois (2007). "When student experiences in classes do not match their prior expectations, they react in negative ways. Students may begin to boycott classes they're unhappy with, they may write complaint letters to administrators, or they may challenge the academic integrity of their professors. Some students may become so disrespectful of the professor that they circulate their feelings in the press, on the internet, and over the airways." In 1965, for example, students at the University of California–Berkeley generated a review of teacher performance in a manual entitled *The Slate Supplement,* and sold it at the campus bookstore. "Most of the opinions in the manual were ill-informed and mean-spirited," recalls Fish. "The opinions weren't from professionals in the field but transient students with little or no stake in the enterprise who would be free (because they were anonymous) to indulge any sense of grievance they happened to harbor in the full knowledge that nothing they said would ever be questioned or challenged. The abuse would eventually affect the careers and livelihoods of faculty members especially the young, nontenured professors" (Selvin 1991). In addition, with the negative exposure, university officials became alarmed that the dissatisfaction would lead to students dropping their courses or leaving the university altogether. With the mounting anxieties, many instructors countered by lowering the expectations in their courses. A survey of faculty found 70% of professors believe that their grading leniency and course difficulty bias student ratings, and 83% admitted making their course easier in response to student evaluations (Ryan, Anderson and Birchler 1980).

This was nicely demonstrated when Peter Sacks, a young journalism instructor, was hired on a tenure track at a small northwest college. At the end of the first semester, Sacks, an accomplished writer but not yet an accomplished teacher, found himself in trouble with student evaluations. When he started, Sacks resolved to maintain a high quality in his courses by emphasizing critical thinking about issues. Although he found it extremely difficult, he stuck with his plan for the entire semester, and as a consequence, received terrible student evaluations. Fearing that he would lose his tenure-track appointment after the spring term, he decided to change his tactics and attempt to achieve higher evaluations by deliberately pandering to his students. At the end of his three-year trial, he had dramatically raised his teaching evaluations and gained tenure. Sacks shamelessly admits he became utterly undemanding and uncritical of his students, giving out easy grades, and teaching to the lowest common denominator (1986). Other researchers have confirmed that lenient grading is the most frequently used faculty strategy to counter abusive student assessment (Howard and Maxwell 1982; Greenwald 1997).

Another problem with the business model is that students truly believe they're paying for their credits and not their education.

Consumers are used to paying for merchandise that can later be returned for a refund with no questions asked. The student confusion over this probably resides in the way universities charge pupils for the credits they're taking (at least for students attending part time or over the summer). If, for example, a high school biology teacher decided to upgrade his or her knowledge of wildflowers and enrolled in a three-credit course at a local college on spring flora, the teacher would be charged for the three credits. If the teacher decided to continue the learning the following semester on summer wildflowers, he or she would again pay for the three credits. It's not hard, therefore, to see how the idea of paying for credits rather than earning them came about.

A final reason why student evaluations are an unreliable way to assess faculty is that most students simply don't know what good teaching is. Undergraduates generally have a vision of how college teaching is conducted from depictions in movies or hearing tales from former students. The most common view is that professors stand before a class and recite, write on the chalkboard, or use PowerPoint slides to get across the information students should know in the lesson (McKeachie 1992).

I asked my students what they thought made a great instructor and was told the best professors move unhurriedly through their notes, speaking at a slow-to-moderate pace, explaining the information the students need to learn. One student told me that good professors don't get sidetracked by superficial chunks of information and don't waste time off the subject. Some students also suggested that competent professors are entertaining when they lecture and frequently use demonstrations and videos to back up their presentations. Many class members said the best professors repeat several times the items that are the most salient and hold review sessions before each exam to reaffirm the important content.

Most contemporary theorists, however, tell us that top instructors don't do most of those things. According to education leaders, competent teachers seldom lecture to a gallery of passive students, but provide experiences and directions that actively challenge class members to think and discover information (Handelsmen et al. 2004). Practiced professors believe understanding is the driving force for learning and spend a great amount of preclass time orchestrating team-based learning situations for the upcoming class. Proponents of student-centered instruction acknowledge that active participation in classes and discovery-based laboratories help students develop the habits of mind that drive science (Udovic et al. 2002). Furthermore, while traditional instructors create factual recall questions for their exams where students reiterate what they were told in class, contemporary teachers challenge students to discover the answers through application, synthesis, or evaluation (Huitt 2004). Quality teachers understand what agronomist George Washington Carver meant in 1927 when he wrote, "I know nothing more inspiring than discovering new information for oneself" (Carver 1998).

Students also believe that the best professors don't expect class members to know information that the professor hasn't covered in lecture. Students don't seem to realize that education is the art of using information, not the art of restating it. College graduates must understand that once they're out of school, they'll depend on their education to get them through life. Often will they have to address unfamiliar questions. As I've stated previously, "Once they're out of college, students can't fall back on the answer, 'I don't know 'cause it wasn't covered by my professor' " (Lord 2007).

Enough has been written on this matter that colleges and universities should justify why they continue to use student evaluations to assess their faculty. "The answer is already known," answers Cahn (1986). "Institutions of higher education provide faculty evaluations to students to assess student satisfaction. Not only are the evaluations easy to grade and inexpensive to administer, but they give the impression of objectivity in comparison with more subjective measures such as letters from observers since student evaluations produce definite numbers."

"The role of the university is leadership, not a servant of consumer demands as the current business model requires," states Wilson (1998). "Universities certainly have a responsibility for the safety, well-being, and satisfaction of the people they serve, but they also have a responsibility to educate the people as well. With their dignity and reputation on the line, the most important responsibility is to certify that their graduates are truly educated. Under the consumer model, the goals of satisfaction and education are sometimes in conflict. It is important, therefore, that the metaphor of students as consumers be replaced by the metaphor of students as apprentices" (Haskell 1997).

References

Cahn, S. 1986. *Saints and scamps: Ethics in academia.* Totowa, NJ: Rowman and Littlefield.

Carver, G.W. 1998. *The all-university celebration.* Iowa City, IA: University Press.

d'Apollonia S., and P. Abrami. 1997. Navigating student ratings of instruction. *American Psychologist* 52 (11): 1198–1208.

Fish, S. 2007. Advocacy and teaching. *Academe* 93 (4): 23–27.

Greenwald, A.G. 1997. Validity concerns and usefulness of student ratings. *American Psychologist* 52 (11): 1182–86.

Handelsman, J., D. Ebert-May, R. Beichner, P. Burns, A. Chang, R. DeHann, J. Gentile, S. Luffefer, J. Stewart, S. Tukgnab, and W. Wood. 2004. Scientific thinking. *Science* 304 (5670): 521–22.

Haskell, R. 1997. Academic freedom, tenure and student evaluation of faculty: Galloping polls in the 21st century. *Education Policy Analysis Archives* 5 (6): 43.

Howard, G., and S. Maxwell. 1982. Linking raters' judgments. *Evaluation Review* 6 (1): 140–46.

Huitt, W. 2004. Bloom et al's taxonomy of the cognitive domain. *Educational Psychology Interactive*. http://chiron.valdosta.edu/whuitt/col/cogsys/bloom.html. Valdosta, GA: Valdosta University Press.

Lord, T. 2007. Putting inquiry to the test: Enhancing learning in college botany. *Journal of College Science Teaching* 36 (7): 56–59.

McKeachie, W. 1992. Student ratings: The validity of use. *American Psychologist* 52 (11): 1218–25

Reisman, D. 1981. *On higher education: The academic enterprise in an era of rising student consumerism*. San Francisco: Jossey Bass.

Remmers, D. 1927. Experimental data on the Purdue rating scale. In *Student ratings of instructors: Issues for improving practice,* eds. M. Theall and J. Franklin. 1990. San Francisco: Jossey Bass.

Ryan, J., J. Birchler, and A. Birchler. 1980. Student evaluation: The faculty responds. *Research in Higher Education* 12 (4): 395–401.

Sacks P. 1986. *Generation X goes to college*. LaSalle, IL: Open Court Press.

Selvin, P. 1991. The raging bull at Berkley. *Science* 251 (4992): 368–71.

Wilson, R. 1998. New research casts doubt on value of student evaluations of professors. *Chronicle of Higher Education* 44 (19): A2–A14.

Udovic, D., D. Morris, A. Dickman, J. Postlethwait, and P. Wetherwax. 2002. Workshop biology: Demonstrating the effectiveness of active learning in an introductory biology course. *Bioscience* 52 (3): 272–81.

Thomas Lord (trlord@grove.iup.edu) *is a professor in the Department of Biology at the Indiana University of Pennsylvania in Indiana, Pennsylvania.*

Notetaking Techniques

I confessed to a dislike of notecards. Apparently, I'm not the only one. Mention notecards, and students often tell horror stories. It's a little like talking about who has the most horrendous scar, a discussion that can prompt participants to expose knees and bare abdomens in public places. One student even mailed me her notecards—50 bibliography cards and 53 notecards, all bound by a metal ring and color coded. She assured me that she didn't want them back—ever. Another student told me she was required to write 20 notecards a day: "If you spelled something wrong or if you put your name on the left side of the notecard rather than the right, your notecards were torn up and you had to do them over."

It is true, of course, that some students find recording information on notecards an enormously useful way of organizing information. And some teachers have realized that it's pretty silly to turn notetaking into an exercise that must be done "correctly" or not at all. For these reasons, I included suggestions about how to use notecards effectively in the first edition of this text. But in good conscience, I can't do it anymore. I no longer believe that 3 × 5 or 4 × 6 index cards are large enough to accommodate the frequently messy and occasionally extended writing that often characterizes genuinely useful notes. Little cards get in the way of having a good conversation with your sources.

If conventional notecards encourage a monologue, then what method will encourage dialogue? Basically any notetaking strategy that encourages the things that you've practiced so far in this chapter: listening and responding, collecting and evaluating. It's that movement back and forth between information and what you think of that information, between your observations of things and your ideas about them, between what you once understood and what you *now* understand, that will involve you in the process of *knowledge making,* rather than simple information retrieval and reporting. Now this probably sounds pretty grandiose. Your research essay will probably not earn space in an academic journal. But as you begin to understand the difference between knowledge and information, you will earn yourself a place in an academic community that values people with their own ideas. Isn't that inviting?

I'm convinced that something as seemingly mundane as notetaking can be a key part of becoming a knower rather than a parrot. One method, in particular, seems especially effective at encouraging dialogue between the researcher and his sources: the double-entry journal. You can use your notebook or computer for this technique.

The Double-Entry Journal

The double-entry approach (see Figure 2) is basically this: Use opposing pages of your research notebook or opposing columns in a Word document—two columns and one row for each source. At the top of the page for each source, write down the bibliographic information for that source. Then, using the left side or column, compile your notes from

Notes from Source (left page or column)	Fastwrite Response (right page or column)
■ Direct quotations, paraphrases, and summaries of material from the source: • of ideas that are important to project • of ideas that are surprising or puzzling or generate some emotional response ■ Be careful to: • include bibliographic information at the top; • include the page number from the source.	■ Focused fastwrite in response to material at left ■ Tips for fastwrite: • Write as long as possible; then look left and find something else to respond to. • Try shifting between stances of believing and doubting. • Use the questions below.

FIGURE 2 Double-Entry Journal Method

a source—paraphrases, summaries, quotes. Put appropriate page numbers in the margin next to borrowed material or ideas. Then on the right side, comment on what you collected from each source. Imagine that the line down the middle of the page—or the spiral binder that divides opposing pages—is a table at which you sit across from an author with something to say about a topic you're interested in. Take care to listen to what the author says through paraphrase, summary, and quotation on the left, and then on the right respond with a fastwrite in which you give your own commentary, questions, interpretations, clarifications, or even feelings about what you heard. Your commentary can be pretty open ended, responding to questions such as the following:

- What strikes you? What was confusing? What was surprising?
- If you assume that this is true, why is it significant?
- If you doubt the truth or accuracy of the claim or fact, what is the author failing to consider?
- How does the information stand up to your own experiences and observations?
- Does it support or contradict your thesis (if you have one at this point)?
- How might you use the information in your paper? What purpose might it serve?
- What do you think of the source?
- What further questions does the information raise that might be worth investigating?
- How does the information connect to other sources you've read?

Refer to this list of questions (and any others that occur to you) as a prompt for the writing on the right side of your journal (or right column of your Word document). There are a variety of ways to approach the double-entry journal. If you're taking notes on the printout of an article or a photocopy from a book, try reading the material first and underlining passages that seem important. Then, when you're done, transfer some of that underlined material—quotes, summaries, or paraphrases—into the left column of your journal. Otherwise, take notes in the left column *as* you read.

While you take notes, or after you've finished, do some exploratory writing in the right column. This territory belongs to you. Here, through language, your mind and heart assert themselves over the source material. Use your notes in the left column as a trigger for writing in the right. Whenever your writing stalls, look to the left. The process is a little like watching tennis—look left, then right, then left, then right. Direct your attention to what the source says and then to what *you* have to say about the source. Keep up a dialogue.

Figures 3 and 4 illustrate how the double-entry journal works in practice. Note these features:

- Bibliographic information is recorded at the top of the page. Do that first, and make sure it's complete.
- Page numbers are included in the far-left margin, right next to the information that was taken from that page. Make sure you keep up with this as you write.
- While the material from the source in the left column may be quite formal or technical, the response in the right column should be informal and conversational. Try to write in your own voice. Find your own way to say things. And don't hesitate to use the first person: *I*.
- The writers often use their own writing to try to question a source's claim or understand better what that claim might be (e.g., "What the authors seem to be missing here..." and "I don't get this quote at all...").
- Seize a phrase from your source, and play out its implications; think about how it pushes your own thinking or relates to your thesis.
- In Figures 3 and 4, the writers frequently pause to ask themselves questions—not only about what the authors of the original sources might be saying but what the writers are saying to themselves as they write. Use questions to keep you writing and thinking.

Prior, Molly. *"Bright On: Americans' Insatiable Appetite for Whiter-Than-White Teeth Is Giving Retailers Something to Smile About."* <u>Beauty Biz</u> 1 Sept. 2005: 36–43. Print.

Teeth are no longer just for eating with—their appearance is becoming more important as a factor in a person's image, and they need to be perfectly white. (36)

Cosmetics companies are now entering territory once reserved for dentists as more and more people care mostly about the aesthetics of their teeth and smile. (36)

"Sephora is so enthusiastic about the [tooth whitening] category, it named 'smile' its fifth retail pillar, joining the four others (makeup, fragrance, skin care and hair care) earlier this year." (37)

"The trend has shed its clinical beginnings and assumed a new identity, smile care. Its new name has been quickly adopted by a growing troupe of retailers, who hope to lure consumers with a simple promise: A brighter smile will make you look younger and feel more confident." (37)

Instead of going to the dentist and taking care of their teeth so they function well, people are investing a cosmetic interest in their teeth. People selling tooth-whitening products hope people associate whiter, more perfect teeth with higher self-esteem and social acceptance. (40)

"What says health, youth and vitality like a great smile?" (40)

I have noticed the increasing amount of importance that people put on the whiteness of their teeth, but this also seems to have increased with the amount of advertising for whitening products on TV and in magazines. I wonder if the whole thing is profit driven: Hygiene companies wanted to make more money, so instead of just selling toothbrushes and toothpaste, they created a whitening product and then worked to produce a demand for it. I almost feel really manipulated, like everyone's teeth were fine the way they naturally existed, and then all the sudden a big company decided it needed to create a new product and sell it by making us feel bad about our smiles, and thus bad about ourselves.

The whole thing is sad, because once something becomes the societal "norm," we start to become obligated to do it. If everyone's teeth are beige, it's no problem when yours are too. But when everyone has sparkling white teeth, then it looks funny if you let yours stay brown. It either says "I don't have the money to whiten my teeth," or "I don't care about my appearance."

Sometimes it feels people might also judge you as being dirty, because white teeth seem healthier and cleaner than brown teeth, or lazy, for not spending the time to whiten your teeth. All those things are negative, and create a negative cloud around our teeth where we once felt good, or at least ambivalent. I don't like the way I'm being told my smile isn't good enough the way it is. I feel like when I smile it should just be about showing happiness and conveying that to others, not a judgment about me as a person.

FIGURE 3   Amanda's Double-Entry Journal. Here, Amanda concentrates on thinking through the implications of the summaries and quotations she collected from an article on teeth whitening.

Greenbaum, Jessica B. "Training Dogs and Training Humans: Symbolic Interaction and Dog Training." <u>Anthrozoos</u> 23.2: 129-141. Web. 10 Jan. 2010.

"The 'traditional' dominance-based method of training endorses obedience by using a human-centric approach that places dogs in a subordinate position in order to maintain a space in the family. The 'reward-based' behavior modification method promotes a dog-centric approach that highlights companionship over dominance...." (129)	Article seems to capture the essence of the debate: Is a well-behaved dog a product of dominance or companionship? Why can't it be both? One of the things that always strikes me about these binaries—either/or—is that it ignores both/and. Dogs will always have some kind of unequal relationship with their owners. Right? They have to. And won't they try to sort out, in their own way, the question of who is in charge?
"The methods we use to train our dogs reflect our perceptions of relationships between human and non-human animals. The socially constructed status of dogs, as pet or companion, influences the philosophy, methods, and training skills used." (129)	This seems key: "the socially constructed status of dogs" has an enormous influence on how we construe our relationship with them. Greenbaum draws the distinction as between "pet" and "companion." Behind those general terms is a whole set of ways in which we "socially construct" pets. A pet can be a companion, right? It doesn't necessarily imply subservience? I keep returning to the binaries that theorists draw. This is exactly the same thing that I notice with dog trainers themselves. There is a "right" and "wrong" way, and this divide is typically described as it is here: between positive reinforcement and negative reinforcement.
Mead discounted idea that animals can engage in symbolic communication with humans: "the ability to think was the ability to say." But article, using Sanders, argues that in a sense, pet owners "speak for" their animals. Sanders's research on police dogs, however, also highlighted the "ambiguity" of dog ownership—they are both companions and "tools." Subjective beings and objective things. (130)	This idea that we "speak for animals" strikes home, and I imagine that people like me who constantly give dogs and cats a human voice are more likely to favor "human-centric" methods. How can you put a shock collar on a dog that can talk back? But I never thought about this "ambiguity" between dogs as "tools" and

---

FIGURE 4   Double-Entry Journal. Here's a double-entry journal entry that uses Word's Table feature to respond to an article I was reading on theories of dog training. I could copy and paste quotes from the original article, a PDF file, and drop them into the left column. Also notice, however, that I rely on summaries as well. Page numbers in parentheses follow borrowed material.

"companions." Though wouldn't this be mostly true of people who train dogs for particular purposes? Is this ambiguity typical of most pet owners who don't.

Fennel argues that while the principle of modeling training on pack behavior makes sense, the method is often misapplied—correction is too harsh or effort to domesticate too extreme. She thinks this is cause of most behavior problems. "Dog guardians have failed as pack leaders" (131)

Must read Fennel's study. Seems like her argument is much like the one I'm thinking about: It may be that dogs do behave in some ways like wild pack animals, but their trainers aren't exactly alpha dogs, either.

FIGURE 4   (Continued)

What I like about the double-entry journal system is that it turns me into a really active reader as I'm taking notes for my essay. That blank column on the right, like the whirring of my computer right now, impatiently urges me to figure out what I think through writing. All along, I've said the key to writing a strong research paper is *making the information your own*. Developing your own thinking about the information you collect, as you go along, is one way to do that. Thoughtful notes are so easy to neglect in your mad rush to simply take down a lot of information. The double-entry journal won't let you neglect your own thinking; at least it will remind you when you do.

The Research Log

The research log is an alternative to the double-entry journal that promotes a similar "conversation" between writer and source but with a few differences. One is that, like Jay Leno, the researcher starts with a monologue and always gets the last word. The standard format of the research log can serve as a template, which can be retrieved whenever you're ready to take notes on another source. Those notes can then be easily dropped into the draft as needed, using the Cut and Paste feature of your word-processing program.

The basic approach is this:

1. Take down the full bibliographic information on the source—article, book chapter, Web page, or whatever (see Figure 5). Then read the source, marking up your personal copy in the usual fashion by underlining, making marginal notes, and so on.
2. Your first entry will be a fastwrite that is an *open-ended response* to the reading under the heading "What Strikes Me Most." For example, you might begin by playing the "believing game,"

Project: The Newest Commodity: The Smile

Citation: Tanner, Marty. "American Choppers." *New York Times*. New York Times, 20 Feb. 2005. Web. 4 Apr. 2009.

Date: 4/5/2009

What Strikes Me Most:
A prosthodontist is a dentist who specializes in making teeth look a certain way. While many people are born with smiles they are proud of, a pros-thodontist can take any smile and modify it in any way. Unfortunately, more and more people are fall-ing into a trap of believing that there is only one "perfect" smile, and they are asking for their own mouths to be modified to create the perfect smile. This disgusts me because I think there should be as many smiles as there are people. It's becoming like a nose job or a face-lift—some modification people make to their appearance to make it less like the countenance they were born with, and more like that "perfect" face. It makes me sad that another thing that is so distinctive to each person has actually become something we want to normalize. As a woman I feel like I'm told to be a size two; have straight, shiny hair; have a little, cute nose; have perfectly arched eyebrows; and have thick, pink lips. Now, too, I have to have the correct length and width teeth that are a sparkly B1 white. It makes me wonder why our culture goes from accepting one part of ourselves as standard and imperfect but accept-able, and makes it into something we need to modify.

I also think the prosthodontist to the stars, Dr. Levine, is really disingenuous in this article. While his job depends on people being unhappy with the way their teeth look, he tries to play the "good guy" card and say that people's smiles are looking too perfect and that people need to have a great set of choppers, but not overly great. He seems to want to make the polite statement

---

FIGURE 5 Amanda's Research Log

that nobody has a perfect smile, but then, through his profession, his job is to make people believe they can get a perfect smile—and they don't already have one. I think that's kind of slimy.

Source Notes:
"Within certain strict boundaries, Levine likes to see some imperfection because it renders the hand of the dentist invisible. This is his art." Many famous people, like actors and actresses, think of their smile as a sort of symbol of their status that they can flash to attract attention. Many of these smiles are exactly the same, with the golden mean the proportion of the length of their top six front teeth, and with each individual tooth having a width that is 80% of the length. There is even a "perfect" amount of tooth that should show when a person's mouth is closed: around 3.7 mm. Patients can wear a fake set of teeth around their home before they have their smiles modified to see if what they imagine as being perfect actually looks bad. They can test drive their new set of teeth for friends and family so they don't end up with a mistake that looks like a pair of too-perfect dentures.

"Smiles are looking too much alike."

"...the man who credits himself with shaping Christie Brinkley's 'iconic American smile.'"

Reality makeover programs like *The Swan* often use a prosthodontist as part of the makeover.

The Source Reconsidered:
When the article mentions Julia Roberts or the "iconic American smile" I know exactly what it means. In my mind, I truly have an image of that smile, and I realize now that that's because every single starlet and commercial model seems to have that smile. Yet, when I look at my friends and all the people around me, there are so many different smiles. I have one friend with really short, stubby teeth that are pretty brown

FIGURE 5 (Continued)

around the edges, and I admit that I notice it. But
when she smiles, I tend to look more at the rest of
her face and the fact that she's really happy than I
do at her imperfect teeth. It's like it's turning some
natural human emotion into some mass-produced carbon
copy. That's why the whole smile-care thing really
bothers me. Changing somebody's nose changes only
their nose. Changing someone's smile seems to control
and modify the way they communicate a feeling, and
that is really bothersome. They are modifying something far more personal than just their appearance;
they are changing the way they emote. That's freaky.

FIGURE 5   (Continued)

exploring how the author's ideas, arguments, or findings are
sensible and then shift to the "doubting game," looking for gaps,
questions, and doubts you have about what the source says. You
could write a response to any or all of the questions suggested
for the double-entry journal. But as the subheading suggests,
you can also begin with this simple, open-ended question:

> What strikes you as the most important thing the author is
> trying to say?

3. Next, mine the source for nuggets. Take notes under the heading
   "Source Notes." These are quotations, summaries, paraphrases,
   or key facts you collect from the reading. They are probably some
   of the things you marked as you read the source initially.
4. Finally, follow up with one more fastwrite under the heading
   "The Source Reconsidered." This is a second, *more focused* look
   at the source in which you fastwrite about what stands out in the
   notes you took. Which facts, findings, claims, or arguments that
   you jotted down shape your thinking now? If the writing stalls,
   skip a line, take another look at your source notes, and seize on
   something else to write about.

Narrative Notetaking

This is the simplest method of all. As you read, mark up or annotate your source in the ways you usually do. After you read through
it carefully, you will fastwrite a rapid summary for at least one full
minute, beginning with the following prompt (see Figure 6):

> What I understand this to be saying is....

The Third Week

Focusing Question: How has cosmetic dentistry changed the way we think of the smile, and what are the repercussions?

Source: Walker, Rob. "Consumed; Unstained Masses." <u>New York Times</u>. New York Times, 2 May 2004. Web. 10 Apr. 2009.

Rapid Summary (one minute):

What I understand this article to be saying is that the American public is getting more and more vain, as evidenced by the fact that tooth whitening is growing in popularity. While only celebrities used to modify the appearance of their teeth, now average people are doing it. Because of the value of appearance in our society, once we realize we can modify the way we look to our advantage, we seem to flock to it quickly. That's what's happening with the whole trend of smile care—we're using whiteners to change the way our teeth look so maybe we will be judged more profitably. And when a large percentage of society decides to buy something, there will always be corporations and retailers standing alongside to reap a profit.

Narrative of Thought (six minutes):

Before I started reading this article I thought that it was the capitalistic profit motive that had introduced whitening products and created a consumer demand for them. Now I understand that all of us as consumers have an equal responsibility with the companies that make and market such products, because we're the ones that buy them and change our standards of beauty. That makes me think that this is a complicated issue. While it's frustrating to feel like I can never be attractive enough, because the standard of attractiveness to which I'm held keeps getting harder and harder to meet, I'm the one that is interested in meeting it in the first place. While it would be easy to denigrate that as vanity, however, I can also see that being judged by others as attractive does have actual benefits, be it a higher salary or better treatment from strangers. In that case I'm put in a tough spot—I can work against the culture that tells me I don't look the right way, and feel negatively judged, or I can conform to it, and feel disappointed that I folded to social pressure. This isn't just an issue about people whitening their teeth for fun, it's about how society changes its standards and how quickly we assimilate to them—and why.

FIGURE 6 Amanda's Narrative Notes

Skip a line, and begin a second episode of fastwriting. Tell the story of your thinking, a narrative of thought that begins with what you initially might have believed about the topic covered in your source, and then how that thinking was influenced by what you read. This time scribble (or type) for as long as you can without stopping, beginning with this prompt.

When I first began reading this, I thought _____, and now I think _____.

Whenever your writing stalls, repeat the prompt again, inserting another discovery from your reading.

Online Research Notebooks

These days, academic researchers frequently work with digital documents, especially PDF files. While it's always a good idea to print out hard copies of anything you use, it's also convenient to annotate and mark up electronic copies. In addition to highlighting passages, it's also possible with some software to insert comments. These can be much like responses in the double-entry journal.

The problem is that most of the software that can annotate PDF files isn't free. For example, while anyone can download Adobe Reader to read PDF documents, you might need to buy Adobe Acrobat to annotate them. There is, however, some free software that can help you organize your digital research files and attach documents to them. That way you can attach your notes for each source to the digital original. The downside, of course, is that these notes aren't keyed to particular passages in the source, but the software is still useful for researchers. Here's a list of a few you might try:

1. *Zotero* (http://zotero.org). I already mentioned this one earlier in *The Curious Researcher*. This is my favorite software for research because it not only organizes digital documents in project folders but also organizes citation information for each source. Zotero is an add-in that only works on the Firefox browser.

2. *Evernote* (http://evernote.com). You can't annotate documents but you can organize your research sources and associated notes and then upload them so they're accessible everywhere you have an Internet connection. The program also runs on all kinds of devices—iPads, iPhones, PCs, Blackberries, and so on. In addition, Evernote has a function that allows you to search your notes by tags or titles.

3. *Google Docs* (http://google.com). Google Docs is a standard for many users who want to organize (and share) documents, and it's even more useful now that it allows documents like PDFs and Word files to remain in their native formats. As with Evernote, you can access your Google Docs wherever you have an Internet connection. (Google Notebook, is no longer supported by the company).

When You're Coming Up Short: More Advanced Searching Techniques

At the end of the third week of the research assignment last semester, Laura showed up at my office, looking pale.

"I spent all night at the library, and I couldn't find much on my topic," she said. "What I *could* find, the library didn't have—it was missing, or checked out, or wasn't even part of the collection. I may have to change my topic."

"I hate libraries!" she said, the color returning to her face.

Laura's complaint is one that I hear often at this point in the research process, especially from students who have dutifully tried to find a narrow focus for their papers, only to realize—they think—that there isn't enough information to make the topic work. They have tried the online catalog, article databases, and the Internet. The students found a few articles but not enough for a ten-page paper. Like Laura, they may decide to broaden their focus or bail out of their topic altogether, even though they're still interested in it.

I always give these frustrated students the same advice: Don't despair yet. And don't give up on your narrow focus or your topic until you've dug more deeply for information. There are still some more specialized databases to try and some nonlibrary sources to consider. You are, in a sense, like the archaeologist who carefully removes the dirt from each layer of a dig site, looking to see what it might reveal. If little turns up, the archaeologist systematically explores the next layer and then the next, until she is convinced she's digging in the wrong place. Student researchers too often give up the dig before they've removed enough dirt, believing too quickly there's nothing there. Some things you might not have considered to help you unearth more useful information are discussed in the following pages.

Advanced Library Searching Techniques

These advanced library searching techniques are listed in the order you might try them.

1. *Vary search terms*. Try using some other search terms suggested by your research so far. You might, for instance, try searching using the names of people who have published on your topic.
2. *Search other databases*. Okay, so you've tried a general subject database like Academic OneFile and even a specialized database like PsycINFO. But have you tried another general database like Academic Search Premier or another specialized database like InfoTrac Psychology? Broaden your coverage.

3. *Check bibliographies.* Academic books and articles always include a list of references at the end. These can be gold mines. Look at all the sources like these that you've collected so far and scan the titles in the bibliographies that seem promising. Find these by searching the library databases.

4. *Consider using interlibrary loan services.* Your campus library will get you that article or book it doesn't have by borrowing the materials from another library. This is an incredibly useful service, often available online. These days delivery of requested materials can take as little as a few days!

5. *Troll government documents.* The U.S. government is the largest publisher in the world. If your research question is related

FIGURE 7 USA.gov is a useful starting point for a search of government documents on your topic.

to some issue of public policy, then there's a decent chance you'll find some government documents on the subject. Try the site USA.gov (see Figure 7), a useful index to the gazillions of government publications and reports.

6. *Ask a reference librarian for help.* If you do, you won't be sorry.

Advanced Internet Searching Techniques

It's more likely that you've tapped out relevant sources on the Internet before you've tapped out those in the library—most of us like to begin with the Internet. But make sure that you've tried some of the following search strategies on the Web.

1. *Vary search terms.* By now, you've gathered enough information on your topic to have some new ideas about terms or phrases that might yield good results. Say you're researching the origins of American blues music, and you discover that among its many traditions is something called the Piedmont style. Try searching using that phrase in quotation marks. Also consider doing Web searches on the names of experts who have contributed significantly to the conversation on your topic.

2. *Use advanced search features.* Few of us use the advanced search page on Google and other search engines. By habit, we just type in a few terms in the simple search window. But advanced searching will allow you to exploit methods that will give you better results—things like phrase searching in conjunction with Boolean operators like AND and OR.

3. *Use multiple search engines.* Don't call for retreat until you've gone beyond Google. Try Yahoo!, Ask.com, and similar search engines. Also try specialized search engines that are relevant to your subjects.

Thinking Outside the Box: Alternative Sources

Sometimes you need to be creative. Try finding sources on your research question in places you don't think to look.

1. *Search blogs.* It's easy to dismiss blogs as merely self-indulgent musings of people with nothing better to do, but some blogs are written by people who really know what they're talking about. Bloggers can be vigilant observers of new developments, breaking news stories, and cutting-edge opinion. There are a number of specialized search engines to scour the blogosphere. Perhaps the best is http://technorati.com.

2. *Search images.* Another source of material you may not have thought of is images available on the Internet. A photograph of a collapsed school building following the 2008 earthquake in central China will do much to dramatize your essay on the vulnerability of buildings to such a disaster. Or a historical essay on lynching in the South might be more powerful with a picture of a murder from the Library of Congress archives (especially see http://memory.loc.gov/). Your campus library may also have a collection of digital images relevant to your project. Remember that if you use them in your essay, images need to be cited like any other source.

3. *Archived radio or podcasts.* Suppose your research question focuses on Martin Luther King Jr. Why not listen to an interview of Taylor Branch, the man who wrote a three-volume biography of the civil rights leader? You can find it on NPR.org (see Figure 8). National Public Radio is a particularly good source for material for academic projects. There are also a variety of search engines that will help you find podcasts on nearly any subject.

4. *Check out YouTube.* It isn't just about laughing babies anymore. YouTube is a rich archive of video that can provide material on many topics. For the project on Martin Luther King Jr., for example, you might watch a video of his last speech. There are,

FIGURE 8 **Searching the Archives at National Public Radio**

of course, other sites that archive video, too. Truveo (http://www.truveo.com/) will help you search them all.

5. *Search iTunes U.* Across the United States, colleges and universities are going online through Apple's iTunes U, putting up video and audio speeches, lectures, and other academic content. You can find iTunes U on iTunes, of course, and you can do a keyword search on multiple sites using "power search." The term "global warming" produced 90 hits, including lectures, opinions, and reports from some of America's top universities.

6. *Local organizations.* The reference librarians on our campus routinely refer students to the state historical society or state law library when relevant to their projects. Local organizations can be rich sources of not only published information but also interviews and artifacts.

Library	**Internet**	**Alternative Sources**
• Vary search terms	• Vary search terms	• Search blogs
• Search other databases	• Use advanced search features	• Search images
• Check bibliographies	• Use multiple search engines	• Listen to archived radio and podcasts
• Use interlibrary loan	• Watch videocasts	• Search iTunes U
• Troll government documents		• Visit local organizations or libraries
• Ask a librarian		

FIGURE 9 **More Advanced Searching Techniques**

The Fourth Week

Getting to the Draft

It is *not* 2 A.M. Your paper is *not* due in 12 hours but in one or two weeks. For some students, beginning to write a research paper this early—weeks before it's due—will be a totally new experience. An early start may also, for the first time, make the experience a positive one. I know that starting early will help ensure writing a better paper.

Still, there are those students who say they thrive on a looming deadline, who love working in its shadow, flirting with failure. "I work best that way," they say, and they wait until the last minute and race to the deadline in a burst of writing, often sustained by energy drinks or strong doses of caffeine. It works for some students. Panic is a pretty strong motivator. But I think most who defend this habit confuse their relief at successfully pulling off the assignment once again with a belief that the paper itself is successful.

Papers done under such pressure often aren't successful, and that is particularly true of the last-minute research paper, where procrastination is especially deadly. Research writing is recursive. You often have to circle back to where you've already been, discovering holes in your research or looking at your subject from new angles. It's hard to fit in a trip back to the library the night before the paper is due, when you've just started the draft and need to check some information. This book is designed to defeat procrastination, and if, in the past few weeks, you've done the exercises, taken thoughtful notes, and attempted a thorough search for information, you probably have the urge to begin writing.

On the other hand, you may feel as though you don't know enough yet about your topic to have anything to say. Or you may be swamped with information, and your head may be spinning. What do you do with it all?

Exploration or Argument?

What you do with it all depends on what kind of essay you're going to write. Working from an inquiry question, your draft can head in two directions:

1. *Argument.* Your discoveries in the past few weeks may have convinced you that a certain answer to your research question is particularly persuasive. Now you want to prove it. Another way to think about this is to ask yourself whether you think you want your readers to *think* or possibly even *do* something about your research topic.

2. *Exploratory essay.* On the other hand, maybe you're still not ready to make a judgment about the best answer to your research question and you want to use your essay to continue exploring it. You are less concerned with trying to get readers to think or do something than you are with helping them to appreciate what you find interesting or complicated about your topic.

Sometimes your research question will lead you toward one kind of essay or the other. Compare these two questions:

- *What should be done about the problem of smoking on campus?* (Argument)
- *How do smoking bans on college campuses influence social relationships between smokers?* (Exploration)

While both questions involve open-ended inquiry into the topic of campus smoking, one more naturally leads ultimately to a claim that is supported by reasons and evidence, and the other to an exploration of possible effects.

Your instructor may also give you guidance about whether your draft should be exploratory or argumentative. Depending on which it is, your focus this week might be a bit different. But first, gather your thoughts on everything you've learned about your topic so far.

EXERCISE 1

Dialogue with Dave

STEP 1: Dave is the reader you imagine when you picture the reader of your essay. He's a pretty nice guy, and smart, too. But first off, like any reader, he wants to know why he should care about the subject you're writing about. Then, once you've got Dave's interest, he has questions about what you're telling him about your topic. Like any conversation, what he asks about depends on the details of what you tell him. This conversation can't be scripted. Just let it develop as you write.

When you assume Dave's persona in this exercise, consider some of the stuff Dave might want to know, like

- Why? Where? Who? When? What?
- What do you mean by _____?
- How do most people see this? How do you see it differently?
- Are you kidding? I didn't know that. What else did you find out?
- Can you give me an example?
- Did that surprise you?
- What other questions does this raise?
- Who does this affect, mostly?
- What should we do about this?
- I'm not sure I believe this. Why do you?
- What do you think we should do about it?

Use the Table feature to format a document on your computer, creating two columns—one for Dave's questions and the other for your answers (see below). Start the conversation with Dave's first question—"What's the big deal about this, anyway?"—and take it from there. *If this is going to be useful, try to keep this conversation going for at least a half hour.*

In Figure 1, you can see part of what Mandy did with this exercise. She was exploring how ideas about beauty communicated through the American mass media influence how girls feel about themselves.

STEP 2: Many conversations like this one move toward some kind of conclusion. Reread what you wrote, and finish the exercise by crafting an answer to Dave's final question: *Okay, this is all very interesting. But based on everything you've learned so far, what's your point?*

S.O.F.T.

Many years ago, I was lucky enough to go to graduate school where a wonderful writer and teacher named Donald Murray taught, and he became both a friend and mentor. One of Don's endearing habits was to take a saying about which he was particularly fond

DAVE	MANDY
What's the big deal about this anyway? Why should I care?	In society today, girls at young ages are being influenced by the media and society that they should be culturally beautiful in order to live a happy life and gain social acceptance. Many girls compete in beauty pageants at young ages and grow up to have psychological and mental disorders from this pressure to be beautiful.
What do you mean by culturally beautiful?	Cultural beauty is where the woman appeals to what is considered attractive to the society at the specific time she is being judged. Cultural beauty is basically meeting society's standards; however, biological beauty for a woman means to be healthy and able to reproduce.
Can you give me an example of this cultural beauty affecting girls at a young age?	Beauty, whether it be male or female, will never disappear in society. It is a primitive goal to be considered socially attractive in society and many people will do anything to gain this social acceptance. Plastic surgery and liposuction are two methods women use to keep their beauty. Also this pressure on women can lead to eating disorders at a young age. The age group that has the highest rates of anorexia or bulimia is the female age group of 17 years old to 19 years old. A lot of this can be related back to their childhoods and the influences they had.

FIGURE 1 **Mandy's Dialogue with Dave**

and print it out on cardboard, which he would then distribute to his students. "Nulla dies sine linea"—never a day without a line—was one of these. Another was "S.O.F.T." This was an acronym for Say One Fricking Thing. Don believed that every piece of writing should say one fricking thing—it may deal with many ideas, but the writer's job was to find the *one* thing he or she wanted most to say about an essay topic.

More formally, we often understand this to mean that writing—especially academic writing—should have a thesis, a point, a theme, and a main idea. Too often, I'm afraid, writers arrive at this too early in their research—ending the inquiry process prematurely—or they don't arrive at it at all, and the essay or paper seems pointless.

In Exercise 1 you moved toward finding your S.O.F.T., and when you did, several things might have happened:

1. You discovered a point, and maybe it was one you didn't expect. Hallelujah! This one might need some fine-tuning but it seems to reflect your understanding of the topic at this point.
2. You arrived at a point, but it doesn't seem quite right. You feel like you're still groping toward a thesis—an answer to your research question—and this one seems forced or too general.
3. You have no clue what might be the S.O.F.T. All you have is more questions. Or perhaps you realize that you simply don't know enough yet to have any idea what you want to say.

If you find yourself in the first situation—you discovered a thesis that seems right—then maybe your draft should be an argumentative essay in which you attempt to prove your point. The second situation might invite you to continue your investigation by writing an exploratory research essay, and the third probably means that you haven't done nearly enough research yet. Actually, you probably need to do more research in every case—and you will as you continue the process.

Organizing the Draft

How you approach writing your first draft this week depends on what you decide about which kind of research essay you think you want to write: an argument or an exploratory essay. Let's look at how the two might differ.

But first the five-paragraph theme. Like a lot of school kids, I learned to write something called the "five-paragraph theme": introduction with thesis; three body paragraphs, each with a topic sentence and supporting details; and conclusion. This was the container into which I poured all of my writing back then. Though it didn't produce particularly interesting writing, the five-paragraph structure was a reliable way to organize things. It was very well suited to out-lines. I vaguely remember this one from sixth grade:

I. China is a really big country.
   A. The population of China is really big.
   B. The geographic size of China is really big.
   C. The economic dreams of China are really big.

What's useful about thinking of structure this way is the notion of hierarchy: Some ideas are subordinated to others, and each idea has some information subordinated under it. A problem with it, however, is the assumption that hierarchy is *always* the best way to organize information. For instance, essays can often make relevant digressions, or they might play with one way of seeing the topic and then another.

Perhaps a more basic problem with forms like the five-paragraph theme is the idea that structure is this kind of inert container that stands apart from the things you put into it and from your particular motives in writing about something.

Yet structure is important. And it's even more important when writers begin a draft with an abundance of information. John McPhee has written popular nonfiction essays on such topics as a guy who still makes birch bark canoes, people who study animal road kill, and his own exploration of Atlantic City using the game Monopoly as a guide. He is a careful and meticulous researcher, accumulating material in multiple binders from his interviews, observations, and reading. By the time he sits down to write, he's looking at pages and pages of notes. McPhee's solution to this problem is to use notecards to organize his information on bulletin boards, moving the cards around until he gets a satisfying arrange-ment. "The piece of writing has a structure inside it," he says, and before he begins drafting he seeks to find it.

If you don't have much information to begin with, structure is less of a problem. You simply end up using everything you have.

I'd like to encourage you, as you start drafting this week, to avoid thinking about the structure of your essay as something set in concrete before you begin. Instead, think of form rhetorically: Who is your audience and what does the assignment say, and what is your purpose in writing about your topic? For example, here are two structures to consider depending on whether your research paper is exploratory or argumentative:

- *Delayed thesis structure*—characteristic of the exploratory essay
- *Question-claim structure*—characteristic of the argumentative paper

However you choose to organize it, your research essay will have certain characteristics. For example, nearly any academic research paper includes the following items:

1. A S.O.F.T.—a point, a claim, a thesis—one main thing you are trying to say about the research question
2. A review of what has already been said by others about your topic
3. Specific information—the evidence or data on which your interpretations, conclusions, assertions, and speculations are based
4. A method of reasoning through the question, some pattern of thought—narrative, argument, essaying—that writer and reader find a convincing way to try to get at the truth of things

Delayed Thesis Structure

In an inquiry-based class, you typically choose a topic because you want to learn what you think. As you work through the research process, as I pointed out earlier, either you arrive at what you think is a persuasive answer to your research question and decide you will argue for it or you believe that you have more to learn and decide you will explore further. This second possibility was my motive in writing "Theories of Intelligence," I didn't want to write an argument. I wanted to write an exploratory essay.

Quite naturally, then, I didn't begin my draft with a thesis—an answer to my questions about why I often felt stupid, despite evidence to the contrary—but sought to use my essay to try to sort this out. If you go with the "delayed thesis" structure in writing your essay, you use the information from your research to think through your research question.

In one version of using the delayed thesis structure, you essentially tell the story of your thinking so that your paper is a kind of "narrative of thought." The plot is something like, "This seems to be the problem and this is the question is raises for me. And here's what this person and that person have said about it, and this is what I think of what they said." The story ends with some kind of statement that addresses this question: "What do I understand now about the question I initially asked that I didn't understand when I first asked it, and what in this new understanding is particularly important?" (See Figure 2.) This last statement is your delayed thesis. You might also include discussion of questions you would like to further explore. As the arrows in Figure 2 show, arriving at a thesis doesn't necessarily mean the end of inquiry. A delayed thesis may end up opening doors rather than closing them.

Figure 3 is a more detailed look at a delayed thesis structure. It highlights five parts that a research essay *might* include and lists some specific options for developing each. Figure 3 might help you think about how to organize your draft this week.

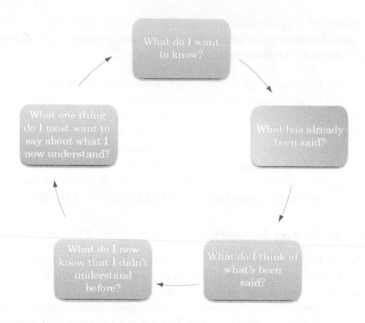

FIGURE 2   **The Delayed Thesis Structure.** This method of thinking through a research question might tell the story of your thinking and of how what you've read and heard has helped you to understand what you didn't understand before about your topic.

Question–Claim Structure

If your initial research question leads you toward an idea about what should be done or what your readers should believe—that is, toward argument—then you'll likely organize your essay differently. Instead of a delayed thesis structure, you might want to use the question–claim structure.

The question–claim structure has some similarities to the delayed thesis structure of the essay—for one thing, it arises from a question—but this method for organizing your draft puts your answer to that question toward the beginning and then proceeds, using your research, to make the most convincing case for that answer (see Figure 4). It's a little like the automobile dealer who, after wandering the lot, decides to put the models he or she most wants to sell in the showroom window. You focus your readers' gaze not on the process of discovery but, rather, on the product of that process: the point you want to make.

The question–claim structure may be the form of the research paper with which you're most familiar. Here's one way to think about

I. **Introduce the research problem or question and then your motive for exploring it. For example:**
   - Tell a story that dramatizes the problem.
   - Describe your own experiences with it.
   - What did you read, observe, or experience that made you curious about it?

II. **Establish the significance of the problem or question and why readers should care about it. For example:**
   - How many other people are affected?
   - What difference will it make in people's lives?
   - Why is this *particular* question significant?

III. **Describe and analyze what has already been written or said by others about the problem or question and how this advances your understanding. For example:**
   - Who has made a significant contribution to the conversation about this?
   - What have they said and how does that relate to your research question?
   - What important questions do these other voices raise for you?

IV. **Explain what you find to be the most persuasive or significant answer to the research question. This is your thesis. For example:**
   - In the end, which voices were most convincing? Why?
   - What might you add to the conversation?
   - What do you want to say?

V. **Describe what you've come to understand about the topic that you didn't fully appreciate when you began the project. What is left to explore?**
   - What difference will the discoveries you made about your question make in your life? In your readers' lives?
   - What do you remain curious about?
   - What questions are unresolved and what directions might more inquiry take if you were to continue?

FIGURE 3   **A Structure for Exploring**

organizing your draft using this approach. This structure has five parts (see Figure 5), each with various options and considerations. It is a structure that you can adapt to your needs.

FIGURE 4 **The Question–Claim Structure.** This structure, which is characteristic of the argumentative research paper, signals the writer's purpose and point early on and then sets out to prove it.

Exploring or Arguing: An Example

Susan was writing an exploratory research essay on the relationship between attendance at preschool and academic success in elementary school. She decided to introduce her topic by describing her own dilemma with her son, Sam. She wanted to send him to preschool, but as a working college student, she wasn't sure she could afford it. Her personal anecdote highlighted the problem many parents face and the question behind her research: Will children who don't attend preschool be at a disadvantage in primary school or not? In the middle section of her essay, Susan reported on several studies that looked at a range of skills that were affected by preschool experience and discussed which of these she found most significant, particularly in the context of her personal interviews with several local teachers. In the second-to-last section of her draft, Susan concluded that preschool does indeed make a difference, particularly in the areas of reading and reasoning.

I. **Introduce the research question or problem that is the focus of the paper. For example:**
   - Provide factual background.
   - Dramatize with an anecdote.
   - Establish the significance of the problem by citing experts or other observers.

II. **What will be your argument or claim in the paper? This is your thesis.**
   - What do you think your readers should *believe* or what do you think they should *do*? State this thesis clearly.

III. **Review the literature. What have others already said about the question or problem? For example:**
   - Cite published studies, interviews, commentaries, experiments, and so on that are relevant to the question or problem.
   - Which ideas or voices seem most important? Are there identifiable camps in the debate, or certain patterns of argument?
   - Address popular assumptions. What do most people believe to be true?

IV. **What are your reasons for believing what you believe and, for each one, what specific evidence did you find that you thought was convincing?**
   - What kinds of evidence will your readers find most persuasive?
   - Are there various kinds of evidence that can be brought to bear?
   - How do your reasons square with those who might disagree with you?

V. **What is the significance of your claim? What's at stake for your audience? What might be other avenues for research? For example:**
   - What should we do? What might happen if we don't act?
   - How does the thesis or claim that you propose resolve some part of the problem? What part remains unresolved?
   - What questions remain?

FIGURE 5   A Structure for Argument

Imagine that Susan wanted instead to write an argumentative research paper, a more conventional form for academic research. Would it be organized differently? While she still might begin with a personal anecdote as a way to dramatize the problem, Susan might choose instead to begin with information, highlighting the statistics and arguments that establish the importance of the problem. How many children in the United States attend preschool? How many don't? What are the trends? Are more parents struggling to find affordable preschools? Are fewer preschools available in disadvantaged areas? Is there a shortage of teachers? A significant difference would be where in the paper Susan puts her thesis. In the argumentative paper, the thesis usually appears toward the beginning (see Figure 3) and is stated explicitly: "I will argue in this essay that the growing number of children in the United States who are being denied a preschool experience will be at a serious disadvantage in reading and reasoning skills when they enter elementary school." Her essay would then go on to methodically establish the truth of this claim using her research. Susan might end her essay by suggesting how elementary teachers could address the learning deficits these children bring into their classrooms or how more children could be given access to preschool.

Preparing to Write the Draft

If research is a little like soup making, then you want to make something hearty, not thin; that's nearly impossible unless you have a lot of information. If you slacked on developing focused knowledge last week and didn't do enough research on your question, then you'll find that you have to use most everything you *do* have to write the first draft. If that happens, your essay will be unfocused and uninformative. Scanty research is one of the most common problems I see in student work at this stage in the process. Your first decision before beginning the draft is whether you've got what it takes to make at least decent soup.

Refining the Question

But you can't really judge the quality of your information until you feel comfortable with your research question. Are you asking the right question? Is it the question that you find most interesting? Is it focused enough? Did you refine it as you learned more about your topic? Does it incorporate the language or terms you may have learned in your reading? Typically, research questions evolve, especially if you are tackling a topic that you initially didn't know much about.

For these kinds of topics, the research questions we often ask initially are broadly informative or questions of definition:

- *What are the theories of dog training?*

As we learn more about our research topic, the questions frequently become more specific—which is far more helpful in guiding research—and reflect our new understandings of the topic. The next generation of questions often moves beyond questions of fact or definition and reflects a *particular* interest in the topic: Is it any good? What does it mean? What should be done? What might be true? What are important causes? (See Figure 6.)

FIGURE 6 **Categories of Questions.** Usually our initial research questions are questions of fact or definition: What is known about this topic? What is it? But a strong research essay needs *to do* something with the facts. One way to think about what a question is trying to do is to place it in one of these additional categories: questions of policy, interpretation, hypothesis, value, or relationship. Before you begin your draft, rethink your question. Can it be more specific? Can you rewrite your question so that it gives you a stronger sense of what you're trying to with your research?

For example, this rewrite of the original research question is a little more specific and also implies value:

- *What are the best theories of dog training?*

The following question is more specific still and incorporates some of the language in the literature:

- *Is there evidence that "dog-centric" approaches to training that reward behavior work better than approaches that emphasize the trainer's dominance over the dog?*

And the following question is even more specific:

- *What is the relationship between the use of shock collars and dog aggression or submission?*

Revisit your research question before you begin your draft. In light of what you've learned about your topic so far, can you rewrite the question so that it provides you with stronger guidance about your purpose in the draft? When you've rewritten your research question, put it on a notecard or sticky note, and put it somewhere on your computer monitor where you can see it as you're writing the draft. Your research question (or thesis) is the sea anchor that will keep you from going adrift.

Refining the Thesis

If you're writing an argumentative essay, then you need to settle on a tentative thesis. It may change as you continue doing the writing and research, but for now you should have a pretty specific statement of what you think. Exercise 1 might have helped nudge you in this direction. Now work with your thesis a bit more.

There is considerable talk about thesis statements. Sometimes it seems like a thesis (or S.O.F.T., main point, central claim, organizing idea, etc.) is a kind of club required to beat an essay into submission, forcing every part of the work into obedience. In this view, there is no room for digression, contrary evidence, opposing views, or uncertainty. Much writing—like the world that writers attempt to explore in that writing—is much messier than that, and that complexity is what makes inquiry interesting.

And yet, when writers discover what they want to say—the answer to the question, the realization about what should be done, or the interpretation that makes the most sense—it's essential that they say it clearly, first for themselves and then for their readers. At this stage in the research process, your thesis is very tentative, but if you spend some time refining it, it will reward you later. A well-stated thesis gives you a sense of direction and can help you to organize both your research and your essay. Just don't be slavish about it. A thesis isn't a club. It isn't even a tool. A thesis is a way of seeing that is made of sand, not stone, and it is continually reshaped by what you learn.

What do we know about the qualities of a good thesis? For one thing, we know that they are not overly broad or obvious. Take this statement, for example:

There are many theories about how to train dogs.

Yep, there sure are. This is not a thesis; it's just an observation and a statement of the obvious. What's missing here is a judgment. The kind of judgment you make in your thesis is related to the kind of question you're asking about your topic (see Figure 6). The observation that there are many theories of dog training is a statement of fact in response to a question of fact. But a thesis is a tentative answer to another kind of question—a question of policy, interpretation, hypothesis, value, or relationship. So if my research question were "What is the *best* method of dog training?" (a question of value), then my thesis might be something like this:

The evidence suggests that "human-centric" approaches to dog training—those that work from the premise that the trainer should be dominant over the dog—are less effective than "dog-centric" approaches, which use positive reinforcement.

Can you see how your thesis is directly related to your research question?

EXERCISE 2

Sharpening Your Point

Even if you're writing an exploratory essay, it's helpful to think about what your thesis might be at this stage in the inquiry process. This is a kind of reality check: What do I think *right now* based on what I've learned? You are invited to change your mind later. If your essay is argumentative, then it's even more important to establish a tentative thesis. The following templates, each based on the kind of question you're asking, might help:

Thesis from a Question of Value

Based on _____, the evidence strongly suggests that _____ is (better / worse, more effective / less effective) than _____.

Example: Based on recent studies comparing how well disciplines teach critical thinking to college students, the evidence suggests that business programs are failing to do a good job teaching reasoning skills to their undergraduates.

Thesis from a Question of Policy

In the debate over _____, I'm persuaded that the most important thing to do is _____.

Example: In the debate over what to do with the overpopulation of wild horses in western rangelands, it's clear that the only effective solution is for the federal agencies to cull the herds.

Thesis from a Question of Interpretation

The pattern in _____ that is most (significant / interesting / obvious) is _____.

Example: Throughout Ken Kesey's *One Flew Over the Cuckoo's Nest*, the character of Nurse Ratched represents everything that sexist men fear: the threat of emasculation by a woman.

Thesis from a Hypothesis Question

Based on my research, the assumption that _____ appears to be (true / false, qualified / unqualified, accurate / inaccurate, difficult to determine / impossible to determine).

Example: My research on Facebook and social intimacy appears to confirm my impression that "friending" can promote connection but can also be used to manipulate and divide.

Thesis from a Relationship Question

There is a (strong / weak) relationship between _____ and _____.

Example: There is a strong relationship between dog owners' views about the need for dominance over their pet and their choice of either "human-centric" or "dog-centric" training methods.

These templates are a bit crude, but try to use them as a starting point to craft a one- or two-sentence thesis that *reflects your current understanding of your topic.* Write this on a sticky note or notecard and, along with your research question, put it on your computer monitor as a reminder when you write the draft.

Deciding Whether to Say *I*

In addition to refining your research question and thesis, there's something else you should wrestle with before you get started: Will you write your essay in first person? You may think that this isn't even a choice. Academic writing is supposed to be faceless, impersonal, and objective, and the best way to maintain this pretense is to religiously avoid ever using the first person in an academic essay.

The ban on the slender "I" from academic prose by teachers and textbooks is based, in part, on the assumption that this is simply the only way to write scholarship, a myth that studies of academic writing prove wrong again and again. Scholarly writing is diverse and discipline specific, and in a number of fields—for example, business, philosophy, English, and linguistics—articles sometimes use the first person and may even include autobiographical material. Another reason that first person is exiled is because it encourages students to write with needless self-references like "I believe that…" or "In my opinion…." As is so often the case with writing, there aren't really "rules" about how things are supposed to be written; these are rhetorical decisions based on your reasons for composing something, to whom you're writing, and what you're writing about.

There are actually good reasons to consider writing this essay in the first person. The most important is this: When a writer stops pretending that the *text* talks instead of the *author* (e.g., "This paper will argue that…") and actually enters into her text, she is much more likely to initiate a genuine conversation with her readers *and* with her sources. This dialogue might very well lead to some new ways of seeing her topic—that is, after all, the purpose of inquiry.

Getting Personal Without Being Personal

Conversation takes place between people, and in writing that embodies conversation, readers sense what Gordon Harvey* called *presence*—an awareness that a writer is making sense of things in his own particular ways, that he has a personal stake in what is being said. This is most easily achieved when the writer *gets* personal by using the first person, sharing personal experiences and perspectives. I hope that you sense my presence in this chapter through my willingness to do such things.

*Harvey, Gordon. "Presence in the Essay." *College English* 56 (1994): 642–54. Print.

Making Your Presence Felt

Here are some ways to establish your presence in your research essay without necessarily using the first person.

- *Control quotation*. Carefully consider how you use the voices of others—where in your essay and for what purpose—as well as what you choose to emphasize in what those voices said.
- *Find your own way of saying things*. Even when talking about what someone else has said, say it in a way that only you can.
- *Find your own way of seeing things*. How do others usually see your topic, and how do you see it differently?
- *Seize opportunities to comment*. More than anything else, what you *do* with information—evaluating it, relating it, defining it, interpreting it, establishing its significance— gives the essay your signature.

But I also want you to see, as Harvey observes, that presence in writing can be registered in ways other than simply talking about yourself. That is, you can write a research essay this week that *doesn't* use the first person or isn't autobiographical and still provides your readers with a strong sense of your presence as an individual writer and thinker. (See the box "Making Your Presence Felt" for some specific suggestions.) This presence may be much more subtle when it's not carried on the first-person singular's sturdy back. But it still makes writing come to life.

Before you begin drafting your essay this week, you'll have to decide how you'd prefer to get personal—explicitly or implicitly. For some of you, the choices may be limited. For instance, if your essay is on the causes of World War I, then integrating your own personal experience with the subject is obviously not an option. Most topics, however, offer the possibility of self-disclosure, and unless your instructor advises otherwise, almost all can accommodate *I*. But when you choose not to get personal in direct ways, you can still establish a strong presence in your essay.

Frankly, one of the best ways to do this isn't self-disclosure *or* first-person writing. The best way to have a strong presence in anything you write is to *find your own way of saying things*. You practice this in your double-entry journal in summaries, paraphrases, and fastwrites. Even if you're borrowing the ideas of someone else—and even bringing their voices into your writing—it is your voice that gives the work your signature.

Starting to Write the Draft: Beginning at the Beginning

John McPhee, one of the masters of the research-based essay, gave a talk some years back about beginnings, which vex many writers.

> The first part—the lead, the beginning—is the hardest part of all to write. I've often heard writers say that if you have written your lead you have written 90 percent of the story. You have tens of thousands of words to choose from, after all, and only one can start the story, then one after that, and so forth. And your material, at this point, is all fresh and unused, so you don't have the advantage of being in the middle of things. You could start in any of many places. What will you choose? Leads must be sound. They should never promise what does not follow.

As McPhee said in his talk, "Leads, like titles, are flashlights that shine down into the story."*

Flashlights or Floodlights?

I love this: *"Leads...are flashlights that shine down into the story."* An introduction, at least the kind I was taught to write in high school, is more like a sodium vapor lamp that lights up the whole neighborhood. I remember writing introductions to research papers that sounded like this:

> There are many critical problems that face soci-
> ety today. One of these critical problems is
> environmental protection, and especially the con-
> servation of marine resources. This paper will
> explore one of these resources—the whale—and the
> myriad ways in which the whale-watching industry
> now poses a new threat to this species' survival.
> It will look at what is happening today and what
> some people concerned with the problem hope will

*McPhee, John. University of New Hampshire, 1977.

happen tomorrow. It will argue that new regulations need to be put into effect to reduce boat
traffic around our remaining whales, a national
treasure that needs protection.

This introduction isn't that bad. It does offer a statement of purpose, and it explains the thesis. But the window it opens on the paper is so broad—listing everything the paper will try to do—that readers see a bland, general landscape. What's to discover? The old writing formula for structuring some papers—"Say what you're going to say, say it, and then say what you said"—breeds this kind of introduction. It also gets the writer started on a paper that often turns out as bland as the beginning.

Consider this alternative opening for the same paper:

Scott Mercer, owner of the whale-watching vessel
Cetecea, tells the story of a man and his son
who decide that watching the whales from inside
their small motorboat isn't close enough. They
want to swim with them. As Mercer and his passengers watch, the man sends his son overboard
with snorkel and fins, and the boy promptly
swims toward a "bubble cloud," a mass of air
exhaled by a feeding humpback whale below the
surface. What the swimmer doesn't know is that,
directly below that bubble cloud, the creature
is on its way up, mouth gaping. They are both
in for a surprise. "I got on the P.A. system and
told my passengers, just loud enough for the guy
in the boat to hear me, that either that swimmer was going to end up as whale food or he was
going to get slapped with a $10,000 fine. He got
out of the water pretty fast."

I think this lead accomplishes nearly as much as the bland version but in a more compelling way. It suggests the purpose of the paper—to explore conflicts between whale lovers and whales—and even implies the thesis—that human activity around whales needs more regulation, a point that might follow the anecdote. This lead is more like McPhee's "flashlight," pointing out the direction of the paper without attempting to illuminate the entire subject in a paragraph. An interesting beginning will also help launch the writer into a more interesting paper, for both reader and writer.

It's probably obvious that your opening is your first chance to capture your reader's attention. But how you begin your research paper will also have a subtle yet significant impact on the rest of it. The lead starts the paper going in a particular direction; it also establishes the *tone*, or writing voice, and the writer's relationships to the subject and the reader. Most writers at least intuitively know this, which is why beginnings are so hard to write.

Writing Multiple Leads

One thing that will make it easier to get started is to write three leads to your paper, instead of agonizing over one that must be perfect. Each different opening you write should point the "flashlight" in a different direction, suggesting different trails the draft might follow. After composing several leads, you can choose the one that you—and ultimately, your readers—find most promising.

Writing multiple openings to your paper might sound hard, but consider all the ways to begin:

■ *Anecdote*. Think of a little story that nicely frames what your paper is about, as does the lead about the man and his son who almost became whale food.

■ *Scene*. Begin by giving your readers a look at some revealing aspect of your topic. A paper on the destruction of tropical rain forests might begin with a description of what the land looks like after loggers have left it.

■ *Profile*. Try a lead that introduces someone who is important to your topic. Amanda's essay on the relationship between the popularity of tooth whitening and our changing notions of beauty might begin, for example, by describing Dr. Levine, the man who determined with mathematical precision the dimensions of the "perfect smile."

■ *Background.* Maybe you could begin by providing important and possibly surprising background information on your topic. A paper on steroid use might start by citing the explosive growth in use by high school athletes in the last ten years. A paper on a novel or an author might begin with a review of what critics have had to say.

■ *Quotation.* Sometimes, you encounter a great quote that beautifully captures the question your paper will explore or the direction it will take. Heidi's paper on whether *Sesame Street* provides children with a good education began by quoting a tribute from *U.S. News and World Report* to Jim Henson after his sudden death.

■ *Dialogue.* Open with dialogue between people involved in your topic. Dan's paper on the connection between spouse abuse and alcoholism began with a conversation between himself and a woman who had been abused by her husband.

■ *Question.* Pointedly ask your readers the questions you asked that launched your research or the questions your readers might raise about your topic. Here's how Kim began her paper on adoption: "Can you imagine going through life not knowing your true identity?"

■ *Contrast.* Try a lead that compares two apparently unlike things that highlight the problem or dilemma the paper will explore. Dusty's paper "Myth of the Superwoman" began with a comparison between her friend Susan, who grew up believing in Snow White and Cinderella and married at 21, and herself, who never believed in princes on white horses and was advised by her mother that it was risky to depend on a man.

■ *Announcement.* Sometimes the most appropriate beginning *is* one like the first lead on whales and whale-watchers mentioned earlier, which announces what the paper is about. Though such openings are sometimes not particularly compelling, they are direct. A paper with a complex topic or focus may be well served by simply stating in the beginning the main idea you'll explore and what plan you'll follow.

EXERCISE 3

Three Ways In

STEP 1: Compose three different beginnings, or leads, to your research paper. Each should be one or two paragraphs (or perhaps more, depending on what type of lead you've chosen and on the length of your

Here are three openings that Amanda crafted for her draft on our cultural obsession with the "perfect smile." Which do you think is strongest?

1. I haven't felt much like smiling recently. It isn't that I've been particularly melancholy or deprived of necessary joy. I've actually been hesitant to smile because lately I've felt insecure about my teeth. I brush and floss every day and see my dentist twice a year, just like any responsible hygiene patient does—but that doesn't seem to be enough anymore. My teeth need to be white. Now when I feel the corners of my mouth pucker upwards and I start to grin at someone, I can't stop thinking about my teeth. What once was a simple visual expression of happiness has become a symptom of my overall doubts about my appearance.

2. Julie Beatty wants people to look at her as a more confident, strong person, so she's doing the only logical thing. She's shelling out over $12,500 for an overhaul on her teeth. While it sounds completely ridiculous to change a person's oral structure to create a different persona, Julie is a member of a booming group of people who are looking to change their smiles to change their lives. Whether or not Julie's straightening, whitening, and tooth reshaping will change her success as an executive is still unknown, but the popularity of cosmetic dentistry and smile care is an undeniable new phenomenon.

3. I can feel individual molecules of air battering at my teeth. It's the middle of the night, but I can't sleep because of the constant pain in my mouth. Even the weight of my lips pressing down on my teeth is agonizing, like I've spent the day being hit in the mouth with a hammer and have exposed nerves protruding throughout. I haven't been beaten up, though. The cause of all my agony is a 10 percent peroxide gel I've been smearing into trays and putting on my teeth for the past week to whiten them. All this pain is due to my vanity and desire for a bit more pearliness in my pearly whites. As I watch the numbers of the clock roll from 2:00 to 4:00, I wonder why I'm putting up with such dental distress just for a more gleaming smile.

FIGURE 7 Amanda's Three Leads*

paper). Think about the many different ways to begin, as mentioned earlier, and experiment. Your instructor may ask you to write the three leads in your research notebook or print them out and bring them to class. (For an example, see Figure 7.)

*These excerpts are reprinted with permission of Amanda Stewart.

STEP 2: Get some help deciding which opening is strongest. Circulate your leads in class, or show them to friends. Ask each person to check the one lead he likes best, that most makes him want to read on.

STEP 3: Choose the lead you like (even if no one else does). To determine how well it prepares your readers for what follows, ask a friend or classmate to answer these questions: Based on reading only the opening of the paper: (a) What do you predict this paper is about? What might be its focus? (b) Can you guess what central question I'm trying to answer? (c) Can you predict what my thesis might be? (d) How would you characterize the tone of the paper?

It's easy to choose an opening that's catchy. But the beginning of your paper must also help establish your purpose in writing it, frame your focus, and perhaps even suggest your main point or thesis. The lead will also establish the voice, or tone, the paper will adopt.

That's a big order for one or two paragraphs, and you may find that more than a couple of paragraphs are needed to do it. If you did Exercise 3, tentatively select the one opening (or a combination of several) you composed that does those things best. I think you'll find that none of the leads you composed will be wasted; there will be a place for the ones you don't use somewhere else in the paper. Keep them handy.

Writing for Reader Interest

You've tentatively chosen a lead for your paper. You've selected it based on how well you think it frames your tentative purpose, establishes an appropriate tone or voice, and captures your readers' attention. Once you've gotten your readers' attention, you want to keep it. Before you continue writing your draft, take some time to explore the four considerations discussed next. Along with your strong lead, drafting with these considerations in mind will help you craft a lively, interesting paper that will help keep readers turning pages:

1. How does your topic intersect with your readers' experiences?
2. Is there a way to put faces on your topic, to dramatize how it affects or is affected by particular people?
3. Can you find an ending that further clarifies, dramatizes, or emphasizes what you've come to understand about the answers to your research question?
4. Are there opportunities to surprise your readers, with interesting facts or arresting arguments, or highlighting a way of seeing something that is unexpected?

Working the Common Ground

Here's how David Quammen, a nature writer, begins an essay on the sexual strategy of Canada geese:

> Listen: *uh-whongk, uh-whongk, uh-whongk, uh-whongk,* and then you are wide awake, and you smile up at the ceiling as the calls fade off to the north and already they are gone. Silence again, 3 A.M., the hiss of March winds. A thought crosses your mind before you roll over and, contentedly, resume sleeping. The thought is: "Thank God I live here, right here exactly, in their path. Thank God for those birds." The honk of wild Canada geese passing overhead in the night is a sound to freshen the human soul. The question is why.*

If you live in Puerto Rico or anywhere beyond the late-night call of geese flying overhead, this lead paragraph may not draw you into Quammen's article on the birds' sexual habits. But for the many of us who know the muttering of geese overhead, suddenly the writer's question—Why is this a sound "to freshen the human soul"?—becomes our question, too. *We want to know what he knows because he starts with what we both know already:* the haunting sound of geese in flight.

David Quammen understands the importance of working the common ground his readers have with him on his topic. In "The Miracle of Geese," his lead draws on an experience that many of us know, and once he establishes that common ground, he takes us into the less familiar territory he encountered while researching Canada geese. And we willingly go. Quammen gives us a foothold on his topic that comes from our own experience with it.

As you write your draft this week, seize common ground with your readers whenever you can. Ask yourself this:

- *What are my readers' own experiences with my topic?*
- *Is there some way in my paper that I can help them see that it's relevant to them?*
- *How can I help them see what they may already know?*

One of my interests in writing an essay about theories of intelligence was the conviction that I'm not alone in wondering whether I'm not all that smart and wondering, too, why these doubts linger despite my success.

*Quammen, David. *The Flight of the Iguana*. New York: Delacorte, 1988, 233. Print.

As you draft your research paper, look for ways to work the common ground between your topic and your readers: What typically is their relationship to what you're writing about? What might they know about the topic but not have noticed? How does it touch their world? What would they want to know from their own experiences with your topic?

Steve, writing a paper about the town fire department that services the university, began by describing a frequent event in his dormitory: a false alarm. He then went on to explore why many alarms are not really so false after all. He hooked his readers by drawing on their common experience with his topic.

Some topics, like geese and divorce and alcoholism, may have very real connections to the lives of your readers. Many people have heard geese overhead, seen families broken apart, or watched parents or friends destroy themselves with booze. As you revise your paper, look for opportunities to encourage readers to take a closer look at something about your topic they may have seen before.

Topics for Which Common Ground Is Hard to Find

Some topics don't yield common ground so directly. They may be outside the direct experiences of your readers. For example, Margaret was a history major, and, thankfully, she had never had the bubonic plague. Neither have the rest of us. But she was interested in writing a research essay on the impact of the fourteenth-century epidemic on the lives of European women. This is an age and a disaster that in some ways is beyond the imagining of modern readers, but a skillful writer will look to highlight some of the similarities between our lives and those of the people she's writing about. One of these connections might be the modern AIDS epidemic in Africa, a disaster of truly epic proportions, though it seems largely ignored by many Americans. Margaret might begin her essay with a brief glimpse at the devastation of families in South Africa today as a way of establishing the relevance of her 500-year-old topic.

Literary topics may also present a challenge in establishing common ground with readers, unless the author or work is familiar. But there are ways. When I was writing a paper on notions of manhood in Wallace Stegner's novels *The Big Rock Candy Mountain* and *Recapitulation,* I brought the idea of manhood home to my readers by describing my relationship with my own father and then comparing it to the relationship of two key characters in the books. Comparison to other more popular works that readers may know can also be a way to establish some common ground.

In writing your paper, imagine the ways in which your topic intersects with the life of a typical reader, and then use your insights to bring the information to life.

Putting People on the Page

Essayist E. B. White once advised that when you want to write about humankind, you should write about a human. The advice to look at the *small* to understand the *large* applies to most writing, not just the research paper.

Ideas come alive when we see how they operate in the world we live in. Beware, then, of long paragraphs with sentences that begin with phrases such as *in today's society,* where you wax on with generalization after generalization about your topic. Unless your ideas are anchored to specific cases, observations, experiences, statistics, and, especially, people, they will be reduced to abstractions and lose their power for your reader.

Using Case Studies

Strangely, research papers are often peopleless landscapes, which is one of the things that can make them so lifeless to read. Lisa wrote about theories of child development, citing studies and schools of thought about the topic yet never applying that information to a real child, her own daughter, two-year-old Rebecca. In his paper decrying the deforestation of the Amazon rain forest, Marty never gave his readers the chance to hear the voices of the Indians whose way of life is threatened. *Ultimately, what makes almost any topic matter to the writer or the reader is what difference it makes to people.*

Candy's paper on child abuse and its effect on language development, for example, opened with the tragic story of Genie, who, for nearly 13 years, was bound in her room by her father and beaten whenever she made a sound. When Genie was finally rescued, she could not speak at all. This sad story about a real girl makes the idea that child abuse affects how one speaks (the paper's thesis)—anything but abstract. Candy gave her readers reason to care about what she learned about the problem by personalizing it.

Sometimes, the best personal experience to share is your own. Have you been touched by the topic? Kim's paper about the special problems of women alcoholics included anecdotes about several women gleaned from her reading, but the paper was most compelling when she talked about her own experiences with her mother's alcoholism.

Using Interviews

Interviews are another way to bring people to the page. In "Why God Created Flies," Richard Conniff brought in the voice of a bug expert, Vincent Dethier, who not only had interesting things to say about flies but also said them with humor and enthusiasm. Heidi's paper on *Sesame Street* featured the voice of a school principal, a woman who echoed the point the paper made about the value of the program. Such research essays are filled not just with information about the topic but also with people who are touched by it in some way.

As you write your paper, look for opportunities to bring people to the page. Hunt for case studies, anecdotes, and good quotes that will help your readers see how your topic affects how people think and live their lives.

Writing a Strong Ending

Readers remember beginnings and endings. We already explored what makes a strong beginning: It engages the reader's interest, it's more often specific than general, and it frames the purpose of the paper, defining for the reader where it is headed. A beginning for a research paper should also state its thesis (as in an argumentative essay) or state the question (as in an exploratory essay).

We haven't said anything yet about endings, or "conclusions" as they are traditionally labeled. What's a strong ending? That depends. If you're writing a formal research paper in some disciplines, the basic elements of your conclusion might be prescribed. For example, you might need to summarize major findings and suggest directions for further research. But often, especially if you're writing a less formal research essay, you'll be able select from a wide range of options. For example, in an argumentative research essay, you might end as Figure 5 suggests, emphasizing what readers should do about the problem and why it matters. Exploratory essays might end with an anecdote, one that illuminates the understandings the writer has discovered. An ending for either kind of essay might suggest new questions, other avenues for research, or a reconsideration of an initial thesis.

Endings to Avoid

The ending of your research paper could be a lot of things, and in a way, it's easier to say what it should *not* be:

■ Avoid conclusions that simply restate what you've already said. This is the "kick the dead horse" conclusion some of us were taught to write in school on the assumption that our readers probably aren't smart enough to get our point, so we'd better repeat it. This approach annoys most readers, who *are* smart enough to know the horse is dead.

■ Avoid endings that begin with *in conclusion* or *thus*. Words such as these also signal to your reader what she already knows: that you're ending. And they often lead into a very general summary, which gets you into a conclusion such as the one mentioned above: dead.

■ Avoid endings that don't feel like endings—that trail off onto other topics, are abrupt, or don't seem connected to what came before them. Prompting your readers to think is one thing; leaving them hanging is quite another.

In some ways, the conclusion of your research paper is the last stop on your journey; the reader has traveled far with you to get there. The most important quality of a good ending is that it add something to the paper. If it doesn't, cut it and write a new one.

What can the ending add? It can add a further elaboration of your thesis that grows from the evidence you've presented, a discussion of solutions to a problem that has arisen from the information you've uncovered, or perhaps a final illustration or piece of evidence that drives home your point.

Student Christina Kerby's research essay on method acting explores the controversy over whether this approach is selfish, subverting the playwright's intentions about a character's identity and replacing it with the actor's focus on her own feelings and identity. Christina's ending, however, first transcends the debate by putting method acting in context: It is one of several tools an actor can use to tap her emotions for a role. But then Christina humorously raises the nagging question about selfishness once more: Can we accept that Juliet is not thinking about the fallen Romeo as she weeps by his side but about her dead cat Fluffy? Here's Christina's ending:

> Acting is no longer about poise, voice quality, and diction only. It is also about feeling the part, about understanding the emotions that go into playing the part, and about possessing the skill necessary to bring those emotions to life within the character.... Whether an actor uses Stanislavski's method of physical actions to unlock the door to her subconscious or whether she attempts to stir up emotions from deep within herself using Strasberg's method, the actor's goal is to create a portrayal that is truthful. It is

possible to pick out a bad actor from a mile away,
one who does not understand the role because she
does not understand the emotions necessary to
create it. Or perhaps she simply lacks the means
of tapping into them.

If genuine emotion is what the masses want,
method acting may be just what every star-struck
actress needs. Real tears? No problem. The
audience will never know that Juliet was not
lamenting the loss of her true love Romeo but
invoking the memory of her favorite cat Fluffy,
who died tragically in her arms.*

An ending, in many ways, can be approached similarly to a lead.
You can conclude with an anecdote, a quotation, a description, a summary, or a profile. Go back to the discussion earlier in this chapter
of types of leads for ideas about types of conclusions. The same basic
guidelines apply.

One of the easiest ways to solve the problem of finding a strong
ending is to have the snake bite its tail. In other words, find some
way in the end of your essay to return to where the piece began.
For example, if your research essay began with an anecdote that
dramatized a problem—say, the destruction of old growth forests in
Washington—you might return to that opening anecdote, suggesting
how the solutions you explored in your essay might have changed the
outcome. If you pose a question in the first few paragraphs, return
to the question in the last few. If you begin with a profile of someone relevant to your topic, return to him or her in the end, perhaps
amplifying on some part of your picture of the person. Although this
approach is formulaic, it often works well because it gives a piece of
writing a sense of unity.

Using Surprise

The research process—like the writing process—can be filled
with discovery for the writer if he approaches the topic with curiosity

---

*Reprinted with permission of Christina B. Kerby.

and openness. When I began researching the *Lobster Almanac,* I was constantly surprised by things I didn't know: Lobsters are bugs; it takes eight years for a lobster in Maine to grow to the familiar one-pound size; the largest lobster ever caught weighed about 40 pounds and lived in a tank at a restaurant for a year, developing a fondness for the owner's wife. I could go on and on. And I did, in the book, sharing unusual information with my readers on the assumption that if it surprised me, it would surprise them, too.

As you write your draft, reflect on the surprising things you discovered about your topic during your research and look for ways to weave that information into the rewrite. Later, after you have written your draft, share it with a reader and ask for his ideas about what is particularly interesting and should be further developed. For now, think about unusual specifics you may have left out.

However, don't include information, no matter how surprising or interesting, that doesn't serve your purpose. Christine's survey on the dreams of college freshmen had some fascinating findings, including some accounts of recurring dreams that really surprised her. She reluctantly decided not to say much about them, however, because they didn't really further the purpose of her paper, which was to discover what function dreams serve. On the other hand, Bob was surprised to find that some politically conservative politicians and judges actually supported decriminalization of marijuana. He decided to include more information about who they were and what they said in his revision, believing it would surprise his readers and strengthen his argument.

Writing with Sources

The need for *documentation*—that is, citing sources—distinguishes the research paper from most other kinds of writing. And let's face it: Worrying about sources can cramp your style. Many students have an understandable paranoia about plagiarism and tend, as mentioned earlier, to let the voices of their sources overwhelm their own. Students are also often distracted by technical details: Am I getting the right page number? Where exactly should this citation go? Do I need to cite this or not?

As you gain control of the material by choosing your own writing voice and clarifying your purpose in the paper, you should feel less constrained by the technical demands of documentation. The following suggestions may also help you weave reference sources into your own writing without the seams showing.

Blending Kinds of Writing and Sources

One of the wonderful things about the research essay is that it can draw on all four sources of information—reading, interviews, observation, and experience—as well as the four notetaking strategies discussed earlier—quotation, paraphrase, summary, and the writer's own analysis and commentary. Skillfully blended, these elements can make music.

Look at this paragraph from Heidi's paper on *Sesame Street*:

```
There is more to this show than meets the eye,
certainly. It is definitely more than just a crowd
of furry animals all living together in the middle
of New York City. Originally intended as an effort
to educate poor, less privileged youth, Sesame
Street is set in the very middle of an urban devel-
opment on purpose (Hellman 52). As Jon Stone, one
of the show's founders and co-producers sees it,
the program couldn't be "just another escapist show
set in a tree house or a badger den" (52). Instead,
the recognizable environment gave something to the
kids they could relate to. "...It had a lot more
real quality to it than, say, Mister Rogers....
Kids say the reason they don't like Mister Rogers
is that it's unbelievable," says Nancy
Diamonti.*
```

The writing is lively here, not simply because the topic is interesting to those of us who know the program. Heidi has nicely blended her own commentary with summary, paraphrase, and quotation, all in a single paragraph. She has also been able to draw on multiple sources of information—an interview, some effective quotes from her reading, and her own observations of *Sesame Street*. We sense that the writer is *using* the information, and is not being used by it.

*Used with permission of Heidi R. Dunham.

Handling Quotes

Avoid the temptation, as Heidi did, to load up your paragraphs with long and unintegrated quotes from your sources. The most common fumble I see with quotations in student papers is what I call "hanging quotes." Embedded in a paragraph is a sentence or two within quotation marks. Though the passage is cited, there's no indication of who said it. Usually this means the writer was uncertain about how to summarize or paraphrase or work *part* of the quotation into his own prose. Here's what I mean:

> The third biggest tattooing movement occurred at the turn of the century: religious tattooing. "When it comes to modern Christian tattoo, it can most likely be traced back to the times of the counterculture movement of the '60s and '70s. While sex, drugs, and rock and roll were waging a war against Christian culture, devoted Christians emerged who wanted to claim back lost Christian territory. One of the ways that they did this was to reclaim the practice of tattoo for God and Jesus, by getting tattoos that were inspired by Christian and religious symbols and images" ("TattooJohnny"). Many Christian preachers and youth group leaders are getting tattoos with Christian themes to combat the satanic images in rock music. Many of the themes include rock-style designs with scripture or crosses that resemble those of the warriors.

Can you see how the long quote just appears in the middle of the paragraph, just floating freely and (aside from a parenthetical citation) unanchored to who said it and why? As a rule, whenever you quote, attribute the source, and *work* with it. Don't just look for opportunities to paraphrase some of it; also comment on what was said: What is interesting about the quote? Why is it significant in the context of what you're talking about? What would you emphasize? (See "Sandwiching Quotes".)

Use quotations selectively. And if you can, blend them into your own sentences, using a particularly striking or relevant part of the original source. To see how this might work, contrast the use of quotes in this paragraph and in the reworked paragraph that follows:

> Black Elk often spoke of the importance of the circle to American Indian culture. "You may have noticed that everything an Indian does is in a circle, and that is because the Power of the World always works in circles, and everything tries to be round....The sky is round, and I have heard that the earth is round like a ball, and so are all the stars." He couldn't understand why white people lived in square houses. "It is a bad way to live, for there is not power in a square."

Here the quotes stand out, separate from the writer's own text, but in the revised paragraph they are worked smoothly into the writer's own prose:

> Black Elk believed the "Power of the World always works in circles," noting the roundness of the sun, the earth, and the stars. He couldn't understand why white people live in square houses: "It is a bad way to live, for there is not power in a square."

Although long quotes, especially if unintegrated, should usually be avoided, occasionally it may be useful to include a long quotation from one of your sources. A quotation that is longer than four lines should be *blocked,* or set off from the rest of the text by indenting it an inch from the left margin. Like the rest of the paper, a blocked quotation is also typed double-spaced. For example:

According to Robert Karen, shame is a particularly modern phenomenon. He notes that in medieval times people pretty much let loose, and by our modern tastes, it was not a pretty sight:

> Their emotional life appears to have been extraordinarily spontaneous and unrestrained. From Johan Huizinga's *The Waning of the Middle Ages*, we learn that the average European town dweller was wildly erratic and inconsistent, murderously violent when enraged, easily plunged into guilt, tears, and pleas for forgiveness, and bursting with psychological eccentricities. He ate with his hands out of a common bowl, blew his nose on his sleeve, defecated openly by the side of the road, made love, and mourned with great passion, and was relatively unconcerned about such notions as maladjustment or what others might think.... In post-medieval centuries, what I've called situational shame spread rapidly.... (61)

Note that the quotation marks are dropped around a blocked quotation. In this case, only part of a paragraph was borrowed, but if you quote one or more full paragraphs, indent the first line of each *three* spaces in addition to the inch the block is indented from the left margin. Note, too, that the writer has introduced this long quote in a way that effectively ties it to his own paper.

We'll examine *parenthetical references* more fully in the next section, but notice how the citation in the blocked quotation above is placed *after* the final period. That's a unique exception to the usual rule that a parenthetical citation is enclosed *before* the period of the borrowed material's final sentence.

Quick Tips for Controlling Quotations

From our discussion so far, you've seen the hazards and the benefits of using quotations. Quotations from your sources can definitely be overused, especially when they seem dumped into the draft, untouched and unexamined, or used as a lazy substitute for paraphrase. But when it works, bringing the voices of others into your own writing can bring the work to life and make readers feel as though there is a genuine conversation going on.

You've also seen some basics on how to handle quotes. Here are some specific tips for doing this effectively.

Grafting Quotes

Frequently, the best way to use quoted material is to graft it onto your own prose. Sometimes you just use a word or phrase:

```
Some words for hangover, like ours, refer prosai-
cally to the cause: the Egyptians say they are
"still drunk," the Japanese "two days drunk," the
Chinese "drunk overnight."*
```

In other situations, especially when you want to add emphasis to what a source has said, you might give over parts of several sentences to a source, like this:

```
The makers of NoHang, on their Web page, say what
your mother would: "It is recommended that you
drink moderately and responsibly." At the same
time, they tell you that with NoHang "you can
drink the night away."
```

Sandwiching Quotes

A sandwich without the bread isn't a sandwich. Similarly, when you use a quotation, especially one that is a full sentence or more, it should be surrounded by your comments about it. Introduce the quotation: Who said it, and why is he or she relevant? When did this person say it and in what context? How does the quote relate to the

---

*Acocella, Joan. "A Few Too Many." *New Yorker* 26 May 2008: 32–37. Print.

current discussion in your essay? Follow up the quotation: What do *you* think is important about what was just said? How does it address an important idea or question? What does the person quoted *fail* to say or to see?

Here's an example of what I mean:

> In fact, even back when leeches were held in con-
> tempt by the medical profession, Sawyer had a
> solid rationale for choosing them as his subject.
> Biology, as taught in the United States had left
> him frustrated: "For sex determination, we'd study
> *Drosophilia,* for physiology we'd study frogs, for
> genetics, bacteria. I thought there was more to be
> learned from studying one organism in detail than
> from parts of many." His American professors dis-
> dained this approach as a throw-back to nineteenth
> century biology.*

See how the writer here sets up the quotation? He provides background on the significance of what Sawyer, the leech biologist, was about to say. The guy was frustrated with how organisms were studied. The quotation is then sandwiched with a comment about how the quote reflects Sawyer's reputation as an antitraditionalist.

Billboarding Quotes

Another way you can control quotations is by adding emphasis to billboard parts of a particular quote. Typically you do this by italicizing the phrase or sentence. Here is an example, taken from the end of a block quotation:

> For the sake of Millennials—and, through them,
> the future of America—the most urgent adult task
> *is to elevate their expectations.* (Emphasis added)
> (Howe and Strauss 365)†

*Conniff, Richard. *Spineless Wonders.* New York: Holt, 1996. Print.
†Howe, Neil, and William Strauss. *Millennials Rising.* New York: Vintage, 2000. Print.

Notice that the parenthetical note that signals the original quote has been altered to give emphasis.

Splicing Quotes

Sometimes you want to prune away unnecessary information from a quotation to place emphasis on the part that matters most to you or to eliminate unnecessary information. Ellipsis points, those three dots (...) you sometimes see at the beginning, middle, or end of a sentence, signal that some information has been omitted.

Take this passage, for example:

```
During the Gen-X child era, the American family

endured countless new movements and trends—

feminism, sexual freedom, a divorce epidemic,

fewer G-rated movies, child-raising handbooks

telling parents to "consider yourself" ahead of

a child's needs, gay rights, Chappaquiddick, film

nudity, a Zero Population Growth ethic, Kramer vs.

Kramer, and Roe v. Wade. A prominent academic in

1969 proclaimed in the Washington Post that the

family needed a "decent burial."
```

That's a pretty long list of movements and trends, and the reader could get a taste without being served up the whole thing. Ellipsis points can help:

```
During the Gen-X child era, the American family

endured countless new movements and trends—

feminism, sexual freedom, a divorce epidemic...,

[and a] prominent academic in 1969 proclaimed

in the Washington Post that the family needed a

"decent burial."
```

When you have to slightly reword the original text or alter the punctuation for a smoother splice, put the alteration in brackets. In the example, for instance, I turned what was a separate sentence in the original into a compound sentence using the conjunction *and*.

Handling Interview Material

The great quotes you glean from your interviews can be handled like quotations from texts. But there's a dimension to a quote from an interview that's lacking in a quote from a book: Namely, you participated in the quote's creation by asking a question, and in some cases, you were there to observe your subject saying it. This presents some new choices. When you're quoting an interview subject, should you enter your essay as a participant in the conversation, or should you stay out of the way? That is, should you describe yourself asking the question? Should you describe the scene of the interview, your subject's manner of responding, or your immediate reaction to what she said? Or should you merely report what was said and who said it?

Christina's essay, "Crying Real Tears: The History and Psychology of Method Acting," makes good use of interviews. Notice how Christina writes about one of them in the middle of her essay:

> During a phone interview, I asked my acting
> teacher, Ed Claudio, who studied under Stella
> Adler, whether or not he agreed with the ideas
> behind method acting. I could almost see him wrin-
> kle his nose at the other end of the connection.
> He described method acting as "self-indulgent,"
> insisting that it encourages "island acting."
> Because of emotional recall, acting has become a
> far more personal art, and the actor began to move
> away from the script, often hiding the author's
> purpose and intentions under his own.*

Contrast Christina's handling of the Claudio interview with her treatment of material from an interview with Dave Pierini later in her essay:

> Dave Pierini, a local Sacramento actor, pointed
> out, "You can be a good actor without using
> method, but you cannot be a good actor without

*Reprinted with permission of Christina B. Kerby.

at least understanding it." Actors are perhaps
some of the greatest scholars of the human psy-
che because they devote their lives to the study
and exploration of it. Aspiring artists are told
to "get inside of the character's head." They are
asked, "How would the character *feel*? How would
the character *react*?"

Do you think Christina's entry into her report of the first interview (with Ed Claudio) is intrusive? Or do you think it adds useful information or even livens it up? What circumstances might make this a good move? On the other hand, what might be some advantages of the writer staying out of the way and simply letting her subject speak, as Christina chooses to do in her treatment of the interview with Dave Pierini?

Trusting Your Memory

One of the best ways to weave references seamlessly into your own writing is to avoid the compulsion to stop and study your sources as you're writing the draft. I remember that writing my research papers in college was typically done in stops and starts. I'd write a paragraph of the draft, then stop and reread a photocopy of an article, then write a few more sentences, and then stop again. Part of the problem was the meager notes I took as I collected information. I hadn't really taken possession of the material before I started writing the draft. But I also didn't trust that I'd remember what was important from my reading.

If, during the course of your research and writing so far, you've found a sense of purpose—for example, you're pretty sure your paper is going to argue for legalization of marijuana or analyze the symbolism on old gravestones on Cape Cod—then you've probably read purposefully, too. You *will* likely know what reference sources you need as you write the draft, without sputtering to a halt to remind yourself of what each says. Consult your notes and sources as you need them; otherwise, push them aside, and immerse yourself in your own writing.

Citing Sources

Like most people I knew back then, I took a typing class the summer between eighth grade and high school. Our instructional texts were long books with the bindings at the top, and we worked on standard Royal typewriters that were built like tanks. I got up to 30 words a minute, I think, which wasn't very good, but thanks to that class, I can still type without looking at the keyboard. The one thing I never learned, though, was how to turn the typewriter roller up a half space to type a footnote number that would neatly float above the line. In every term paper in high school, my footnotes collided with my sentences.

I'm certain that such technical difficulties were not the reason that most academic writers in the humanities and social sciences have largely abandoned the footnote method of citation for the parenthetical one, but I'm relieved, nonetheless. In the current system, borrowed material is parenthetically cited in the paper by indicating the author of the original work and the page the borrowed material was taken from or the date the work was published. These parenthetical citations are then explained more fully in the "Works Cited" page at the end of your paper where the sources themselves are listed.

By now, your instructor has probably told you which method of citing sources you should use: the Modern Language Association (MLA) style or the American Psychological Association (APA) style. Most English classes use MLA.

Driving Through the First Draft

You have an opening, a lot of material in your notes—much of it, written in your own words—and maybe an outline. You've considered some general methods of development, looked at ways to write with sources, and completed a quick course in how to cite them. Finish the week by writing through the first draft.

Writing the draft may be difficult. All writing, but especially research writing, is a recursive process. You may find sometimes that you must circle back to a step you took before, discovering a gap in your information, a new idea for a thesis statement, or a better lead or focus. Circling back may be frustrating at times, but it's natural and even a good sign: It means you're letting go of your preconceived ideas and allowing the discoveries you make *through writing* to change your mind.

It's too early to worry about writing a research paper that's air-tight, with no problems to solve. Too often, student writers think they have to write a perfect paper in the first draft. You can worry about plugging holes and tightening things up next week. For now, write a draft, and if you must, put a reminder on a piece of paper and post it on the computer next to your thesis statement or research question. Look at this reminder every time you find yourself agonizing over the imperfections of your paper. The reminder should say, "It Doesn't Count."

Keep a few other things in mind while writing your first draft:

1. *Focus on your tentative thesis or your research question.* In the draft, consider your thesis a theory you're trying to prove but that you're willing to change. If your paper is more exploratory than argumentative, use your focusing question as a reminder of what you want to know. Remember, your question and thesis can change, too, as you learn more about your subject.

2. *Vary your sources.* Offer a variety of different sources as evidence to support your assertions. Beware of writing a single page that cites only one source.

3. *Remember your audience.* What do your readers want to know about your topic? What do they need to know to understand what you're trying to say?

4. *Write with your notes.* If you took thoughtful notes during the third week—carefully transforming another author's words into your own, flagging good quotes, and developing your own analysis—then you've already written at least some of your paper. You may only need to fine-tune the language in your notes and then plug them into your draft.

5. *Be open to surprises.* The act of writing is often full of surprises. In fact, it should be, because *writing* is *thinking,* and the more you think about something, the more you're likely to see. You might get halfway through your draft and discover the part of your topic that *really* fascinates you. Should that happen, you may have to change your thesis or throw away your outline. You may even have to reresearch your topic, at least somewhat. It's not necessarily too late to shift the purpose or focus of your paper (though you should consult your instructor before totally abandoning your topic at this point). Let your curiosity remain the engine that drives you forward.

The Fifth Week

Revision Is Re-seeing (or Breaking Up Is Hard to Do)

My high school girlfriend, Jan, was bright, warm hearted, and fun, and I wasn't at all sure I liked her much—at least at first. Though we had a lot in common—we both loved sunrises over Lake Michigan, bird watching, and Simon and Garfunkel—I found Jan a little intimidating, a little too much in a hurry to anoint us a solid "couple." But we stuck together for three years, and as time passed, I persuaded myself—despite lingering doubts—that I couldn't live without her. There was no way I was going to break my white-knuckled hold on that relationship. After all, I'd invested all that time.

As a writer, I used to have similar relationships with my drafts. I'd work on something very hard, finally finishing the draft. I'd know there were problems, but I'd developed such a tight relationship with my draft that the problems were hard to see. And even when I recognized some problems, the thought of making major changes seemed too risky. Did I dare ruin the things I loved about the draft? These decisions were even harder if the draft had taken a long time to write.

Revision doesn't necessarily mean you have to sever your relationship with your draft. It's probably too late to make a complete break with the draft and abandon your topic. However, revision does demand finding some way to step back from the draft and change your relationship with it, trying to see it more from the reader's perspective than the writer's. Revision requires that you loosen your grip. And when you do, you may decide to shift your focus or rearrange the information. At the very least, you may discover gaps in information or sections of the draft that need more development. You will certainly need to prune sentences.

Revision, as the word implies, means "re-seeing" or "reconceiving," trying to see what you failed to notice with the first look. That can be hard. Remember how stuck I was on that one picture of the lighthouse? I planted my feet in the sand, and the longer I stared through the camera lens, the harder it was to see the lighthouse from any other angle. It didn't matter that I didn't particularly like what I was seeing. I just wanted to take the picture.

You've spent more than four weeks researching your topic and the last few days composing your first draft. You may find that you've spent so much time staring through the lens—seeing your topic the way you chose to see it in your first draft—that doing a major revision is about as appealing as eating cold beets. How do you get the perspective to "re-see" the draft and rebuild it into a stronger paper?

Global Revision: Revising for Purpose, Thesis, and Structure

Your instinct when you revise may be to take out the microscope rather than the binoculars. But if revision is a process of re-seeing—of not just shutting things down but opening them up—then your rewrite this week should begin with the whole rather than with the details. Rather than trying to "fix" the small things—grammar, citations, diction, and so on—take the large view. Ask these questions: What is my draft trying to do? How well does it do it? And, especially, will it make sense to someone else?

Writer- to Reader-Based Prose

Writing theorist Linda Flower distinguishes between "writer-based prose" and "reader-based prose." When we first start writing about something in notebooks, journals, and sometimes first drafts, we are our own audience. Sure, we might have a vague sense that someone else will be reading what we write, but often our energies are focused on whether it makes sense to us. "Writer-based prose" like this often works from the tacit assumption that readers and writers share the same understanding and knowledge about a topic. As a result, writers may assume that certain things that should be explained don't need to be. Writers may also assume that the things they find interesting or relevant their readers will find interesting or relevant. In "reader-based prose," writers have confronted these assumptions. They have revised their work with their readers in mind.

Reading anything is work. Most of us are willing to do the work if we sense an author is taking us somewhere interesting. More specifically, readers must trust that writers know what they're doing—the writers have a destination in mind, they are reliable guides, and the journey will likely yield something worth knowing or thinking about.

One way to see if your draft research essay is sufficiently "reader-based" is to determine whether it does three things that all essays must do (see Figure 1):

■ *Have a clear purpose*: What exactly did you want to find out in this investigation of your topic? What is your research question?
■ *Establish why the question (and its answer) is significant*: What stake might readers have in your inquiry?
■ *Say one main thing*: Among the possible answers to the question you pose, which one seems most persuasive, most significant, or most revealing?

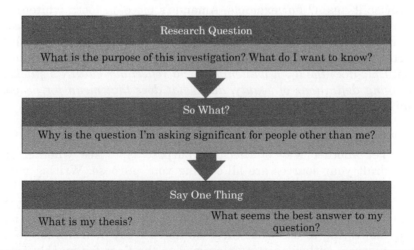

FIGURE 1 Three Things the Essay Must Do. As you revise your draft, you can measure your progress by asking whether you've answered these three basic questions: *Is the question I'm asking clear and sufficiently limited? Have I answered the "So what?" question? Is there one most important thing I'm trying to say?* If your draft explicitly answers each of these, then the boat at least will float and have a clear destination.

Is It Organized Around a Clear Purpose?

Purpose, like a torch, lights the way in the darkness. It illuminates one part of your subject, helping to guide you in the direction you want to go. You should determine whether the purpose of your paper is clear and examine how well the information is organized around that purpose.

Presumably, by now you know the purpose of your essay. You know, for instance, whether you're exploring or arguing. But what exactly are you exploring or arguing? Your ability to state this purpose as clearly as you can is a great foundation for revision this week. Try completing one of the following sentences:

For an exploratory essay: The main purpose of my essay on _____ is to explore _____. In particular, I will consider the questions raised by _____ and _____ as well as _____.

For an argument essay: Because of _____ and _____ as well as _____, in this essay I am arguing _____.

Another way of getting at purpose is to clarify your research question, something that you were working on last week. Is it time to revise it again? For example, Amanda's piece on tooth whitening began with this research question: *How has cosmetic tooth whitening changed the way Americans feel about their teeth?* After a few clarifications she made as she learned more, Amanda had this question: *How does the tooth whitening trend reflect our culture's quickly changing definitions of beauty, and what does that mean for people who don't fit that definition?*

Go back to the beginning. What was your initial research question? What is it now?

Yet another way of checking purpose is to see whether in your draft your sources are all serving your purpose. Writing with research is a wrestling match. You're the 120-pound weakling, who may not have written many college research essays before, trying to take on the heavyweight experts on your topic. You're fighting for your life, trying to use what these authorities say or think for your own purpose, without getting slammed to the floor for meekly submitting a report rather than an essay. The challenge is to get control of the information, to muscle it to the ground using the strength of your purpose. Establishing this control is one of the hardest parts of drafting research papers. Two extreme responses to this problem are giving up entirely and turning your paper over to your sources (letting them do all the talking) and pretending that you're not really wrestling with anyone and writing a paper that includes only your own opinions. Neither option is what you want.

Who won the wrestling match in your draft? To what extent did you have a coherent purpose and succeed in using other people's ideas and information in the service of your purpose? One way to see who is getting the upper hand in the draft is to mark it up, noting where you've given control to your sources and where you've taken it back. Exercise 1 can graphically illustrate who is winning the wresting match. To what extent is your purpose in the essay enabling you to *use* the information you've gathered to explore your research question or prove your point? The exercise will also reveal how well you've managed to surround your research with your own analysis, interpretations, arguments, and questions.

EXERCISE 1

Wrestling with the Draft*

For this exercise you'll use two highlighters, each a different color.

1. Choose a random page or two of your draft, somewhere in the middle.
2. First mark the parts in which you're a less active author. As you read the page, highlight every sentence that reports facts, quotes sources, or otherwise presents information or ideas that belong to someone else.
3. Now, using the other highlighter, mark the parts in which you're a more active author. Read the same page or pages again, but this time highlight every sentence or paragraph that represents *your* ideas, analysis, commentary, interpretation, definition, synthesis, or claims.
4. Repeat the previous steps with two more pages of your draft.

Which color dominates? Are you turning over too much of the text to your sources? Are you ignoring them and rattling on too much about what you think? Or does your source use seem appropriate to support your purpose?

*This exercise is adapted from one I borrowed from my colleague Dr. Mike Mattison, who borrowed it from his former colleagues at the University of Massachusetts–Amherst. Thanks to all.

In addition, look at the pattern of color. What do you notice about this pattern? Are you taking turns paragraph by paragraph with your sources, or is your own analysis and commentary nicely blended *within* paragraphs, so that the information is always anchored to your own thoughts? Do you surround quoted passages with your own voice and analysis? Who wins the wrestling match? See Figure 2 for an example of this exercise.

Does It Establish Significance?

So what? That's the blunt question here. Any reader will need a *reason* to care about what you have to say. So what reasons might there be for someone to care about a research essay on theories

Our tooth whiteners are safer, and a study by James W. Curtis, DMD, discovered that bleaching through carbamide peroxide actually decreases the amount of plaque on teeth, but we're still doing it for beauty reasons rather than health ones (Nuss 28).

In her article "Bright On," Molly Prior notes that Procter & Gamble and Colgate-Palmolive revolutionized the whitening industry by bringing over-the-counter whiteners to drugstores everywhere at the turn of the twenty-first century (39). No longer did people have to pay high prices for professional whitening—they could do it themselves, at home, for a reasonable cost. In the past, a patient had to eat a bill of $1,000 for a laser whitening treatment, or $10,000 for a full set of veneers; now a package of Crest Whitestrips retails for only $29.99 (Gideonse). Suddenly, whiter teeth were available to everyone. While a shining smile once indicated wealth and the ability to splurge on cosmetic dentistry, it became affordable to the dentally discolored masses eager to emulate the lifestyles of the people they saw in magazines and on television.

Companies didn't create whitening products to fill a demand created by the public for whiter teeth. While Hollywood glitterati did pay high prices for iconic smiles, most people seemed happy with functional teeth. However, companies saw money to be made in creating a whiter norm for teeth, so they barraged the airwaves with advertisements featuring people complaining about the dullness and imperfection of their teeth. Natural teeth were denigrated as ugly. Crest and Colgate-Palmolive wanted to make money, so appealed to the American obsession with beauty to secure a financial reason to smile.

FIGURE 2 Amanda Wins the Wrestling Match. The sections of text highlighted in gray are passages from Amanda's sources, and the sections highlighted in blue are passages in which she is commenting, clarifying, asserting, or interpreting. Notice the balance between gray and blue. Clearly Amanda has a strong authorial presence. Also notice how quotations are surrounded by her commentary. By controlling quotations like this, she is also using rather than being used by her sources.

> As Jonathan Levine, DDS, notes, "It's lately seeming much harder to go broke by overestimating the vanity of the American public" (Walker). The companies succeeded in making mouthfuls of money, netting $450 million dollars and getting 45 percent of Americans to try some form of whitening (Prior 42). In effect, they appealed to our egos to get to our pocket books.

FIGURE 2   (Continued)

of intelligence, or an investigation of video game addiction, or an argument about what should be done about dog poop in city parks? In other words, what stake might readers have in the question you are exploring? Your mother will think nearly anything you write is significant. But what might make someone else consider that you have important things to say? Here are five possible reasons. Do any apply to your draft and, if so, do you emphasize the significance of your inquiry enough?

Readers may find your discussion of a topic significant if:

1. *It raises questions they want to know the answer to.* As a pet owner, I'm interested in theories of dog training because Fred digs in the garden.
2. *It helps them to see what they've seen before in a way they haven't seen it.* Is the destruction of jack pines in Yellowstone National Park really being caused by global warming and not the drought, as I had assumed?
3. *It amplifies what they may already know and care about, leading to new learning.* I play video games and know they're habit forming, but I didn't know what was happening in my brain because I played them.
4. *It moves them emotionally.* The story of the failure of Haitian relief efforts in protecting the health and welfare of children is heartbreaking. Something should be done about it. But what?
5. *It takes a surprising point of view.* The research leads you to believe that decriminalizing marijuana will actually reduce its use.

You should be able to read your draft and see exactly where you establish the significance of your project to your readers, perhaps touching on one or more of the five reasons above. Is this content sufficient or is there more you might say?

Does It Say One Thing?

When I write an exploratory essay, I'm essentially in pursuit of a point and, not infrequently, it playfully eludes me. Just when I think I've figured out exactly what I'm trying to say, I have the nagging feeling that it's not quite right—it's too simplistic or obvious, it doesn't quite account for the evidence I've collected, or it just doesn't capture the spirit of the discoveries I've made. A thesis is often a slippery fish—just when I think I've figured out what I think, I start to think something else.

A thesis can present different problems in an argumentative essay. It can become a club—rigid and unyielding—that we use to beat a draft into submission. Yet, the very reason to do research is to *test* your ideas about things, and as your draft evolves, so should your thesis.

Now is a good time to consider revising your thesis again. Does it accurately capture what you're trying to say—or *think* you're trying to say? Is it specific enough? Is it interesting?

Using a Reader

If you wanted to save or improve a relationship, you might ask a friend for advice. Then you'd get the benefit of a third-party opinion, a fresh view that could help you see what you may be too close to see.

A reader can do the same thing for your research paper draft. She will come to the draft without the entanglements that encumber the writer and provide a fresh pair of eyes through which you can see the work. Your reader can tell you what kind of guide you are in the draft: Is it clear where you're headed, why it's significant, and what your most important discovery is?

Your instructor may be that reader, or you might exchange drafts with someone else in class. You may already have someone whom you share your writing with—a roommate, a friend. Whomever you choose, try to find a reader who will respond honestly *and* make you want to write again.

What will be most helpful from a reader at this stage? Comments about your spelling and mechanics are not critical right now. You'll deal with those factors later. For now, the most useful feedback will focus on whether there's a disconnect between what you *intend* in your draft and how a reader understands those intentions.

EXERCISE 2

Directing the Reader's Response

Though you could ask your reader for a completely open-ended reaction to your paper, the following questions might help her focus on providing comments that will help you tackle a revision:

1. After reading the draft, what would you say is the main question the paper is trying to answer or focus on?
2. In your own words, what is the main point?
3. What did you learn about the topic after reading the paper that you didn't fully appreciate *before* you read it? Is this something you find significant or interesting? If so, why?

How your reader responds to the first two questions will tell you a lot about how well you've succeeded in making the purpose and thesis of your paper clear. The answer to the third question will too, but it may also tell you whether you've established the significance of your project.

Reviewing the Structure

In addition to focusing on your paper in terms of its purpose and thesis, this global revision is also about focusing on structure. If you did Exercise 1, about purpose, you've already begun to take a closer look at the structure of your essay. There are various other ways of focusing on structure, including using your thesis.

Using Your Thesis to Revise

The payoff for crafting a stronger thesis is huge. As you will see in Exercise 3, a thesis can help you decide what to put in it and what to leave out, and in research-based writing, this is a decision that comes up again and again.

EXERCISE 3

Cut-and-Paste Revision

Try this cut-and-paste revision exercise (a useful technique inspired by Peter Elbow and his book *Writing with Power*)*:

1. On a notecard or sticky note, write your thesis or main idea. Make sure that it is plainly stated and fully captures what you think you're trying to say in your research essay. Set it aside.

*Elbow, Peter. *Writing with Power*. New York: Oxford University Press, 1981. Print.

2. Photocopy or print two copies of your first draft (one-sided pages only). Save the original; you may need it later.

3. Cut apart a copy of your research paper, paragraph by paragraph. (You may cut it into even smaller pieces later.) Once the draft has been completely disassembled, shuffle the paragraphs—get them wildly out of order so the original draft is just a memory.

4. Retrieve the notecard or sticky note with your thesis on it, and set it before you. Now work your way through the stack of paragraphs and make two new stacks: one of paragraphs that are relevant to your thesis and one of paragraphs that don't seem relevant, that don't seem to serve a clear purpose in developing your main idea. Be as tough as a drill sergeant as you scrutinize each scrap of paper. What you are trying to determine is whether each piece of information, each paragraph, is there for a reason. Ask yourself this question as you examine each paragraph:

> *Does this paragraph (or part of a paragraph) develop my thesis and further the purpose of my paper, or does it seem an unnecessary tangent that could be part of another paper with a different focus?*

For example,

- Does it provide important *evidence* that supports my main point?
- Does it *explain* something that's key to understanding what I'm trying to say?
- Does it *illustrate* a key concept?
- Does it help establish the *importance* of what I'm trying to say?
- Does it raise (or answer) a *question* that I must explore, given what I'm trying to say?

You might find it helpful to write on the back of each relevant paragraph which of these specific purposes it serves. You may also discover that *some* of the information in a paragraph seems to serve your purpose while the rest strikes you as unnecessary. Use your scissors to cut away the irrelevant material, pruning back the paragraph to include only what's essential.

5. You now have two stacks of paper scraps: those that seem to support your thesis and serve your purpose and those that don't. For now, set aside your "reject" pile. Begin to reassemble a very rough draft, using what you've saved. Play with order. Try new leads, new ends, new middles. As you spread out the pieces of information before you, see if a new structure suddenly emerges. *But especially, look for gaps—places where you should add information.* On a piece of paper, jot down ideas for material you might add; then cut up this paper as

well and insert these in the appropriate places. You may rediscover uses for information in your "reject" pile as well. Mine that pile, if you need to.

6. As a structure begins to emerge, reassemble the draft by taping together the fragments of paper, including the ideas for new information and any rejects you've decided to use after all. Don't worry about transitions; you'll deal with those later. When you're done with the reconstruction, the draft might look totally unlike the version you started with.

Examining the Wreckage. If you did Exercise 3, as you dealt with the wreckage your scissors wrought on your first draft, you might have discovered that the information in your draft suggested a revision of your thesis, pointed toward another thesis, or simply suggested your thesis was unworkable.

To your horror, you may have found that your "reject" pile of paragraphs is bigger than your "save" pile. If that's the case, you won't have much left to work with. You may need to reresearch the topic (returning to the library or going online this week to collect more information) or shift the focus of your paper. Perhaps both. But even if your cut-and-paste went well, you will likely need to do more research this week, to fill the gaps you found. That's perfectly normal.

To your satisfaction, you may have discovered that your reconstructed draft looks familiar. You may have returned to the structure you started with in the first draft. If that's the case, it might mean your first draft worked pretty well; breaking it down and putting it back together confirmed that and showed you where you might need to prune and fine-tune.

When Jeff cut up "The Alcoholic Family," he discovered immediately that much of his paper did not seem clearly related to his point about the role outsiders can play in helping the family of an alcoholic. His "reject" pile had paragraph after paragraph of information about the roles that other family members take on when there's an alcoholic in the house. Jeff asked himself, What does that information have to do with the roles of outsiders? He considered changing his thesis to say something about how each family member plays a role in dealing with the drinker. But Jeff's purpose in writing the paper was to discover what *he,* as an outsider, could do to help.

As Jeff played with the pieces of his draft, he began to see two things. First of all, he realized that some of the ways members behave in an alcoholic family make them resistant to outside help; this insight allowed him to salvage some information from his "reject" pile by more clearly connecting the information to his main point. Second, Jeff knew he had to go back to the well: He needed to return to the library and recheck his sources to find more information on what family friends can do to help.

When you slice up your draft and play with the pieces, you are experimenting with the basic architecture of your essay. If the result is going to hold up, certain fundamentals must be in place. You need to be transforming your draft in a direction that is making it more "reader based," with a clear purpose, significance, and point.

Other Ways of Reviewing the Structure

Exercise 3, "Cut-and-Paste Revision," invited you to experiment with the organization of your draft by disassembling and then rebuilding your essay, imagining different ways to order information. Its starting point was the thesis. There are other starting points for an examination of structure. Here are a few of these alternative starting points:

Type of Essay.   The structure of a research essay is partly a function of the type of essay—of whether you are writing an exploratory or an argumentative essay. Depending on the type of essay you're writing, return to Figure 2 or 4 in the last chapter for an idea about about how to organize your paper.

Lead.   How you begin your paper has a huge influence on how it develops from there. A lead or introduction should not only draw readers in but also dramatize or introduce the dilemma, problem, question, or argument that is the focus of your inquiry. You might find a stronger lead buried in the middle of your draft. Try it as an alternative introduction and follow it from there.

Logical Structure.   In a very general sense, most writing can be said to be structured by either narrative or logic. Essays that focus on the writer's experience tend to rely on some form of narrative structure, though it may not be chronological. Essays that focus on a subject other than the writer often rely on structures that reflect a pattern of reasoning. (And many research essays might employ both types of structures because they can be experiential *and* focused on a subject other than the writer.) Most of us have more experience with narrative structures; after all, part of being human is telling stories. Logical structures are less familiar. They usually spring from either a question or thesis (or both) and are designed to methodically explore a question or prove a point. Consider various ways essays might do this:

- Thesis to proof
- Problem to solution
- Question to answer
- Comparison and conrast
- Cause and effect, or effect and cause
- Known to unknown or unknown to known
- Simple to complex

Review your draft with these possible structures in mind. You may see a way to strengthen it by reshaping its structure to better fit one of these structures. Remember that while your research essay might generally use one of the logical structures, often a piece of writing that generally uses one structure uses others as microstructures. For example, an essay that has a comparison-and-contrast structure might have elements of narrative.

Re-researching

I know. You thought you were done digging. But as I said last week, research is a recursive process. (Remember, the word is *research,* or "look again.") You will often find yourself circling back to the earlier steps as you get a clearer sense of where you want to go. I want to emphasize this. It's actually *unusual,* after you've written a draft, to discover that you're done with research. This means returning to the library databases, trying a different Google search, going back to interview someone, or returning to the field for more observations. You've got the skills now to do this. Make time for it.

As you stand back from your draft, looking again at how well your research paper addresses your research question or thesis, you'll likely see holes in the information. They may seem more like craters. Jeff discovered he had to reresearch his topic, returning to the library to hunt for new sources to help him develop his point. Because he had enough time, he repeated some of the research steps from the third week. This time, though, he knew exactly what he needed to find.

You may find that you basically have the information you need but that your draft requires more development. Candy's draft on how child abuse affects language included material from some useful studies from the *Journal of Speech and Hearing Disorders,* which showed pretty conclusively that abuse cripples children's abilities to converse. At her reader's suggestion, Candy decided it was important to write more in her revision about what was learned from the studies, because they offered convincing evidence for her thesis. Though she could mine her notes for more information, Candy decided to recheck the journal databases to look for any similar studies she may have missed.

Finding Quick Facts

If you're lucky, the holes of information in your research paper draft will not be large at all. What's missing may be an important but discrete fact that would really help your readers understand the point you're making. For example, in Janabeth's draft on the impact of divorce on father–daughter relationships, she realized she was missing an important fact: the number of marriages that end in divorce in the United States. This single piece of information could help establish the significance of the problem she was writing about. And Janabeth could obtain it by simply looking online.

One of the Internet's greatest strengths is its usefulness in searching for specific facts. What are the ingredients in a Big Mac? How high is the Great Wall of China? How many high school kids in Illinois go on to college? What does a map of Brazilian deforestation look like? A quick click or two and the Web can yield a rich harvest of facts and information. Google and similar search engines are naturally where we start looking for that kind of information, and because what you want to know is pretty specific, there's a good chance you'll find what you're looking for. But there are some particularly useful statistical references on the Web that you might want to check out as well.

Facts on the Web

General

- *American Factfinder* (http://factfinder.census.gov). A rich site maintained by the U.S. Census Bureau. It includes data on population and economic trends, both national and local.
- *FedStats* (http://www.fedstats.gov). A superstore of statistical resources that allows users to find information from all U.S. government agencies.
- *Refdesk.com* (http://refdesk.com). Links to the usual references—dictionaries, biographical indexes, encyclopedias, and government information.
- *STATS America* (http://www.statsamerica.org). Search page allows users to find a range of data for states and counties in the United States, including facts on demographics, economics, education, and the workforce.

Subject Specific

Crime

- *National Criminal Justice Reference Service* (http://www.ncjrs.org/search.html). Allows keyword searches to find not just facts but articles on crime, drug abuse, corrections, juvenile justice, and more.

Education

- *National Center for Educational Statisics* (http://nces.ed.gov). The U.S. Department of Education site includes statistics on everything related to schooling in the United States and also features an annual report on the state of education.

Economics

- *Bureau of Economic Analysis* (http://www.bea.gov/). This U.S. Department of Commerce site includes statistics on key economic indicators, trade, corporate profits, and much more.

Energy

- *U.S. Energy Information Administration* (http://www.eia.doe.gov/). Includes use forecasts, environmental impacts, reserves, alternative energy information, and much more.

(*continued*)

Health

- *National Center for Health Statistics* (http://www.cdc.gov/nchs). Offers information about injuries, diseases, lifestyles, death rates, and more provided by the Centers for Disease Control.

International

- *U.N. Food and Agricultural Organization* (http://www.fao.org/corp/statistics/en/). The FAO site allows users to search for not just statistics on food and hunger but also for information on such topics as world foresty practices and water issues.
- *NationMaster* (http://www.nationmaster.com). Drawing in part from the *CIA Factbook* and UN information, Nation-Master will also generate interesting maps and graphics on a wide range of subjects.

In addition to these Web resources, the standard print texts for researchers hunting down facts and statistics are still quite useful. They include the *Statistical Abstracts of the United States,* the *Information Please Almanac, Facts on File,* and the *World Almanac Book of Facts*—all published annually. A number of these are now available on the Web.

Like the online sources mentioned, these fact books can be especially valuable resources when you need to plug small holes in your draft. But even if you're not sure whether you can glean a useful statistic from one of these sources, they might be worth checking anyway. There's a good chance you'll find something useful.

Local Revision: Revising for Language

Most of my students have the impression that revision begins and ends with concerns about language—that it's about *how* they say it rather than *what* they say. Revising for language is really a tertiary concern (though an important one) to be addressed after the writer has dealt with global revision: clear purpose, significance, and thesis as well as structure.

Once you're satisfied that your paper's purpose is clear, that it provides readers with the information they need to understand what you're trying to say, and that it is organized in a logical, interesting way, *then* focus your attention on the fine points of *how* it is written. Begin with voice.

Listening to the Voice

Listen to your paper by reading it aloud to yourself. You may find the experience a little unsettling. Most of us are not used to actively listening to our writing voices. But your readers will be listening.

As you read, ask yourself: Is this the voice you want readers to hear? Does it seem appropriate for this paper? Does it sound flat or wooden or ponderous in any places? Does it sound anything like you?

If revising your writing voice is necessary for any reason, begin at the beginning—the first line, the first paragraph—and rely on your ears. What sounds right?

You may discover that you begin with the right voice but lose it in places. That often happens when you move from anecdotal material to exposition, from telling a story to explaining research findings. To some extent, a shift in voice is inevitable when you move from one method of development to another, especially from personal material to factual material. But examine your word choices in those passages that seem to go flat. Do you sometimes shift to the dry language used by your sources? Can you rewrite that language in your own voice? When you do, you will find yourself cutting away unnecessary, vague, and pretentious language.

Rewriting in your own voice has another effect, too: It brings the writing to life. Readers respond to an individual writing voice. When I read David Quammen, it rises up from the page, like a hologram, and suddenly I can see him as a distinct individual. I also become interested in how he sees the things he's writing about.

Avoid Sounding Glib

Beware, though, of a voice that calls more attention to itself than the substance of what you're saying. As you've no doubt learned from reading scholarly sources, much academic writing is voiceless, or at least seems to be, partly because what's important is not *who* the writer is but *what* he has to say.

Sometimes, in an attempt to sound natural, a writer will take on a folksy or overly colloquial voice, which is much worse than sounding dry and flat. What impression does the following passage give you?

```
The thing that really blew my mind was that
marijuana use among college students had actually
declined in the past ten years! I was psyched to
learn that.
```

Ugh!

As you search for the right voice in doing your revision, look for a balance between flat prose, which sounds as if it were manufactured by a machine, and folksy prose or flowery prose, or any other style of prose that would distract the reader from what's most important: what you're trying to say.

Tightening Seams Between What You Say and What They Say

One of the basic challenges of writing with sources is integrating them seamlessly. In the past, you may have practiced the "data dump" strategy, or simply dropping factual information into your papers in little or big clumps. Of course, this won't do. Not only does it make the writing horribly dull, but it means that you're not *making use* of the information you worked so hard to find. Surrounding your sources with your own prose and purposes is an important skill you need to learn, and it's something we looked at Exercise 1 earlier in this chapter.

In particular, think about the following points:

■ *Find your own way of saying things.* This is one of the best ways to take possession of information.

■ *Surround factual information with your own analysis.* Provide a context for any quotation you use. Comment on the significance of a fact or statistic. Look for ways to connect any information to your research question or thesis.

■ *Make analogies or comparisons.* Is something like something else? Advocates for addressing climate change, for example, have used an extended analogy of a bathtub to illustrate how easy it is to ignore a problem until it's too late. You start the water running, get involved in, say, a computer game, and then have to decide when to check whether the tub is full. How long do you wait? What goes into this calculation?

Verbal Gestures

Burke's metaphor for the knowledge-making process is he imagined a parlor full of people having an ongoing conversation about what might be true—arguing, agreeing, raising questions, suggesting new ideas, critiquing old ideas, everyone trying to push the conversation along. Any roomful of people in a conversation about things that cause disagreement is also a roomful of gestures. People wave off a point. They nod in assent. They raise a single finger to raise a new question or make a new point. They invite someone to step forward to speak and ask another to step aside.

Similarly, an essay that is a writer's conversation with others about a question that matters to all of them also includes words and phrases that serve as verbal gestures. Some are gestures that invite some people in the room to provide *background* on the question so that everyone understands what has already been said. Other gestures signal *analysis,* or a closer examination and critique of something someone said. Sometimes these verbal gestures signify *speculation*; the writer just isn't quite sure what to think for sure but maybe.... Or they might indicate *agreement or disagreement*—the writer is taking sides with a particular idea, position, or way of seeing.

Consider whether verbal gestures like these will help you manage the conversation about your topic. Go through your draft, and identify those moments in which you seem to be providing background, analyzing something, agreeing or disagreeing, or speculating. Might some of the following language help you signpost that material?

BACKGROUND

Among the most important voices on _____, the most relevant to this inquiry are _____.

Most people _____.

The major sources of controversy are _____.

One idea emerges again and again, and it's _____.

Like most people, I believed that _____.

The unanswered questions are _____.

This much is clear, _____.

_____'s most important contribution is _____.

Most relevant is _____.

ANALYSIS

The most relevant point is _____.

In comparison,...

In contrast,...

What is most convincing is _____.

What is least convincing is _____.

What's most interesting is _____.

The surprising connection is _____.

Paradoxically,...

Actually,...

What isn't clear is _____.

SPECULATION

Perhaps...

Maybe...

It's possible that _____.

AGREEMENT AND DISAGREEMENT

Indeed...

Obviously...

Alternatively...

While others have argued that _____, I think _____.

On balance, the most convincing idea is _____.

What _____ has failed to consider is _____.

The more important question is _____.

Based on my research, _____.

A better explanation is _____.

It's hard to argue with _____.

What I understand now that I didn't understand before is _____.

Scrutinizing Paragraphs

Is Each Paragraph Unified?

Each paragraph should be about one idea and organized around it. You probably know that already. But applying this notion is a particular problem in a research paper, where information abounds and paragraphs sometimes approach marathon length.

If any of your paragraphs seem too long (say, over a page or even verging on a page), look for ways to break them up into shorter paragraphs. Is more than one idea embedded in the long version? Are you explaining or examining more than one thing?

Even short paragraphs can lack unity, so look at those, too. Do any present minor or tangential ideas that belong somewhere else? Are any of these ideas irrelevant? In other words, should the information in the paragraph be moved into another paragraph of your paper, or should the paragraph just be cut? The cut-and-paste exercise (Exercise 3) may have helped you with this already.

Scrutinizing Sentences

Using Active Voice

Which of these two sentences seems more passive, more lifeless?

```
Steroids are used by many high school athletes.
```

or

```
Many high school athletes use steroids.
```

The first version, written in the passive voice, is clearly the more limp of the two. It's not grammatically incorrect. In fact, you may have found texts written in the passive voice to be pervasive in the reading you've done for your research paper. Research writing is plagued by passive voice, and that's one of the reasons it can be so mind numbing to read.

Passive voice construction is simple: The subject of the sentence is not the thing *doing the action* of the verb but, rather, the thing *acted upon* by the verb. For instance, in the following pair, the *active voice* sentence has as its subject Clarence, who does the action of kicking, but the passive sentence has the dog as the subject, which was kicked:

```
Clarence kicked the dog.
```

versus

```
The dog was kicked by Clarence.
```

Sometimes, in passive sentences the subject of the corresponding active sentence may be missing altogether, as in:

```
The study was released.
```

Who or *what* released it?

If you have passive sentences, you can remedy the problem by using *active voice* to push the doer of the action up front in the sentence or adding a doer if it is missing. For example:

```
Many high school athletes use steroids.
```

A telltale sign of passive voice is that it usually requires a form of the verb *to be* (*is, was, are, were, am, be, being, been*). For example:

```
Alcoholism among women has been extensively
studied.
```

Search your draft for *be's,* and see if any sentences are written in the passive voice. (Some word-processing programs will search for you.) Unless this is a sentence that is more appropriate in passive voice, make the passive sentence active. To make a sentence active, move its doer from after the verb into subject position or supply the appropriate doer if the sentence doesn't have one.

Using Strong Verbs

Though this may seem like nitpicking, you'd be amazed how much writing in the active voice can revitalize research writing. The use of strong verbs can have the same effect.

As you know, verbs make things happen. Some verbs can make the difference between a sentence that crackles and one that merely hums. Instead of this:

```
The study suggested that the widespread assumption
that oral sex is common among American teenagers
might be wrong.
```

write this:

```
The study shattered the common belief that
American teens increasingly indulge in oral sex.
```

Just because you're writing about people's ideas doesn't mean you can't use strong verbs. See the box "Verbs for Discussing Ideas", which was compiled by a colleague of mine, Cinthia Gannett. If you're desperate for an alternative to *says* or *argues,* check out the 135 alternatives this box offers.

Varying Sentence Length

Here's part of a research essay on the promise of wind energy. When you read it, I think you'll find the writing choppy. What's going on? One way to understand the problem is to count the number of syllables in each sentence. That's the number in the parentheses.

Verbs for Discussing Ideas

accepts	critiques	implies	refutes
acknowledges	declares	infers	regards
adds	defends	informs	rejects
admires	defies	initiates	relinquishes
affirms	demands	insinuates	reminds
allows	denies	insists	repudiates
analyzes	describes	interprets	resolves
announces	determines	intimates	responds
answers	diminishes	judges	retorts
argues	disagrees	lists	reveals
assaults	disconfirms	maintains	reviews
assembles	discusses	marshalls	seeks
asserts	disputes	narrates	sees
assists	disregards	negates	shares
believes	distinguishes	observes	shifts
buttresses	emphasizes	outlines	shows
categorizes	endorses	parses	simplifies
cautions	enumerates	perceives	states
challenges	exaggerates	persists	stresses
claims	experiences	persuades	substitutes
clarifies	experiments	pleads	suggests
compares	explains	points out	summarizes
complicates	exposes	postulates	supplements
concludes	facilitates	praises	supplies
condemns	formulates	proposes	supports
confirms	grants	protects	synthesizes
conflates	guides	provides	tests
confronts	handles	qualifies	toys with
confuses	hesitates	quotes	treats
considers	highlights	ratifies	uncovers
contradicts	hints	rationalizes	urges
contrasts	hypothesizes	reads	verifies
convinces	identifies	reconciles	warns
criticizes	illuminates	reconsiders	

Source: Reproduced with permission of Cinthia Gannett.

The idea of alternative energy is sweeping the country and numerous other developed nations. (29) People are beginning to recyle more plastic and metals. (16) They are also more interested in energy efficiency. (16) Wind energy is among the renewable resources sprouting up around the United States. (25) Wind energy affects the environment, wildlife, society, humans, and politics. (23)

It's not hard to see that the sentence length, measured by syllables, doesn't vary much. There are three sentences in the passage that run between 23 and 29 syllables, and the others are both 16. In addition, the structure of these sentences doesn't vary much. Each has just one main clause. Prose that doesn't vary much in sentence length or structure is invariably boring to read. So what can you do about it?

- *Vary sentence length*. Do a syllable count on a paragraph in your draft that seems clunky, and you'll probably find that you need to vary sentence length. Develop the instinct to follow a long sentence, for example, with a short punchy one from time to time.
- *Combine sentences*. This often works wonders. Can you use puncuation or conjunctions like *or*, *but*, and *and* to join separate sentences together? For example, you might take this sequence of sentences in the passage on wind energy:

    People are beginning to recyle more plastic and metals. (16) They are also more interested in energy efficiency. (16)

and revise it through sentence combining to read like this:

    People are beginning to recycle more plastic and metals, and they're also more interested in energy efficiency. (32)

Notice that you now have a compound sentence. In varying length, you'll often also be varying structure.

Editing for Simplicity

Thoreau saw simplicity as a virtue. He demonstrated this not only by spending time beside Walden Pond but also by writing prose while living there. Thoreau writes clearly and plainly.

Somewhere, many of us got the idea that simplicity in writing is a vice—that the long word is better than the short word, that the complex phrase is superior to the simple one. The misconception is that to write simply is to be simple minded. Research papers, especially, suffer from this mistaken notion. They are often filled with what writer William Zinsser calls *clutter*.

EXERCISE 4

Cutting Clutter

The following passage is an example of cluttered writing at its best (worst?). It contains phrases and words that often appear in college research papers. Read the passage once. Then take a few minutes and rewrite it, cutting as many words as you can without sacrificing the meaning. Look for ways to substitute a shorter word for a longer one and to say in fewer words what is currently said in many. Try to cut the word count by half.

The implementation of the revised alcohol policy in the university community is regrettable at the present time due to the fact that the administration has not facilitated sufficient student input, in spite of the fact that there have been attempts by the people affected by this policy to make their objections known in many instances.

(55 words)

Avoiding Stock Phrases

A place to begin cutting unnecessary clutter in your essay is to hack away at stock phrases. Like many types of writing, the language of the college research paper is littered with words and phrases that find their way to the page as inevitably as drinking root beer prompted my 12-year-old daughter and her friends to hold burping contests. In each case, the one just seems to inspire the other. Following is a list of stock phrases that I often find in research papers. There is nothing grammatically wrong with these. It's simply that they are old, tired phrases, and you can say the same thing more freshly with fewer words. Look for them in your draft and then edit them out.

TIRED PHRASES	BETTER ALTERNATIVES
Due to the fact that...	*Because...*
At this point in time...	*Now...*
In my opinion,...	*(Unnecessary. We know it's your opinion.)*
A number of...	*Many.../Some...*
A number of studies point to the fact that...	*Many/some researchers conclude (or argue)...*
In the event of...	*If...*
In today's society...	*Today we...*
In conclusion,...	*(Omit. If you're at the end of the paper, you're probably concluding.)*
Until such time as...	*Until...*
Referred to as...	*Called...*
It should be pointed out that...	*(Omit. You are pointing it out.)*
Is in a position to...	*Can*
It is a fact that...	*(Omit. Just state the fact, ma'am.)*
It may be said that...	*(Omit. Just say it.)*
There can be little doubt that...	*It's likely...*
It is possible that...	*Perhaps...*

Preparing the Final Manuscript

I wanted to title this section "Preparing the Final Draft," but it occurred to me that *draft* doesn't suggest anything final. I always call my work a draft because until it's out of my hands, it never feels finished. You may feel that way, too. You've spent five weeks on this paper—and the last few days, disassembling it and putting it back together again. How do you know when you're finally done?

For many students, the deadline dictates that: The paper is due tomorrow. But you may find that your paper really seems to be coming together in a satisfying way. You may even like it, and you're ready to prepare the final manuscript.

Considering a "Reader-Friendly" Design

As consumers of texts these days—especially online—we are constantly influenced by visual rhetoric even if we aren't aware of it. "Eye-tracking" studies, for example, suggest that there is a sequence in how we look at a Web page: Most readers typically read a Web page in an upsidedown "L" pattern, reading across the top of the page and then down the left side. Print advertisers are also acutely aware of visual rhetoric for obvious reasons—text works better with images if they are designed to work together.

A research essay like the one you're working on right now would seem to have little to do with visual rhetoric. The form of an academic paper, particularly if the emphasis is on text—and it usually is—seems largely prescribed by the Modern Language Associaton or the American Psychogical Association. Some papers in the social sciences, for example, require certain sections (abstract, introduction, discussion of method, presentation of results, and discussion of results), and these sections need to be clearly defined with subheadings, making it easy for readers to examine the parts they're most interested in. You probably discovered that in your own reading of formal research. You'll likely learn the formats research papers should conform to in various disciplines as you take upper-level courses in those fields.

While you should document your paper properly, you may have some freedom to develop a format that best serves your purpose. As you consider format in revising, keep readers in mind. How can you make your paper more readable? How can you signal your plan for developing the topic and what's important? Some visual devices might help, including:

- Subheadings
- Bulleted lists (like the one you're reading now)
- Graphs, illustrations, tables
- Block quotes
- Underlining and paragraphing for emphasis
- White space

Long, unbroken pages of text can appear to be a gray, uninviting mass to the reader. All of the devices listed help break up the text, making it more "reader friendly." Subheadings, if not overused, can also cue your reader to significant sections of your paper and how they relate to the whole. Long quotes, those over four lines, should be blocked, or indented one inch from the left margin, so they're distinct from the rest of the text. Bullets—dots or asterisks preceding brief lines of text—can be used to highlight a list of important information. Graphs, tables, and illustrations also break up the text but, more importantly, they can also help clarify and explain information.

Using Images

Thanks to digital imaging, it's easier than ever to find pictures and use them in papers. As you probably know, Google allows users to do keyword searching specifically for images. You're writing an essay on the nutritional problems with fast food? You won't have any trouble finding a picture of a Big Mac that you can drop into your essay. Even better, perhaps you're writing your essay on a historical event, a local controversy, or perhaps a profile. With a few clicks you may find a less generic and more relevant image: a photograph of your profile subject or of the Civil War battle that you're analyzing.

You can do this. But should you?

That's up to your instructor, of course. But if she allows it, any visual addition to your essay—and especially an image—needs to do much more than take up space or break up gray text. It must do work. What kind of work can an image do?

■ *Pictures can dramatize a moment, situation, or outcome that you emphasize in your text*: a photograph of the space shuttle's missing insulation in a paper arguing for an end to funding space exploration programs; a picture of the shootings of students on the Kent State campus in 1970 in a paper exploring campus violence.

■ *Pictures can contribute to difficult explanations.* Like a well-crafted analogy, an image can help readers to see more clearly what you're trying to explain. To explain quantitative data, you typically turn to tables and charts. But how can you use pictures? Use images that don't simply reinforce what you say in words but that also amplify what you say. An obvious example: If you're writing about a painting, then surrounding an image of a work with your textual explanations will bring your words to life. Readers simply have more to work with in understanding what you want them to see.

■ *A sequence of pictures can tell a story or illustrate a process.* A disturbing example of this is a series of photos of a meth addict—usually police booking shots—that tell the story of addiction to the drug in the steady deterioration of a user's face. Pictures of Brazilian rainforest before and after logging can help make an argument about loss of biodiversity.

Following MLA Conventions

I've already mentioned that formal research papers in various disciplines may have prescribed formats. If your instructor expects a certain format, he has probably detailed exactly what that format should be. But in all likelihood, your essay for this class doesn't need to follow a rigid form. It will, however, probably adhere to the basic Modern Language Association (MLA) guidelines.

Proofreading Your Paper

You've spent weeks researching, writing, and revising your paper. You want to stop now. That's understandable, no matter how much you were driven by your curiosity. But before you sign off on your research paper, placing it in someone else's hands, take the time to proofread it.

I was often so glad to be done with a piece of writing that I was careless about proofreading it. That changed about ten years ago, after I submitted a portfolio of writing to complete my master's degree. I was pretty proud of it, especially an essay about dealing with my father's alcoholism. Unfortunately, I misspelled that word—*alcoholism*—every time I used it. Bummer.

Proofreading on a Computer

Proofreading used to necessitate gobbing on correction fluid to cover up mistakes and then trying to line up the paper and type in the changes. Writing on a computer, you're spared from that ordeal. The text can be easily manipulated.

Software programs can, of course, also help with the actual job of proofreading. Most word-processing programs, for example, come with spelling and grammar checkers. These programs will count the number of words in your sentences, alerting you to particularly long ones, and will even point out uses of passive voice. While these style-checkers may not be all that helpful because of their dubious assumptions about what constitutes "good" style, spell-checkers are an invaluable feature. You probably already know that.

Some writers proofread on screen. Others find they need to print out their paper and proofread the hard copy. They argue that they catch more mistakes if they proofread on paper than if they proofread on screen. It makes sense, especially if you've been staring at the screen for days. A printed copy of your paper *looks* different, and I think you see it differently—maybe with fresher eyes and a more energetic attitude. You might notice things you didn't notice before. Decide for yourself how you want to proofread.

Looking Closely

You've already edited the manuscript, pruning sentences and tightening things up. Now proofread for the little errors in grammar and mechanics that you missed. Aside from misspellings (usually typos), some pretty common mistakes appear in the papers I see. For practice, see if you can catch some of them in the following exercise.

EXERCISE 5

Picking Off the Lint

I have a colleague who compares proofreading to picking the lint off an outfit, which is often your final step before heading out the door. Examine the following excerpt from a student paper. Proofread it, catching as many mechanical errors as possible. Note punctuation mistakes, agreement problems, misspellings, and anything else that seems off.

In an important essay, Melody Graulich notes
how "rigid dichotomizing of sex roles" in most
frontier myths have "often handicapped and confused male as well as female writers (187)," she
wonders if a "universel mythology" (198) might
emerge that is less confining for both of them.
In Bruce Mason, Wallace Stegner seems to experiment with this idea; acknowledging the power of
Bo's male fantasies *and* Elsa's ability to teach
her son to feel. It is his strenth. On the other
hand, Bruces brother chet, who dies young, lost
and broken, seems doomed because he lacked sufficient measure of both the feminine and masculine.

```
He observes that Chet had "enough of the old
man to spoil him, ebnough of his mother to
soften him, not enough of either to save him
(Big Rock, 521)."
```

If you did this exercise in class, compare your proofreading of this passage with that of a partner. What did each of you find?

Ten Common Things to Avoid in Research Papers

The following is a list of the ten most common errors (besides misspelled words) made in research papers that should be caught in careful proofreading. A number of these errors occurred in the previous exercise.

1. Commonly confused words, such as *your* instead of *you're*. Here's a list of others:

their/there/they're	advice/advise
know/now	lay/lie
accept/except	its/it's
all ready/already	passed/past

2. Possessives. Instead of *my fathers alcoholism,* the correct form is *my father's alcoholism.* Remember that if a singular noun ends in *s,* still add *'s*: *Tess's laughter.* If a noun is plural, just add the apostrophe: *the scientists' studies.*

3. Vague pronoun references. The excerpt in Exercise 5 ends with the sentence, *He observes that Chet....* Who's *he?* The sentence should read, *Bruce observes that Chet....* Whenever you use the pronouns *he, she, it, they,* and *their,* make sure each clearly refers to someone or something.

4. Subject and verb agreement. If the subject is singular, its verb must be, too:

```
The perils of climate change are many.
```

What confuses writers sometimes is the appearance before the verb of a noun that is not really the subject. Exercise 5 begins, for example, with this sentence:

```
In an important essay, Melody Graulich notes
how "rigid dichotomizing of sex roles" in most
```

```
frontier myths have "often handicapped and con-
fused male as well as female writers."
```

The subject here is not *frontier myths* but *rigid dichotomizing,* a singular subject. The sentence should read:

```
In an important essay, Melody Graulich notes
how "rigid dichotomizing of sex roles" in most
frontier myths has "often handicapped and con-
fused male as well as female writers."
```

The verb *has* may sound funny, but it's correct.

5. Punctuation of quotations. Note that commas belong inside quotation marks, not outside. Periods belong inside, too. Colons and semicolons are exceptions—they belong *outside* quotation marks. Blocked quotes don't need quotation marks at all unless there is a quote within the quote.

6. Commas. Could you substitute periods or semicolons? If so, you may be looking at *comma splices* or *run-on sentences.* Here's an example:

```
Since 1980, the use of marijuana by college stu-
dents has steadily declined, this was something
of a surprise to me and my friends.
```

The portion after the comma, *this was...,* is another sentence. The comma should be a period, and *this* should be capitalized.

7. Parenthetical citations. In MLA style, there is no comma between the author's name and page number: (Marks 99).

8. Dashes. Though they can be overused, dashes are a great way to break the flow of a sentence with a related bit of information. You've probably noticed I like them. In a manuscript, type dashes as *two* hyphens (- -), not one. Most word-processing programs will automatically turn the hypens into a solid dash, which is what you want.

9. Names. After mentioning the full name of someone in your paper, normally use her *last name* in subsequent references. For example, this is incorrect:

```
Denise Grady argues that people are genetically
predisposed to obesity. Denise also believes
```

```
that some people are "programmed to convert

calories to fat."
```

Unless you know Denise or for some other reason want to conceal her last name, change the second sentence to this:

```
Grady also believes that some people are

"programmed to convert calories to fat."
```

One exception to this is when writing about literature. It is often appropriate to refer to characters by their first names, particularly if characters share last names (as in Exercise 6).

10. Colons and semicolons. A colon is usually used to call attention to what follows it: a list, quotation, or appositive. A colon should follow an independent clause. For example, this won't do:

```
The most troubling things about child abuse

are: the effects on self-esteem and language

development.
```

In this case, eliminate the colon. A semicolon should be used as a period, separating two independent clauses. It simply implies the clauses are closely related. Semicolons should not be used as if they were colons or commas.

Using the "Find" or "Search" Function

Use the "Find" or "Search" function in your word-processing program to help you track down consistent problems. You simply tell the computer what word or punctuation to look for, and it will locate all occurrences in the text. For example, if you want to check for comma splices, search for commas. The cursor will stop on every comma, and you can verify if you have used it correctly. You can also search for pronouns to locate vague references or for words (like those listed in item 1) that you commonly misuse.

Avoiding Sexist Language

One last proofreading task is to do a *man* and *he* check. Until recently, sexism wasn't an issue in language. Use of words such as *mankind* and *chairman* was acceptable; the implication was that the terms applied to both genders. At least, that's how use of the terms was defended when challenged. Critics argued that words such as *mailman* and *businessman* reinforced ideas that only men could fill these roles. Bias in language is subtle but powerful. And it's often unintentional. To avoid sending the wrong message, it's worth making the effort to avoid sexist language.

If you need to use a word with a *man* suffix, check to see if there is an alternative. *Congressperson* sounds pretty clunky, but *representative* works fine. Instead of *mankind,* why not *humanity?* Substitute *camera operator* for *cameraman.*

Also check use of pronouns. Do you use *he* or *his* in places where you mean both genders? For example:

```
The writer who cares about his topic will bring it

to life for his readers.
```

Because a lot of writers are women, this doesn't seem right. How do you solve this problem? You can ask your instructor what she prefers, but here are some guidelines:

1. Use *his or her, he or she,* or the mutation *s/he.* For example:

```
The writer who cares about his or her topic will

bring it to life for his or her readers.
```

This is an acceptable solution, but using *his or her* repeatedly can be awkward.

2. Change the singular subject to plural. For example:

```
Writers who care about their topics will bring

them to life for their readers.
```

This version, which also avoids discriminatory language, sounds much better.

3. Alternate *he* and *she, his* and *hers* whenever you encounter an indefinite person. If you have referred to writers as *he* in one discussion, refer to them as *she* in the next. Alternate throughout.

Looking Back and Moving On

This book began with your writing, and it also will end with it. More than a month ago, you began your inquiry project, and even if you're still not happy with your essay, you probably learned some things that influenced the way you think about yourself as a writer, about the nature of research in a university, and how to solve typical problems that arise when you're writing research-based papers.

In this final exercise, you'll do some thinking about all of this in your journal, or perhaps on a class blog or discussion board.

EXERCISE 6

Another Dialogue with Dave

Draw a line down the middle of a blank page in your journal, or create two columns in a Word document. Ask each of these questions by writing them into the left column, and then fastwrite your response in the right column. Spend *at least* three minutes with each question.

Question	YOU
1. "Hey you, I think you can't really say that one opinion is better than another one. Don't you agree?"	
2. "There's all this stuff in the book about research as a process of discovery. What did you discover?"	
3. "What do you figure was the most challenging problem you had to solve while working on this research project? How did you solve it?"	
4. "After all this work, what do you take away from this experience? What have you learned that you can *use*?"	

Writing a Personal Essay

From Chapter 3 of *The Curious Writer*, Fourth Edition. Bruce Ballenger. Copyright © 2014 by Pearson Education, Inc. All rights reserved.

Writing a personal essay can be like seeing an old picture of yourself. This publicity photograph of my mother (an actress), my older brother, and me in the 1950s returns me to that world—a time when fathers were often missing from the picture.

Writing a Personal Essay

Learning Objectives

In this chapter, you'll learn to

1 Use personal experiences and observations to drive inquiry.

2 Apply the exploratory thinking of personal essays to academic writing.

3 Identify the characteristics of personal essays in different forms.

4 Use invention strategies to discover and develop a personal essay topic.

5 Apply revision strategies that are effective for shaping narratives.

Writing About Experience and Observations

Most us were taught and still believe that we need to know what we are going to write before we actually pick up the pen or sit in front of the computer. My student Lynn was typical.

"I think I'll write about my experience organizing the street fair," she told me the other day. "That would be a good topic for a personal essay, right?"

"Do you think so?" I said.

"Well, yes, because I already know a lot about it. I'll have a lot to write about."

"Okay, but is there anything about this experience that you want to understand better?" I said. "Anything about it that makes you curious?"

"Curious? It was just a street fair," she said.

"Sure, but is there something about what happened that makes you want to look at the experience again? Is there a chance that you might learn something about yourself, or about street fairs, or about the community, or about people, or…?"

Lynn was clearly sorry she asked. What I should have said was much more to the point: The best personal essay topics are those that are an itch you need to scratch. These tend not to be topics you have already figured out. While the topics can be familiar to you, the results of your inquiry are usually much better if you don't yet know what you think about your topics and you're interested to learn more about them. The best topics ask to be written about because they make you wonder *Why did I do that? What does that mean? Why did that happen? How did I really feel? What do I really think?*

Unlike most other forms of inquiry, the personal essay invites an initial display of confusion or uncertainty from writers regarding their subjects. In other words, the personal essay can be, and often is, a vehicle for writers to work through their thinking and feeling on a subject, directly in front of their readers.

The personal essay is a vehicle for writers to work through their thinking and feeling on a subject, directly in front of their readers.

As a form, the *personal* essay places the writer at center stage. This doesn't mean that once she's there, her responsibility is to pour out her secrets, share her pain, or confess her sins. Some essays do have these confessional qualities, but more often they do not. Yet a personal essayist, no matter the subject of the essay, is still *exposed*. There is no hiding behind the pronoun *one*, as in "one might think" or "one often feels," no lurking in the shadows of the passive voice: "An argument will be made that…" The personal essay is first-person territory.

In this sense, the personal essay is much like a photographic self-portrait. Like a picture, a good personal essay tells the truth, or it tells *a* truth about the writer/subject, and it often captures the writer at a particular moment in time. This explains why the experience of taking a self-portrait, or confronting an old picture of oneself taken by someone else, can create the same feeling of exposure that writing a personal essay often does.

But it does more. When we gaze at ourselves in a photograph, we often see it as yanked from a larger story about ourselves, a story that threads its way through our lives and gives us ideas about who we were and who we are. This is what the personal essay demands of us: We must somehow present ourselves truthfully and measure our past against the present. In other words, when we hold a photograph of ourselves, we know more than the person we see there knew, and as writers of the personal essay, we must share that knowledge and understanding with readers.

Though the personal essay may be an exploration of a past experience, it needn't always be about memories. A personal essay can instead focus on some aspect of writers' present lives, just as long as it raises questions that interest them. Why is it so irritating to overhear certain cell phone conversations? Why do I have an obsession with zombie-killing apps? What does it feel like to be an international student in Idaho? All of these kinds of questions might lead to a personal essay, and the challenge of writing about the present is the same as writing about the past: What do I understand about this now that I didn't understand when I started writing about it?

Motives for Writing a Personal Essay

1

Use personal experiences and observations to drive inquiry.

Essai was a term coined by the sixteenth-century French nobleman Michel de Montaigne, a man who endured plague epidemics, the bloody civil war between French Catholics and Protestants, and his own bouts of ill health. His tumultuous and uncertain times, when old social orders and intellectual traditions were under assault, proved to be ideal ferment for the essay. The French verb *essaier* means "to attempt" or "to try," and the essay became an opportunity for Montaigne to work out his thoughts about war, the education of children, the evils of doctors, and the importance of pleasure. The personal essay tradition inspired by Montaigne is probably unlike what you are familiar with from school. The school essay is often formulaic—a five-paragraph theme or thesis-example paper—while the personal essay is an open-ended form that allows for uncertainty and inconclusiveness. It is more about the process of coming to know than presenting *what* you know. The personal essay attempts *to find out* rather than *to prove*.

It is an ideal form of inquiry if your purpose is exploratory and if you're particularly interested in working out the possible relationships between your subject and yourself. Because the personal essay is openly subjective, the writer can't hide. The intruding *I* confronts the writer with the same questions over and over again: *Why does this matter to me? What do I make of it? How does this change the way I think of myself and the way I see the world?* Because of this, one of the principal dangers of the personal essay is that it can become narcissistic; it can go on and on about what the writer thinks and feels, and the reader can be left with that nagging question—*So what?* The personal essayist must always find some way to hitch the particulars of his or her experience to something larger—an idea, a theme, or even a feeling that readers might share.

On the other hand, one of the prime rhetorical advantages of the personal essay is its subjectivity. Because it is written with openness and honesty, the essay can be a very intimate form, inviting the reader to share in the writer's often concealed world. The *ethos* of personal essayists, or their credibility, revolves around the sense that they are ordinary people writing about ordinary things. In the personal essay, we often get to see the face sweating under the mask. Honesty is one of the essay's primary virtues, and because the form allows for uncertainty and confusion, the writer doesn't need to pretend that he has *the* answer or that he knows more than he lets on about his subject.

The Personal Essay and Academic Writing

In some ways, the personal essay might seem like a dramatic departure from the kind of academic writing you've done in other classes. Openly subjective and sometimes tentative in its conclusions, the personal essay is a relatively open form that is not predictably structured like much academic writing. Additionally, the tone of the personal essay is conversational, even intimate, rather than impersonal and removed. So, if your sociology or economics professor will never ask for a personal essay, why bother to write one in your composition class?

It's a fair question. While the pleasures of personal essay writing can be reason alone to write these essays, there are also other important reasons, related to your academic work:

- Because of your connection to the subject matter, the personal essay, more than any other form, gives you an opportunity to use exploration as a

2
Apply the exploratory thinking of personal essays to academic writing.

method of inquiry, and to practice those habits of mind that are so important to academic inquiry: suspending judgment, tolerating ambiguity, and using questions to challenge easy assumptions.

- For this same reason, the essay is especially conducive to the kind of thinking typical of academic inquiry: a movement back and forth between critical and creative thinking. In many ways, the personal essay is *inductive* like scientific thinking; it looks closely at the data of experience and attempts to infer from that information theories about the way things are.

- The essay emphasizes the *process* of coming to know about yourself and your subject, exposing your reasoning and the ways you use knowledge to get at the truth of things. Reflecting on these things can tell you a lot about how you think.

Finally, the personal essay and academic writing are actually not that far apart. We often assume that "academic" is supposed to be "objective," that self and subject should never mix. "Never use I" is supposedly the rule, and never, ever talk about yourself in an academic paper. These *are* common conventions, especially in the sciences. One reason for this is that the appearance of objectivity gives research more authority. Another is that in many disciplines attention generally needs to be on the data and not the author.

And yet a surprising number of academic articles make use of the first person, and not just in the humanities, where you might expect a more subjective perspective. The first person—and a more personal approach to scholarship—is evident in many disciplines, including literary criticism, business, anthropology, education, nursing, and even geology. This first-person writing often tells a story, sometimes through a case study, a narrative of the writer's experiences, or an account of his or her intellectual journey.

In any case, don't let the relative rarity of the first person in scholarship fool you into not seeing that there's something personal in even the most formal academic writing. It's *always* personal. What we choose to write about, the questions that interest us, and our particular ways of seeing are always at work, even in academic prose. True, the sciences use methods to minimize the researcher's biases. But it's impossible to eliminate them. Whenever anyone—scientist or humanist—uses language to communicate discoveries, they enter a social marketplace where words have meanings that are negotiated with others. For writers—any kind of writers—language is a social currency.

> The essay, more than any other form, gives you an opportunity to use exploration as a method of inquiry.

But most important, much of what you are asked to write in college is about what *you* think. Not what your instructor thinks, or what the textbook author thinks, or what someone said in a journal. All of these things provide you with something to think about. You decide what you want to say. One of the great things about the personal essay is that it insists on flushing writers out into the open. You can't hide in the wings, concealed in the shadow of other people's opinions or someone else's findings. What *you* think is what the essay is all about.

Features of the Form

Feature	Conventions of the Personal Essay
Inquiry questions	What does it mean to me? What do I understand about this now that I didn't then?
Motives	Self-discovery is often the motive behind writing a personal essay—the essay is in first person, and the essayist is center stage.
Subject matter	Essayists often write about quite ordinary things; they find drama in everyday life, past or present. Personal essays can be about taking a walk, breaking up on Facebook, the housefly on your beer glass. In some ways, the real subject of a personal essay is the writer herself and how she makes sense of her world.
Structure	Essays often tell stories, but, unlike fiction, they both show *and* tell, using both narrative and exposition, sometimes alternating between the two.
	When about the past, there are two narrators in the essay—the "then-narrator" and "now-narrator." One describes what happened and the other what the narrator makes *now* of what happened.
	The thesis may come near the end rather than at the beginning. And the essay isn't necessarily chronological.
Sources of information	Like any essay, the personal essay might use all four sources of information—memory, observation, reading, and interview. But it is likely to lean most heavily on memory and observation.
Language	Personal essays work in two registers—the more general language of reflection and the very specific detail of experience and observation. This specific language is often sensory: What did it look like exactly? What did you hear? How did it feel?

3

Identify the characteristics of personal essays in different forms.

Prose+

Josh Neufeld's "A Matter of Perspective" is a kind of personal essay. The theme—the idea that we have moments in our lives when we feel very, very small—speaks not only to Josh's experience, but our own. A graphic essay such as this one exploits image and text in combination, amplifying the power of each.

READINGS

▶ Personal Essay 1

Try this exercise: Think about things, ordinary objects, that you have held onto all these years because you simply can't throw them away. They *mean* something to you. They are reminders of another time, or a turning point in your life, or a particular moment of joy, or sadness, or perhaps fear. Consider a few of mine: a green plaster Buddha, handmade; a glow-in-the-dark crucifix; an old pair of 7 × 50 Nikon binoculars; a 1969 Martin D 28 guitar; a brown-handled flathead screwdriver with a touch of red nail polish on the handle; a homemade lamp made from a wooden wallpaper roller; a red dog's collar. While they are meaningless to you, naturally, to me each of these objects carry a charge; they remind me of a story, a moment, a feeling. The personal essay makes space for writers to explore the meanings of such ordinary things.

Taking Things Seriously: 75 Objects with Unexpected Meanings, the book from which the following short essay was taken, is a gallery of objects—a bottle of dirt, a Velveeta Cheese box, a bear lamp, a pair of shells, and more—that are displayed along with the meditations on their significance by the writers who have carefully kept them as reminders on a shelf, in a closet, by their beside. Laura Zazulak's short essay focuses on a doll that she snatched from a neighbor's trash can. Just telling a story about what happened is not enough in an essay. The essay must have something to say to someone else. As you read Zazulak's brief piece, consider what that might be.

Every Morning for Five Years
Laura Zazulak

Every morning for five years, I was not so welcomingly greeted by my middle-aged, developmentally disabled neighbor across the street. Scotty never smiled and seemed to hate everyone. He never left the perimeter of his mother's lawn and apparently didn't know how to do anything but rake, shovel, take out the trash, and yell in a high-pitched voice. I'd pull out of my driveway and see him there, wearing a neon orange hunting cap, raking absolutely nothing at the same spot that he'd raked the day before. I'd think to myself, "Don't make eye contact!" But I always did. He'd stare at me and neither of us would blink.

Near the end of my fifth year on the street, Scotty stopped coming out of his house. At first, I was thankful. But as time passed, I began to worry. Then one Saturday morning in the middle of January I noticed that his window was wide open. Later that day, a police car showed up. Maybe Scotty and his mother got into one of their screaming

(continued)

1

2

(continued)

matches again? Then a funeral-home van pulled up and they brought out Scotty's body. Although it came as a surprise to me to discover that he knew how miserable his life was, he had killed himself.

3 The next day Scotty's uncle came over and began furiously carting things off to the dump. He left behind a garbage can in the driveway piled with all of Scotty's earthly possessions. I noticed two little pink feet sticking up into the air.

4 After dark, I crept across the street to the garbage can, armed with a travel-sized bottle of hand sanitizer. I looked left, then right. I dashed forward, tugged at the feet, and then ran as fast as I could back into my own backyard with my prize. Only then did I look at what I'd rescued. I would like you to meet Mabel.

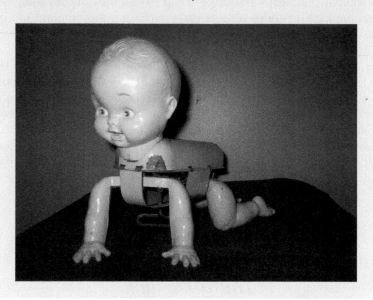

Inquiring into the Essay

Throughout *The Curious Writer*, I'll invite you to respond to readings, using questions. The following questions, therefore, encourage you to explore (*What do I think about this?*), explain (*What do I understand that this is saying?*), evaluate (*What's my judgment about this?*), and reflect to discover (*How does this work?* or *How am I thinking about it?*) and shape what you think about the reading. I encourage you to write while you read and after. Try that now. As soon as you finish your first reading of "Every Morning for Five Years," open up your journal and on the right-hand page fastwrite your response to the explore and explain questions above. Write for at least three minutes. Then go back to Zazulak's essay and on the left-hand page jot down sentences or passages from it that you think are important to your understanding of it. (I call this type of journaling the double-entry journal technique.) Build your responses to the questions that follow from these first thoughts about what you just read.

1. **Explore.** All of the essays in the book *Taking Things Seriously*, from which the piece you just read was taken, have this to say: It is remarkable how much meaning we can invest in the ordinary when we take the time to notice. This is an idea you can explore on your own. Brainstorm a list of objects that might have "unexpected significance" for you. Choose one and fastwrite about it for four minutes. Then skip a line, choose another, and write for another four minutes. If this is interesting to you, repeat this over a few days and create a collage of brief stories that four or five objects inspired. Are there any themes that seem to run through all of them? Do they speak to each other in any way?

2. **Explain.** Explain how, read together, the photograph and the essay work together to create meanings that might not be apparent if they were read separately.

3. **Evaluate.** Personal essays like "Every Morning for Five Years" *imply* their meaning rather than state it explicitly. In that way, an essay like this one is more like a short story. Make an argument for your own understanding of the meaning of Zazulak's essay, and use passages from the piece to support your claim.

4. **Reflect.** One of the features of the personal essay is two narrators: the "now-narrator" and the "then-narrator." One looks back on experience from the present, applying knowledge that the "then-narrator" did not have. From this comes fresh insight. But these two narrators aren't always obvious. Can you see them in this essay?

▶ Personal Essay 2

America is a nation of immigrants, whose stories often haunt their children. Judith Ortiz Cofer moved from Puerto Rico as a child with her family in the mid-1950s to a barrio in Paterson, New Jersey. There she became both part of and witness to a familiar narrative, that of the outsider who finds herself wedged between two worlds, two cultures, and two longings: the desire to return "home" and the desire to feel at home in the new place. While this is a story most immigrants know well, it is also a deeply personal one, shaded by particular places, prejudices, and patterns.

In "One More Lesson," Cofer describes both of the places that competed for her sense of self—the Puerto Rico of her childhood, where she spent time as a child while her Navy father was away at sea, and an apartment in New Jersey, where she would go when he returned.

One More Lesson

Judith Ortiz Cofer

1   I remember Christmas on the Island by the way it felt on my skin. The temperature dropped into the ideal seventies and even lower after midnight when some of the more devout Catholics—mostly older women—got up to go to church, *misa del gallo* they called it; mass at the hour when the rooster crowed for Christ. They would drape shawls over their heads and shoulders and move slowly toward town. The birth of Our Savior was a serious affair in our *pueblo*.

2   At Mamá's house, food was the focal point of *Navidad*. There were banana leaves brought in bunches by the boys, spread on the table, where the women would pour coconut candy steaming hot, and the leaves would wilt around the sticky lumps, adding an extra tang of flavor to the already irresistible treat. Someone had to watch the candy while it cooled, or it would begin to disappear as the children risked life and limb for a stolen piece of heaven. The banana leaves were also used to wrap the traditional food of holidays in Puerto Rico: *pasteles*, the meat pies made from grated yucca and plantain and stuffed with spiced meats.

3   Every afternoon during the week before Christmas Day, we would come home from school to find the women sitting around in the parlor with bowls on their laps, grating pieces of coconut, yuccas, plantains, cheeses—all the ingredients that would make up our Christmas Eve feast. The smells that filled Mamá's house at that time have come to mean anticipation and a sensual joy during a time in my life, the last days of my early childhood, when I could still absorb joy through my pores— *when I had not yet learned that light is followed by darkness, that all of creation is based on that simple concept, and maturity is a discovery of that natural law.*

4   It was in those days that the Americans sent baskets of fruit to our barrio—apples, oranges, grapes flown in from the States. And at night, if you dared to walk up to the hill where the mango tree stood in the dark, you could see a wonderful sight: a Christmas tree, a real pine, decorated with lights of many colors. It was the blurry outline of this tree you saw, for it was inside a screened-in-porch, but we had heard a thorough description of it from the boy who delivered the fruit, a nephew of Mamá's, as it had turned out. Only, I was not impressed, since just the previous year we had put up a tree ourselves in our apartment in Paterson.

5   Packages arrived for us in the mail from our father. I got dolls dressed in the national costumes of Spain, Italy, and Greece (at first we could not decide which of the Greek dolls was the male, since they both wore skirts); my brother got picture books; and my mother, jewelry that she would not wear, because it was too much like showing off and might attract the Evil Eye.

6   Evil Eye or not, the three of us were the envy of the pueblo. Everything about us set us apart, and I put away my dolls quickly when I discovered that my playmates would not be getting any gifts until *Los Reyes*—the Day of the Three Kings, when Christ received His gifts—and that even then it was more likely that the gifts they

found under their beds would be practical things like clothes. Still, it was fun to find fresh grass for the camels the night the Kings were expected, tie it in bundles with string, and put it under our beds along with a bowl of fresh water.

The year went by fast after Christmas, and in the spring we received a telegram from Father. His ship had arrived in Brooklyn Yard. He gave us a date for our trip back to the States. I remember Mother's frantic packing, and the trips to Mayagüez for new clothes; the inspections of my brother's and my bodies for cuts, scrapes, mosquito bites, and other "damage" she would have to explain to Father. And I remember begging Mamá to tell me stories in the afternoons, although it was not summer yet and the trips to the mango tree had not begun. In looking back I realize that Mamá's stories were what I packed—my winter store. 7

Father had succeeded in finding an apartment outside Paterson's "vertical barrio," the tenement Puerto Ricans called *El Building*. He had talked a Jewish candy store owner into renting us the apartment above his establishment, which he and his wife had just vacated after buying a house in West Paterson, an affluent suburb. Mr. Schultz was a nice man whose melancholy face I was familiar with from trips I had made often with my father to his store for cigarettes. Apparently, my father had convinced him and his brother, a look-alike of Mr. Schultz who helped in the store, that we were not the usual Puerto Rican family. My father's fair skin, his ultra-correct English, and his Navy uniform were a good argument. Later it occurred to me that my father had been displaying me as a model child when he took me to that store with him. I was always dressed as if for church and held firmly by the hand. I imagine he did the same with my brother. As for my mother, her Latin beauty, her thick black hair that hung to her waist, her voluptuous body which even the winter clothes could not disguise, would have been nothing but a hindrance to my father's plans. But everyone knew that a Puerto Rican woman is her husband's satellite; she reflects both his light and his dark sides. If my father was respectable, then his family would be respectable. We got the apartment on Park Avenue. 8

Unlike El Building, where we had lived on our first trip to Paterson, our new home was truly in exile. There were Puerto Ricans by the hundreds only one block away, but we heard no Spanish, no loud music, no mothers yelling at children, nor the familiar *¡Ay Bendito!*, that catch-all phrase of our people. Mother lapsed into silence herself, suffering from *La Tristeza*, the sadness that only place induces and only place cures. But Father relished silence, and we were taught that silence was something to be cultivated and practiced. 9

Since our apartment was situated directly above where the Schultzes worked all day, our father instructed us to remove our shoes at the door and walk in our socks. We were going to prove how respectable we were by being the opposite of what our ethnic group was known to be—we would be quiet and inconspicuous. 10

I was escorted each day to school by my nervous mother. It was a long walk in the cooling air of fall in Paterson and we had to pass by El Building where the children poured out of the front door of the dilapidated tenement still answering their 11

(continued)

(continued)

mothers in a mixture of Spanish and English: "Sí, Mami, I'll come straight home from school." At the corner we were halted by the crossing guard, a strict woman who only gestured her instructions, never spoke directly to the children, and only ordered us to "halt" or "cross" while holding her white-gloved hand up at face level or swinging her arm sharply across her chest if the light was green.

12   The school building was not a welcoming sight for someone used to the bright colors and airiness of tropical architecture. The building looked functional. It could have been a prison, an asylum, or just what it was: an urban school for the children of immigrants, built to withstand waves of change, generation by generation. Its red brick sides rose to four solid stories. The black steel fire escapes snaked up its back like an exposed vertebra. A chain-link fence surrounded its concrete playground. Members of the elite safety patrol, older kids, sixth graders mainly, stood at each of its entrances, wearing their fluorescent white belts that criss-crossed their chests and their metal badges. No one was allowed in the building until the bell rang, not even on rainy or bitter-cold days. Only the safety-patrol stayed warm.

13   My mother stood in front of the main entrance with me and a growing crowd of noisy children. She looked like one of us, being no taller than the sixth-grade girls. She held my hand so tightly that my fingers cramped. When the bell rang, she walked me into the building and kissed my cheek. Apparently my father had done all the paperwork for my enrollment, because the next thing I remember was being led to my third-grade classroom by a black girl who had emerged from the principal's office.

14   Though I had learned some English at home during my first years in Paterson, I had let it recede deep into my memory while learning Spanish in Puerto Rico. Once again I was the child in the cloud of silence, the one who had to be spoken to in sign language as if she were a deaf-mute. Some of the children even raised their voices when they spoke to me, as if I had trouble hearing. Since it was a large troublesome class composed mainly of black and Puerto Rican children, with a few working-class Italian children interspersed, the teacher paid little attention to me. I re-learned the language quickly by the immersion method. I remember one day, soon after I joined the rowdy class when our regular teacher was absent and Mrs. D., the sixth-grade teacher from across the hall, attempted to monitor both classes. She scribbled something on the chalkboard and went to her own room. I felt a pressing need to use the bathroom and asked Julio, the Puerto Rican boy who sat behind me, what I had to do to be excused. He said that Mrs. D. had written on the board that we could be excused by simply writing our names under the sign. I got up from my desk and started for the front of the room when I was struck on the head hard with a book. Startled and hurt, I turned around expecting to find one of the bad boys in my class, but it was Mrs. D. I faced. I remember her angry face, her fingers on my arms pulling me back to my desk, and her voice saying incomprehensible things to me in a hissing tone. Someone finally explained to her that I was new, that I did not speak English. I also remember how suddenly her face changed from anger to anxiety. But I did not forgive her for hitting

me with that hard-cover spelling book. Yes, I would recognize that book even now. It was not until years later that I stopped hating that teacher for not understanding that I had been betrayed by a classmate, and by my inability to read her warning on the board. *I instinctively understood then that language is the only weapon a child has against the absolute power of adults.*

I quickly built up my arsenal of words by becoming an insatiable reader of books.   15

Inquiring into the Essay

Here's another chance to use writing to think about what you've just read. On a right-hand notebook page (or top of a Word document), finish your first reading of Cofer's essay with a fastwrite that explores and explains your reaction to and understanding of what you just read. Then on the left-hand page (or below your initial fastwrite in a Word document) collect some sentences or passages from the essay that seem relevant to your first thoughts.

1. **Explore.** In the 1950s and 1960s, many saw America as a "melting pot." The idea was that although we may have many different immigrant backgrounds, we should strive toward some common "Americanism." For some this is still a powerful idea, but for others the melting pot metaphor reflects cultural dominance and even prejudice, a demand that differences be ignored and erased rather than celebrated. In your journal, write about your own feelings on this controversy. Tell the story of a friend, a relative, a neighbor who was an outsider. Tell about your own experience. What did it mean to assimilate, and at what cost?

2. **Explain.** Explain what you understand Cofer to mean in the second-to-last sentence of the essay: *I instinctively understood then that language is the only weapon a child has against the absolute power of adults.* To arrive at this explanation, consider exploring your thinking first. Fastwrite for one full minute without stopping, beginning with "The first thing I think when I read this is…And then I think…And then…"

3. **Evaluate.** What might this essay be asserting about cultural assimilation in America during the 1950s and 1960s? Would such an assertion still be relevant?

4. **Reflect.** One of the most common reasons students cite for liking a story is that "they could relate to it." Usually, this seems to mean that the author's and reader's experience coincide somehow: "I've felt like that" or "That happened to me, too." Does this mean that an American reader from the Chicago suburbs won't ever "relate to" a story by a child-soldier in Uganda? And can an Anglo reader of Cofer's essay genuinely "relate to" her experience as an American of Puerto Rican descent? Reflect on what it means to "relate to" something you read by talking about your experience reading Cofer's essay.

Seeing the Form

Photo Essays

In 1997, Brooklyn photographer Lauren Fleishman was living in France when she met the love of her life. When the affair ended, she composed a photo essay about the relationship, with the poignant title "You Would Have Loved Him, Too." She assembled 29 images, including shots of handwritten notes from her former lover, into a visual personal essay. One of her photographs for that series is included here. Fleishman is a professional photographer, but people create photo essays all the time on sites such as Flickr. Though the authors may not be consciously composing essays, these photographic series often do what personal essays do, but without words: They tell a story.

THE WRITING PROCESS

Inquiry Project **Writing a Personal Essay**

Watch
the Animation on
Writing Memoirs
in your MyLab

Here are some approaches to writing a personal essay as an inquiry project—a traditional essay and some multimodal methods. Your instructor will give you further guidance on the details of the assignment.

Inquiry questions: What does it mean to me? What do I understand about this now that I didn't understand then?

Write a personal essay on a topic that you find confusing or that raises interesting questions for you. Topics need not be personal, but they should arise from your own experiences and observations. The essay should offer a central insight about what you've come to understand about yourself and/or the topic. In other words, you will "essay" into a part of your life, past or present, exploring the significance of some memories, experiences, or observations. Your motive is personal discovery—reaching that new insight.

Your essay should do all the following:

- Do more than tell a story. There must be a *purpose* behind telling the story that speaks in some way to someone else. It should, ultimately, answer the *So what?* question.

- Include some reflection to explain or speculate about what you understand *now* about something that you didn't understand *then*. Your essay should have both a then-narrator and a now-narrator, one who remembers what happened and the other who sees what happened with the understanding you have now.

- Be richly detailed. Seize opportunities to *show* what you mean rather than simply explain it.

Prose+

Write your essay as a radio essay/podcast, and digitally record yourself reading the piece, using Audacity, GarageBand, or other audio software. This essay should be no longer than 2 to 3 minutes. The incorporation of music is optional. Keep the following in mind:

- This is a conversational medium. Write the piece like you talk.

- Be concise. Don't waste any words.

- The point (S.O.F.T.— say one fucking thing) of your essay should be clearly stated.

- Emphasize story, and avoid long stretches of exposition.

Write your essay to then publish on the web using Blogger, Wordpress, or other blogging software. You can use the site throughout the semester to post personal essays on other topics, and use this experience in a final paper to explore some aspect of the theme "The Public and the Personal." Some tips for writing a personal essay in this form include:

- Craft a good title for your essay so search engines and RSS readers will notice your piece.

- People who read unfamiliar blogs will often merely glance at them first. Write your essay to get your readers' attention and make it easily "scannable." Use subheadings, images, boxes, and so on.

- Write with voice. Your essay should have a strong persona that you can imagine using in almost any blog you write.

Write a personal essay modeled after "Every Morning for Five Years". Begin with a digital photograph of an object that is meaningful to you, and then explore its significance.

Writing Beyond the Classroom

Essaying "This I Believe"

The essay genre, which has been around for about five hundred years, is a vibrant and increasingly common form of writing on the radio and online audio. Why? One reason might be that the intimacy of the essay—the sense of a writer speaking directly to a reader without the masks we often wear when we write—seems particularly powerful when we hear

A public dialogue about belief—one essay at a time.

this i believe®

the voice of writing embodied in speech. Certainly, the ease with which we can "publish" essays as podcasts accounts for the explosion of online essayists.

This I Believe, a program heard on public radio (thisibelieve.org), is typical of radio programs that actively seek to broadcast student essays (which are subsequently published as podcasts). The program was begun in the 1950s by famed journalist Edward R. Murrow, who invited radio listeners and public figures to submit very brief (350–500 word) essays that stated some core belief that guided their "daily lives." As revived by the nonprofit organization This I Believe, the program is enormously popular and features work from people from all walks of life, including college students who may have written a "This I Believe" essay in their writing courses.

The program's website offers this advice to essayists:

1. Find a way to succinctly and clearly state your belief.

2. If possible, anchor it to stories.

3. Write in your own voice.

4. "Be positive," and avoid lecturing the listener.

What Are You Going to Write About?

With the personal essay, nearly anything goes. Essayists write about everything from their struggles with eating disorders, adjusting to life after military service, or dealing with the loss of a sibling to what we typically consider utterly commonplace things: a walk, negotiating use of an armrest with a fellow airplane passenger, a fondness for weird hats. Whatever you write about, what matters most is that you've chosen the topic because you aren't quite sure what you want to think about it. Write about what confuses you, what puzzles you, or what raises itchy questions.

4 Use invention strategies to discover and develop a personal essay topic.

The process for discovering a topic (see Figure 1) begins simply with what I call opening up, or generating lots of material. Open the warehouse of memory and walk around, or open your eyes and look around you *now*. Just collect some things, without judging their value for this project. Next, narrow things down. Make some judgments. Decide on an experience or observation that raises the most interesting questions—about how you feel or what it means. Now try out this topic by generating more material that focuses on it. Finally, make some judgments about what (if anything) all this writing has helped you to understand about yourself or the topic. These insights help you to clarify what your essay might really be about. The essayist Vivian Gornick writes that personal essays have both a *situation* and a *story*. The situation is what happened—the doctor told you when you were twelve that your leg was broken. The story is what you understand *now* about the significance of that situation. Maybe that time of walking on crutches gave you insight into a kind of suffering that you otherwise wouldn't have known, and this inspired the empathy you feel now for a disabled friend.

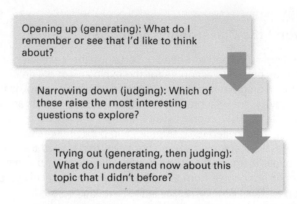

Figure 1 A process for discovering a personal essay topic

Generate material about possible situations to write about, narrow them down, and then focus on trying to discover the larger story you might be trying to tell.

Opening Up

Watch
the Animation on
Writing Reflections
in your MyLab

Even if you've already got an idea for a personal essay topic, spend some time exploring the possibilities before you make a commitment. It doesn't really take much time, and there's a decent chance that you'll discover a great topic for your essay you never would have thought of otherwise.

The journal prompts that follow will get you going. What you're after is to stumble on an interesting topic. Actually, it's more like stumbling through the *door* to an interesting topic—a door that gives you a look at what you might fruitfully explore with more-focused writing. Try several prompts, looking for a topic that might, after some writing, raise questions such as these:

- *Am I uncertain about what this might mean?*
- *Is this topic more complicated than it seemed at first?*
- *Might I understand these events differently now than I did then?*

Listing Prompts. Lists can be rich sources of topic ideas. Let them grow freely, and when you're ready, use an item as the focus of another list or an episode of fastwriting. The following prompts should get you started thinking about both your experiences and your observations.

1. Make a list of experiences you've had that you can't forget. Reach into all parts and times of your life.

2. Make a list of things that bug you. Think about everyday things like people with Apple computer fetishes or friends who send text messages in the middle of a serious conversation.

When they work, writing prompts open a door to promising topics. More-focused writing later will help you to explore the room and generate the information that may lead to a sketch or draft.

Fastwriting Prompts. Early on, fastwriting can help you settle on a narrower topic, *if* you allow yourself to write "badly." Then use a more focused fastwrite, trying to generate information and ideas within the loose boundaries of your chosen topic.

1. Choose an item from a list you've created to use as a prompt. Just start fastwriting about the item; perhaps start with a story, a scene, a situation, a description. Follow the writing to see where it leads.

One Student's Response

Lauren's Journal: Lists of Things That Bug Me

People who write in library books

Dead batteries

Goatheads in bicycle tires

Bad instructions

Spitting

Bad beer

Profane football fans

Global warming deniers

2. Most of us quietly harbor dreams—we hope to be a professional dancer, a good father, an activist, a marketing executive, an Olympic luger, or a novelist. Begin a fastwrite in which you explore your dreams. When the writing stalls, ask yourself questions: *Where did this dream come from? Do I still believe in it? In what moments did it seem within reach? In what moments did it fade?* Plunge into those moments.

3. What was the most confusing time in your life? Choose a moment or scene that stands out in your memory of that time, and, writing in the present tense, describe what you see, hear, and do. After five minutes, skip a line and choose another moment. Then another. Make a collage.

4. What do you consider "turning points" in your life, times when you could see the end of one thing and the beginning of something else? Fastwrite about one of these for seven minutes.

Visual Prompts. Images trigger ideas, and so can more-visual ways of thinking. Let's try both. Boxes, lines, arrows, charts, and even sketches can help us see more of the landscape of a subject, especially connections between fragments of information that aren't as obvious in prose. The clustering or mapping method is useful to many writers early in the writing process as they try to discover a topic. (See the "Inquiring into the Details" box for more details on how to create a cluster.) Figure 2 shows my cluster from the first prompt listed here.

1. What objects would you most regret losing in a house fire? Choose a most-treasured object as the core for a cluster. Build a web of associations from it, returning to the detail in the core whenever a strand dies out.

2. Find a photograph from your past, perhaps like the one from mine that opens this chapter. Fastwrite about what you see in the picture, what you don't see, and a story that it inspires.

3. Draw a long line on a piece of paper in your journal. This is your life. Divide the line into segments that seem to describe what feels like distinct times in your life. These don't have to correspond to familiar age categories such as adolescence or childhood; they could correspond to periods in your life you associate with a place, a relationship, a dilemma, a job, a personal challenge, and so on. In any case, make the segments chronological. Examine your timeline, and, as a fastwrite prompt, put two of these periods in your life together. Explore what they had in common, particularly how the earlier period might have shaped the later one. See Figure 3 for a sample timeline.

4. Get on Google Earth. Find the town or city where you were born or lived as a young child. Zoom in on your neighborhood. Fastwrite about what this makes you remember. Alternatively, find the house you live in now. Using the "street view" feature, "walk" down the street, stopping at the homes of interesting neighbors that you know or have observed. With the image on the screen, fastwrite in your journal, telling yourself stories about the people in your neighborhood.

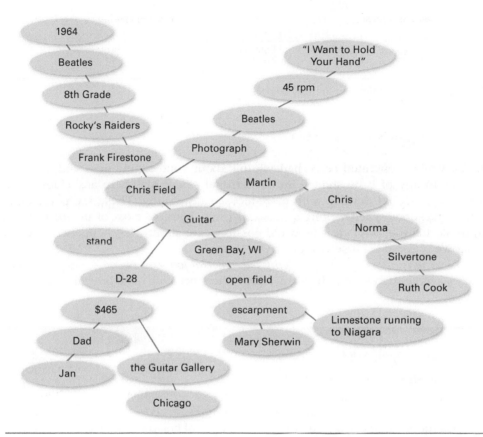

Figure 2 A cluster built around the one object I would most regret losing in a house fire: my Martin guitar

Research Prompts. Things we hear, see, or read can be powerful prompts for personal essays. It's tempting to believe that personal essays are always about the past, but just as often essayists are firmly rooted in the present, commenting and pondering on the confusions of contemporary life. In that sense, personal essayists are researchers, always on the lookout for material. Train your eye with one or more of the following prompts.

1. Put this at the top of a journal page: "Things People Do." Now go outside and find a place to observe people. Write down a list of everything you see people doing. Choose one action you find interesting and fastwrite about it. Is it weird? Why?

2. Look up the definition of "infatuation." Write it down on the top of a journal page, and then write for five minutes about your experience and observations of infatuations with people, things, places, ideas.

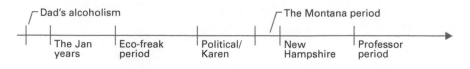

Figure 3 A sample timeline from my own life

Narrowing Down

Okay, you've generated some bad writing about your experiences and observations. Can any of it be shaped into a personal essay? Are there any clues about a topic you could develop with more-focused fastwriting? These are particularly tough questions when writing a personal essay, because most of us are inclined to think that the only one who could possibly care about what happened to us or what we observe is ourselves (or maybe Mom).

Don't make the mistake of judging the material too soon or too harshly. Personal essayists write successfully about any topic—often including quite ordinary things—so

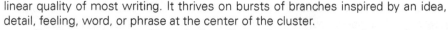

Inquiring into the Details

Clustering or Mapping

A method of visual thinking and invention, clustering (or mapping), is a refreshing alternative to the linear quality of most writing. It thrives on bursts of branches inspired by an idea, detail, feeling, word, or phrase at the center of the cluster.

Clusters are in code. If you look at Figure 2, my cluster on the word *guitar*, the items in the cluster won't say to you what they say to me, because I'm familiar with their meaning and you, of course, can't be. For me, each strand suggests a story, an idea, or a feeling that I might explore. In this same way, any cluster you make will be in a code that only you fully understand.

How do you cluster?

1. Begin with a blank page in your journal. Choose a core word, phrase, name, idea, detail, or question; write it in the middle of the page and circle it.

2. Relax and focus on the core word or phrase, and when you feel moved to do so, build a strand of associations from the core, circling and connecting each item. Write other details, names, dates, place names, phrases, and so on—whatever comes to mind.

3. When a strand dies out, return to the core and begin another. Keep clustering until the page looks like a web of associations. Doodle, darkening lines and circles, if that helps you relax and focus.

4. When you feel the urge to write, stop clustering and use one of the strands as a prompt for journal work.

don't give up on a promising topic this early in the game. But first, how do you decide what's promising?

What's Promising Material and What Isn't? The signs of a promising personal essay topic include the following:

- **Abundance.** What subject generated the most writing? Do you sense that there is much more to write about?
- **Surprise.** Did you see or say something you didn't expect about a topic?
- **Confusion.** What subject raises questions you're not sure you can answer easily?

In the personal essay, this last item—confusion and uncertainty—may yield the most-fertile topics. All of the questions listed at the beginning of "Opening Up," are related in some way to a feeling that some experience or observation—even if it's familiar to you—has yet to yield all of its possible meanings.

Questions About Purpose and Audience. Who cares about my middling career as a high school cross-country runner? Who cares that I grew to love that gritty neighborhood in Hartford? Who cares that I find high school reunions weird? When we write about ourselves, we can't help but wonder why anyone, other than ourselves, *would* care. Maybe they won't. But if you discover something about your life that helps you to understand it better—even in a small way—you will begin to find an audience. After all, we are interested in understanding our own, often ordinary lives, and perhaps we can learn something from you.

To find an audience for a personal essay, you have to discover something to say about your experiences and observations that speak to others—a theme that you could express in a "we statement."

Obviously, why you're writing and for whom will profoundly influence your approach. That's a fundamental principle of rhetoric, one that you applied when you jotted that note to your teacher explaining the late assignment or texted your friend about your new bicycle. Although it is useful to consider your purpose and audience early on, make sure you don't let purpose and audience considerations squeeze off your writing. You always want to be open to the unexpected places your writing might lead you, especially in the early stages of the process. Being too vigilant about what readers think can discourage you from welcoming the messy accidents that can make for helpful discoveries.

Trying Out

Recently, I began working on a personal essay about my experiences going to high school reunions. I went to my fortieth last fall. As I generated "bad writing" on the subject of high school reunions, I kept returning to the same question: If I find these reunions generally weird and unsatisfying, why do I keep going? Using this inquiry question, I tried out my topic with the focused fastwrite that follows:

Last fall, I went to my 40th high school reunion...I had been to the 10th and the 20th, both of which required travel, once from the East coast and once from the West. I have no idea why I went to the effort...I didn't like high school...and I don't have many friends left in the Chicago suburb where I grew up. Why does anyone go to a high school reunion? I wonder if I've gone because...like it or not...high school is part of the narrative of our growing up that is at once mysterious and utterly familiar. I can remember everything...my failure to make the swim team that my brother was a star on...breaking the mercury barometer in physics class with my elbow while cleaning chalk erasers at the window...the sexual thrill of sitting on a bench next to Suzie Durment at a football game and feeling her thigh press close to mine. And yet I can't explain so much of high school...It just doesn't make sense. Why would I run cross country for four years and absolutely hate every minute of it?...How could I so thoroughly mishandle the kindness and affection of Jan Dawe, my first serious girlfriend?...And why all those years did I still pine for Lori Jo Flink, a girl from the 7th grade?...I guess that's one reason I go to my high school reunion...To enjoy the melancholy of seeing Lori Jo again and to relish the bittersweet taste of rejection....She always comes...Yet when I did see her this time it wasn't the same. We had a very brief conversation... "I looked you up on the Internet," she said, and was promptly swept to the dance floor by Larry Piacenza...She looked me up on the Internet...This should have given me a thrill but it didn't...Why not?...These days I've been stripping the siding off so many old narratives about myself, stories that I've mistaken for walls that bear weight...Perhaps I tossed Lori Jo on that pile of discarded lumber...along with the desire to attend another high school reunion. As I'm counting the gifts of middle age, I gladly add this one.

What I hope you notice in my focused writing on reunions is how I keep using questions to tease out meaning, starting with a question I've never really asked myself before: Why do I go to high school reunions? Why would anyone? These inquiry questions pulled me out of the sea of experience and onto the mountain of reflection (highlighted passages), where I begin to see a possible answer: I go to reunions to revive old stories about myself that may no longer matter. In the personal essay, judging involves *reflection*. What do we make of what happened then that we didn't quite see until now? What might our observations of the world around us now *say* about that world and, maybe more important, about ourselves?

Questions for Reflection. Thinking with writing is a movement back and forth between the creative and critical minds. In a way, personal essays and other narrative genres make this movement of the mind visible. In the essays you read earlier in the chapter, you may have noticed that some of the pieces seem to subtly shift from situation to story, from narrative to exposition, memory to reflection. This movement often has to do with time. You remember that something happened, recently or long ago. You describe what you remember, traveling back in time. But you aren't really a time traveler. You write from the present, and it is the present that allows you to understand what you couldn't have understood in the past. This is the source of reflection in the personal essay.

One way of thinking about this is in terms of the then-narrator and the now-narrator. The two narrators collaborate to make meaning. But it is the now-narrator who provides the judgment. Now that you've tried out your topic, put yourself in the now-narrator's perspective, answering questions such as these:

- What do you understand now about this topic that you didn't fully understand when you began writing about it? Start some writing with this phrase: "As I look back on this now, I realize that…"

- What seems to be the most important thing you're trying to say so far?

- How has your thinking changed about your topic? Finish this seed sentence as many times as you can in your notebook: *Once I thought* _____, *and now I think* _____.

Writing the Sketch

Throughout *The Curious Writer*, I'll encourage you to write what I call "sketches." As the name implies, this is a first look at something roughly drawn. It is a pretty rough draft of your piece, perhaps no more than about 300 words, with a tentative title. Though it may be sketchy, your sketch should be reader-based prose. You want someone else to understand what it's about. Don't assume they know what you know. When you need to, explain things.

Watch
the Video on
Writing Personal Narratives
in your MyLab

A sketch is a good starting point for a personal essay in any mode. If you're working on a radio essay, for example, the sketch will be much the same as one that you write for a conventional essay. It's simply a very early script.

Choose your most promising material, and tell the story. If it's drawn from memory, incorporate both what happened then and what you make of it now. If it's built on observations, make sure they are detailed, anchored to particular times and places, and in some way significant.

You may or may not answer the "So what?" question in your sketch, though you should try. Don't muscle the material too much to conform to what you already think; let the writing help you figure out what you think.

To summarize, then, in a sketch try to do the following:

- Have a tentative title.

- Keep it relatively short.

- Write it fast.

- Don't muscle it to conform to a preconceived idea.

- Write to be read, with an audience in mind.

- Make it specific instead of general.

▶ Student Sketch

Amanda Stewart's sketch, "Earning a Sense of Place," faintly bears the outlines of what might be a great personal essay. When they succeed, sketches are suggestive; it is what they're not quite saying that yields promise. On the surface, "Earning a Sense of Place" could seem simply a piece about Amanda's passion for skiing. So what? And yet, there are lines here that point to larger ideas and unanswered questions. For example, Amanda writes that the "mental reel" of her swishing down a mountain on skis is "the image that sustains me when things are hard, and when I want to stop doing what is right and start doing what is easy." Why is it that such a mental image can be sustaining in hard times? How well does this work? The end of the sketch is even more suggestive. This really might be a piece about trying to find a "sense of place" that doesn't rely on such images; in a sense, the sketch seems to be trying to say that joy on the mountain isn't enough.

The pleasure of writing and reading a sketch is looking for what it might teach you, learning what you didn't know you knew.

I've highlighted portions of the text to illustrate a revision exercise that follows Amanda's essay.

Earning a Sense of Place
Amanda Stewart

1   The strings to my earflaps stream behind me, mixing with my hair as a rooster-tail flowing behind my neck. Little ice crystals cling to the bottom of my braid and sparkle in the sunlight. The pompom on top of my hat bobs up and down as I arc out, turning cleanly across the snow. I suck in the air, biting with cold as it hits my hot lungs, and breathe deep as I push down the run.

2   This is what I see when I picture who I want to be. It's the image that sustains me when things are hard, and when I want to stop doing what is right and start doing what is easy. I have made so many terrible decisions in the past that I know how far astray they lead me; I don't want that. I want the girl in the mental reel in her quilted magenta jacket and huge smile. She's what I grasp at when I need help getting through the day.

3   She's an amalgam of moments from the past mixed with my hopes for the future. I love to ski, and have since my parents strapped little plastic skis onto my galoshes when I was a year and a half old. From that day I flopped around our snow-covered yard, I've been in love with skiing. It's the only time I feel truly comfortable. Day to day I often feel so awkward. I wonder if my hair is right, or if my clothes fit. Last night, my roommate had a boy over, and as he sat on the couch talking to me, all I felt was discomfort and awkwardness. I didn't know what to say, felt judged, felt out of place. I never feel that way on skis. Even floundering in heavy, deep snow, or after a fall that has packed my goggles with snow

and ripped the mittens off my hands I know exactly what to do. I'm a snow mermaid, only comfortable in my medium. I often wish I could trade in my walking legs for something like a tail that is more truly me.

My dad's coffee cup at home says, "I only work so I can ski," and for him, it's true. Sometimes I feel like I only push through my daily life so I can get to the next mountain and zip up my pants and go. I don't want to live like that though: it's too much time looking forward to something, and not enough looking at what I'm living in. I need to appreciate my life as it is, snowy cold or sunny warm. That sense of place I have on skis can probably be earned here on the flat expanses of campus just as easily as I got it pushing myself down the bunny slopes so long ago. I just have to earn it.

4

Moving from Sketch to Draft

Here's the journey with the assignment you've taken so far:

Watch
the Animation on
**Writing Narration
Essays**
in your MyLab

1. You've generated some "bad writing," openly exploring possibilities for personal essay topics while suspending judgment.

2. You landed on a tentative topic.

3. You tried out this topic through more writing, some of it still "bad."

4. Your critical mind took over as you began to judge what you have so far. What questions does this material raise for you? What might it *mean?* With judgment comes a growing concern for audience. Why would they care about this?

5. You tried out the topic in a sketch. It's written with an audience in mind.

At the heart of the process I'm describing is a movement from "writer-based" to "reader-based" prose. This movement occurs with any type of writing, but it's particularly tricky with the personal essay. When you're writing about yourself, there is always this: *Who cares?*

The movement from sketch to draft must address this question. But how?

Evaluating Your Own Sketch. One way to assess whether your sketch might be meaningful to someone other than you is to look for the balance between narrative and reflection, or the then-narrator and the now-narrator. Try this:

- Take two highlighters, each a different color.

- Go through your sketch from beginning to end, using one color to highlight text that's story-telling, what happened or what you saw, and then use the other color to highlight text that is explanatory, more-general commentary about what happened or what you saw. What's the pattern of color?

There are several possibilities here.

1. **One color dominates.** Your sketch is mostly narrative or mostly summary, all then-narrator or all now-narrator. A personal essay that is mostly narrative

usually fails to address the "So what?" question. It seems to tell a story without a purpose. On the other hand, a personal essay that is all explanation fails to engage readers in the writer's *experiences*. It's all telling and no showing. Personal essays must both show *and* tell.

2. **One color dominates except at the end.** Typically, there is all narrative until the very end, when the writer briefly reflects, much like the formula for a fable, with its moral at the end. This can seem predictable to readers. But you can work with it in revision by taking the reflection at the end and using it to reconceive the essay *from the very beginning*. Can you take the ending and use the insight to organize your thinking in a revision?

3. **The colors alternate.** Sometimes this is the most interesting type of personal essay, because the two narrators are in genuine collaboration, trying to figure out what happened and what it *means*.

In my markup of Amanda's sketch, you can see how there is some shifting in the pattern of color. But exposition dominates. Her revision might need more story, more *showing* readers what happened that has made her think the things she now thinks.

If our personal experiences and observations are to mean anything to someone else, then they must, at the very least, both show and tell. They should, through details, descriptions, and scenes, invite an audience into the sea of our experiences. But they must also be clear about the *reason* behind the invitation—about what we have come to understand and want our audience to understand. In revising your sketch, focus on these two concerns above all.

Reflecting on What You Learned. Thinking through writing is the dialectical method that moves back and forth between creative thinking and critical thinking, generating and judging. Highlighting the two narrators in your sketch is a way to actually see yourself thinking that way *in your own writing*—or not, depending on the patterns of color you see. Make a journal entry about this. In your sketch, which of the two narrators is more active, and why do you think that's so? In a revision of this sketch, how might you address any imbalance between the two? Where could the now-narrator tell more, or where could the then-narrator show more?

Developing

In the last section, you focused on using a sketch to identify the *purposes* of telling someone else about your memories, experiences, or observations. For example, in the sample sketch, Amanda seems to be telling us about her love for skiing because it suggests a longing that most of us feel: to transfer the confidence we feel in one part of our lives to every part. The key to developing your draft is to arrive at a fuller understanding of what your purpose is in telling your own stories *and then rebuild your essay around that insight from the beginning*.

In other words, as you begin your revision, focus on exploring the answer to these questions:

- What might this essay be saying, not only about me, but more generally about people who find themselves in similar situations?

- What questions does it raise that might be interesting, not only to me, but also to others who may not know me?

Fastwrite in your journal about these questions for as long as you can. One word of caution, though, and I can't stress it enough: YOU DO NOT NEED TO BE PROFOUND. Most of us aren't philosophers or really deep thinkers. We are ordinary people who are just trying to make sense of our lives and work towards those little insights that make us understand things a little better.

As you get a grip on the purpose behind your essay, you can focus your efforts on developing those parts of the narrative that are relevant. What scenes, anecdotes, details, observations, facts, stories, and so on might focus your attention—and later your readers' attention—on what you're trying to say about the topic?

For this, try some of the following strategies:

- *Explode a moment.* Choose a scene or moment in the story or stories you're telling that seems particularly important to the meaning of the essay. Reenter that moment and fastwrite for a full seven minutes, using all your senses and as much detail as you can muster.

- *Make lists.* Brainstorm a list of details, facts, or specifics about a moment or scene that was part of an experience or about an observation. Then list other experiences or observations that seem connected to this one (see "Cluster" below).

- *Research.* Do some quick-and-dirty research that might bring in other voices or more information that will deepen your consideration of the topic.

- *Cluster (or fastwrite).* Try to move beyond narrating a single experience or observation and discover others that might help you see important patterns. For example, let's say your sketch is about your experience working with the poor in Chile. Have you had other encounters with extreme poverty (or extreme wealth)? Can you describe them? What do they reveal about your feelings or attitudes about poverty or your reactions to what happened in Chile?

Drafting

Some of my students get annoyed at all the "stuff" I encourage them to do before they begin a first draft of a personal essay. In some cases, all the journal work isn't necessary; the writer very quickly gets a strong sense of direction and feels ready to begin composing. But from the beginning, I've encouraged you to gravitate toward topics that you find confusing, and with that kind of material, exploratory writing is time well spent. Remember, too, that journal writing counts as writing.

It not only offers the pleasures of surprise, but can ultimately make the drafting process more efficient by generating material that you won't have to conjure up during those long, painful periods of staring at the computer screen, wondering what to say next.

As you begin drafting, keep in mind what you've learned from your writing so far. For example:

■ What is the most important question that is behind your exploration of the topic?

■ What do you understand now that you didn't understand fully when you started writing about it?

■ How can you show *and* explain how you came to this understanding?

■ Have you already written a strong first line for the draft? Can you find it somewhere in all your journal writing?

Draft with your reader in mind. As you draft, ask yourself,

What does the reader most need to know to understand my thinking and feelings about this topic? What should I show about what happened, to give the reader a clear sense of what happened?

Methods of Development. Narrative is an especially useful method of development for personal essays. How might you use it to develop your subject?

Narrative. Narrative can work in a personal essay in at least three ways. You can use it to:

1. Tell an extended story of what happened.

2. Tell one or more anecdotes, or brief stories, that somehow address the question behind your interest in the topic.

3. Tell the story of your thinking as you've come to understand something you didn't understand before.

Often, a single essay uses narrative in all three types of ways.

Consider beginning your draft with the anecdote or the part of the story you want to tell that best frames the question, dilemma, or idea that is the focus of your essay (see "Inquiring into the Details: More Than One Way to Tell a Story"). If you're writing about the needless destruction of a childhood haunt by developers, then consider opening with the way the place looked *after* the bulldozers were done with it—description related to the end of your narrative.

Time in writing is nothing like real time. You can ignore chronology, if it serves your purpose. You can write pages about something that happened in seven minutes or cover twenty years in a paragraph. The key is to tell your story or stories in ways that emphasize what's important.

Using Evidence. How do you make your essay convincing, and even moving, to an audience? It's all in the details. Like most stories, the personal essay thrives on particularity: What exactly did it look like? What exactly did she say? What exactly did it sound and smell like at that moment? Evidence that gives a personal essay authority are details that make a reader believe the writer can be trusted to observe keenly and to remember accurately. All of the professional essays in this chapter are rich in detail. There is the neighbor with the "neon orange hunting cap" who rakes the same spot every day in Laura Zazulak's "Every Morning for Five Years," and the wilting banana leaves that curl around the coconut candy in Judith Ortiz Cofer's "One More Lesson." This focus on the particular—what it *exactly* looked like, smelled like, felt like, sounded like—makes an essay come alive for both writer and reader.

As you draft your essay, remember the subtle power of details. Tell, but always show, too.

Inquiring into the Details

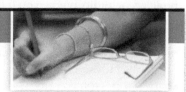

More Than One Way to Tell a Story

This is my daughter Julia telling a story:

"And she was like..."

"And then I was like..."

"And then she was like..."

When we think about organizing experiences—something that personal essays try to do—we immediately think of narrative, and then, naturally, we think of the most common narrative structure: chronology. This is Julia's method of oral storytelling, as it is for most of us.

Yet in essay writing, strict chronology—this happened and then this and then this—may not be the best way to tell a story. Once locked into a strictly chronological narrative, you may feel compelled to tell the *whole* story. While chronological storytelling might be a good way to remember what happened as you explore your experiences in your journal or in early drafts, what you need to do in your essay is to tell those *parts* of the story (or stories) that are relevant to the question you're exploring or the thing you're trying to say.

Structure in the personal essay, as in all writing, must be a servant to purpose. Simply put, purpose is how you might answer a potential reader who wants to know this: *So what?* Why should I read this? Organize a narrative essay with the *So what?* question in mind. That may mean that you start a narrative essay in the part of the story that illuminates the question you're exploring, the idea you're trying to understand. Typically, this won't be the beginning of the story ("The alarm clock went off at 6 AM, and I was groggy from sleep"); it may be the middle or even the end.

Judith Ortiz Cofer, for example, opens her story about her struggles as a young Puerto Rican immigrant to the United States in the 1950s with an anecdote about her memories of Christmas on the island. The Christmas anecdote frames the narrative's controlling idea: that in life "light is followed by darkness" and that

> **One Student's Response** (*continued*)
>
> this is an immutable fact. The most important part of organizing a personal narrative is not how you tell what happened. It is what you *now* think about the significance of what happened. It is this shift from past to present—from what you remember and what you understand about it now that you didn't then—that is the most important structure of all.

Workshopping

Sharing a personal essay with peers might present some special challenges. After all, in this kind of essay, you're really putting yourself out there. You're honestly talking about yourself, and about *your* experiences and observations. If your essay is a podcast or radio piece, you'll be sharing not only your writing but also your voice, and my students tell me that in a spoken essay, it's nearly impossible to lie. It's a kind of writing that, as E. B. White once said, should not indulge "in deceit or in concealment," for the writer "will be found out in no time."

Under these circumstances, it's hard not to feel a least a little vulnerable when sharing a personal essay. (If this is a real source of anxiety, talk to your instructor.) But you will find that exactly *because* the personal essay is personal, your peers will be enthusiastic readers of your work. The key is to channel that enthusiasm towards a response that will help you revise.

At this stage in writing the personal essay—the first full draft—what you may need most are responses that address the things you've worked on most in your sketch: Does the draft clearly answer the "So what?" question (purpose)? Is it clear what the one main thing is that the essay is trying to say (meaning)? All other revision concerns are subordinate to these questions. Why? Because without a clear purpose and clear sense, it's impossible to make any judgments about content.

Annie Dillard, a writer of many nonfiction books and essays, once said that she believed that the biggest challenge in writing comes down to this basic question: *What to put in and what to leave out.* In a narrative essay such as the one you're working on, you might conclude that the answer to the question is equally simple: You tell the "whole" story. Yet the truth is that you never do, even in telling a story to friends. We shape and shade a story depending on our motive for telling it. The same is true in prose. Your purpose and what you are trying to say are the two things that determine what belongs in a story and what doesn't. So this is where you should begin.

Questions for Readers. The following grid, which focuses on these two key concerns, can help you to guide your peers' response to your first draft.

Questions for Peer Reviewers	
1. Purpose	What would you say this essay is about? Do you have a clear sense of *why* I'm writing about this topic?
2. Meaning	Most essays need to say one fricking thing (S.O.F.T.). What would you say is the point of this draft? What is the main thing I seem to be saying about this topic?

Reflecting on the Workshop. After the workshop session, do a follow-up entry in your notebook that summarizes what you heard, what made sense and what didn't, and how you plan to approach the next draft. Your instructor may ask you to share this information in a cover letter submitted with the revision.

Revising

Revision is a continual process—not a last step. You've been revising—"reseeing" your subject—from the first messy fastwriting in your journal. But the things that get your attention vary depending on where you are in the writing process. With your draft in hand, revision becomes your focus through what I'll call "shaping and tightening your draft."

5

Apply revision strategies that are effective for shaping narratives.

Shaping. In your draft, you made a tentative commitment to your topic, hoping that you could shape it into something that might have meaning for someone other than you. Fundamentally, you've been trying to figure out *what you're trying to say* and then rebuild your essay so that this is both clear and convincing. In a personal essay, you might also want it to be moving.

Shaping focuses on larger concerns first: purpose and meaning—the very largest concerns, which you've looked at if you workshopped your draft—and the next-to-largest concerns of information and organization. It starts with knowing what your essay is about—your inquiry question and maybe your theme—and then revising to make every element of the draft focused on that question or idea.

What to Cut and What to Add. Ryan wrote a personal essay about the epic battles he had with his brother growing up. He realized writing it that, while they didn't exactly hate each other, they certainly behaved like they did back then. The purpose of Ryan's essay was to explore a question: *Why were these sibling rivalries so intense, and how do they shape the brothers' relationships today?* As he reflects on what he wrote and understands what he wanted to convey, Ryan can make the decisions that Dillard says revision demands: what to cut and what to add. Ryan will cut the part that focuses on his father, because it does little to help readers see the brothers' rivalry. He will add more about the chess game in which they finally came to blows. A key to revising a personal essay, then, is this:

Given my essay's purpose and meaning, what should I cut and what should I add?

- What information—scenes, descriptions, observations, explanations—is no longer relevant to the purpose and meaning?

- What information is missing that should be added to help readers understand and, in a small way, experience, so that they will appreciate my point?

The Question of Time. Revising a narrative essay also involves the question of time. Consider this in two ways:

1. Where will information come from to develop your story—from the past or from the present? The then-narrator is master of the past. What happened? And then what? The now-narrator is charged with commenting from the present. What do I make of what happened from where I sit now? Personal essays that tell stories need information from both past and present.

2. How does time organize the information in the draft? Do you tell your story chronologically? Is that the best way to structure the essay? What might happen, for example, if you begin in the middle of the story, or even at the end? Will that better dramatize the question or dilemma that you're exploring?

Research. I'm not talking about extensive research, but about quick searches for background information, relevant facts, and maybe even something on what other writers or experts have said. Here's an example. I was writing an essay in which I recalled a total solar eclipse that happened in August 1964. Did it really? A quick web search confirmed it, but I also got information about exactly how long it lasted, and this information helped strengthen the scene I was writing. Say you're writing an essay about iPhone infatuation. Why not look up a definition of "infatuation" and then do some quick research on how students use their iPhones in a typical day?

Other Questions for Revision. Make sure you address the following questions as you revise:

- Does the draft begin in a way that gives your readers a sense of where the essay is going? Is your purpose clear? (This is especially important for podcast essays.)

- Is there too much explaining? Narrative essays are usually built on the backbone of story—anecdote, scene, description. This is how we help the audience appreciate, in some small way, the experiences that have inspired the insights we want to share. Personal essays *do* need to tell, but they must also *show*.

- By the end of your essay, does the reader appreciate the significance of the story you're telling? Have you said what you need to say about how, though it's your experience, the meaning you discover might apply to others as well?

Polishing. When you are satisfied with the shape of your draft, focus on paragraphs, sentences, and words. Are your paragraphs coherent? How do you manage transitions? Are your sentences fluent and concise? Are there any errors in spelling or syntax?

Before you finish your draft, work through the following checklist:

✓ Every paragraph is about one thing.

✓ The transitions between paragraphs aren't abrupt.

✓ The length of sentences varies in each paragraph.

✓ Each sentence is concise. There are no unnecessary words or phrases.

✓ You've checked grammar, particularly for verb agreement, run-on sentences, unclear pronouns, and misused words (*there/their*, *where/were*, and so on). (See the Handbook for help with these grammar issues.)

✓ You've run your spellchecker and proofed your paper for misspelled words.

Watch
the Animation on
How to Edit
in your MyLab

▶ Student Essay

Military veterans often bring their rich, complicated experiences into my writing classes, and because what they've seen and done often raises questions they can't easily answer, they learn to love the personal essay. Seth Marlin served in Iraq. In the essay "Smoke of Empire," he remembers that during his first night in the country, there was a stench he didn't recognize. It turns out this was the smell of things—often perfectly good things—burning. The refuse of war. This memory inspires a meditation on war, waste, and empire.

The piece was written for the radio, and Seth produced an audio essay using Audacity software that blended his voice reading of "Smoke of Empire" with music that gave the essay even more power. As you read Seth's essay, keep in mind that he wrote it with the idea that his audience would hear it a single time. Consider as you read it how that changes his approach to the writing. You can also listen to the essay at bruceballenger.com.

Smoke of Empire

Seth Marlin

1   When I was in Iraq, we used to have this rotating detail. Call it "*Hajji*-watch." Bring in local guys, pay them ten bucks to move sandbags, haul trash. Post a couple soldiers with rifles in case anyone gets froggy. Locals try to sell you stuff, turn them down. They ask for soap, shampoo, toothpaste, say you don't have any. That's the order they drill into you: *Do Not Buy, Sell, or Give Items to Local Nationals.*

2   Locals were poor. Dirt poor. Steal the gloves out of your pocket if they thought they'd get some use. Who could blame them? One guy I saw stole a bedroll once; another, maybe fifteen, jacked a soccer-ball, said it was for his little brother. Our squad-leader said it was contraband, said the ball would be waiting for him when he came back next week, soon as he got a memorandum from the base-commander.

3   That kid never got his ball, you kidding me? Lot of poor guys with families; that line stretched two miles up the road back into town. He'd have been lucky to get in at all. I doubt he ever got that ball back; most likely, it just went to the burn-pit.

* * *

4   Fun fact: Wars generate waste. The Department of Defense estimates that its wars each generate ten pounds of garbage per service member per day. At over 150,000 service members deployed, that's a lot of trash. Unfortunately, the locals tend not to cotton to your leaving messes all over their soil; thus, in the name of diplomacy, the invaders have to clean up after themselves. On places like Joint Base Balad, all that refuse goes to one place: the burn-pit.

Picture a base, fifteen miles across, set in a swath of palm-dotted farmland. Now picture on part of that a landscape of hills, valleys, and craters—all of it garbage, all bigger than a dozen football fields. Now picture that on fire. Through the haze, you might see the figures who manage all that incoming drek—orange-turbaned Sikhs wearing blue jumpsuits, some of them wearing goggles and surgical masks if they're lucky. These pits are typically run by private contractors; OSHA guidelines mean little to nothing here. Your tax dollars at work.

5

My first night in Iraq, I remember looking west from my trailer and being surprised to see a sunset of blazing orange. It was at least two hours after dusk, and the stars were out, at least a couple anyway. Then I realized that *that wasn't sunlight I was seeing*—that it was *flames*. Those weren't clouds I was seeing, but rather smoke. I didn't know what all that was yet, only that it took up half the northern sky. But oh, I learned. The first thing I learned about was the smell, like burning oak-leaves mixed with scorched plastic and warping aluminum. Wood, fabric, paper, metal—if it burned, they burnt it. If not, they threw something on it until it did. On a clear day it threw smoke a half-mile high; on the cold days during the rainy season, October through March, the flames got tamped down by the constant downpour. Made the world smell like a half-smoked cigarette, all wet soot and chemicals. Made you gag passing through it on your way to the motor pool. During the summer months the ashes blew into the town just north of us, a little two-rut burg called Yethrib. Turned the air gray, sent hot embers raining down on the farmers' fields. Sitting in a tower on a weeklong rotation of guard-duty, I remember watching one day as some hundred-odd acres of sunflower, sorghum, and lentils went up in flames. An entire season's crops destroyed, in a part of the country where the median income was two dollars a day.

6

* * *

I remember convoying home from bridge-sites late at night; I used to peer over the steering-wheel and look for the banded floodlights, the blood-red haze of smoke. Waste never sleeps. On a bulletin-board in my platoon's Ops office, I remember they'd posted a memo signed by two Air-Force lieutenants-colonel. The memo cited the effects of long-term exposure to the smoke, expressed outrage at the lack of incinerators, ordered the memo posted in every company headquarters, every permanent file of every soldier in service on that base. I'm sure that memo's still in my record somewhere; then again, the VA does have a tendency to lose things.

7

I saw a lot of strange, scary, moving things during my time deployed. Sunrises over the Tigris, Sumerian ruins, farmers praying in their fields at dawn. But the image that sticks with me is the burn-pit. Why? Maybe because the sight of all that waste, made tangible, left some mark on me, like tracking mud on floors as a guest, uninvited. War is consumption, I've realized. Conspicuous consumption. It's embarrassing, really: this is the democracy we bring to a foreign nation, consumption and waste. Look at all we've got. Fast-food, electronics, medicine. You can't have any, and we're going to burn it all right in front of you.

8

(continued)

(continued)

9   You know, the last night I was writing this I pulled up Google Earth, pinned down where I was posted. Our old motor-pool was taken down, bulldozed over; our old living-areas and trailers had been carted away. Even the burn-pit was silent, but it still sits there, like a grease-stain you can see from the air. Big sign in English: "NO DUMPING," it says, while behind it sits a mountain of blackened, twisted steel. The Balad pit may sit quiet now, but I'll bet even money those fires are still going elsewhere.

10   All day. Every day. The smoke of consumption, of Empire.

Evaluating the Essay

Discuss or write about your response to Seth Marlin's essay, using some or all of the following questions.

1. What do you understand this essay to be saying about war, empire, and waste? Where does it say it most clearly or memorably?

2. Throughout this chapter, I've promoted the idea that personal essays have two narrators—the now-narrator and the then-narrator. Are they both present in "Smoke of Empire"? Where?

3. What is the main thing you might take away from reading this piece and apply when you write or revise your own personal essay?

4. This piece was written to be heard rather than read, and the writer assumed that it would be heard only once. Imagine this rhetorical situation: You're in the car listening to the radio driving to campus and you hear Seth reading "Smoke of Empire." Because he's not in the car with you, you don't have to be polite. You don't even know him. You can change the station if what you hear doesn't interest you. What special demands does this situation make on *how* a personal essay is written? How might it affect the writing and organization of a piece?

Using What You Have Learned

Let's revisit the list of things at the beginning of this chapter that I hoped you'd learn.

1. **Use personal experiences and observations to drive inquiry.** Even before you read this chapter, you've told stories about yourself—we all do all the time—but it rarely occurs to us that these stories can be a source of insight even in some academic situations. The questions that drive our inquiry into

how we understand our lives are no less important than the questions that inspire us to explore other subjects. In fact, Montaigne, the first essayist, believed that self-knowledge is the most important knowing of all.

2. **Apply the exploratory thinking of personal essays to academic writing.** Next time you get a writing assignment in another class, start the work by "essaying" the topic—by developing a quick list of questions and responding to them. One great template for exploring almost any topic is a relationship question: What is the relationship between _____ and _____? For example, "What is the relationship between tutoring programs for college athletes and academic success?" Rather than trying to come up with a quick answer, spend some time fastwriting to find out what *you* think based on what you've read, heard, experienced, or observed. What you discover might lead to a thesis later.

3. **Identify the characteristics of personal essays in different forms.** Personal essays lend themselves to different forms, and if you know what a personal essay looks like, you can write yours in one of these different forms. Some of the most vibrant examples of the genre are podcasts, radio essays, or photographic essays. With the availability of free software for digitally recording your voice, publishing an essay online is easier than ever. The blog is also an extremely popular new form of the personal essay. Though these media can work with almost any form of writing, they seem to lend themselves especially to autobiographical work. There's something about hearing the writer's voice in a podcast or the easy intimacy of the blog that encourages personal essays.

4. **Use invention strategies to discover and develop a personal essay topic.** When I suggest using invention strategies, I mean this in two ways. First, you can use techniques such as fastwriting and clustering to discover a topic for personal writing. But perhaps more important, you can use such invention techniques to generate *insight*—not just an idea about something to write about, but discoveries about what you think about that topic.

5. **Apply revision strategies that are effective for shaping narratives.** The story—whether it's a recollection of what happened or our experience observing what is happening—is one of the most basic ways we all organize information: This happened, and then this, and then this…Yet chronology isn't always the best way to organize information from experience in writing, and, more important, story isn't just about what happened. It's also a "narrative of thought," or the story of what we now make of what happened. Even if you never write another personal essay, you can use narrative to tell the story of what you first thought about a subject and what you came to understand.

Complete Additional Exercises and Practice on this chapter in your MyLab

Text Credits

Credits are listed in order of appearance.

"Every Morning for Five Years" by Laura Zazulak. Reprinted by permission of the author.

"One More Lesson" is reprinted with permission from the publisher of Silent Dancing: A Partial Remembrance of a Puerto Rican Childhood by Judith Ortiz Cofer (© 1990 Arte Publico Press–University of Houston).

"This I Believe," is a registered trademark of This I Believe, Inc. Used with permission.

Photo Credits

Credits are listed in order of appearance.

Photo 1: Bruce Ballenger

Photo 2: Originally published in the Unexpected World of Nature # 3 (Thirteen/WNET, 2008). Copyright © 2008 Josh Neufeld

Photo 3: "Mable" Laura Zazulak

Photo 4: Lauren Fleishman Photography

Photo 5: Rottenman/Fotolia

Inquiring into the Details icon. Frederick Bass/Getty Images

One Student's Response icon. Purestock/Getty Images

Writing Beyond the Classroom icon. Fuse/Getty Images

Guide to MLA Style

Appendix A contains guidelines for preparing your essay in the format recommended by the Modern Language Association, or MLA, a body that, among other things, decides documentation conventions for papers in the humanities. The information here reflects the most recent changes by the MLA, as described in the group's definitive reference for students, the *MLA Handbook for Writers of Research Papers,* 7th edition. By the way, the American Psychological Association (APA) is a similar body for the social sciences, with its own documentation conventions. You will find it fairly easy to switch from one system to the other once you've learned both (Table 1, summarizes the important differences). Appendix A covers MLA conventions.

Checklist Before Handing in a Paper in MLA Style

- My paper has a title but no separate title page (unless my instructor has said otherwise).
- My name, the instructor's name, the course, and the date are in the upper left-hand corner of the first page.
- All my pages are numbered using my last name next to the appropriate page number.
- My Works Cited list begins on a new page.
- Everything, including my Works Cited page(s), is double-spaced.
- Every page of the paper's text is readable.
- There are no commas in my parenthetical citations between the author's name and the page number.
- All my parenthetical citations are *before* the periods at the ends of sentences, unless the citation appears at the end of a blocked quote.
- The entries in my Works Cited page(s) are listed alphabetically, and every line after the first one in an entry is indented a half inch.

Part One of this appendix, "Citing Sources in Your Essay," will be particularly useful as you write your draft; it provides guidance on how to parenthetically cite the sources you use in the text of your essay. Part Two, "Formatting Your Essay," will help you with formatting the manuscript, something you will likely focus on after revising; it includes guidelines for margins, pagination, and tables, charts, and illustrations. Part Three, "Preparing the Works Cited Page," offers detailed instructions on how to prepare your bibliography at the end of your essay; this is usually one of the last steps in preparing the final manuscript. Finally, Part Four presents a sample research essay in MLA style, which will show you how it all comes together.

Directory of MLA Style

Citing Sources in Your Essay

1.2.1   When You Mention One Author
1.2.2   When You Mention More Than One Author
1.2.3   When There Is No Author
1.2.4   Works by the Same Author
1.2.5   Works by Different Authors with the Same Name
1.2.6   Indirect Sources
1.2.7   Personal Interviews
1.2.8   Several Sources in a Single Citation
1.2.9   An Entire Work
1.2.10 A Volume of a Multivolume Work
1.2.11 A Literary Work
1.2.12 An Online Source

Preparing the Works Cited Page

3.2 Citing Books, in Print and Online

3.2.1   A Book with One Author
3.2.2   A Book with Two or Three Authors
3.2.3   A Book with More Than Three Authors
3.2.4   Several Books by the Same Author
3.2.5   An Entire Collection or Anthology
3.2.6   A Work in a Collection or Anthology
3.2.7   An Introduction, Preface, Foreword, or Prologue
3.2.8   A Book with No Author
3.2.9   An Encyclopedia Article
3.2.10 A Book with an Institutional Author
3.2.11 A Book with Multiple Volumes
3.2.12 A Book That Is Not a First Edition
3.2.13 A Book Published Before 1900
3.2.14 A Translation
3.2.15 Government Documents

3.2.16 A Book That Was Republished

3.3 Citing Articles, in Print and Online

3.3.1 A Journal or Magazine Article

3.3.2 A Newspaper Article

3.3.3 An Article with No Author

3.3.4 An Editorial

3.3.5 A Letter to the Editor

3.3.6 A Review

3.3.7 An Abstract

3.4 Citing Web Pages and Other Online Sources

3.4.1 A Web Site or Page from a Web Site

3.4.2 An Online Posting

3.4.3 An E-mail Message

3.4.4 A Sound Clip or Podcast

3.4.5 An Online Video

3.4.6 An Interview

3.4.7 A Blog Entry or Blog Comment

3.4.8 An Online Image

3.5 Citing Other Sources

3.5.1 An Interview

3.5.2 Surveys, Questionnaires, and Case Studies

3.5.3 Recordings

3.5.4 Television and Radio Programs

3.5.5 Films, Videos, and DVDs

3.5.6 Artwork

3.5.7 An Advertisement

3.5.8 Lectures and Speeches

3.5.9 Pamphlets

Part One: Citing Sources in Your Essay

1.1 When to Cite

Before examining the details of how to use parenthetical citations, remember when you must cite sources in your paper:

1. Whenever you quote from an original source
2. Whenever you borrow ideas from an original source, even when you express them in your own words by paraphrasing or summarizing
3. Whenever you borrow from a source factual information that is *not common knowledge*

The Common Knowledge Exception

The business about *common knowledge* causes much confusion. Just what does this term mean? Basically, *common knowledge* means facts that are widely known and about which there is no controversy.

Sometimes, it's really obvious whether something is common knowledge. The fact that the Super Bowl occurs in late January or early February and pits the winning teams from the American Football Conference and National Football Conference is common knowledge. The fact that President Ronald Reagan was once an actor and starred in a movie with a chimpanzee is common knowledge, too. But what about Carolyn's assertion that most dreaming occurs during rapid eye movement (REM) sleep? This is an idea about which all of her sources seem to agree. Does that make it common knowledge?

It's useful to ask next, How common to whom? Experts in the topic at hand or the rest of us? As a rule, consider the knowledge of your readers. What information will not be familiar to most of your readers or may even surprise them? Which ideas might even raise skepticism? In this case, the fact about REM sleep and dreaming goes slightly beyond the knowledge of most readers, so to be safe, it should be cited. Use common sense, but when in doubt, cite.

1.2 The MLA Author/Page System

The Modern Language Association (MLA) uses the author/page parenthetical citation system.

The Basics of Using Parenthetical Citation

The MLA method of in-text parenthetical citation is fairly simple: As close as possible to the borrowed material, you indicate in parentheses the original source (usually, the author's name) and the page number in the work that material came from. For example, here's how you'd cite a book or article with a single author using the author/page system:

```
From the very beginning of Sesame Street
in 1969, kindergarten teachers discovered that
incoming students who had watched the program
already knew their ABCs (Chira 13).*
```

The parenthetical citation here tells readers two things: (1) This information about the success of *Sesame Street* does not

---

*This and the following "Works Cited" example are used with permission of Heidi R. Dunham.

originate with the writer but with someone named *Chira,* and (2) readers can consult the original source for further information by looking on page 13 of Chira's book or article, which is cited fully at the back of the paper in the Works Cited. Here is what readers would find there:

```
                     Works Cited

Chira, Susan. "Sesame Street at 20: Taking

     Stock." New York Times 15 Nov. 1989: 13.

     Print.
```

Here's another example of a parenthetical author/page citation, from another research paper. Note the differences from the previous example:

```
"One thing is clear," writes Thomas Mallon,

"plagiarism didn't become a truly sore point

with writers until they thought of writing as

their trade.... Suddenly his capital and iden-

tity were at stake" (3-4).
```

The first thing you may have noticed is that the author's last name—Mallon—was omitted from the parenthetical citation. It didn't need to be included because it had already been mentioned in the text. *If you mention the author's name in the text of your paper, then you only need to parenthetically cite the relevant page number(s).* This citation also tells us that the quoted passage comes from two pages rather than one.

Placement of Citations. Place the citation as close as you can to the borrowed material, trying to avoid breaking the flow of the sentences, if possible. To avoid confusion about what's borrowed and what's not—particularly if the material you're borrowing spans more than a sentence—when possible mention the name of the original author *in your paper* in a way that clarifies what you've borrowed. Note that in the next example the writer simply cites the source at the end of the paragraph, not naming the source in the text. As a result, it is hard for the reader to figure out whether

Citations That Go with the Flow

There's no getting around it: Parenthetical citations can be like stones on the sidewalk. Readers stride through a sentence in your essay and then have to step around the citation at the end before they resume their walk. Yet citations are important in academic writing because they help readers know who you read or heard that shaped your thinking. And you can write your citations in such a way that they won't trip up readers. As a result, your essay will be more readable. Try these techniques:

- Avoid lengthy parenthetical citations by mentioning the name of the author in your essay. That way, you usually only have to include a page number in the citation.
- Try to place citations where readers are likely to pause anyway—for example, at the end of the sentence or right before a comma.
- Remember you *don't* need a citation when you're citing common knowledge or referring to an entire work by an author.
- If you're borrowing from only one source in a paragraph of your essay, and all of the borrowed material comes from a single page of that source, don't repeat the citation over and over again with each new bit of information. Just put the citation at the end of the paragraph.

Blager is the source of the information in the entire paragraph or just in part of it:

> Though children who have been sexually abused
> seem to be disadvantaged in many areas,
> including the inability to forge lasting
> relationships, low self-esteem, and crippling
> shame, they seem advantaged in other areas.
> Sexually abused children seem to be more
> socially mature than other children of their
> same age group. It's a distinctly mixed
> blessing (Blager 994).

In the following example, notice how the ambiguity about what's borrowed and what's not is resolved by careful placement of the author's name and parenthetical citation in the text:

> Though children who have been sexually abused
> seem to be disadvantaged in many areas,
> including the inability to forge lasting rela-
> tionships, low self-esteem, and crippling shame,
> they seem advantaged in other areas. Accord-
> ing to Blager, sexually abused children seem to
> be more socially mature than other children of
> their same age group (994). It's a distinctly
> mixed blessing.

In this latter version, it's clear that Blager is the source for one sentence in the paragraph, and the writer is responsible for the rest. When you first mention authors, use their full name, and when you mention them again, use only their last names. Also note that the citation is placed *before* the period of the sentence (or last sentence) that it documents. That's almost always the case, except at the end of a blocked quotation, where the parenthetical reference is placed *after* the period of the last sentence. The citation can also be placed near the author's name, rather than at the end of the sentence, if it doesn't unnecessarily break the flow of the sentence. For example:

> Blager (994) observes that sexually abused chil-
> dren tend to be more socially mature than other
> children of their same age group.

1.2.1 WHEN YOU MENTION ONE AUTHOR

It's generally good practice in research writing to identify who said what. The familiar convention of using attribution tags such as "According to Fletcher,..." or "Fletcher argues..." and so on helps readers attach a name with a voice or an individual with certain claims or findings. As just discussed, when you mention the author of a source in your sentence, the parenthetical citation includes only the page number. For example,

> Robert Harris believes that there is "widespread uncertainty" among students about what constitutes plagiarism (2).

As was also discussed, the page number could come directly after the author's name.

> Robert Harris (2) believes that there is "widespread uncertainty" among students about what constitutes plagiarism.

1.2.2 WHEN YOU MENTION MORE THAN ONE AUTHOR

Often your sources will have more than one author. If the book or article has two or three authors, list all their last names in the parenthetical citation, with *and* before the final author; for example:

> (Oscar and Leibowitz 29)

If your source has more than three authors, you can either list them all or use the first author and *et al.*:

> (Kemp et al. 199)

1.2.3 WHEN THERE IS NO AUTHOR

Occasionally, you may encounter a source whose author is anonymous—that is, who isn't identified. This isn't unusual with pamphlets, editorials, government documents, some newspaper articles, online sources, and short filler articles in magazines. If you can't parenthetically name the author, what do you cite?

Most often, cite the title (or an abbreviated version, if the title is long) and the page number. If you abbreviate the title, begin with the word under which it is alphabetized in the Works Cited list. For example:

> Simply put, public relations is "doing good and getting credit" for it (*Getting Yours* 3).

Here is how the publication cited above would be listed at the back of the paper:

Works Cited

Getting Yours: A Publicity and Funding Primer

    for Nonprofit and Voluntary Organizations.

    Lincoln: Contact Center, 2008. Print.

As with other sources, for clarity, it's often helpful to mention the original source of the borrowed material in the text of your paper. Refer to the publication or institution (e.g., the American Cancer Society or Department of Defense) you're citing or make a more general reference to the source. For example:

An article in *Cuisine* magazine argues that the

best way to kill a lobster is to plunge a knife

between its eyes ("How to Kill" 56).

or

According to one government report, with the

current minimum size limit, most lobsters end up

on dinner plates before they've had a chance to

reproduce ("Size" 3-4).

Note the abbreviation of the article titles; for example, the full title for "How to Kill," listed in the Works Cited, is "How to Kill a Lobster." Note also that article titles are in quotation marks and book titles are italicized.

1.2.4 WORKS BY THE SAME AUTHOR

Suppose you end up using several books or articles by the same author. Obviously, a parenthetical citation that merely lists the author's name and page number won't do because it won't be clear *which* of several works the citation refers to. In this case, include the author's name, an abbreviated title (if the original is too long), and the page number. For example:

The thing that distinguishes the amateur from

the experienced writer is focus; one "rides off

in all directions at once," and the other finds

```
one meaning around which everything revolves

(Murray, Write to Learn 92).
```

The Works Cited list would show multiple works by one author as follows:

```
                    Works Cited

Murray, Donald M. Write to Learn. 8th ed. Boston:

    Heinle, 2004. Print.

---. A Writer Teaches Writing. Boston:

    Heinle, 2004. Print.
```

It's obvious from the parenthetical citation which of the two Murray books is the source of the information. Note that in the parenthetical reference, no punctuation separates the title and the page number, but a comma follows the author's name. If Murray had been mentioned in the text of the paper, his name could have been dropped from the citation.

How to handle the Works Cited list is explained more fully later in this appendix, but for now, notice that the three hyphens used in the second entry signal that the author's name in this source is the same as in the preceding entry.

1.2.5 WORKS BY DIFFERENT AUTHORS WITH THE SAME NAME

How do you distinguish between different authors who have the same last name? Say you're citing a piece by someone named Lars Anderson as well as a piece by someone named Kelli Anderson. The usual in-text citation, which uses the last name only (Anderson 2), wouldn't help the reader much. In this situation, add the author's first initial to the citation: (L. Anderson 2) or (K. Anderson 12).

1.2.6 INDIRECT SOURCES

Whenever you can, cite the original source for material you use. For example, if an article on television violence quotes the author of a book and you want to use the quote, try to hunt down the book. That way, you'll be certain of the accuracy of the quote and you may find some more usable information.

Sometimes, however, finding the original source is not possible. In those cases, use the term *qtd. in* to signal that you've quoted or paraphrased material that was quoted in your source and initially appeared elsewhere. In the following example, the citation signals that the quote from Bacon was in fact culled from an article by Guibroy, rather than from Bacon's original work:

> Francis Bacon also weighed in on the dangers of imitation, observing that "it is hardly possible at once to admire an author and to go beyond him" (qtd. in Guibroy 113).

1.2.7 PERSONAL INTERVIEWS

If you mention the name of your interview subject in your text, no parenthetical citation is necessary. If you don't mention the subject's name, cite it in parentheses after the quote:

> The key thing when writing for radio, says one journalist, is to "write to the sound if you've got great sound, and read your stuff aloud" (Tan).

Regardless of whether you mention your subject's name, you should include a reference to the interview in the Works Cited. In this case, the reference would look like this:

> Works Cited
>
> Tan, Than. Personal interview. 28 Jan. 2011.

1.2.8 SEVERAL SOURCES IN A SINGLE CITATION

Suppose two sources both contributed the same information in a paragraph of your essay. Or, even more likely, suppose you're summarizing the findings of several authors on a certain topic—a fairly common move when you're trying to establish a context for your own research question. How do you cite multiple authors in a single citation? Use author names and page numbers as usual, and separate them with a semicolon. For example,

> A whole range of studies have looked closely at the intellectual development of college students, finding that they generally assume

```
"stages" or "perspectives" that differ from sub-
ject to subject (Perry 122; Belenky et al. 12).
```

Sample Parenthetical References for Other Sources

MLA format is pretty simple, and we've already covered some of the basic variations. You should also know the following five additional variations:

1.2.9 AN ENTIRE WORK

If you mention an author's name and his or her work in the text but don't refer to specific details, no citation is necessary. The work should, however, be listed in the Works Cited. For the following example, Edel's book would be listed in the Works Cited.

```
Leon Edel's Henry James is considered by many to
be a model biography.
```

1.2.10 A VOLUME OF A MULTIVOLUME WORK

If you're working with one volume of a multivolume work, it's a good idea to mention which volume in the parenthetical reference. The citation below attributes the passage to the second volume, page 3, of a work by Baym and other authors. The volume number is always followed by a colon, which is followed by the page number:

```
By the turn of the century, three authors
dominated American literature: Mark Twain,
Henry James, and William Dean Howells (Baym
et al. 2: 3).
```

1.2.11 A LITERARY WORK

Because so many literary works, particularly classics, have been reprinted in so many editions, and readers are likely using different editions, it's useful to give readers information about where a passage can be found regardless of edition. You can do this by listing not only the page number but also the chapter number—and any other relevant information, such as the section or volume—separated from the page number by a semicolon. Use arabic rather than roman numerals.

```
Izaak Walton warns that "no direction can be
given to make a man of a dull capacity able to
make a Flie well" (130; ch. 5).
```

When citing poems or plays, instead of page numbers, cite line numbers for poems and act, scene, and line numbers, separated with periods, for plays. For example, (Othello 2.3.286) indicates act 2, scene 3, line 286 of that play.

1.2.12 AN ONLINE SOURCE

If you're using material from a book on your Kindle or iPad, you'll notice that there are "location numbers" or percentages rather than page numbers. (Other e-text devices may have page numbers.) And you've probably already noticed that many online documents don't have page numbers or don't have permanent ones. What should you do when you want to cite sources that don't have page numbers?

When a document or Web page lacks permanent page numbers, you can cite just the author, but you may be able to alert readers to a more general location: "In the first chapter, Payne argues that...." If the source is authorless, the citation would just include a title, as in this citation of an article from the Web:

```
Many women who wait to begin a family may won-
der if prior birth control choices negatively
affect their fertility. It's not uncommon, for
instance, for a woman to take oral contracep-
tives for 10 years or longer. The birth control
pill itself doesn't affect long-term fertility
("Infertility: Key Q and A").
```

On the other hand, PDF files frequently have permanent pagination, particularly if the document is a copy of the original article. In that case, the page numbers should be used in your citation.

Part Two: Formatting Your Essay

2.1 The Layout

There is, well, a certain fussiness associated with the look of academic papers. The reason for it is quite simple—academic disciplines generally aim for consistency in format so that readers of scholarship know exactly where to look to find what they want to know. It's a matter of efficiency. How closely you must follow the MLA's requirements for the layout of your essay is up to your instructor, but it's really not that complicated. A lot of what you need to know is featured in Figure A1.

2.1.1 PRINTING

Print your paper on white, 8½ × 11-inch paper. Make sure the printer has sufficient ink or toner.

2.1.2 MARGINS AND SPACING

The old high school trick is to have big margins so you can get the length without the information. Don't try that trick with this paper. Leave one-inch margins at the top, bottom, and sides of your pages. Indent the first line of each paragraph a half inch, and indent

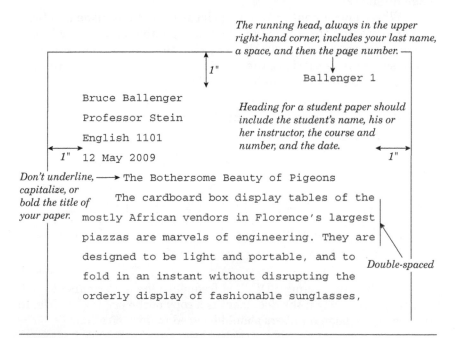

FIGURE 1   The Basic Look of an MLA-Style Paper

blocked quotes an inch. Double-space all of the text, including blocked quotes and Works Cited.

2.1.3 TITLE

Your paper doesn't need a separate title page; the title will go on your first page of text. On that page, one inch from the top on the upper left-hand side, type your name, your instructor's name, the course name and number, and the date. Below that, type the title, centered on the page. Begin the text of the paper below the title. For example:

```
Karoline Ann Fox

Professor Dethier

English 401

15 December 2008
            Metamorphosis, the Exorcist,
                  and Oedipus
Ernst Pawel has said that Franz Kafka's The
Metamorphosis...*
```

Note that everything is double spaced. The title is not italicized (although italics would be used for the name of a book or other work that should be italicized), underlined, or boldfaced.

2.1.4 HEADER WITH PAGINATION

Make sure that every page is numbered. That's especially important with long papers. Type your last name and the page number in the upper right-hand corner, flush with the right margin: `Ballenger 3`. Don't use the abbreviation *p.* or a hyphen between your name and the number.

2.1.5 PLACEMENT OF TABLES, CHARTS, AND ILLUSTRATIONS

With MLA format, papers do not have appendixes. Tables, charts, and illustrations are placed in the body of the paper, close to the text that refers to them. Number tables and charts consecutively (Table 1, Table 2, and so on; Fig. 1, Fig. 2, and so on; notice the abbreviation of "Figure"). Place the title of a table above it, flush left. Place the caption for a chart or illustration below it. For tables, charts, and illustrations that are borrowed, give full citations. This

---

*Reprinted with permission of Karoline A. Fox.

Table 1
Percentage of Students Who Self-Report Acts of Plagiarism

Acts of Plagiarism	Never/ Rarely	Some- times	Often/ Very Freq.
Copy text without citation	71	19	10
Copy paper without citation	91	5	3
Request paper to hand in	90	5	2
Purchase paper to hand in	91	6	3

Source: Scanlon, Patrick M., and David R. Neumann; "Internet Plagiarism among College Students," *Journal of College Student Development* 43.3 (2002): 379. Print.

FIGURE 2 Example of Format for a Table.

information goes at the bottom of a table or at the end of a caption for a chart or illustration. See Figure A2 for an example of a table formatted according to MLA guidelines.

2.2 Some Style Considerations

2.2.1 HANDLING TITLES

The general MLA rule for capitalization of titles is that the writer should capitalize the first letters of all principal words in a title, including any that follow hyphens. Words not capitalized include articles (*a, an,* and *the*), prepositions (*for, of, in, to,* and so on), coordinating conjunctions (*and, or, but, for*), and *to* in infinitives. However, these words are capitalized if they appear at the beginning or end of the title.

In May 2008, the MLA updated its citation style, and among the changes is a no-brainer in this era of word processing: a shift to *italicizing* titles of works rather than <u>underlining</u> them. The APA figured this out about a decade ago.

The new rules for deciding whether to italicize a title or place it in quotation marks (the usual alternative) makes this distinction:

1. If the work is "published independently," italicize it. These works are typically books, Web sites, online databases, TV broadcasts, plays, periodicals, and so on.
2. If the title is part of a larger work—say, an article in a periodical or an episode of a TV program—then place it in quotation marks.

Here are some examples:

The Curious Researcher (book)

A Streetcar Named Desire (play)

"Once More to the Lake" (essay in a collection)

New York Times (newspaper)

"Psychotherapy" (encyclopedia article)

"Funny Talking Animals" (YouTube clip)

2.2.2 STYLE RELATED TO SOURCES AND QUOTATIONS

Names.   Though it may seem as if you're on familiar terms with some of the authors you cite by the end of your research project, it's not a good idea to call them by their first names. Give the full names of people you cite when you first mention them, and then give only their last names if you mention them again.

Ellipsis Points.   Those are the three dots (or four if the omitted material comes at the end of a sentence where they join a period) that indicate you've left out a word, phrase, or even whole section of a quoted passage. It's wise to use ellipsis points and omit material when you want to emphasize part of a quotation and don't want to burden your reader with unnecessary information, but be careful to preserve the basic intention and idea of the author's original statement. Ellipsis points can come at the beginning of a quotation, in the middle, or at the end, depending where it is you've omitted material. For example,

> "After the publication of a controversial
> picture that shows, for example, either dead
> or grieving victims . . ., readers in telephone
> calls and in letters to the editor, often
> attack the photographer for being tasteless . . ."
> (Lesser 56).

Quotations.   Quotations that run more than four lines long should be blocked, or indented one inch from the left margin. The first sentence of any paragraphs within a blocked quotation should be indented an additional quarter inch. The quotation should be double spaced. Quotation marks should not be used. The parenthetical citation is placed *after* the period at the end of the quotation. A colon is a customary way to introduce a blocked quotation. For example,

> Chris Sherman and Gary Price, in *The Invisible Web*, contend that much of the Internet, possibly most, is beyond the reach of researchers who use conventional search engines:
>
> > The problem is that vast expanses of the Web are completely invisible to general-purpose search engines like AltaVista, HotBot, and Google. Even worse, this "Invisible Web" is in all likelihood growing significantly faster than the visible Web that you're familiar with. It's not that search engines and Web directories are "stupid" or even badly engineered. Rather, they simply can't "see" millions of high-quality resources that are available exclusively on the Invisible Web. So what is this Invisible Web and why aren't search engines doing anything about it to make it visible? (xxi)

Part Three: Preparing the Works Cited Page

The Works Cited page ends the paper. (This may also be called the "References Cited" or "Sources Cited" page, depending on the preference of your instructor.) Occasionally, instructors may want another kind of source list along with or instead of a Works Cited list: An "Annotated List of Works Cited" includes a brief description of each source; a "Works Consulted" list includes not only the sources you cited but also others that shaped your thinking; a "Content Notes" page, keyed to superscript numbers in the text of the paper, lists short asides that are not central enough to the discussion to be included in the text itself.

The Works Cited page is the workhorse of most college papers. Works Cited is essentially an alphabetical listing of all the sources you quoted, paraphrased, or summarized in your paper. If you have used MLA format for citing sources, your paper has numerous parenthetical references to authors and page numbers. The Works Cited page provides complete information on each source cited in the text for the reader who wants to know. (In APA format, this page is called "References" and is slightly different in how items are listed.)

3.1 Format

Alphabetizing the List

Works Cited follows the text of your paper on a separate page. After you've assembled complete information about each source you've cited, put the sources in alphabetical order by the last name of the author. If the work has multiple authors, alphabetize by the last name of the first one listed. If the source has no author, then alphabetize it by the first key word of the title. If you're citing more than one source by a single author, you don't need to repeat the name for each source; simply place three hyphens followed by a period (- - - .) for the author's name in subsequent listings.

Indenting and Spacing

Type the first line of each entry flush left, and indent subsequent lines of that entry (if any) a half inch. Double-space between each line and each entry. For example:

Hall 10

Works Cited

Biernacki, Patrick. *Pathways from Heroin Addic-*
tion. Philadelphia: Temple UP, 1986. Print.

Brill, Leon. *The De-Addiction Process.* Spring-
field: Thomas, 1972. Print.

Epstein, Joan F., and Joseph C. Gfroerer. "Heroin
Abuse in the United States." *National Clear-*
inghouse for Alcohol and Drug Information.

US Dept. of Health and Human Services,

    Aug. 1997. Web. 24 Nov. 2008.

Hall, Lonny. Personal interview. 1 Mar. 2009.

Kaplan, John. *The Hardest Drug: Heroin and Pub-*

    lic Policy. Chicago: U of Chicago P, 1983.

    Print.

"Methadone." *Encyclopaedia Britannica.* 1999 ed.

    1999. CD-ROM.

Shaffner, Nicholas. *Saucerful of Secrets: The*

    Pink Floyd Odyssey. New York: Dell, 1992.

    Print.

Strang, John, and Michael Gossop. *Heroin Addic-*

    tion and Drug Policy: The British System.

    New York: Oxford UP, 1994. Print.

Swift, Wendy, et al. "Transitions between Routes

    of Heroin Administration: A Study of Cauca-

    sian and Indochinese Users in South-Western

    Sydney, Australia." *Addiction* (1999): 71-82.

    Print.

3.2 Citing Books, in Print and Online

You usually need three pieces of information to cite a book: the name of the author or authors, the title, and the publication information. Information you need to cite for an online text depends on whether the book is also available in print. The following chart shows the basics for citing in-print and electronic books.

CITING A BOOK IN PRINT	CITING AN E-BOOK
1. Author(s)	1. Author(s)
2. *Title*	2. *Title*
3. Edition and/or volume (if relevant)	3. Edition and/or volume (if relevant)

(continued)

4. Where published, by whom, and date	4. If also in print, where published, by whom, and date; in any case, sponsoring organization, date of electronic publication
5. Medium: Print	5. Medium: Web
	6. Date of access
SAMPLE CITATION: BOOK IN PRINT	**SAMPLE CITATION: E-BOOK (WEB ONLY)**
Donald, David H. *Lincoln.* New York: Simon & Schuster, 1995. Print.	Lincoln, Abraham. *The Writings of Abraham Lincoln.* B & R Samizdat Express, 2009. Web. 28 Jan. 2011.

Author(s). Authors' names should appear as they do in the source. Only list an author's name with initials if it appears that way on the title page. You don't need to include titles or degrees that sometimes follow an author's name (e.g., Diana Rosenstein PhD).

Title. As a rule, the titles of books are italicized, with capitalization of the first letters of the first word and all principal words, including in any subtitles. Titles that are not italicized are usually those of pieces found within larger works, such as poems and short stories in anthologies. These titles are set off by quotation marks. Titles of religious works (the Bible, the Koran) are neither italicized nor enclosed within quotation marks. (See the guidelines in "Handling Titles," in Part Two.)

Edition. If a book doesn't indicate any edition number, then it's probably a first edition, a fact you don't need to cite. Look on the title page. Signal an edition like this: *2nd ed., 3rd ed.,* and so on. If you're citing a multivolume work, include the total number of volumes in the citation following the book's title, using the abbreviation *vols.* (e.g. 2 vols.).

Publication Information. For any book that has been published in print, this includes place, publisher, and date. Look on the title page to find out who published the book. Publishers' names are usually shortened in the Works Cited list; for example, *St. Martin's Press, Inc.,* is shortened to *St. Martin's.*

What publication place to cite may be unclear when several cities are listed on the title page. Cite the first one. For books published outside the United States, add the country name along with the city to avoid confusion.

The date a book is published is usually indicated on the copyright page. If several dates or several printings by the same publisher are listed, cite the original publication date. However, if the book is a revised edition, give the date of that edition. One final variation: If you're citing a book that's a reprint of an original edition, give both dates. For example:

```
Stegner, Wallace. Recapitulation. 1979. Lincoln:

    U of Nebraska P, 1986. Print.
```

This book was first published in 1979 and then republished in 1986 by the University of Nebraska Press.

Online books also often appear in print, and in such cases your citation will include all the usual print publication information. For all online books you must give the date of electronic publication and the organization that is sponsoring the electronic text. These organizations range from commercial sponsors like Amazon to nonprofit groups like Project Gutenberg. You can usually find the name of the sponsor either on the text itself or on the Web page from which you downloaded it.

Medium.   Following the publication information, you indicate the medium—Print or Web. Capitalize the word and follow it with a period.

Date of Access.   For electronic sources, the citation also includes the date you accessed the title. In the example that follows, notice the form for the date, as well as the print publication information and the sponsoring organization:

```
Badke, William. Research Strategies: Finding

    Your Way Through the Information Fog.

    Lincoln: Writers Club P, 2000. iUniverse.

    Web. 12 July 2008.
```

Page Numbers.   Normally, you don't list page numbers of a book in your Works Cited. The parenthetical reference in your paper specifies the particular page or pages the material you borrowed is from. But if you use only part of a book—an introduction or an essay— list the appropriate page numbers following the publication date.

A period should follow the page numbers. Notice in this example that if the author(s) or editor(s) of the entire work also wrote the introduction or essay you're citing, the second mention in that citation uses last name only:

> Lee, L. L., and Merrill Lewis. Preface. *Women,*
>
>   *Women Writers, and the West.* Ed. Lee and
>
>   Lewis. Troy: Whitston, 1980. v-ix. Print.

Sample Book Citations

The examples that follow show the form for some common variations on the basic book citation format just shown. Although most of the examples are for printed books, the corresponding online sources work in much the same way. Remember that for an online source you would give print publication information if the source has also been published in print and would in any case give the sponsoring organization and date of electronic publication, indicate Web as the medium, and give the date of access.

3.2.1 A BOOK WITH ONE AUTHOR

> Armstrong, Karen. *The Spiral Staircase.* New
>
>   York: Knopf, 2004. Print.

In-Text Citation: (Armstrong 22)

3.2.2 A BOOK WITH TWO OR THREE AUTHORS

If a book has two authors, give the second author's names uninverted.

> Ballenger, Bruce, and Michelle Payne. *The Curi-*
>
>   *ous Reader.* New York: Longman, 2006. Print.

In-Text Citation: (Ballenger and Payne 14)

Cite a book with three authors like this:

> Bloom, Lynn Z., Donald A. Daiker, and Edward M.
>
>   White, eds. *Composition Studies in the New*

Millenium. Carbondale: Southern Illinois
UP, 2003.

In-Text Citation: (Bloom, Daiker, and White 200)

3.2.3 A BOOK WITH MORE THAN THREE AUTHORS

If a book has more than three authors, you may list the first and substitute the term *et al.* for the others.

Jones, Hillary, et al. *The Unmasking of Adam*.
Highland Park: Pegasus, 1992. Print.

In-Text Citation: (Jones et al. 21-30)

3.2.4 SEVERAL BOOKS BY THE SAME AUTHOR

Baldwin, James. *Tell Me How Long the Train's Been*
Gone. New York: Dell-Doubleday, 1968. Print.
---. *Going to Meet the Man*. New York: Dell-
Doubleday, 1948. Print.

In-Text Citation: (Baldwin, *Going* 34) or (Baldwin,
Tell Me How Long 121)

3.2.5 AN ENTIRE COLLECTION OR ANTHOLOGY

Crane, R. S., ed. *Critics and Criticism: Ancient*
and Modern. Chicago: U of Chicago P, 1952.
Print.

In-Text Citation: (Crane xx)

3.2.6 A WORK IN A COLLECTION OR ANTHOLOGY

The title of a work in a collection should be enclosed in quotation marks. However, if the work was originally published as a book, its title should be italicized.

Jones, Robert F. "Welcome to Muskie Country." *The Ultimate Fishing Book*. Ed. Lee

Eisenberg and DeCourcy Taylor. Boston: Houghton, 1981. 122-34. Print.

In-Text Citation: (Jones 131)

Bahktin, Mikhail. *Marxism and the Philosophy of Language. The Rhetorical Tradition.* Ed. Patricia Bizzell and Bruce Herzberg. New York: St. Martin's, 1990. 928-44. Print.

In-Text Citation: (Bahktin 929-31)

3.2.7 AN INTRODUCTION, PREFACE, FOREWORD, OR PROLOGUE

Scott, Jerie Cobb. Foreword. *Writing Groups: History, Theory, and Implications.* By Ann Ruggles Gere. Carbondale: Southern Illinois UP, 1987. ix-xi. Print.

In-Text Citation: (Scott x-xi)

Rich, Adrienne. Introduction. *On Lies, Secrets, and Silence.* By Rich. New York: Norton, 1979. 9-18. Print.

In-Text Citation: (Rich 12)

3.2.8 A BOOK WITH NO AUTHOR

Merriam-Webster Dictionary Online. Encyclopedia Britannica, 2011. Web. 8 Feb. 2011.

In-Text Citation: (*Merriam-Webster* 444)

3.2.9 AN ENCYLOPEDIA ARTICLE

"City of Chicago." *Encyclopaedia Britannica.* 1999 ed. Print.

In-Text Citation: ("City of Chicago" 397)

For online encyclopedias, as for other online sources, include the name of the sponsor of the Web site and the date you accessed the site. Notice the in-text citation for this source without page numbers.

"Diarrhea." *Columbia Encyclopedia Online.* 6th

ed. Columbia UP, 2008. Web. 10 June 2008.

In-Text Citation: ("Diarrhea")

Wikipedia raises eyebrows among many academics who don't consider it a particularly authoritative source, but should you need to cite it, include the date and time of the latest revision of the page you're citing. You can find that date at the bottom of the page.

"Flesh Fly." *Wikipedia.* Wikimedia Foundation, 27

January 2011. Web. 28 January 2011.

In-Text Citation: ("Flesh Fly")

3.2.10 A BOOK WITH AN INSTITUTIONAL AUTHOR

Hospital Corporation of America. *Employee Bene-*

fits Handbook. Nashville: HCA, 2004. Print.

In-Text Citation: (Hospital Corporation of America 5-7)

3.2.11 A BOOK WITH MULTIPLE VOLUMES

If you are using material from more than one volume of a multivolume work, include the number of volumes in the work between the title and publication information. In your in-text citations, indicate the relevant volume.

Baym, Nina, ed. *The Norton Anthology of American*

Literature. 6th ed. 2 vols. New York:

Norton, 2002. Print.

In-Text Citation: (Baym 2: 3)

If you use only one volume of a multivolume work, indicate which one along with the page numbers. The in-text citation includes only the page number.

> Baym, Nina, ed. *The Norton Anthology of American*
>
> *Literature.* 6th ed. Vol 2. New York:
>
> Norton, 2002. Print.

In-Text Citation: (Baym 1115)

3.2.12 A BOOK THAT IS NOT A FIRST EDITION

Check the title page to determine whether the book is an edition other than the first (2nd, 3rd, 4th, etc.); if no edition number is mentioned, assume it's the first. Put the edition number right after the title.

> Ballenger, Bruce. *The Curious Researcher.* 5th
>
> ed. Boston: Longman, 2007. Print.

In-Text Citation: (Ballenger 194)

Citing the edition is necessary only for books that are *not* first editions. This includes revised editions (*Rev. ed.*) and abridged editions (*Abr. ed.*).

3.2.13 A BOOK PUBLISHED BEFORE 1900

For a book published before 1900, it's usually unnecessary to list the publisher.

> Hitchcock, Edward. *Religion of Geology.* Glasgow,
>
> 1851. Print.

In-Text Citation: (Hitchcock 48)

3.2.14 A TRANSLATION

> Montaigne, Michel de. *Essays.* Trans. J. M.
>
> Cohen. Middlesex: Penguin, 1958. Print.

In-Text Citation: (Montaigne 638)

3.2.15 GOVERNMENT DOCUMENTS

Because of the enormous variety of government documents, citing them properly can be a challenge. Because most government documents do not name authors, begin an entry for such a source with the level of government (United States, State of Illinois, etc., unless it is obvious from the title), followed by the sponsoring agency, the title of the work, and the publication information. Look on the title page to determine the publisher. If it's a federal document, then the Government Printing Office (abbreviated *GPO*) is usually the publisher.

```
United States. Bureau of the Census. Statistical

    Abstract of the United States. Washington:

    GPO, 1990. Print.
```

In-Text Citation: (United States, Bureau of the Census 79-83)

3.2.16 A BOOK THAT WAS REPUBLISHED

A fairly common occurrence, particularly in literary study, is to find a book that was republished, sometimes many years after the original publication date. In addition, some books first appear in hard cover and then are republished in paperback. To cite one, put the original date of publication immediately after the book's title, and then include the more current publication date, as usual, at the end of the citation. Do it like so:

```
Ballenger, Bruce, and Barry Lane. Discover-

    ing the Writer Within: 40 Days to More

    Imaginative Writing. 1989. Shoreham:

    Discover Writing P, 2008. Print.
```

In-Text Citation: (Ballenger and Lane 31)

3.3 Citing Articles, in Print and Online

Citations for articles from periodicals—magazines, newspapers, journals, and other such publications that appear regularly—are similar to those for books but include somewhat different information.

As with books, citations for online articles have their own special requirements. The following chart shows, in the appropriate order, the elements for citations for a print article and an article from the Web or your library's online databases. As the following pages show, the elements actually included vary a bit depending on specifics of the source.

PRINT ARTICLE	ARTICLE FROM A DATABASE OR THE WEB
1. Author(s)	1. Author(s)
2. "Article Title"	2. "Article Title"
3. *Periodical Title*	3. *Periodical Title*
4. Volume and issue	4. Volume and issue
5. Date published	5. Date published
6. Page numbers	6. Page numbers, if any (usually present in versions also in print)
7. Medium: Print	7. *Database* or Sponsor
	8. Medium: Web
	9. Date of access
SAMPLE CITATION: PRINT ARTICLE	**SAMPLE CITATION: DATABASE ARTICLE**
Martinello, Marian L. "Learning to Question for Inquiry." *Educational Forum* 62 (1998): 164-71. Print.	Greenebaum, Jessica B. "Training Dogs and Training Humans: Symbolic Interaction and Dog Training." *Anthrozoos: An Interdisciplinary Journal of the Interactions of People & Animals* 23.2 (2010): 129-41. *ArticleFirst*. Web. 28 Jan. 2011.

Author(s). List the author(s)—one, two, or three or more—as you would for a book citation.

Article Title. Unlike book titles, which are italicized, article titles are usually enclosed in quotation marks. Capitalize same as book citations.

Periodical Title. Italicize periodical names, dropping introductory articles (*Aegis*, not *The Aegis*). Capitalize as for book citations. If you're citing a newspaper your readers may not be familiar with, include in the title—enclosed in brackets but not italicized—the city in which it was published. For example:

> MacDonald, Mary. "Local Hiker Freezes to Death."
>
> *Foster's Daily Democrat* [Dover, NH] 28 Jan.
>
> 1992: 1. Print.

Volume Number. Most academic journals are numbered as volumes (or, occasionally, feature series numbers); the volume number should be included in the citation. Popular periodicals sometimes have volume numbers, too, but these are not included in the citations. Indicate the volume number immediately after the journal's name. Omit the tag *vol.* before the number.

Issue Number. Most scholarly journals have issue numbers as well as volume numbers. Include the issue number in your citation if one is given. Follow the volume number with a period and then the issue number, with no spaces. Volume 12, issue 1, would appear in your citation as "12.1."

Date(s). When citing popular periodicals (newspapers, magazines, and so on), include the day, month, and year of the issue you're citing—in that order—following the periodical name. Academic journals are a little different. Because the issue number indicates when the journal was published within a given year, just indicate that year. Put it in parentheses following the volume number and before the page numbers. For example,

> Elstein, David. "Training Dogs to Smell Off-
>
> Flavor in Catfish." *Agricultural Research*
>
> 52.4 (2004): 10.

Electronic-source citations usually include two dates: the date of publication and the date of access (when you visited the site and retrieved the document). There is a good reason for listing both dates: Online documents are changed and updated frequently—when you retrieved the material matters.

Page Numbers. The page numbers of the article follow the volume and issue or date. Just list the pages of the entire article, omitting abbreviations such as *p.* or *pp.* It's common for articles in newspapers and popular magazines *not* to run on consecutive pages. In that case, indicate the page on which the article begins, followed by a "+": (12+).

Newspaper pagination can be peculiar. Some papers wed the section (usually a letter) with the page number (A4); other papers simply begin numbering anew in each section. Most, however, paginate continuously. See the following sample citations for newspapers for how to deal with these peculiarities.

Online sources, which often have no pagination at all, present special problems. If the article you're using from an online source also appeared in print, then you'll often find the same page numbers that are in the print version. But if an article appeared only online and has no page numbers, all you can do is signal that's the case, using the abbreviation *n. pag.* (no pages).

Databases. The availability of full-text versions of many articles through the campus library's databases makes it possible for researchers to retrieve materials without hiking to the library. In recent years these databases have evolved to be highly user friendly, not only enabling researchers to easily search multiple databases at once but also offering them nifty features like citation formatting. Citations for an article you've found on such a database should contain the same information as one for the print version, with the addition of the name of the database (in italics). Here's an example:

> Winbush, Raymond A. "Back to the Future: Campus Racism in the 21st Century." *Black Collegian* Oct. 2001: 102-03. *Expanded Academic ASAP.* Web. 12 Apr. 2002.

In-Text Citation: (Winbush 102)

When citing an abstract from a library database, include the word "abstract" in the citation. For example,

> Erskine, Ruth. "Exposing Racism, Exploring Race." *Journal of Family Therapy* 24

```
(2002): 282-97. Abstract. EBSCO Online

    Citations. Web. 3 Dec. 2002.
```

In-Text Citation: (Erskine)

Medium. As with books, indicate the medium of the source (Print, Web).

Sample Periodical Citations

3.3.1 A JOURNAL OR MAGAZINE ARTICLE

Cite articles from print magazines like this (notice that for a monthly magazine only the month and year are given):

```
Oppenheimer, Todd. "The Computer Delusion."

    Atlantic Monthly July 1997: 47-60. Print.
```

In-Text Citation: (Oppenheimer 48)

```
Zimmer, Marc. "How to Find Students' Inner

    Geek." Chronicle of Higher Education 12

    Aug. 2005: B5. Print.
```

In-Text Citation: (Zimmer B5)

Cite print journal articles like this:

```
Allen, Rebecca E., and J. M. Oliver. "The

    Effects of Child Maltreatment on Language

    Development." Child Abuse and Neglect 6.2

    (1982): 299-305. Print.
```

In-Text Citation: (Allen and Oliver 299-300)

Online articles usually come from either a library database or a periodical's Web site. The key thing you need to know is whether the article is online only or also appeared in print, as in the latter case you need to include information on the print version as well.

Cite an article that appeared online only like this:

Beyea, Suzanne C. "Best Practices of Safe Medi-

  cine Administration." *AORN Journal* Apr.

  2005. Web. 26 Aug. 2005.

In-Text Citation: (Beyea)

For this document without page or paragraph numbers, simply give the author's name. Or avoid parenthetical citation altogether by mentioning the name of the source in your essay (for example: "According to Suzanne Beyea, medications are . . .").

Cite an online article that also appeared in print like this (this example is from a library database):

Liu, Eric Zhi Feng, and Chun Hung Liu. "Devel-

  oping Evaluative Indicators for Educa-

  tional Computer Games." *British Journal*

  of Educational Technology 40.1 (2009):

  174-78. *Academic Search Complete.* Web.

  5 Feb. 2009.

In-Text Citation: (Liu and Liu 174)

3.3.2 A NEWSPAPER ARTICLE

Some newspapers have several editions (late edition, national edition), each of which may contain different articles. If an edition is listed on the masthead, include it in the citation.

Mendels, Pamela. "Internet Access Spreads to

  More Classrooms." *New York Times* 1 Dec.

  1999, late ed.: C1+. Print.

In-Text Citation: (Mendels C1)

Some papers begin numbering pages anew in each section. In that case, include the section number if it's not part of pagination.

Brooks, James. "Lobsters on the Brink." *Portland*
Press 29 Nov. 1999, sec. 2: 4. Print.

In-Text Citation: (Brooks 4)

Increasingly, full-text newspaper articles are available online using library databases such as Newspaper Source or through the newspapers themselves. As when citing other online articles, you'll need to include the database in italics if you used a database (e.g., *Newspaper Source*) and the date of access.

Cite a newspaper article from a database like this:

"Lobsterman Hunts for Perfect Bait." *AP Online* 7
July 2002. *Newspaper Source*. Web. 13 July
2008.

In-Text Citation: ("Lobsterman")

An entry for an article from a newspaper's Web site would include both the title of the online site (in italics) and the name of the publication, even if they're the same, as in this example:

Wiedeman, Reeves. "A Playwright Whose Time Seems
to Be Now." *New York Times*. New York Times.
9 Feb. 2011. Web. 10 Feb. 2011.

In-Text Citation: (Reeves)

3.3.3 AN ARTICLE WITH NO AUTHOR

"The Understanding." *New Yorker* 2 Dec. 1991:
34-35. Print.

In-Text Citation: ("Understanding" 35)

3.3.4 AN EDITORIAL

"Paid Leave for Parents." Editorial. *New York*
Times 1 Dec. 1999: 31. Print.

In-Text Citation: ("Paid Leave" 31)

To cite an editorial found online, include date of access. Unsigned editorials would begin with the title.

McGurn, William. "Obama, Religion, and the Pub-
    lic Square." Editorial. *WSJ.com*. Wall Street
    Journal. 8 June 2008. Web. 10 June 2008.

In-Text Citation: (McGurn)

3.3.5 A LETTER TO THE EDITOR

Ault, Gary Owen. "A Suspicious Stench." Letter.
    Idaho Statesman 18 Aug. 2005: 14. Print.

In-Text Citation: (Ault 14)

Wood, Bradford. "Living with a Disability, in a
    Caring Setting." Letter. *Washington Post*.
    27 Jan. 2011. Web. 28 Jan. 2011.

In-Text Citation: (Wood)

3.3.6 A REVIEW

Page, Barbara. Rev. of *Allegories of Cinema:
    American Film in the Sixties*, by David E.
    James. *College English* 54 (1992): 945-54.
    Print.

In-Text Citation: (Page 945-46)

O'Connell, Sean. "Beauty Is as Bardam Does."
    Rev. of *Biutiful*. *WashingtonPost.com*.
    Washington Post. 28 Jan. 2011. Web. 28
    January, 2011.

In-Text Citation: (O'Connell)

3.3.7 AN ABSTRACT

It's usually better to have the full text of an article for research purposes, but sometimes all you can come up with is an abstract, or short summary of the article that highlights its findings or summarizes its argument. Online databases frequently offer abstracts when they don't feature full-text versions of an article.

To cite an abstract, begin with information about the full version, and then include the information about the source from which you got the abstract. Unless the title of the source makes it obvious that what you are citing is an abstract (i.e., as with *Psychological Abstracts*), include the word "abstract" after the original publication information, but don't italicize it or put it in quotation marks. In this example, the source of the abstract is a periodical database:

```
Edwards, Rob. "Air-raid Warning." New Scientist
     14 Aug. 1999: 48-49. Abstract. MasterFILE
     Premier. Web. 1 May 2009.
```

In-Text Citation: (Edwards)

The following citation is from the print version of *Dissertation Abstracts International,* a useful source of abstracts (notice that the word "abstract" isn't needed because this source just contains abstracts):

```
McDonald, James C. "Imitation of Models in the
     History of Rhetoric: Classical, Belletris-
     tic, and Current-Traditional." U of Texas,
     Austin. DAI 48 (1988): 2613A. Print.
```

In-Text Citation: (McDonald 2613A)

3.4 Citing Web Pages and Other Online Sources

3.4.1 A WEB SITE OR PAGE FROM A WEB SITE

If you're citing a Web site, you're referring to either the entire site or a particular page. A citation for an entire Web site includes the author's name, though it's rare for an entire site to have identifiable authors. Lacking an author or compiler, begin with the Web site's name (in italics), the sponsoring organization and date published, medium of publication, and date of access. For example,

> *Son of Citation Machine.* Landmark Project, 2009.
>
> Web. 12 Feb. 2009.

In-Text Citation: (*Son of Citation Machine*)

More commonly, though, you'll be citing a page on a Web site, and this must include, along with all the Web site information mentioned above, the title of the Web page itself (in quotation marks). Begin with the author of the Web page, if there is one, as in this example:

> Rogers, Scott. "The Stupid Vote." *The Conserva-*
>
> *tive Voice.* Salem Web Network, 7 June 2008.
>
> Web. 10 June 2008.

In-Text Citation: (Rogers)

Here's a citation for a page with an institutional sponsor rather than an author:

> "ESL Instructors and Students." *The OWL at*
>
> *Purdue.* Purdue Online Writing Lab, 2011.
>
> Web. 8 Feb. 2011.

In-Text Citation: ("ESL Instructors")

Finally, here is a citation for a Web page with no author or institutional sponsor (notice it begins with the title of the Web site):

> "Urban Wildlands." Center for Biological
>
> Diversity, n.d. Web. 28 Jan. 2011.

In-Text Citation: ("Urban Wildlands")

3.4.2 AN ONLINE POSTING

An online post can be a contribution to an e-mail discussion group like a listserv, a post to a bulletin board or usenet group, or an entry on a WWW forum. The description "Online posting" is included if there is no title. (The title is usually drawn from the message subject line). List the author's name, Web site name, the date the material was posted, the medium, and the access date, as you would for other online citations.

> Justin, Everett. "Team Teaching in Writing-
>
>   Intensive Courses in a Science Context."
>
>   *Writing Program Administration Listserv*
>
>   Arizona State University, 29 Jan. 2011.
>
>   Web. 8 Feb. 2011.

In-Text Citation: (Justin)

3.4.3 AN E-MAIL MESSAGE

> Kriebel, David. "Environmental Address." Message
>
>   to the author. 8 June 2008. E-mail.

In-Text Citation: (Kriebel)

3.4.4 A SOUND CLIP OR PODCAST

Cite an audio clip from a Web site like this:

> Gonzales, Richard. "Asian American Political
>
>   Strength." *Morning Edition.* Natl. Public
>
>   Radio, 27 May 2008. Web. 12 July 2008.

In-Text Citation: (Gonzales)

A citation for a podcast should explicitly say that is the medium. For example,

> Johnson, Roberta. "Climate Changes, People
>
>   Don't." *This American Life.* Natl.
>
>   Public Radio, 14 Jan. 2011. Podcast.
>
>   8 Feb. 2011.

In-Text Citation: (Johnson)

3.4.5 AN ONLINE VIDEO

"Daughter Turns Dad In." Online video clip. *CNN.*

  com. Cable News Network, 4 Apr. 2008. Web.

  10 Apr. 2008.

In-Text Citation: ("Daughter Turns")

Shimabukuro, Jake. "Ukelele Weeps by Jake Shima-

  bukuro." Online video clip. *YouTube.* You

  Tube, 4 Apr. 2008. Web. 6 Apr. 2008.

In-Text Citation: (Shimabukuro)

3.4.6 AN INTERVIEW

Boukreev, Anatoli. Interview. *Outside.* Mariah

  Media, 14 Nov. 2007. Web. 27 May 2008.

In-Text Citation: (Boukreev)

3.4.7 A BLOG ENTRY OR BLOG COMMENT

For a blog entry, include the author's name (or screen name), title of the entry, the phrase "Weblog entry," name of the blog, sponsoring organization (if any), date of update, the medium, and your date of access.

Dent, Shirley. "Written on the Body: Literary

  Tattoos." Weblog entry. *The Blog: Books.*

  Guardian News and Media, 9 June 2008. Web.

  10 June 2008.

In-Text Citation: (Dent)

If you want to cite a comment on a blog—and sometimes they're pretty interesting—then include the author's name (or screen name); a title, if there is one, or the first few words of the post if there isn't one; "Weblog comment"; and the date it was posted. Then include the information on the blog that is the subject of the comment.

MargotBlackSheep. "Tattoos Exist in Every Cul-
     ture." Weblog comment. 10 June 2008. Dent,
     Shirley. "Written on the Body: Literary
     Tattoos." *The Blog: Books.* Guardian News
     and Media, 9 June 2008. Web. 10 June 2008.

In-Text Citation: (MargotBlackSheep)

3.4.8 AN ONLINE IMAGE

Online images often don't give you much to go on. If there is a name of the artist and a title of the image, include them. If not, at least describe the image, and include the name of the sponsoring organization or site and when you downloaded it.

"China Town Engulfed." Online image. 12 May 2008.
     BBC News. BBC, 8 June 2008. Web. 10 June
     2008.

3.5 Citing Other Sources

3.5.1 AN INTERVIEW

If you conducted the interview yourself, list your subject's name first, indicate what kind of interview it was (telephone interview, e-mail interview, or personal interview), and provide the date.

Hall, Lonny. Personal interview. 1 Mar. 2005.

In-Text Citation: (Hall)

Or avoid parenthetical reference altogether by mentioning the subject's name in the text: According to Lonny Hall, ...

If you're citing an interview done by someone else (perhaps from a book or article) and the title does not indicate that it was an interview, you should include it after the subject's name. Always begin the citation with the subject's name.

Stegner, Wallace. Interview. *Conversations with
     Wallace Stegner.* By Richard Eutlain and
     Wallace Stegner. Salt Lake: U of Utah P,
     1990. Print.

In-Text Citation: (Stegner 22)

3.5.2 SURVEYS, QUESTIONNAIRES, AND CASE STUDIES

If you conducted the survey or case study, list it under your name and give it an appropriate title.

Ball, Helen. "Internet Survey." Boise State U,

1999. Print.

In-Text Citation: (Ball)

3.5.3 RECORDINGS

Generally, list a recording by the name of the performer and italicize the title. Also include the recording company, and year. (If you don't know the year, use the abbreviation *n.d.*. Include the medium (CD, Audiocassette, LP, etc.).

Orff, Carl. *Carmina Burana.* Cond. Seiji Ozawa.

Boston Symphony. RCA, n.d. CD.

In-Text Citation: (Orff)

When citing a single song from a recording, put it in quotation marks:

Larkin, Tom. "Emergence." *Oceans.* Enso,

1997. CD.

In-Text Citation: (Larkin)

3.5.4 TELEVISION AND RADIO PROGRAMS

List the title of the program (italicized), the station, and the date. If the episode has a title, list that first in quotation marks. You may also want to include the name of the narrator or producer after the title.

All Things Considered. Interview with Andre

Dubus. Natl. Public Radio. WBUR, Boston,

12 Dec. 1990. Radio.

In-Text Citation: (*All Things Considered*)

"U.S. to Limit Sales Related to Amphetamine

Scourge." *All Things Considered.* Natl.

Public Radio. WBUR, Boston, 18 Aug. 2005.

Radio.

In-Text Citation: ("U.S. to Limit")

3.5.5 FILMS, VIDEOS, AND DVDS

Begin with the title (italicized), followed by the director, the distributor, and the year. You may also include names of writers, performers, or producers. End with the date and any other specifics about the characteristics of the film or video that may be relevant (length and size).

Saving Private Ryan. Dir. Steven Spielberg.

Perf. Tom Hanks, Tom Sizemore, and Matt

Damon. Paramount, 1998. Videocassette.

In-Text Citation: (*Saving*)

You can also list a video or film by the name of a contributor you'd like to emphasize.

Capra, Frank, dir. *It's a Wonderful Life.* Perf.

Jimmy Stewart and Donna Reed. RKO Pictures,

1946. Film.

In-Text Citation: (Capra)

3.5.6 ARTWORK

List each work by artist. Then cite the title of the work (italicized), the year of its creation, and where it's located (institution and city). If you've reproduced the work from a published source, include that information as well.

Homer, Winslow. *Casting for a Rise.* 1889. Hirschl

and Adler Galleries, New York. *Ultimate*

Fishing Book. Ed. Lee Eisenberg and DeCourcy

Taylor. Boston: Houghton, 1981. Print.

In-Text Citation: (Homer 113)

3.5.7 AN ADVERTISEMENT

To cite an advertisement in a periodical, first list the company behind the ad, then the word "Advertisement," and then the publication information.

```
Volkswagen. Advertisement. Men's Health August
     2005: 115. Print.
```

In-Text Citation: (Volkswagen)

3.5.8 LECTURES AND SPEECHES

List the name of the speaker, followed by the title of the address (if any) in quotation marks, the name of the sponsoring organization, the location, and the date. Also indicate what kind of address it was (lecture, speech, etc.).

```
Naynaha, Siskanna. "Emily Dickinson's Last
     Poems." Sigma Tau Delta, Boise, 15 Nov.
     2011. Lecture.
```

In-Text Citation: Avoid the need for parenthetical citation by mentioning the speaker's name in your text.

```
In her presentation, Naynaha argued that
Dickinson...
```

3.5.9 PAMPHLETS

Cite a pamphlet as you would a book.

```
New Challenges for Wilderness Conservationists.
     Washington: Wilderness Society, 1973.
     Print.
```

In-Text Citation: (New Challenges)

Note: If no page numbers are listed, use *n. pag.*

Part Four: Student Paper in MLA Style

Ashley Carvalho's essay, "Patching Up Belfast," is a compelling research essay on the innovations in trauma care that emerged from decades of death during the conflict between Catholics and Protestants in Northern Ireland. During a semester abroad in Ireland, Ashley experienced the legacy of the conflict firsthand—through the colorful murals on public buildings, the lingering tension on the faces of Belfast residents, and, most of all, the words of several of the doctors who cared for victims. She combines first-hand observations, interviews, and other research to tell an amazing story of the courage and inventiveness of Belfast's health care providers, particularly those at Royal Victoria Hospital, which was at the epicenter of the violence. "Patching Up Belfast" is an inspiring example of how a writer can take a personal experience and use research to make it richer and more meaningful for both reader and writer.

Ashley Carvalho

Prof. Jill Heney

English 201

10 November 2010

Patching Up Belfast

It was May of 1972, and from his vantage point in a pub on the Malone Road, Colin Russell saw the thick, inky pall of smoke erupt and curdle blackly over Belfast city center. Mere seconds had gone by when, right on cue, the pub's telephone trilled. Before the barman could answer, before his ruddy face could pale slightly, and even before his eyes could flash uneasily to Colin and his mouth could speak the words "Dr. Russell, it's for you," Colin knew by the sinking feeling in his gut that it was the hospital, calling him in despite the fact he was off duty. It wasn't the first time this scenario had happened, and, disturbingly, it wouldn't be the last. "Tell them I'm on my way"—and Colin was out the door, leaving behind an untouched pint and a pubful of people expecting the worst.

Take a walk down any major West Belfast thoroughfare, particularly near the Catholic Falls and Protestant Shankill roads, and you'll see Northern Ireland's history splashed vividly

Ashley uses a "scene lead" to dramatize the purpose of her essay—an examination of the medical innovations that came from the tragedy of northern Ireland's "Troubles."

Carvalho 2

onto walls, sides of houses and buildings, like so many pages torn from a giant coloring book. The infamous political
murals of West Belfast illustrate a range
of visceral emotions: vengeance, hatred,
sorrow, desperation, and, above all, fe-
rocious pride. Even before the Troubles,
mural-painting had been a conduit of
self-expression for Belfast natives, but
the way these sentiments are expressed
has changed over the years. At the height
of the conflict, the sentiments behind
the murals that sprang up almost over-
night were those of aggression and anger.
Nowadays, new murals continue to appear
almost weekly, but most focus on moving
toward a brighter, more peaceful future,
not only for Belfast, but also for the
world (see fig. 1).

Just as art can be inspired by tragedy, the violence and wartime atmosphere
of the Troubles have also resulted in the
creation of some of the most innovative
medical treatments the world has seen, and
it is this violence that provided a stimulus to Northern Ireland's hospitals to
make progress in medicine. Like the mural
painters, Northern Ireland's doctors and
surgeons expressed their frustration and

Carvalho 3

Fig. 1 Graffiti, Peace Wall, Belfast.

despair through their work. From something bad, they created good.

Although the deep-seated divide between Catholics and Protestants frequently put Northern Ireland in national news headlines from 1968 onward, the roots of sectarianism—the opposition between Nationalist Catholics and Unionist Protestants in Northern Ireland—date back to the seventeenth century, to the time of Oliver Cromwell. In 1649, Cromwell led English forces in an invasion of Ireland to suppress Catholic power, and,

Images can enhance a paper if they add something to the discussion.

Carvalho 4

within three years, Cromwell's forces defeated the major Irish cities and their armies (Bardon 140-1). This paved the way for English and Scottish Protestants to begin settling in the North of Ireland, alongside the Irish Catholics who already inhabited the area. With the close proximity of Catholics and Protestants concentrated in the North, the stage was set for the sectarianism that fueled the fire of the Troubles, and still lingers in today's Belfast.

Throughout the Troubles, Catholics and Protestants were seemingly at loggerheads, pitted against one another, which leads to the common misconception that the Troubles was primarily a religious conflict. But the religious identity of these groups is a secondary association; the conflict is predominantly political. Republican and Nationalist parties envision a united Ireland that includes Northern Ireland and is independent of British influence, whereas Loyalists and Unionists desire Northern Ireland to remain a part of the powerful United Kingdom and separate from the Republic of Ireland (McKittrick and McVea 26-28).

Here Ashley addresses an assumption that she believes most readers share about her topic. It's not that simple, she suggests, and then explains why.

Carvalho 5

In 1968, the violence of the Troubles began with several small sparks born from a housing allocation dispute that soon became a full-fledged conflagration, and Northern Ireland's history was to be forever transformed (McKittrick and McVea 40-4). Over the next three decades, violence raged in streets and city centers throughout Northern Ireland, resulting in casualties of a type and scale previously unseen in Northern Ireland's hospitals. In a setting where only one murder had been recorded in the preceding decade, Northern Ireland's hospitals were suddenly inundated with Troubles victims as the civil conflict became a part of daily life (D'Sa 51). Over the thirty-year period of the Troubles, nearly 3,600 people were killed, and over ten times that number injured as a result of the violence (McKittrick and McVea 324-8). From a medical perspective, numbers of this magnitude are difficult to cope with in any capacity, and Northern Ireland's hospitals had to quickly mobilize the resources, personnel, and expertise to face the violence of the Troubles head-on.

Dr. Colin Russell is not a superhero, and he doesn't claim to be. As a surgeon who worked in Belfast's Royal Victoria

Carvalho 6

Fig. 2 Royal Victoria Hospital, Belfast.

Hospital (see fig. 2) during the peak of the Troubles, Russell witnessed almost daily the tragedy of lives left wrecked by human hands, but rarely does he lose his composure speaking about his memories. In fact, I can't help but smile along with him as he remembers not the horror but the exhilaration, the sheer thrill of playing a healing role in the Troubles. In the sitting room of his spacious, secluded South Belfast home, Russell and his wife, Pat, sit opposite me. "I would be dishonest if I denied that there was an excitement about working during the Troubles." Russell says, opting for a conversational interview rather than a rigid question-and-answer session.

If you use figures or tables in your paper, make sure you refer to them in the text.

Carvalho 7

"At night, there was an almost wartime atmosphere prevailing in the hospital. We were only people, confined together, under pressure, and emotions ran high. But us doctors, we were not immune to getting upset" (Russell).

In his mid-seventies now, Russell's face still retains a youthful quality, a perpetual, boyish eagerness for education and understanding. For Russell, the time of the Troubles was a hands-on learning experience. He began his postgraduate schooling not as a surgeon, but as a dentist. After completing a five-year dentistry course at Queen's University Belfast, Russell realized as the course progressed that the aspect of dentistry that interested him most was surgery. Upon gaining a post as a dental surgeon in the Royal Victoria Hospital, Russell became increasingly frustrated; with his dental degree, he simply didn't have enough education and expertise to work in the hospital's surgical wards. So, in 1967, he went back to Queen's University, this time as a medical student. Graduating in 1971, just as the brewing political turmoil began to froth and boil over, Russell was appointed to the surgical house staff of the Royal Victoria, and the

Carvalho 8

bulk of his surgical training and career
was spent at the Royal Victoria during the
height of the Troubles—specifically, the
1970s and early 1980s.

The outbreak of the Troubles was a
critical moment, a point of no return, not
only for Russell but also for countless
other medical trainees working in Belfast's hospitals at the turn of the decade. Speak to any of these individuals,
and the odds are that they can pinpoint
the exact moment when, for them, everything changed. Siobhan,* a doctor at both
the Royal Victoria and Belfast City hospitals, attributes her life-changing moment to the introduction of internment. On
August 9, 1971, Northern Ireland's prime
minister demanded the large-scale arrest
and imprisonment, without trial, of suspected IRA members in the hopes that civil
violence would lessen with the IRA locked
away. Siobhan, only a junior doctor at the
time, recalls what August 9, 1971, symbol-
ized for her:

> I remember looking out from the second
> floor of the West wing of the Roy-
> al Victoria, where my bedroom was at

*Name has been changed at the request of the interviewee.

Carvalho 9

that time, and seeing scores of troop
carriers arrive silently, in the dead
of night. One minute, Dunville Park
across the road was as it ever was.
The next moment, it was surrounded
by a host of camouflaged vehicles,
silently moving in and taking their
places in a massed migration influx.
My life, our lives, would never be
the same again. Like seeing Kennedy
shot, like seeing a man land on the
moon, like seeing the Twin Towers
falling, it was a salient moment in
history, one which I will never forget.

Quotations that are four or more sentences are "blocked" by indenting one inch from the left margin. And, by the way, what a great quotation!

As the largest and best-equipped
hospital in all of Northern Ireland, the
Royal Victoria experienced a recurring influx of patients injured in riots, and
the hospital's proximity to the Falls Road
meant that it was often the center
of the riot zones. In the nearly thirty
years of violence, the Royal Victoria accommodated victims of rioting
episodes almost nightly (Clarke 114-8).
These were peppered in between frequent
terrorist bombings, and the combination
of the two types of incidents produced a
steady stream of casualties. Secondly, and

equally problematic, was the need for the
hospital and its employees to remain neu-
tral throughout the conflict. This proved
difficult for some, particularly during
the many high-stress, emotionally charged
incidents the violence of the Troubles
produced. Many of the injured that arrived
in the hospital's Accident and Emergency
Department following a bombing or shoot-
ing were friends or relatives of the medical personnel. Still others who sought
medical care from the hospital were para-
militaries or members of a wrongdoing sec-
tarian gang. Within the highly politicized
milieu of the Troubles, where one's religious and political views could be figured
out just by learning one's name (during
the Troubles and even today, a Gerald
O' Callahan or an Aisling Murphy would be
categorized as a Republican Irish Catholic
while a Richard Carrington or an Elizabeth Montgomery would be assumed a Unionist Protestant), shrugging off the shroud
of politics and throwing on the neutrality
cloak wasn't exactly easy. But healthcare
providers in Northern Ireland sidestepped
this difficulty and continued to provide
high-quality, nonbiased healthcare to the
injured.

Carvalho 11

In the hospital ward, medical personnel looked after civilians, terrorists,
freedom fighters, innocent bystanders,
policemen, and soldiers alike, curious but
never aware of who was who, or who fired
the deadly bullet or detonated the lethal
bomb, or who was Catholic or Protestant.
In tense situations, Siobhan focused on
her work: "I learned very early on to be
apolitical and to never, ever comment on
any political incident one way or another,
to my colleagues or to my patients.
My role was to care always and to cure
if possible."

The most catastrophic weapon
appeared on the stage of the Troubles
at the end of 1971. Worried that the British army would not be able to contain the
IRA, and wanting to exercise their newfound
strength, the loyalist Ulster Volunteer
Force (UVF) in conjunction with the Ulster
Defense Association (UDA) placed a fifty-
pound bomb in a small North Belfast Catholic pub called McGurk's Bar. The explosion
killed fifteen people and injured many more
(McKittrick and McVea 75). This incident
marked the debut of the bomb as a means for
paramilitary organizations to influence
Belfast's street politics.

Carvalho 12

Bombings provided a sizeable stimulus to Belfast's healthcare services in two ways: first, to develop a system that could provide comprehensive care to the sheer numbers of those injured in a bombing incident and, second, to create new methods of treatment to address the variety of injuries produced in a bomb blast. For example, the McGurk's Bar bombing resulted in a wide range of injury patterns, the worst of which included crush injuries, burn injuries, cranial injuries, lacerations from projectiles, and carbon monoxide poisoning (Gillespie 37-40).

Regarded as the most violent year of the Troubles, 1972 brought with it an unparalleled level of violence, and the state of civil conflict in Northern Ireland closely resembled civil war. The events of this year placed a higher strain on Belfast's hospital services than any other year of the Troubles, not necessarily because the incidents of violence were the most catastrophic, but because they occurred with an unpredictable and terrifying frequency. One month into the year, the infamous Bloody Sunday in Londonderry left thirteen dead and another thirteen injured when British troops openly fired upon a

A sentence like this firmly reattaches the essay to its thesis much like a tack pins down loose fabric so that it keeps its shape.

large illegal march. Enraged, Republican
supporters bolstered the IRA with money,
guns, and men, and violence was loosed upon
the streets throughout Northern Ireland
(Coogan 674-5). Riots, shootings, and
bombings began to occur with alarming regu-
larity. On March 4th, the IRA slipped a
six-pound bomb inside one of the shopping
bags carried by two sisters. Having decided
to stop for tea, the girls, unknowingly
carrying the bomb, entered the Abercorn,
a popular restaurant in Belfast city center. The girls were killed immediately and
at least one hundred others were injured
(Gillespie 47-9). For the first time in its
history, the Royal Victoria used a documented disaster plan to care for the masses
of the injured (McKittrick and McVea 78).

Bomb injuries presented an entirely
new set of challenges to Belfast's hospitals. Colin Russell, who worked in the
Royal Victoria that day, recalled that
mass-casualty on this large a scale was
an entirely new experience, one that the
hospital and its staff weren't totally
ready for. "There were horrific injuries," Russell remembers. Making matters
worse, this particular bomb was designed
to explode outward, rather than upward as

Carvalho 14

most bombs do, and the shockwaves from
the blast careened along the Abercorn's
wooden floors. Trying to contain my horror, I winced inwardly as Russell showed
me some slides containing photographs of
the horrific injuries that came into the
Royal that day: a chair leg shot through
someone's thigh, pieces of an amputated
limbs placed on green towels in the surgical wards, unable to be reunited with
the bodies of their owners, faces charred
beyond recognition. But none of this prepared me for the emotional shock that came
next from Russell's memories: "I remember
the senior anesthetist who was on call at
the time, working on one of the victims
of the bombing in the operating room. He
was completely unaware of the fact that
the two sisters who were carrying the bomb
and who were killed in the blast were his
daughters" (Russell).

The medical progress made in Northern
Ireland's hospitals during the Troubles
speaks to the remarkable ability of the
medical personnel to rise to the challenges posed by the civil violence.
Developments in disaster planning, triage,
and organization in Northern Ireland's
hospitals went hand-in-hand with the

Carvalho 15

creation of specific medical treatments
to address the needs of civil violence
victims. Throughout the Troubles, paramilitary violence generated casualties that
varied greatly in the type and pattern of
injury as well as in the numbers of injured, calling attention to the need for
a comprehensive, all-encompassing system
of treatment. In Northern Ireland's hospitals, the seamless joining of the methods
of disaster planning and the methods of
medical treatment enabled these hospitals
to meet the demands of mass casualty terrorist incidents head-on throughout the
decades of civil violence.

The innovation of Belfast's medics is clearly seen in the treatment of
punishment injuries. These injuries were
different from other types of injury seen
during the Troubles because they were
completely nonsectarian; in a bizarre
twist of vigilante justice, Protestants
would shoot Protestants, and Catholics
would shoot Catholics, usually for some
sort of wrongdoing on the victim's part.
A certain subset of punishment injury
termed "kneecapping," whereby the victim
was shot from close range in the back of
the legs, is unique to Northern Ireland

This paragraph is a typical example of how well Ashley reports information from her research but finds her own way of saying things (e.g. "in a bizarre twist of vigilante justice") and characterizing them.

Carvalho 16

alone and, as such, necessitated a unique
form of surgical treatment (Nolan 405-6).
If an individual were suspected of a serious crime, such as rape or murder, he would
be punished with gunshots through the el-
bows and ankles in addition to the knees—
the proverbial "six pack"—although this
type of punishment was much less common.

Throughout the thirty-year period
of violence, some 2,500 people in Northern Ireland sustained a kneecapping injury
(Williams 79). The high prevalence of this
type of injury and the severe destruction
of knee vasculature that it caused presented a whole host of challenges to trauma
surgeons during the Troubles, and it wasn't
long before they developed effective methods of treatment. Belfast's trauma surgeons
learned to reconnect the damaged blood ves-
sels in the knee using an ingenious system of shunts and vein grafts, and toward
the end of the Troubles most kneecapping
injuries were repaired successfully and
quickly, the victim up and walking within a
matter of months (D'Sa 38-9).

But however clever Belfast's trauma
surgeons proved to be, the paramilitary
organizations tried to be more clever. In
response to the surgical developments made

Carvalho 17

by trauma surgeons during the Troubles,
the IRA changed its methods of kneecapping
in order to cause further damage and
to hinder surgeons in repairing the knee
vasculature, which in turn prompted
surgeons to again reinvent treatment
methods in reaction.

The method created in Belfast to
restructure severely fractured skulls
might be the most resourceful of all
medical developments during the Troubles. This method was created in the mid
1970s and was the brainchild of a dental surgeon, George Blair, and a neuro-
surgeon, Derrick Gordon, in the Royal
Victoria. Skull fractures like the ones
seen during the Troubles posed a real
challenge to neurosurgeons, not least
because of the bony defects that resulted in the skull, but also the fact
that pieces of the skull were often
lost, leaving the underlying brain layers completely exposed. Gordon and Blair
devised a method of treatment in which a
material used to make impressions of the
teeth called alginate was poured into
a light metal cap, which was placed on
the patient's head to make an impression
of the fractured skull. Then, titanium

metal was poured into the impression to make a plate, which was fitted into the patient's skull. Titanium, as a fairly light yet inert metal, was perfect for the job. Later research showed that the success rate for this procedure was at least 90 percent (Roy 544). Today, this treatment method is used in hospitals worldwide.

Even today, the tension isn't completely gone from Belfast's streets. It will still take another couple of generations for the emotional sting of the Troubles to lose its poignancy and for the painfully sharp memories of the violence to soften around the edges. But even now, the hope of Belfast's overwhelming majority is one of peace, of moving away from a violent, harrowing past and toward a brighter future. In terms of the developments and progress in medicine achieved by Northern Ireland's healthcare workers, Northern Ireland's medics left a legacy of tenacity, determination, and strength of spirit. Just as the mural-painters fought the Troubles by expressing themselves through art, the medics fought the Troubles in their

Carvalho 19

Fig. 3 Rainbow in a Troubled Sky, Belfast.

own way: by patching up Belfast and healing the city. In finding a silver lin-
ing within the black stormclouds of the
Troubles, placing a rainbow (see fig. 3)
in Belfast's perpetually grey skies, and
creating good from bad, these medics are
truly remarkable.

Carvalho 20

Works Cited

Bardon, Jonathan. *A History of Ulster*. Belfast:
    The Blackstaff Press, 1992. Print.

Clarke, Richard. *The Royal Victoria Hospital
    Belfast: A History 1797-1997*. Belfast:
    Blackstaff, 1997. Print.

Coogan, Tim Pat. *The Troubles: Ireland's Ordeal
    and the Search for Peace*. New York:
    Palgrave, 1996. Print.

D'Sa, Airres Barros. "Symposium Paper: Manage-
    ment of Vascular Injuries of Civil Strife."
    British Journal of Accident Surgery 14.1
    (1982): 51-57. Print.

---. "A Decade of Missile-Induced Vascular
    Trauma." *Annals of the Royal College of
    Surgeons of England* 64 (1982): 37-44.
    Print.

Gillespie, Gordon. *Years of Darkness: The Trou-
    bles Remembered*. Dublin: Gill & Macmillan,
    2008. Print.

McKittrick, David, and McVea, David. *Making Sense
    of the Troubles*. London: Penguin, 2001.
    Print.

Nolan P. C., and G. McCoy. "The Changing Pat-
    tern of Paramilitary Punishments in North-
    ern Ireland." *Injury* 27.6 (1996): 405-06.
    Print.

The Works Cited list begins a new page at the end of your paper.

Carvalho 21

Roy, Douglas. "Gunshot and Bomb Blast Injuries: A
    Review of the Experience in Belfast." *Jour-
    nal of the Royal Society of Medicine* 75.7
    (1982): 542-45. Print.

Russell, Colin. Personal interview. Oct. 2010.

Siobhan. Personal interview. Sept. 2010.

Williams, John. "Casualties of Violence in North-
    ern Ireland." *International Journal of
    Trauma Nursing* 3.3 (1997): 78-82. Print.

APPENDIX

Guide to APA Style

The American Psychological Association (APA) style is, like MLA style, commonly used for documenting and formatting college papers. APA style is the standard for papers in the social and behavioral sciences as well as in education and business. In those disciplines, the currency of the material cited is often especially important. Therefore, APA style's author/date citation system emphasizes the date of publication, in contrast to MLA's author/page system.

Checklist Before Handing in a Paper in APA Style

- My paper is double spaced throughout, including the References list.
- I have a running head on each page, including a page number in the upper right-hand corner.
- I've cited page numbers in my paper whenever I've quoted a source.
- I've "blocked" every quotation that is longer than 40 words.
- Whenever possible, I've mentioned the names of authors I cite in my paper and put the date of the appropriate publication next to their names.
- I've doubled-checked the accuracy of DOIs and URLs of electronic sources that I included in my References.
- The References begin on a new page and are organized alphabetically by the authors' last names.
- In article and book titles cited, only the first words of titles and subtitles are capitalized; the remaining words are not capitalized unless they would ordinarily be capitalized.

I think you'll find APA style easy to use, especially if you've had some practice with MLA. Converting from one style to the other is easy (for some key differences between the two, see Table 1). Appendix covers what you need to know about APA style, including how and when to cite sources in your essay (Part One) and how to assemble the References page (Part Three). The discussion of conventions for formatting your paper (Part Two) offers guidance on pagination, layout, and various specifics of style. Finally, you can see what APA style looks like in a paper like the one you're writing (Part Four).

TABLE 1 Key Differences Between MLA and APA Formats

MLA	APA
Capitalizes most words in book and article titles on Works Cited page.	Capitalizes only the first word and proper nouns in book and article titles on References page.
Uses author's full first and last name on Works Cited page.	Uses author's last name along with first and middle initials on References page.
Uses the word "and" to combine authors' names in in-text citations and on Works Cited page if there is more than one author for a source.	Uses an ampersand (&) to combine authors' names in in-text citations and on References page if a source has more than one author.
In-text citations use author's last name and pages cited.	In-text citations use author's last name and date; page numbers aren't required except for quotations.
In-text citations use no punctuation between author's name and page number.	In-text citations use a comma between author's last name and date.
Page numbers are listed simply as a number in in-text citations.	Page numbers are denoted with a "p." or "pp." in in-text citations.
There is no separate title page.	There is a title page with running head.
Running head contains author's last name and the page number.	Running head contains the first words of the paper's title and the page number.
No subheadings occur within the paper.	Subheadings often occur within the paper. Paper often begins with an abstract.
Tables and figures are integrated into the body of the paper.	Tables and figures can be integrated or in an appendix.

The *Publication Manual of the American Psychological Association** is the authoritative reference on APA style, and the sixth edition, published in 2010, features some updates, including some new guidelines for referencing electronic sources. The APA Web site now includes some free tutorials on the citation style, narrated by a guy who seems really excited about it. Though the information in the section that follows should answer your questions, check the manual when in doubt.

Directory of APA Style

Citing Sources in Your Essay

1.1.1 A Work by One Author

1.1.2 A Work by Two Authors

1.1.3 A Work by Three to Five Authors

1.1.4 A Work by Six or More Authors

1.1.5 An Institutional Author

1.1.6 A Work with No Author

1.1.7 Two or More Works by the Same Author

1.1.8 Authors with the Same Last Names

1.1.9 Several Sources in a Single Citation

1.1.10 Indirect Sources

1.1.11 New Editions of Old Works

1.1.12 Interviews, E-mail, and Letters

1.1.13 A Web Site

Preparing the References List

3.2 Citing Books, in Print and Online

3.2.1 A Book with One Author

3.2.2 A Book with Two Authors

3.2.3 A Book with Three to Seven Authors

3.2.4 A Book with Eight or More Authors

3.2.5 A Book with an Institutional Author

3.2.6 A Book with No Author

3.2.7 An Encyclopedia Entry

3.2.8 A Chapter in a Book

3.2.9 A Book with an Editor

3.2.10 A Selection in a Book with an Editor

3.2.11 A Republished Work

3.2.12 A Government Document

3.3 Citing Articles, in Print and Online

3.3.1 A Journal Article

3.3.2 A Journal Article Not Paginated Continuously

(continued)

Publication Manual of the American Psychological Association. 6th ed. Washington DC: APA, 2010. Print.

3.3.3	A Magazine Article	**3.4**	**Citing Other Sources**
3.3.4	A Newspaper Article	3.4.1	An Entire Web Page
3.3.5	An Article with No Author	3.4.2	A Film, DVD, or Online Video
3.3.6	An Article on a Web Site	3.4.3	A Television Program
3.3.7	An Abstract	3.4.4	An Audio Podcast
3.3.8	A Book Review	3.4.5	A Blog
3.3.9	An Editorial	3.4.6	A Wiki
3.3.10	A Letter to the Editor	3.4.7	Online Discussion Lists
3.3.11	A Published Interview	3.4.8	A Musical Recording

Part One: Citing Sources in Your Essay

1.1 The APA Author/Date System

The Basics of Using Parenthetical Citation

The author/date system is pretty uncomplicated. If you mention the name of the author in text, simply place the year her work was published in parentheses immediately after her name. For example:

```
Herrick (2006) argued that college testing was
biased against minorities.
```

If you mention both the author's name and the date in the text of your essay, then you can omit the parenthetical citation altogether. For example:

```
In 2006, Herrick argued that college testing was
biased against minorities.
```

If you don't mention the author's name in the text, then include that information parenthetically. For example:

> A New Hampshire political scientist (Bloom,
> 2008) recently studied the state's presidential
> primary.

Note that the author's name and the year of her work are separated by a comma.

When to Cite Page Numbers.   If the information you're citing came from specific pages (or chapters or sections) of a source, that information may also be included in the parenthetical citation, as in the example below. Including page numbers is essential when quoting a source.

> The first stage of language acquisition is
> called *caretaker speech* (Moskowitz, 1985,
> pp. 50—51), in which children model their
> parents' language.

Or, if the author's name is mentioned in the text:

> Moskowitz (1985) observed that the first stage
> of language acquisition is called *caretaker
> speech* (pp. 50-51), in which children model
> their parents' language.

1.1.1 A WORK BY ONE AUTHOR

> Herrick (2006) argued that college testing was
> biased against minorities.
>
> *or*
>
> One problem with college testing may be bias
> (Herrick, 2006).

1.1.2 A WORK BY TWO AUTHORS

When a work has two authors, always mention them both whenever you cite their work in your paper. For example:

```
Allen and Oliver (1998) observed many cases of
child abuse and concluded that maltreatment
inhibited language development.
```

Notice that if the authors' names are given in a parenthetical citation, an ampersand is used:

```
Researchers observed many cases of child abuse
and concluded that maltreatment inhibited lan-
guage development (Allen & Oliver, 1998).
```

1.1.3 A WORK BY THREE TO FIVE AUTHORS

If a source has three to five authors, mention them all the first time you refer to their work. However, in any subsequent references give the name of the first author followed by the abbreviation *et al.* For example, here's what a first mention of a multiple author source would look like:

```
The study found that medical students sometimes
responded to an inquiry-based approach by becom-
ing more superficial in their analyses (Balas-
oriya, Hughes, & Toohey, 2011).
```

Subsequent mentions use the convention *et al.*:

```
Though collaboration is supposed to promote
learning, in one case it actually hindered it
(Balasoriya et al., 2011).
```

1.1.4 A WORK BY SIX OR MORE AUTHORS

When citing works with six or more authors, *always* use the first author's name and *et al.*

1.1.5 AN INSTITUTIONAL AUTHOR

When citing a corporation or agency as a source, simply list the year of the study in parentheses if you mention the institution in the text:

```
The Environmental Protection Agency (2007)
issued an alarming report on global warming.
```

If you don't mention the institutional source in the text, spell it out in its entirety, along with the year. In subsequent parenthetical citations, abbreviate the name. For example:

```
A study (Environmental Protection Agency [EPA],
2007) predicted dire consequences from continued
global warming.
```

And later:

```
Continued ozone depletion may result in wide-
spread skin cancers (EPA, 2007).
```

1.1.6 A WORK WITH NO AUTHOR

When a work has no author, cite an abbreviated title and the year. Place article or chapter titles in quotation marks, and italicize book titles. For example:

```
The editorial ("Sinking," 2007) concluded that
the EPA was mired in bureaucratic muck.
```

1.1.7 TWO OR MORE WORKS BY THE SAME AUTHOR

Works by the same author are usually distinguished by the date; these would rarely be published in the same year. But if they are, distinguish among works by adding an *a* or *b* immediately following the year in the parenthetical citation. The References list will also have these suffixes. For example:

```
Douglas's studies (1986a) on the mating
habits of lobsters revealed that the females
are dominant. He also found that the female
lobsters have the uncanny ability to smell a
loser (1986b).
```

This citation alerts readers that the information came from two works by Douglas, both published in 1986.

1.1.8 AUTHORS WITH THE SAME LAST NAMES

In the rare case that you're using sources from different authors with the same last name, distinguish between them by including the first initials of each author whenever you mention them in your paper, even if the publication dates differ:

```
M. Bradford (2010) and L. S. Bradford (2008)
both noted that Americans are more narcissistic.
```

1.1.9 SEVERAL SOURCES IN A SINGLE CITATION

Occasionally, you'll want to cite several sources at once. Probably the most common instance is when you refer to the findings of several relevant studies, something that is a good idea as you try to establish a context for what has already been said about your research topic. When listing multiple sources within the same parenthetical citation, order them as they appear in the References and separate them with semicolons. For example:

```
A number of researchers have explored
the connection between Internet use and
depression (Sanders, Field, & Diego, 2000;
Waestlund, Norlander, & Archer, 2001).
```

1.1.10 INDIRECT SOURCES

If you discover, say, a great quotation or idea from someone who is mentioned in another author's book or article, try to track down the original source. But when you can't find it, signal parenthetically that you're using an indirect source, using the phrase *as cited in*.

```
De Groot's study on chess expertise (as cited in
Kirschner, Sweller, & Clark, 2006) is...
```

The only source you'll include in your References list is the source you used; it isn't necessary to include the indirect source.

1.1.11 NEW EDITIONS OF OLD WORKS

For reprints of older works, include both the year of the original publication and that of the reprint edition (or the translation).

```
Pragmatism as a philosophy sought connection
between scientific study and real people's lives
(James, 1906/1978).
```

1.1.12 INTERVIEWS, E-MAIL, AND LETTERS

Interviews and other personal communications are not listed in the references at the back of the paper, because they are not *recoverable data,* but they are parenthetically cited in the text. Provide the initials and last name of the subject (if not mentioned in the text), the nature of the communication, and the complete date, if possible.

```
Nancy Diamonti (personal communication, November
12, 1990) disagrees with the critics of Sesame
Street.
      In a recent e-mail, Michelle Payne (personal
communication, January 4, 2011) complained
that....
```

1.1.13 A WEB SITE

When referring to an *entire* Web site, cite the address parenthetically in your essay. Do not include a citation for an entire Web site in your References list.

```
The Centers for Disease Control (http://www.cdc
.gov) is a reliable source for the latest health
information.
```

If you're quoting from a Web site, you should cite the date of online publication, if available, and the page number, if available. (When simply referring to a part of a Web site, just use the date, if available, not the page number.) However, most Web documents that aren't also available in print do not have page numbers. What do you do in that case? If you can, use a heading or short title from the source that helps readers to locate the part of the document where they can find the material you cited. Then add a paragraph number using the abbreviation *para.*

> According to Cesar Milan (2010), it's essential that dog owners establish themselves as "pack leaders" ("Why Does CDC Teach Wolf Pack Theory?" para. 2).

Part Two: Formatting Your Essay

2.1 Formatting the Essay and Its Parts

2.1.1 PAGE FORMAT AND HEADER

Papers should be double spaced, with at least 1-inch margins on all sides. Number all pages consecutively, beginning with the title page; using the header feature in your word processor, put the page number in the upper right-hand corner. In the upper left-hand corner of each page, beginning with the title page, give an abbreviated title of the paper in uppercase letters. As a rule, the first line of all paragraphs of text should be indented five spaces or a half inch.

2.1.2 TITLE PAGE

Unlike a paper in MLA style, an APA-style paper sometimes has a separate title page. The title page includes the title of the paper, the author, and the author's affiliation (e.g., what university she is from). As Figure 1 shows, this information is double spaced, and each line is centered. The upper left of the title page has the abbreviated title in uppercase letters, preceded by "Running head" and a colon, and the upper right has the page number.

2.1.3 ABSTRACT

Though it's not always required, many APA-style papers include a short abstract (between 150 to 250 words) following the title page. See Figure 2. An abstract is essentially a short summary of the paper's contents. This is a key feature, because it's usually the first

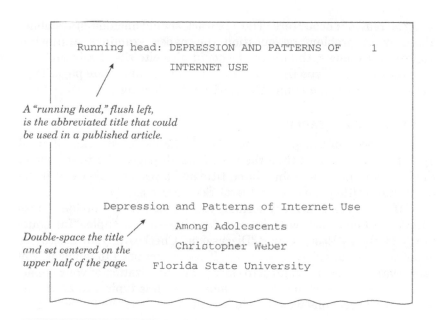

Running head: DEPRESSION AND PATTERNS OF   1
                    INTERNET USE

A "running head," flush left,
is the abbreviated title that could
be used in a published article.

                Depression and Patterns of Internet Use
                        Among Adolescents
Double-space the title
and set centered on the   Christopher Weber
upper half of the page.   Florida State University

FIGURE 1   **Title Page in APA Style**

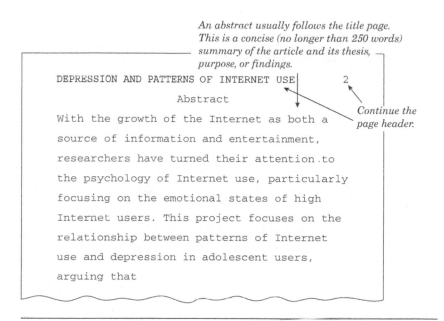

An abstract usually follows the title page.
This is a concise (no longer than 250 words)
summary of the article and its thesis,
purpose, or findings.

DEPRESSION AND PATTERNS OF INTERNET USE   2

                        Abstract

With the growth of the Internet as both a   *Continue the*
                                                 page header.
source of information and entertainment,

researchers have turned their attention to

the psychology of Internet use, particularly

focusing on the emotional states of high

Internet users. This project focuses on the

relationship between patterns of Internet

use and depression in adolescent users,

arguing that

FIGURE 2   **The Abstract Page**

thing a reader encounters. The abstract should include statements about what problem or question the paper examines and what approach it follows; the abstract should also cite the thesis and significant findings. Type the title "Abstract" at the top of the page. Type the abstract text in a single block, without indenting.

2.1.4 BODY OF THE PAPER

The body of the paper begins with the centered title, followed by a double space and then the text. Like all pages, the first page of the body will have an abbreviated title and a page number ("3" if the paper has a title page and abstract). See Figure 3.

If your paper is fairly formal, you might need to divide it into specific sections, each with its own heading—for example, "Introduction," "Method," "Results," and "Discussion." Check with your instructor about whether to follow this format. If you do not need to follow it, you can create your own headings to clarify the organization of your paper.

In the formal structure mentioned, which is typical in academic journals, the sections would include content such as the following:

- Introduction: Why does your research question matter? What has already been said about it? What is the hypothesis you'll be exploring?

DEPRESSION AND PATTERNS OF INTERNET USE   3

Depression and Patterns of Internet Use Among

Adolescents

Before Johnny Beale's family got a new

computer in August 2008, the sixteen-year-old

high school student estimated that he spent

about twenty minutes a day online, mostly

checking his e-mail. Within months, however,

Beale's time at the computer tripled, and he

admitted that he spent most of his time

playing games. At first, his family noticed

Center the title of the paper and double-space to begin the body of the text.

FIGURE 3   The Body of the Paper in APA Style

- Method: How did you test your hypothesis? What you say here depends on the kind of study you're doing.
- Results: What did you find?
- Discussion: How do you interpret the findings? To what extent do they support—or fail to support—your initial hypothesis? What are the implications of these discoveries?

2.1.5 HEADINGS

If you use headings, the APA specifies the following hierarchy:

Centered, Boldface, Uppercase and

Lowercase (Level 1)

Flush Left, Boldface, Uppercase and

Lowercase (Level 2)

    Indented, boldface, lowercase, ending with period, **running into paragraph.** (Level 3)

    Indented, boldface, italicized, lowercase, **ending with period, running into paragraph.** (Level 4)

    Indented, italicized, lowercase, ending with a period, running into paragraph. (Level 5)

Five levels of headings

A paper, particularly a short one, will rarely use all five levels of headings. In fact, it's much more common for a student paper to use just two or possibly three.

2.1.6 HANDLING QUOTED MATERIAL

When you borrow words, phrases, or passages from another author, typically the material must be contained in quotation marks. Usually, it is smoothly integrated with attribution (*According to Ballenger, . . .*) and parenthetical citation including page numbers, into your own sentences and paragraphs. For example,

According to Ellison, Steinfeld, and Lampe (2007), Facebook and other social networking sites offer researchers an "ideal"

chance to investigate "offline and online
connection" (p. 12).

But if the quoted material is longer than 40 words, it should be
"blocked." Indent the entire quoted passage five spaces or a half inch
from the left margin, and omit the quotation marks. For example,

According to Perfetti's (2003) book on women in
the Middle Ages and laughter,

> Laughter is both a defense mechanism and
> a weapon of attack, essential to groups
> struggling to be taken seriously by the
> rest of society. But it is perhaps women,
> more than any other group, who have had the
> most complicated relationship with humor
> in Western culture. People of every reli-
> gion, nationality, ethnicity, class, and
> occupation have at some time found them-
> selves the butt of an offensive joke and
> told to lighten up because "it's just a
> joke." But it is women who have been told
> that their refusal to laugh at jokes made
> at their expense shows that they don't have
> a sense of humor at all. So a woman has to
> assert her right not to laugh at offensive
> jokes but simultaneously prove that she is
> capable of laughter or risk being seen as
> a humorless spoilsport: a balancing act
> requiring a quick wit. (p. viii)

Notice that blocked quotations are double spaced and that the
parenthetical reference is placed *after* the period rather than before it.

If you omit material from an original source—a common method
of using just the relevant information in a sentence or passage—use
ellipsis points (...). For example,

The study (Lampe, 2010) noted that "student athletes in U.S. universities are highly visible.... They are often considered to be representatives of the university, and may be the most visible spokespeople for, in some cases..." (p. 193).

2.1.7 REFERENCES LIST

All sources cited in the body of the paper are listed alphabetically by author (or title, if anonymous) in the list titled "References," as shown in Figure 4. This list should begin a new page, and it is double spaced throughout. The first line of each entry is flush left; subsequent lines are indented a half inch. Explanation of how to cite various types of sources in the References list follows (see "Part Three: Preparing the References List").

2.1.8 TABLES AND FIGURES

Should you include a table, chart, or photograph in your paper? Sure, if you're certain that it adds something to your discussion and if the information it presents is clear and understandable. If you use a table (and with programs like Excel and Word they are incredibly easy to generate), place it in the manuscript as close as

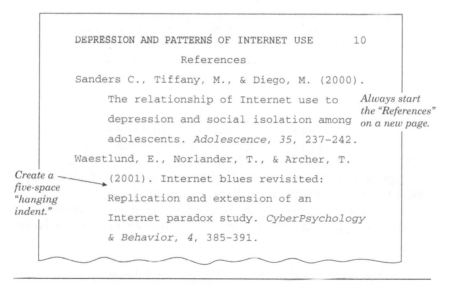

FIGURE 4 **The References Page**

you can to where you mention it. Alternatively, you can put your tables and figures in an appendix. Tables should all be double spaced. Type a table number at the top, flush left. Number tables "Table 1," "Table 2," and so on, corresponding to the order in which they are mentioned in the text. The title, in italics, should be placed on the line below the number. Tables that you put in an appendix should be labeled accordingly. For Example, Table 1 in Appendix A would be numbered Table A1.

Figures (graphs, charts, photographs, and drawings) are handled similarly to tables. They are numbered consecutively beginning with "Figure 1." This figure number, below the figure itself, is followed by a title and, if needed, a caption (see Figure 5). Captions are often helpful to explain a chart, photograph, drawing, or other figure. As with tables, insert figures in your paper as close as you can to where you refer to them or, alternatively, put them in an appendix.

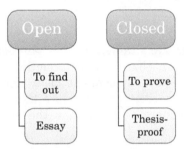

Figure 1. Two Broad Categories of Writing Assignments. Open-ended and more closed writing assignments each are characterized by a different motive and result in a different genre.

FIGURE 5   **Example of Format for a Figure**

2.1.9 APPENDIX

This is a seldom-used feature of an APA-style paper, though you might find it helpful for presenting specific material that isn't central to the discussion in the body of your paper: a detailed description of a device described in the paper, a copy of a blank survey, a table, or the like. Each item, placed at the end of the paper following the References page, should begin on a separate page and be labeled "Appendix" followed by "A," "B," and so on, consecutively.

2.1.10 NOTES

Several kinds of notes might be included in a paper. The most common is *content notes*, or brief commentaries by the writer keyed to superscript numbers in the body of the text. These notes are useful for discussion of key points that are relevant but might be distracting if explored in the text of your paper. Present all notes, numbered consecutively, on a page titled "Footnotes" (placed after the References page but before any appendixes) or at the bottom of the relevant page. Notes should be double spaced. Begin each note with the appropriate superscript number, indented like the first line of a paragraph; subsequent lines of a note are not indented.

2.2 Some Style Considerations

2.2.1 USE OF ITALICS

The APA guidelines for *italicizing* call for its use when:

- Giving the titles of books, periodicals, films, and publications that appear on microfilm.
- Using new or specialized terms, but only the first time you use them (e.g., "the authors' *paradox study* of Internet users...").
- Citing a phrase, letter, or word as an example (e.g., "the second *a* in *separate* can be remembered by remembering the word *rat*").

Use quotation marks around the titles of articles or book chapters mentioned in your essay.

2.2.2 TREATMENT OF NUMBERS

Numbers 9 and below that don't represent precise measurements should be spelled out, and numbers 10 and above should be expressed as numerals. Any numbers that begin a sentence or represent a commonly used fraction (e.g., "one-quarter of the sample") should be spelled out.

Part Three:
Preparing the References List

All parenthetical citations in the body of the paper correspond to a complete listing of sources in the References list. The format for this section was described earlier in this appendix (see "References List" in Part Two).

3.1 Order of Sources and Information

Order of Sources

List the references alphabetically by author last name or by the first key word of the title if there is no author. This alphabetical principle has a few complications:

- You may have several sources by the same author. If these sources weren't published in the same year, list them in chronological order, the earliest first. If the sources were published in the same year, include a lowercase letter to distinguish them. For example:

```
Lane, B. (2007a). Verbal medicine...

Lane, B. (2007b). Writing...
```

- Because scholars and writers often collaborate, you may have several references in which an author is listed with several *different* collaborators. List these alphabetically using the second author's last name. For example,

```
Brown, M., Nelson, A. (2002)

Brown, M., Payne, M. (1999)
```

Order of Information

A Reference list entry for a periodical or book includes this information, in order: author, date of publication, book title or, for articles, article title followed by periodical title, and publication information. Here are some basics about each of these entry parts; details and examples follow. Remember that all entries should be double spaced and that the first line of each should begin flush left and all subsequent lines should be indented.

Author or Authors. List all authors—last name, comma, and then initials. Invert all authors' names. Use commas to separate authors' names; add an *ampersand* (&) before the last author's name. When citing an edited book, list the editor(s) in place of the author, and add the abbreviation *Ed.* or *Eds.* in parentheses after the last editor's name. End the list of names with a period.

Date. After the last author's name, in parentheses list the year the work was published. If the source is a magazine or newspaper, also include the month and day; for example "(2011, April 4)." If a source doesn't list any date, use the abbreviation *n.d.* in parentheses. Add a period after the closing parenthesis.

Book Title or Article Title.   Use a period at the end of each title, and style titles as follows:

- *Book titles* are italicized. Only the first word of titles and sub-titles are capitalized; all other words are lowercase unless ordinarily capitalized. For example:

  The curious researcher: A guide to writing

      research papers.

  Sound reporting.

- *Article titles* are given without italics or quotation marks. As with book titles, capitalize only the first word of the title and any subtitle.

  Student athletes on Facebook.

  Oyster apocalypse? Truth about bivalve

      obliteration.

Periodical Title and Publication Information.   Periodical titles are italicized, like book titles; unlike book and article titles, they use both uppercase and lowercase. Add the volume number (if any), also italicized and separated from the title with a comma. If each issue of the periodical starts with page 1, then also include the issue number in parentheses immediately after the volume number. End the entry, following a comma, with the page numbers of the article. For example, you might have *Journal of Mass Communication, 10*, 138–150. Use the abbreviation *p.* (for one page) or *pp.* (for more than one page) only if you are citing a newspaper.

Publication Information for Books.   List the city and state or country of publication (use postal abbreviations for states) and then, following a colon, the name of the publisher, followed by a period.

Bringing these elements together, a print book citation would look like this in APA style:

Blakeswell, S. (2010). *How to live or a lite of*

    Montaigne. New York, NY: Other Press.

And a print periodical citation would look like this:

```
Alegre, A. (2011). Parenting styles and
     children's emotional intelligence. What do
     we know? The Family Journal, 19, 56-62.
```

Digital Sources.   In many ways citing an electronic source is the same as citing a print one—you'll include author, title, and publication information. But there are also some significant differences. Online material may appear in different versions—say, as a talk and an article based on that talk—and because electronic sources may come and go, it's hard to be certain that readers will be able to find a particular source. APA has been making changes in an effort to meet the special challenges posed by online material. Basically, the organization recommends that you identify where the article or document is located using one of two methods:

1. Include the URL (Web address)

Or, preferably,

2. Cite the DOI (digital object identifier)

The digital object identifier is a unique number that is assigned to an electronic document. Journal articles these days almost all have a DOI, which is often listed on the first page of a document. Because these numbers are stable and unique to each source, they are the preferred method of citing the location of an electronic source.

For example, here's a typical citation of an online document that has no DOI.

```
Perina, K, Flora, P., & Marano, H. P. (2011,
     January 1). Who are you? (And what do you
     think of me?) Psychology Today. Retrieved
     from http://www.psychologytoday.com
     /articles/201012/who-are-you-and-what
     -do-you-think-me
```

A journal article with a DOI would be cited like this:

```
O'Neil, J. (2011). The privatization of
     public schools in New Zealand. Journal
     of Education Policy, 26, 17-31. doi:
     10.1080/02680939.2010.493227
```

3.2 Citing Books, in Print and Online

3.2.1 A BOOK WITH ONE AUTHOR

Cite a print book like this:

Barry, J. M. (2004). *The great influenza: The epic story of the deadliest plague in history.* New York, NY: Viking.

In-Text Citation: (Barry, 2004) *or* According to Barry (2004),...

Cite a book that only appears electronically like this:

Burnheim, J. (2006). *Is democracy possible? The alternative to electoral politics.* Retrieved from http://setis.library.usyd .edu.au/democracy/index.html

In-Text Citation: (Burnheim, 2006) *or* According to Burnheim (2006),...

For an electronic book that is also available in print, include information in brackets about how it appeared digitally. For example,

Gwynne, S.C. (2010). *Empire of the summer moon* [iBook version]. Retrieved from http:// www.apple.com/us/ibooks

In-Text Citation: (Gwynne, 2010) *or* According to Gwynne (2010),...

3.2.2 A BOOK WITH TWO AUTHORS

Graff, G., Birkenstein, C., & Durst, Russell (2009). *They say, I say.* New York, NY: Norton.

In-Text Citations: (Graff, Birkenstein, & Durst, 2009); after first citing all the names, you can subsequently use the first author's name followed by *et al.*

3.2.3 A BOOK WITH THREE TO SEVEN AUTHORS

Belenky, M., Clinchy B. M., Goldberger, N. R.,
    & Tarule, J. M. (1986). *Women's ways of*
    knowing: The development of self, voice,
    and mind. New York, NY: Basic Books.

In-Text Citation: (Belenky, Clinchy, Goldberger, & Tarule, 1986) when mentioned first, and (Belenky et al., 1986) thereafter.

3.2.4 A BOOK WITH EIGHT OR MORE AUTHORS

For a work with eight or more authors, give the first six authors followed by an ellipsis (…) and the final author. For example,

Jones, B., Doverman, L. S., Shanke S., Forman,
    P., Witte, L. S., Firestone, F. J., ...
    Smith, L. A. (2011). *Too many authors spoil*
    the soup. New York, NY: Oyster Press.

In-Text Citation: (Jones et al., 2011)

3.2.5 A BOOK WITH AN INSTITUTIONAL AUTHOR

American Red Cross. (2007). *Advanced first aid*
    and emergency care. New York, NY: Doubleday.

In-Text Citation: (American Red Cross, 2007)

or

The book *Advanced First Aid and Emergency Care*
    (2007) states that...

3.2.6 A BOOK WITH NO AUTHOR

The Chicago manual of style (16th ed.). (2010).
    Chicago, IL: University of Chicago Press.

In-Text Citations: `(Chicago Manual of Style, 2010)`

or

`According to the` *Chicago Manual of Style* `(2010),...`

3.2.7 AN ENCYCLOPEDIA ENTRY

Cite an article from a print encyclopedia like this:

`Hansen, T. S. (2003). Depression. In` *The new encyclopaedia Britannica* `(Vol. 12, pp. 408-412). Chicago, IL: Encyclopaedia Britannica.`

In-Text Citations: `(Hansen, 2003)` *or* `Hansen (2003) defines depression as...`

Cite an article from an online encyclopedia like this:

`Diarrhea. (2008). In` *Columbia encyclopedia* `(6th ed.). Retrieved from http://www .encyclopedia.com/doc/1E1-diarrhea.html`

In-Text Citations: `("Diarrhea," 2008)` *or* `According to the Columbia Encyclopedia (2008), diarrhea...`

3.2.8 A CHAPTER IN A BOOK

`Kuhn, T. S. (1996). The route to normal science. In` *The structure of scientific revolutions* `(pp. 23-34). Chicago, IL: University of Chicago Press.`

In-Text Citations: `(Kuhn, 2006)` *or* `Kuhn (2006) argues that...`

3.2.9 A BOOK WITH AN EDITOR

`Crane, R. S. (Ed.). (1952).` *Critics and criticism.* `Chicago, IL: University of Chicago Press.`

In-Text Citations: (Crane, 1952) *or* In his preface, Crane (1952) observed that . . .

3.2.10 A SELECTION IN A BOOK WITH AN EDITOR

McKeon, R. (1952). Rhetoric in the Middle Ages. In R. S. Crane (Ed.), *Critics and criticism* (pp. 260-289). Chicago, IL: University of Chicago Press.

In-Text Citations: (McKeon, 1952) *or* McKeon (1952) argued that . . .

3.2.11 A REPUBLISHED WORK

James, W. (1978). *Pragmatism*. Cambridge, MA: Harvard University Press. (Original work published 1907).

In-Text Citations: (James, 1907/1978) *or* According to William James (1907/1978), . . .

3.2.12 A GOVERNMENT DOCUMENT

U.S. Bureau of the Census. (1991). *Statistical abstract of the United States* (111th ed.). Washington, DC: U.S. Government Printing Office.

In-Text Citations: (U.S. Bureau, 1991) *or* According to the U.S. Census Bureau (1991), . . .

3.3 Citing Articles, in Print and Online

3.3.1 A JOURNAL ARTICLE

Cite a print journal article like this:

Blager, F. B. (1979). The effect of intervention on the speech and language of children. *Child Abuse and Neglect, 5,* 91-96.

In-Text Citations: (Blager, 1979) *or* Blager (1979) stated that . . .

For a journal article, include the DOI, if available:

Wang, F., McGuire, P., & Pan, E. (2010). Applying technology to inquiry-based learning in early childhood education. *Early Childhood Education Journal, 37,* 381-389. doi: 10.1007/s10643-009-0634-6

In-Text Citations: When first mentioned cite all three (Wang, McGuire, & Pan, 2010) *or* Wang, McGuire, and Pan (2010) argue that... Subsequent mentions can use *et al.*: (Wang et al., 2010).

For a journal article with no DOI, include the URL of the database or the online journal's homepage:

Kaveshar, J. (2008). Kicking the rock and the hard place to the curb: An alternative and integrated approach to suicidal students in higher education. *Emory Law Journal, 57*(3), 651-693. Retrieved from http://find .galegroup.com/itx/start.do?prodId=AONE

In-Text Citations: (Kaveshar, 2008) *or* According to Kaveshar (2008), . . .

3.3.2 A JOURNAL ARTICLE NOT PAGINATED CONTINUOUSLY

Most journals begin on page 1 with the first issue of the year and continue paginating consecutively for subsequent issues. A few journals, however, start on page 1 with each issue. For these, include the issue number in parentheses following the italicized volume number:

> Williams, J., Post, A. T., & Strunk, F. (1991).
>
> The rhetoric of inequality. *Attwanata,*
>
> *12*(3), 54-67.

In-Text Citation: (Williams, Post, & Strunk, 1991) *or* Williams, Post, and Strunk (1991) argue that . . . When first mentioned, cite all three authors and subsequently you can use *et al.*: (Williams et al., 1991).

3.3.3 A MAGAZINE ARTICLE

To cite print articles, include the year, month, and (if present) day published.

> Moore, Peter. (2003, August). Your heart will
>
> stop. *Men's Health.* 142-151.

In-Text Citations: (Moore, 2003) *or* Moore (2003) observed that . . .

Cite online articles like this:

> O'Hehir, A. (2008). Beyond the multiplex. *Salon.*
>
> *com.* Retrieved from http://www.salon.com
>
> /ent/movies/btm/

In-Text Citations: (O'Hehir, 2008) *or* According to O'Hehir (2008), . . .

3.3.4 A NEWSPAPER ARTICLE

Cite print articles like this:

> Honan, W. (1991, January 24). The war affects
>
> Broadway. *New York Times*, pp. C15-16.

In-Text Citations: (Honan, 1991) *or* Honan (1991) said that "Broadway is a battleground" (p. C15).

Cite online articles like this:

```
Englund, W., DeYoung, K., & Willgoren, D.

    (2011, February 4). Huge protests con-

    tinue for 11th day as Obama administration

    weighs Egypt options. The Washington Post.

    Retrieved from http://www.washingtonpost.com
```

In-text Citations: (Englund, DeYoung, & Willgoren, 2011) *or* According to Englund et al.,...

3.3.5 AN ARTICLE WITH NO AUTHOR

If there is no author, a common situation with newspaper articles, alphabetize using the first significant word in the article title. For example:

```
New Hampshire loud and clear. (1998, February 19).

    The Boston Globe, p. 22.
```

In-Text Citations: ("New Hampshire," 1998) *or* In the article "New Hampshire loud and clear" (1998),...

3.3.6 AN ARTICLE ON A WEB SITE

Note that this citation includes the abbreviation *n.d.* because the article did not include a date.

```
Lopez, M. (n.d.). Intellectual development of

    toddlers. National Network for Childcare.

    Retrieved from http://www.nncc.org/Child

    .Dev/intel.dev.todd.html
```

In-Text Citations: (Lopez, n.d.) *or* According to Lopez (n.d.),...

3.3.7 AN ABSTRACT

The growth of online databases for articles has increased the availability of full-text versions and abstracts of articles. While it is almost always better to use the full article, sometimes an abstract itself contains some useful information. Typically, there are two situations in which you might choose to cite just an abstract: when you're working with an original print article or when you've culled the abstract from a database like *Biological Abstracts*. In the first case, include the term *Abstract* in brackets following the title and before the period.

For example,

Renninger, A. K. (2009). Interest and identity

    development in instruction: An inductive

    model [Abstract]. *Educational Psychologist,*

    44, 105-118.

In-Text Citation: (Renninger, 2009) *or* Renninger (2009) claims that...

If the abstract was from a database or some other secondary source, include the name of that source. The term *Abstract* in brackets isn't necessary in this case. For example,

Garcia, R. G. (2002). Evolutionary speed

    of species invasions. *Evolution, 56,*

    661-668. Abstract retrieved from *Biological*

    Abstracts.

In-Text Citations: (Garcia, 2002) *or* Garcia (2002) argues that...

3.3.8 A BOOK REVIEW

Cite a review that's in print like this:

Dentan, R. K. (1989). A new look at the brain

    [Review of the book *The dreaming brain*

    by J. Allen Hobsen]. *Psychiatric Journal,*

    13, 51.

In-Text Citations: (Dentan, 1989) *or* Dentan (1989) argued that...

Cite an online review like this:

Benfey, C. (2008). Why implausibility sells
    [Review of the book *Painter in a savage*
    land by Miles Harvey]. *Slate.* Retrieved
    from http://www.slate.com/id/2193254/

In-Text Citations: (Benfey, 2008) *or* Benfey (2008)
argued that...

3.3.9 AN EDITORIAL

Editorial: Egypt's agonies. [Editorial] (2011,
    February 2). *The New York Times.* Retrieved
    from http://www.nytimes.com/2011/02/04
    /opinion/04fr1.htm

In-Text Citations: ("Egypt's Agonies," 2011) *or The*
New York Times (2011) argued...

3.3.10 A LETTER TO THE EDITOR

Hill, A. C. (1992, February 19). A flawed his-
    tory of blacks in Boston [Letter to the
    editor]. *The Boston Globe*, p. 22.

In-Text Citations: (Hill, 1992) *or* Hill (1992) complained that...

3.3.11 A PUBLISHED INTERVIEW

Personal interviews are usually not cited in an APA-style paper.
Published interviews are cited as follows:

Cotton, P. (1982, April). [Interview with
    Jake Tule, psychic]. *Chronicles Magazine,*
    pp. 24—28.

In-Text Citations: (Cotton, 1982) *or* Cotton (1982) noted that . . .

3.4 Citing Other Sources

3.4.1 AN ENTIRE WEB PAGE

If you're referring to an entire Web site in the text of your essay, include the address parenthetically. However, there is no need to include it in the Reference list. For example:

The Google Scholar search engine (http://scholar .google.com) is considered good for academic research.

3.4.2 A FILM, DVD, OR ONLINE VIDEO

Hitchcock, A. (Producer & Director). (1954).

   Rear window [Film]. United States: MGM.

In-Text Citations: (Hitchcock, 1954) *or* In *Rear Window*, Hitchcock (1954) . . .

Here's how to cite an online video:

Price, P. (Writer).(2008, April 4). *Research-*

   ing online: Five easy steps [Video file].

   Retrieved from http://www.youtube.com/watch?

   v=Ylp9nJpGak4&feature=related

In-Text Citations: (Price, 2008) *or* In *Researching Online*, Price (2008) . . .

3.4.3 A TELEVISION PROGRAM

Burns, K. (Executive producer). (1996). *The*

   West [Television broadcast]. New York,

   NY, and Washington, DC: Public Broad-

   casting Service.

In-Text Citations: (Burns, 1996) *or* In Ken Burns's (1996) film, . . .

3.4.4 AN AUDIO PODCAST

Kermode, M. (2008, June 20). The edge of
love. *Mark Kermode and Simon Mayo's Movie Reviews* [Audio podcast]. Retrieved from
http://www.bbc.co.uk/fivelive/entertainment
/kermode.shtml

In-Text Citations: (Kermode, 2008) *or* In his latest review, Kermode (2008) decried. . .

3.4.5 A BLOG

Shen, H. (2008, June 4). Does your password
meet the test? [Web log post]. Retrieved
from http://googleblog.blogspot.com/2008
/06/does-your-password-pass-test.html

In-Text Citations: (Shen, 2008) *or* Our passwords are vulnerable, says Shen (2008), because. . .

3.4.6 A WIKI

How to use Audacity for podcasting. (n.d.).
Retrieved from http://sites.google.com/a
/biosestate.edu/podcasting-team/Home

In-Text Citation: ("Audacity," n.d.)

3.4.7 ONLINE DISCUSSION LISTS

These include listservs, electronic mailing lists, newsgroups, and online forums, with the method of citation varying slightly depending on the specific type of source. For example,

Hord, J. (2002, July 11). Why do pigeons lift
        one wing up in the air? [Online forum
        comment]. Retrieved from rec://pets.birds
        .pigeons

In-Text Citations: (Hord, 2002) *or* Hord asks (2002)...

Note that the citation includes the subject line of the message as the title, and bracketed information about the source, in this case an online forum comment. For listservs use "[Electronic mailing list message]."

3.4.8 A MUSICAL RECORDING

Wolf, K. (1986). Muddy roads [Recorded by
        E. Clapton]. On *Gold in California* [CD].
        Santa Monica, CA: Rhino Records. (1990).

In-Text Citations: (Wolf, 1986, track 5) *or* In
Wolf's (1986) song, . . .

Part Four: Student Paper in APA Style

Patricia Urbick has set her sights on a career in the Air Force, and so her research essay on military policies that limit women's roles in combat has personal meaning. In "In the Fight," Patricia calls for an end to combat exclusion policies, arguing that such policies ignore the key roles military women are already playing in combat situations. Her essay, written in APA style, is a traditional argument, organized around a claim that Patricia sets out to prove. It's a deeply personal essay, nonetheless, because, among other reasons, the ultimate outcome of the argument has huge implications for Patricia's military career. For those of us who aren't in the armed forces, "In the Fight" lifts a curtain on an issue that deserves more attention.

IN THE FIGHT   1

In the Fight: Women and Combat Exclusion

Patricia Urbick

Boise State University

A running head is an abbreviated title. This will appear, along with page numbers, on every page, including the title page.

IN THE FIGHT   2

Abstract

    Polling data suggest that while most
Americans support women in the military,
they are deeply divided over whether women
should have combat roles. Current military
policies exclude women from combat though
unofficially they are assuming a greater
role on the front lines. The policies that
deny women an opportunity to serve alongside men in combat should be changed so
female service members receive the recognition and benefits they deserve.

IN THE FIGHT   3

In the Fight: Women and Combat Exclusion

　　"Women are in the military, and there
　　they will remain."

　　　　　　　　　—Retired U.S. Navy Commander
　　　　　　　　　　　Darlene M. Iskra, PhD

　　　　The presence of women in the military
elicits responses ranging anywhere from
absolute condemnation to enthusiastic support. An 83-percent majority of the American
public is supportive of women serving in
noncombatant military roles; however, ap-
proval ratings dip 30 points once the topic
of women serving in combatant roles is
broached. Older Americans, in particular,
are against women serving in combat (CBS
News, 2010).

　　　　While this poll does demonstrate that
a slight majority of Americans overall
approve of women in combat (a lukewarm
53 percent), I think that support would
increase if Americans knew that women are
already involved in day-to-day combat
operations in our current conflicts. There
is a pressing need to eliminate the combat exclusion laws because military women
deserve the recognition and care that come
with their service.

　　　　The most virulent opponents of wom-
en's military service claim that since

IN THE FIGHT   4

the integration of women in 1948 there

has been a dangerous "feminization" of

the U.S. military, with military readi-

ness and effectiveness sacrificed to a

pernicious social experiment (Mitchell,

1998, pp. xv-xvii). To some, this could

appear to be a viable objection. After

all, Department of Defense (DoD) policies

on things like living quarters, rations,

and families have evolved drastically

since the integration of women began more

than 60 years ago. However, this is not

a softening of the DoD's expectations of

its troops. Better food and quarters in-

deed *followed* women into military life,

and these were necessary changes demanded

by women who wanted to improve provisions

for all military personnel, not just

women (Holm, 1992).

> *Here Patricia makes a move that is characteristic of a well-crafted argument: She presents the claims of critics of her thesis.*

    As a member of the military myself,

I can testify that current members owe a

debt of gratitude to these women who had

everyone's health and comfort in mind.

The physical conditions that my comrades-

in-arms and I are often required to serve

under can be difficult and uncomfortable

enough. Without the initiative for bet-

ter food and housing as begun by mili-

tary women in the 1940s, these operating

conditions could be far less tolerable.

> *This self-disclosure makes Patricia's argument even more persuasive because it establishes her credibility. She speaks with authority about the military because she serves.*

IN THE FIGHT   5

  There has also been dramatic trans-
formation in policies concerning military
women's families—and military families in
general—since female integration; however, these changes were necessary so the
military could retain qualified women in
its ranks. Before 1975, DoD regulations
stipulated that "women [be] forced out of
the military if they became pregnant or
even if they married someone with children. . . . If an unmarried woman became
pregnant, she would receive a punitive
discharge and little to no support for her
prenatal care" (Iskra, 2010, pp. 26, 41).
These antiquated policies contributed to
unnecessarily high rates of women leaving the military and made the lives of
those who wished to stay needlessly complicated. For example, when my own mother
became pregnant while in the military in
1979, she was counseled to have an abortion. She joined the Air Force at the age
of 17 and was already a competent elec-
trician. And although regulations had
changed four years prior, much of the
mindset within the workplace had not;
so because my mother was at the time a
scared 19-year-old with few advisors and
fewer options, she did as she was told

IN THE FIGHT   6

(J. Anderson, personal communication,

November 9,2010).

     Eventually, the Department of Defense

adjusted its policies. By the mid-1970s,

DoD recognized that forcing a woman to

choose between having a career and having

a family was preposterous, especially

in light of the women's rights move-

ments of the sixties and seventies. More

importantly, the DoD changed its poli-

cies because it saw the benefit of allowing

women who were experts in their fields to

remain in their jobs after the birth of

their first child. Clearly, when making

demographic decisions, the military leader-

ship is more concerned with what benefits

national security than in orchestrating any

kind of social change. As Commander Iskra

(2010) observes, "The military reflects

social change—it does not initiate it" (p. 24).

     Women have been allowed to partici-

pate in air and surface naval combat since

1992 and 1994, respectively (Iskra, 2010).

Since the mid-1990s, women have repeatedly

proven themselves in countless naval and

aviation missions. One example of many is

the accomplishments of Air Force Colonel

Martha McSally. As the first woman fighter

pilot in combat for the United States

*Note that per-
sonal interviews
are cited in
the text of your
paper but aren't
included in
the list of
references.*

Air Force, she has distinguished herself
as a top A-10 pilot in both Kuwait and
Afghanistan beginning in the mid-1990s;
she became the first female squadron commander of a fighter squadron while sta-
tioned at Davis-Monthan Air Force Base in
Tucson, Arizona; in 2006 she was selected to attend the Air War College, which
trains senior personnel in strategic air
and space forces employment; and she con-
tinues to contribute extensively to the
security missions of the U.S. armed forces
(Bergquist, 2010).

Colonel McSally is just one of many
women who have proven their dedication
and capability in the air and on the sea.
Women have demonstrated the same courage, skill, and honor as their male counterparts. It stands to reason, then, that
women will display the same character
traits in ground combat as they have
in air and naval combat. It's time for
legislation allowing for the official
inclusion of women in every aspect of
ground combat operations.

Critics of such a move would cite
aeronautical disasters such as the fatal
crash of Navy pilot Kara Hultgreen in
1994 or any number of adulterous cases

IN THE FIGHT   8

involving female aviators as evidence that
women cannot be trusted with multimillion-
dollar machinery (or co-ed work envi-
ronments) and, by extension, that women
cannot be trusted with the lives of their
comrades-in-arms (Mitchell, 1998). However, it is important to remember that fatal
crashes and adulterous affairs occurred
long before women came onto the scene and
that the well-publicized weaknesses of a
few should not be used to judge the abilities and potentials of such a diverse
group as American military women.

The challenges in today's military
conflicts demand the best of every soldier, sailor, and airman, regardless of
gender. Military women have proven on the
Army's and Marines' training grounds that
they handle the same tasks as men. As a
group, women's average scores are five
percent higher than men's average scores
(Burke, 2004). By policy, however, commanders are not allowed to deploy some of
their most talented soldiers for no other
reason than that they are women. As Marine
Brigadier General Thomas V. Draude said,
"These units deploy with the best men,
but not necessarily the best Marines" (as
cited in Iskra, 2010, p. 3).

Patricia nicely makes an assertion—that commanders can't use some of their best soldiers simply because they are women—and then uses a quotation from a commander that supports the assertion.

IN THE FIGHT   9

    Some commanders recognize that
combat exclusion laws are outdated, and
they already employ women on combat missions, but under different official guis-
es. Currently, when a commander needs to
use a woman on a mission, she will be
placed in the combat unit under the official status of a "temporary assignment"
or "combat support," all the while performing the same duties and service as
her male counterparts (Iskra, 2010).

    Women in combat and forward-operating
units aren't just there because they're
good soldiers. They are also needed in
some conflicts because men are forbidden
by local law and custom to touch native
women for any reason. Women soldiers and
Marines are needed on many missions to
conduct business involving native wom-
en and children, whether it is performing personal searches, guarding them,
or calming them down after a distress-
ing event (McLachlan & Sommers, 2008).
These women execute the same tasks, fight
in the same battles, and run the same
risks as their brothers-in-arms yet do
not receive the same benefits as the men
do. They may be denied combat pay, combat
recognition in the form of awards and

IN THE FIGHT   10

decorations, opportunities for promotion,
and, most importantly, care for combat-
related stress and injuries. Put simply,
women are already engaged in combat. Why
not make it legal?

In the changing terrain of twenty-
first century warfare, the time has come
to eliminate combat exclusion laws. Women
who already engage in combat deserve the
recognition and treatment that accompany
combatant status, and women of the future
military deserve the chance to prove themselves on the battlefield and further
their careers just as their brothers-in-
arms have done for centuries. This will
not result in some fictional "feminization"
of the military but will allow it to use
the best minds rather than a select group
based on gender. Women are needed on the
battlefields of America's wars, not as a
dangerous social experiment but because
they provide additional talent and flexibility to execute vital missions. It is
time to recognize the abilities and potential of American military women by passing
legislation that gives them the rights and
responsibilities that every male soldier
takes part in. It is time to repeal the
combat exclusion laws.

IN THE FIGHT   11

References

Bergquist, C. (2010). Air Force Lt. Col. Martha McSally: First female pilot in combat reflects on career. *The Face of Defense* (Dec. 6, 2006). Retrieved from http://www.defense .gov/home/faceofdefense/fod/2006-12 /f20061207a.html

Burke, C. (2004). *Camp all-American, Hanoi Jane, and the high-and-tight: Gender, folklore, and changing military culture.* Boston, MA: Beacon Press.

CBS News (Producer). (15 Aug. 2009). Poll: 53% support women in combat roles. *CBS News*. Retrieved from http://www.cbsnews .com/stories/2009/08/15/opinion/polls /main5244312.shtml

Holm, J. (1992). *Women in the military: An unfinished evolution.* Novato, CA: Presidio.

Iskra, D. (2010) *Women in the United States Armed Forces: A guide to the issues.* Santa Barbara, CA: Praeger Security International.

McLaclan, M., & Sommers, D. (Directors). (2008). *Lioness* [Film]. United States: Chicken and Eggs Production.

Mitchell, Brian. (1998). *Women in the military: Flirting with disaster.* Washington, DC: Regnery Publishing.

Always begin the references on a new page.

Understanding Research Assignments

About 15 years ago, in a dark, dimly lit basement floor of the University of New Hampshire library, I discovered the textbook that may have had the very first research paper assignment for undergraduates. Charles Baldwin's 1906 *A College Manual of Rhetoric* encouraged students to write essays based on reading that emphasized "originally" compiling facts so that the writer gives "already known" information his "own grouping and interpretation." In an article that year, Baldwin noted that "from the beginning a student should learn that his use of the library will be a very practical measure of his culture."

In the century since Baldwin's book, the college research paper has become probably the most common genre of student writing in the university. It is a fixture in composition classes and many other courses that require a "term paper." Naturally, this is why there are books like this—to help students understand these assignments and give them guidance in the process of writing them. As you know, this book emphasizes the research *essay* rather than the formal research paper. My argument is that this more exploratory, possibly less formal, researched piece is the best way to introduce you to the spirit of inquiry that drives most academic research. The habits of mind that come from essaying, along with the research and writing skills that essaying develops, should help you whenever you're asked to write a paper that involves research.

There's another skill that's invaluable when you encounter a research paper assignment in another class: knowing how to interpret what exactly you're being asked to do. This involves reading your writing assignment rhetorically. In other words, analyze the *situation* for each assignment: How does it fit into other writing projects in the course? What particular purpose does this assignment have? What do you know about the instructor's particular attitudes about research and about writing? How do you figure out the best approaches to the research project? Apparently, this analysis can pose a huge problem for students. In one study, for example, 92 percent of students said that the most frustrating part of doing research was figuring out what their professor wanted.*

Instructors aren't trying to be obtuse. They want you to understand the assignment, and most have made an effort to be clear. While there's not much you can do about *how* the assignment is conceived or described, you can be savvier at analyzing the assignment's purpose and guidelines.

I've recently conducted a review of research paper assignments from courses across the disciplines, and actually there are striking similarities among them. I tried to read them as a student would, actively looking for guidance about how to approach the assignment and also alert to subtleties that students might miss. In the following sections, I break this rhetorical analysis into parts, drawing on what I learned.

Analyzing the Purpose of the Assignment

One of the things I hear most often from my students who have research assignments in other classes is that the instructor "doesn't want my opinion in the paper." Frankly, I'm often skeptical of this. College writing assignments typically are about what or how you think. But because research papers involve considerable time collecting and considering the ideas of others, it's easy to assume that you're supposed to be a bystander.

Actually, even some instructors seem to equate the term "research paper" with merely reporting information. "This is not a research paper," said one assignment. "The idea here is not to pack in as much information as you can, but instead to present a thoughtful and clearly written analysis." Another noted that "although this is a research paper, the focus is fundamentally on your own analysis and interpretation...."

*Head, Alison. "Beyond Google: How Do Students Conduct Academic Research?" *First Monday* 12.8, 6 Aug. 2007. Web. 30 Mar. 2008.

What these instructors are at pains to point out is that, contrary to what you might think, they are actively interested in what you think. They want students to *do* something with the information they collect. But merely having an opinion isn't enough. As one assignment put it, "You are not being graded on your opinion, but your ability to communicate and support a point of view (your thesis)."

Writing a convincing, well-supported paper is straightforward enough. But why do the project in the first place? What is the purpose of writing a research paper? The assignments I reviewed sometimes talk about encouraging "critical thinking" or helping students enter "a scholarly conversation." A few talk about "advancing your knowledge" about a topic or learning the conventions of research writing in a particular discipline. But many, unfortunately, just focus on a requirement that your paper make an argument.

Argumentative Research: Open or Closed?

The language that research assignments use to emphasize argument is quite often very explicit: "You are to write a research paper in which you make an argument related to some aspect of life in Southeast Asia." Not much ambiguity there. Similarly, some assignments ask that you "take a position" on a topic. Argumentative research papers are most often organized around a thesis, and some assignment descriptions go to great lengths to explain what makes a strong one (usually, sufficiently narrow, addressing a significant question, and explicitly stated).

What may not be obvious, however, is how much latitude you have in letting your research revise your thesis or even dramatically change your initial point of view. Most often, instructors *expect* the research to change your thinking, and they often use the term "working thesis" to describe your initial position. These are the more open-ended assignments that might specify that the crafting of a final thesis can occur late rather than early in the research process. These are also assignments that emphasize a focus on a *research question*.

More rarely, an assignment will imply a closed approach: First identify a thesis, and then seek evidence from your research that will support it. This is the conventional thesis-support model in which the expectation is that you will use your thesis, and not your research question, to dictate not just the structure of your paper but also the goal of your research. These kinds of assignments tend not to mention that a thesis might be revised and are silent on how it arises from a research question or problem. Always ask your instructor about whether your reading of the assignment as more closed-ended is accurate. The key questions are these:

Questions to Ask Your Instructor About the Thesis

- Where should the thesis in this assignment come from?
- What process do you suggest for arriving at it?
- Finally, might it be revised—even substantially—later in the process?

In a more open-ended research paper, the inquiry-based methods directly apply. For example, crafting a researchable question is an important route to coming up with a strong working thesis, and the dialogue or double-entry journal can help you think through how your research might develop or revise that thesis. The strict thesis-support paper seems to have little opportunity for inquiry. Indeed, the emphasis in these assignments is frequently on the formal qualities of the paper—how well it's organized around and supports a thesis, the proper use of citations, and mechanical correctness. Developing an outline at the front end of the project is usually helpful.

Audience

For whom are you writing? So much hinges on the answer to this question: the tone of the paper, how specialized its language might be, the emphasis you give on providing background on the research question, and the degree to which you stress reader interest. Despite the importance of audience, research paper assignments frequently fail to mention it at all. This omission can often mean that you are writing for your instructor. But it actually might surprise you how often this isn't intended to be the case. Particularly if your assignment includes peer review of drafts or class presentations, you may be writing for a more general audience. Sometimes this is explicit: "Your paper should be understood by a broader audience than scholars in your field. You will have to explain concepts and not expect your audience to understand in-house jargon." If the audience for your paper isn't clear, ask your instructor this simple question:

Question to Ask Your Instructor About the Audience

- Who is the audience for this assignment—readers like the instructor who are knowledgeable about the topic and/or readers who are not?

Extent of Emphasis on Formal Qualities

An essay like "Theories of Intelligence" is relatively informal: It's casual in tone, has a strong individual voice, and is structured to explore a question—*to find out* rather than *to prove*. It certainly has a thesis, but it is a delayed thesis, appearing not in the introduction but toward the end of the essay. The essay is organized around the writer's questions, not around making a point and logically providing evidence to support it. It does, however, have some formal qualities, including careful citation and attribution, the marshalling of appropriate evidence to explore the topic, and a sensible organization that moves from question to answers.

Research paper assignments in other classes are likely to put considerably more emphasis on a structure based on logic and reasoning. Put another way, these papers differ from an exploratory essay like "Theories of Intelligence" in that they report the *products* of the process of thinking about and researching the question, rather than describe the *process* of thinking and researching the question. The chief product, of course, is your thesis—the thing you are trying to say—and typically you're expected to place this in the introduction of your paper. Fairly often, research paper assignments instruct you to state your thesis or position explicitly in a sentence. Along with a thesis, however, many assignments, in keeping with the approach of this book, ask that you develop a research question from which the thesis then emerges. These are the open assignments we discussed earlier. As one put it, "[The] introduction should make three points: It should briefly introduce your question and its significance, state your answer, and orient the reader regarding your way of proceeding. This is the place to say, 'I'm going to argue....'" Patricia Urbick's essay, in which she argues that the policies that exclude military women from combat should be abolished, is a great example of this kind of paper.

Also pay close attention to what context the assignment asks you to establish for your research question—course discussion, literature review, or both. Some instructors are keen on having you write a paper that in some way extends the course's readings or discussion points. Others want you to become familiar with the scholarly conversation that might extend beyond the class. Here's a question to ask about this:

Question to Ask Your Instructor About the Context

- What is the more important context for establishing the significance of my research question or thesis—what we talked about in class or what I discover when I review the relevant literature?

The logical structure of an argumentative research paper doesn't vary much, although in some disciplines you will be instructed to use the organizational conventions of the field; for example, scientific papers might require an abstract, introduction, methods, results, discussion, and conclusion, in that order. Generally, the body of your paper must draw on evidence from your research to support your thesis, though frequently your assignment requires that you also consider opposing points of view. How are they misguided? In what ways do they fail to address your research question? Also pay attention to whether your assignment asks you to tightly tether each paragraph to the thesis using topic sentences that address how that paragraph supports it.* If so, you might find it useful to outline the topic sentences before you draft your essay.

Because one of the aims of teaching research writing is to help you understand its conventions, assignments almost always discuss the need for proper citation, correct format, a required number of scholarly sources, and so on, as well as attention to grammar and mechanics. You need to determine the relative importance of these conventions. Some research paper assignments, for example, devote much more ink to describing the required format—location of page numbers, font, margins—and the need for "perfect" grammar than they do a discussion of the research process, formulating a thesis, or the larger goals of the assignment. In this case, you might give these

---

*Some instructors heavily stress the use of topic sentences in paragraph writing, though there is considerable evidence that much writing, including academic prose, doesn't consistently feature topic sentences.

conventions more attention. If you're not sure how to weigh them, ask this question:

Question to Ask Your Instructor About the Importance of Formal Qualities

- When you evaluate the paper, what is the relative importance of getting the format right? Do you give that concern as much weight as the quality of my thesis or the soundness of my thinking?

As you know, this book encourages essays in which writers have a strong presence. The easiest way to do this is to enter the text directly by using the first person. Research paper assignments rarely mention whether you can use "I." Silence on this question usually means that you should not. One of the conventions of much academic writing is a more formal register, the sense that the paper speaks rather than the writer. Yet a considerable number of the assignments I reviewed encouraged students to write with "voice" and lively, vigorous prose. The most effective way to inject voice into your research writing is to find your own way of saying things, something that "writing in the middle"—the notetaking strategies encouraged in this book—should help you with. Assignments that say nothing about voice or style probably expect what one assignment described as writing that is "formal in tone, working to establish an authoritative, critical, and analytical voice." If you're unsure about this, consider asking your instructor the following question:

Question to Ask Your Instructor About Tone

- Should the voice in my paper mimic the scholarly sources I'm reading, or can it be somewhat less formal, perhaps sounding a bit more like me?

Types of Evidence: Primary or Secondary

As you move from a general audience (people who may know little about your topic) to a more specialized audience (people who know more), the tone and structure of your paper will change. So will the types of evidence that will make your argument persuasive. In popular writing—say, articles in *Wired* or *Discover* or op-ed pieces in the newspaper—the types of evidence that writers use to convince readers are quite varied. Personal experience and observation, for instance, are often excellent ways to support a point. But as you begin writing research papers in academic disciplines, you need to pay attention to what your instructor considers *appropriate* evidence in that field and for that particular assignment. Scientific papers, for example, often rely on experimental data. Literature papers lean most heavily on evidence culled from the literary text you're writing about. Papers in anthropology might rely on field observations.

Sometimes assignments explicitly talk about appropriate evidence for your paper. More often they do not. Generally speaking, research papers that are assigned in lower-division courses won't require you to conduct experiments or generate field notes. They will likely ask you to draw evidence from already published, or secondary, sources on your topic. But this isn't always the case. A history paper, for example, might require that you study a primary text, perhaps letters by historical figures, political documents, or archived newspapers. This is something you need to know. If the types of evidence you should use in your paper aren't clear, ask this question:

Question to Ask Your Instructor About Evidence

■ What types of evidence should I rely on for this paper? Primary or secondary sources? And is personal experience and observation, if relevant, appropriate to use?

In the spirit of writing a conventional conclusion, let me restate what might be apparent by now: The most important thing you must do when you get a research assignment is read the handout carefully, considering what you've already learned in the class about writing in that discipline. I read a lot of research paper assignments, and they usually provide very good guidance. But if they don't, that's never an excuse for floundering. Ask, ask, ask. Your instructor wants you to.

Handbook

This guide assumes that you, like other writers, sometimes have problems getting your sentences to come out right. These are problems in *usage*: how to use verbs, modifiers, and pronouns, for example. This discussion focuses on those problems, explaining the *how* more than the *what*, treating those problems as matters of writing, not of grammar. It avoids grammatical jargon as much as possible but defines terms where necessary for understanding the problem. This guide also gives you a quick review of punctuation, mechanics, spelling, style, and basic grammar. It also offers tips for ESL writers. Refer to this guide while writing and when your instructor suggests sections for you to study.

Here's how the sections are arranged:

1. Sentence Boundaries
  1A Fragments
  1B Comma Splices
  1C Fused Sentences

2. Sentence Inconsistencies
  2A Parallelism
  2B Coordination and Subordination
  2C Mixed Sentences
  2D Shifts

3. Problems with Modification
  3A Dangling and Misplaced Modifiers
  3B Restrictive and Nonrestrictive Modifiers
  3C Adjectives and Adverbs

4. Verbs
  4A Tense
  4B Voice
  4C Mood
  4D Subject–Verb Agreement

5. Pronouns
  5A Pronoun Case
  5B Pronoun Reference

From Handbook of *The Curious Writer*, Fourth Edition. Bruce Ballenger. Copyright © 2014 by Pearson Education, Inc. All rights reserved.

5C Pronoun Agreement
5D Relative Pronouns

6. Style
6A Conciseness
6B Appropriate Language

7. Punctuation
7A End Punctuation
7B Semicolon
7C Comma
7D Colon
7E Dash
7F Quotation Marks
7G Other Marks

8. Mechanics and Spelling
8A Capitalization
8B Abbreviation
8C Apostrophe
8D Hyphens
8E Italics (Underlining)
8F Numbers
8G Spelling

9. Review of Basic Grammar
9A Parts of Speech
9B Subjects and Predicates
9C Objects and Complements
9D Phrases
9E Clauses
9F Basic Sentence Patterns
9G Types of Sentences

10. Tips for ESL Writers
10A Articles
10B Verbs
10C Adjectives and Adverbs
10D Prepositions
10E Participles

1 Sentence Boundaries

Learning Objectives

1 Recognize and correct sentence fragments.

2 Recognize and correct comma splices.

3 Recognize and correct fused sentences.

Sentence boundaries are marked by end punctuation (7A): periods, question marks, or occasionally exclamation points. Because they mark the ends of sentences, each mark of end punctuation must be preceded by at least one independent clause (a complete statement containing a subject and a verb and not beginning with a subordinating word). Errors in sentence boundaries involve inappropriate punctuation: periods where commas or no punctuation should go, and commas or no punctuation where periods or semicolons should go. To develop your own sense of which marks to use, think of periods, semicolons, and commas as *strongest* to *weakest*. The weakest mark, the comma, is not interchangeable with the strongest mark, the period, and usually not with the semicolon. But periods and semicolons, depending on the writer's choice, *are* often interchangeable. The following discussions regarding sentence boundary errors are based on this reasoning.

1A Fragments

Sentence fragments are errors in which partial sentences are treated as sentences— begun with a capital letter and ended with a period. The fragment may be a subordinate clause, a phrase, or a combination of subordinate elements. What makes each a fragment is that it lacks a subject or a verb, or that it begins with a subordinating word. Only independent clauses can make independent statements.

1
Recognize and correct sentence fragments.

Subordinate Clause Fragment

Recognition. A subordinate clause has a subject and a verb but cannot make an independent statement because of the connector that implies it is only part of a sentence. Here are two lists of the most common subordinating connectors.

Subordinating conjunctions, arranged by function

Time	Place
after	where
before	wherever
once	
since	Cause
until	as
when	because
whenever	since
while	

Contrast	Condition
although	even if
even though	if
though	
while	Result
	in order that
Alternative	so
than	so that
whether	that

Relative pronouns

who (whom, whose)	whoever (whomever, whosever)
which	whichever
that	
what	whatever
where	wherever
when	whenever
why	
unless	
whereas	

Any clause beginning with one of these words is *subordinate* and should not be written as a sentence. Here are examples of clause fragments (italicized):

> The Vikings revolutionized shipbuilding with the keel. *Which allowed their ships to go faster and farther without stopping for supplies.*

> Norway's Lapps are believed to be a nomadic people of Asian heritage. *Who follow reindeer herds through Norway's cold, rugged land.*

> *Because the northern part of Norway is so far north.* It has long periods during the summer when the sun shines 24 hours a day.

Correction. There are mainly two ways of correcting clause fragments: (1) attaching them to the preceding or following sentence and (2) removing or changing the subordinating connector. These sentences illustrate both types of correction:

> The Vikings revolutionized shipbuilding with the keel. *This innovation* allowed their ships to go faster and farther without stopping for supplies. The subordinating word of the fragment is changed.

> Norway's Lapps are believed to be of Asian heritage—nomadic people who follow reindeer herds through Norway's cold, rugged land. The fragment is connected to the preceding sentence with a dash.

> Because the northern part of Norway is so far north, it has long periods during the summer when the sun shines 24 hours a day. The fragment is connected to the following sentence with a comma.

Phrase Fragment

Phrase fragments lack a subject, a verb, or both. The most common phrases written as fragments are *verbal phrases* and *prepositional phrases*.

Watch
the Animation on
Sentence Fragments
in your MyLab

Recognition. A *verbal phrase* is a word group made up of a verb form and related modifiers and other words. As opposed to *verb phrases*, which are made up of verb parts (such as *has been gone*), a verbal phrase is constituted with a *verbal*, a word formed from a verb but not functioning as a verb. *Going*, for example, is a verbal, as is *gone*. You probably wouldn't write "Charles going to St. Louis" or "Charles gone to St. Louis." Instead, you would add helping verbs: "Charles *is going* to St. Louis" and "Charles *has gone* to St. Louis."

There are three kinds of verbals: gerunds, participles, and infinitives. Gerunds end in *-ing*; participles end in either *-ing* (present) or *-ed* (regular past); infinitives have no ending but are usually introduced by *to*. Here arc a few examples of how verbals are formed from verbs:

Verb	Present participle and gerund	Past participle	Infinitive
snap	snapping	snapped	to snap
look	looking	looked	to look
want	wanting	wanted	to want
go	going	gone	to go
has	having	had	to have

Verbals function primarily as adjectives and nouns, most often in verbal phrases.

In the following examples, the italicized verbal phrases are fragments because they are written as sentences:

Eero Saarinen designed the 630-foot Gateway Arch for the St. Louis riverfront. *Imagining a giant stainless steel arch.* Participial phrase modifying Eero Saarinen.

Critics said that cranes could not reach high enough. *To lift the steel sections into place.* Infinitive phrase modifying high.

Under Saarinen's plan, a derrick would creep up the side of each leg of the arch. *Lifting each plate into position.* Participial phrase modifying derrick.

Saarinen knew that precision was of utmost importance. In *building the arch.* Gerund phrase as object of preposition In.

Correction. Verbal phrase fragments can be corrected in one of two ways: (1) by connecting them to a related sentence or (2) by expanding them to a sentence. Both ways are illustrated next.

Eero Saarinen designed the 630-foot Gateway Arch for the St. Louis riverfront. *He imagined a giant stainless steel arch.* The verbal fragment is expanded to a sentence.

Critics said that cranes could not reach high enough *to lift the steel sections into place.* The verbal fragment is connected to a related sentence.

Under Saarinen's plan, a derrick would creep up the side of each leg of the arch, *lifting each plate into position*. The verbal fragment is connected to a related sentence.

Saarinen knew that precision was of utmost importance in *building the arch*. The gerund phrase, object of the preposition *In*, is connected to a related sentence.

Recognition. A *prepositional phrase* is a word group made up of a preposition and its object. Together they contribute meaning to a sentence, usually modifying a noun or a verb. Like subordinating conjunctions, prepositions show relationships, such as time, place, condition, cause, and so on. Here are some of the most common prepositions:

about	concerning	onto
above	despite	out
according to	down	out of
across	during	outside
after	except	over
against	except for	past
along	excepting	regarding
along with	for	since
among	from	through
around	in	throughout
as	in addition to	till
at	in back of	to
because of	in place of	toward
before	in spite of	under
behind	inside	underneath
below	instead of	unlike
beneath	into	until
beside	like	up
between	near	up to
beyond	next	upon
but	of	with
by	off	within
by means of	on	without

In the following examples, prepositional phrases have been written as sentences and are therefore fragments:

The Vikings were descendants of Teutonic settlers. *Like most of today's Norwegians.*

Norway is a land of natural beauty. *From its fjord-lined coast to frigid Lapland.*

Correction. Prepositional phrase fragments also can be corrected (1) by connecting them to a related sentence or (2) by expanding them to a sentence.

The Vikings were descendants of Teutonic settlers, *like most of today's Norwegians.* **or** *Like most of today's Norwegians*, the Vikings were descendants of Teutonic settlers. The prepositional phrase is connected to a related sentence.

Norway is a land of natural beauty. *Its charm extends from its fjord-lined coast to frigid Lapland.* The prepositional phrase is expanded to a sentence.

Incomplete Thoughts

Sometimes fragments are simply errors in punctuation: The writer uses a period when a comma or no punctuation would be correct. A more difficult type of fragment to correct is the incomplete thought, such as this one:

A large concrete dock 50 feet short of a wooden platform anchored in the middle of the bay.

In this fragment, something is missing, and, as a result, a reader doesn't know what to make of the words "large concrete dock." With fragments of this sort, the writer needs to insert the missing information. The fragment might be revised like this:

A large concrete dock juts out, stopping 50 feet short of a wooden platform anchored in the middle of the bay.

Acceptable Fragments

You probably encounter fragments every day. Titles are often fragments, as are answers to questions and expressions of strong emotion.

Titles: *The Curious Writer*, "A Fire in the Woods"

Answer to question: "How many more chairs do we need?" "Fifteen."

Expression of strong emotion: "What a great concert!"

And much advertising utilizes fragments:

Intricate, delicate, exquisite. Extravagant in every way.

Another successful client meeting. Par for the course.

Common as they are in everyday life, fragments are usually unacceptable in academic or business writing. Even though professional writers and advertising writers sometimes use them for emphasis, there are rarely cases when you will need intentional fragments for the effective expression of your thoughts in school or business.

1B Comma Splices

Comma splices consist of two independent clauses (clauses that can stand alone as sentences) improperly joined together by a comma in the same sentence. Here are two examples:

2
Recognize and correct comma splices.

The economy of Algeria is in trouble, many citizens blame the government.

The death of any soldier is tragic, however, death by friendly fire is particularly disturbing.

Recognition. The first step in avoiding comma splices is to identify them. Because they happen only in sentences with at least two independent clauses, you can test your sentences by substituting periods for your commas. If you end up with complete sentences, you probably have a comma splice. In testing the first of the two preceding examples, we come up with the following result:

The economy of Algeria is in trouble.

Many citizens blame the government.

Both of these clauses obviously qualify as complete sentences, so they must be independent clauses. They therefore cannot be connected with a comma. Remember this simple rule of punctuation: *Periods and commas are not interchangeable*. If a period is correct, a comma is not.

Watch
the Animation on
Comma Splices
in your MyLab

Correction. You can revise comma splices using five different strategies.

1. Separate the independent clauses using a comma and a *coordinating conjunction*. The list of coordinating conjunctions is short:

and	or	for	yet
but	nor	so	

   To correct a comma splice, begin the second independent clause with one of these conjunctions, preceded by a comma. For example:

   The economy of Algeria is in trouble, *and* many citizens blame the government.

2. Separate the independent clauses using a semicolon (with or without a transitional adverb). Semicolons are often interchangeable with periods and therefore can be used to separate independent clauses. For example:

   The economy of Algeria is in trouble; many citizens blame the government.

   The death of any soldier is tragic; *however*, death by friendly fire is particularly disturbing.

   In the second example, *however* is a transitional adverb. Unlike coordinating conjunctions, *transitional adverbs* are not conjunctions and so do not join sentence elements. They do, however, connect ideas by showing how they relate to one another. Like conjunctions, they can show addition, contrast, result, and other relationships. Here are some of the common transitional adverbs, arranged by function:

Addition	Examples
in addition	for example
also	for instance
moreover	in fact
next	specifically
then	
finally	

Comparison	Contrast
likewise	however
similarly	nevertheless
in comparison	on the contrary
	on the other hand
Result	otherwise
therefore	
consequently	Time
then	meanwhile
as a result	subsequently
	finally
	then

A semicolon should always precede the transitional adverb that begins the second independent clause. A comma usually follows the transitional adverb, although in some instances, as in the following example, the comma is omitted:

> Air bags deflate within one second after inflation; *therefore*, they do not interfere with control of the car.

Some comma splices result when writers use transitional adverbs as if they were coordinating conjunctions. If you have trouble distinguishing transitional adverbs from coordinating conjunctions, remember that none of the coordinating conjunctions is longer than three letters, and all of the transitional adverbs are four letters or longer. Also, keep in mind that transitional adverbs are movable within the sentence, while coordinating conjunctions are not; for example, the preceding example could be rewritten as:

> Air bags deflate within one second after inflation; they do not *therefore* interfere with control of the car.

3. Make one of the independent clauses subordinate to the other by inserting a subordinating conjunction. When one of the clauses explains or elaborates on the other, use an appropriate subordinating conjunction to make the relationship between the two clauses more explicit (see 1A Fragments for a list of subordinating conjunctions). Consider the following comma splice and its revision:

> Henry forgot to fill in his time card on Friday, he is going to have a hard time getting paid for the overtime he put in last week.
>
> *Because* Henry forgot to fill in his time card on Friday, he is going to have a hard time getting paid for the overtime he put in last week.

4. Rewrite one of the independent clauses as a modifying phrase. A *modifying phrase* serves as an adjective or adverb within a sentence. By rewriting one

of the independent clauses as a phrase, you can eliminate unneeded words. For example, consider the following comma splice and its revision:

> The celebrity couple smiled for the cameras, they were glowing of wealth and fame.

> The celebrity couple smiled for the cameras, glowing of wealth and fame. Here *glowing of wealth and fame* acts as an adjective modifying the noun *couple.*

5. Punctuate each independent clause as a separate sentence. No law of grammar, punctuation, or style says you must present the two independent clauses together within one sentence, so you won't be cheating if you write them as two separate sentences. The example from before is perfectly acceptable written as follows:

> The economy of Algeria is in trouble. Many citizens blame the government.

It may be to your advantage to divide long and/or complex independent clauses into separate sentences; doing so may help convey your meaning to readers more clearly.

1C Fused Sentences

3

Recognize and correct fused sentences.

Fused sentences, sometimes called *run-on sentences*, are similar to comma splices. However, instead of a comma between the two independent clauses, there is no punctuation—the two independent clauses simply run together. For example:

> The United States has 281 lawyers per 100,000 people Japan has only 11 attorneys per 100,000.

> The World Cup is the most popular sporting event in the world you would never know it based on the indifferent response of the average American.

Recognition. Unlike the comma splice, there is no punctuation in the fused sentence to guide you to the end of the first independent clause and the beginning of the second. As a result, it can be more challenging to identify independent clauses within fused sentences, particularly if the sentence also contains modifying phrases or dependent clauses set off by commas. The best way to do this is to read from the beginning of the sentence (reading aloud may help) until you have found the end of the first independent clause. Consider the following example:

> Even though I was still sick with the flu, I attended the awards banquet as my family watched, the coach presented me with the trophy for most valuable player.

This fused sentence contains two subordinate clauses (*Even though I was still sick with the flu* and *as my family watched*), each one attached to one of the two independent clauses (*I attended the awards banquet* and *the coach presented me with the trophy*).

Correction. Revise fused sentences using any one of the same five strategies employed for correcting comma splices (see 1B Comma Splices for more information on each strategy).

Watch
the Animation on
**Fixing Run-on
Sentences**
in your MyLab

1. Separate the independent clauses using a comma and a coordinating conjunction. For example:

   The United States has 281 lawyers per 100,000 people, *but* Japan has only 11 attorneys per 100,000.

2. Separate the independent clauses using a semicolon (with or without a transitional adverb). For example:

   The United States has 281 lawyers per 100,000 people; Japan has only 11 attorneys per 100,000.

   The World Cup is the most popular sporting event in the world; *however*, you would never know it based on the indifferent response of the average American.

3. Make one of the independent clauses subordinate to the other by inserting a subordinating conjunction. The newly formed dependent clause should explain the remaining independent clause. For example, consider the following fused sentence and its revision:

   I run a marathon my feet get sore.

   Whenever I run a marathon, my feet get sore.

4. Rewrite one of the independent clauses as a modifying phrase. Remember, modifying phrases act as adjectives or adverbs. Consider the following fused sentence and its revision:

   Last night the tomcats fought outside my window they were crying and hissing for what seemed like hours.

   Last night the tomcats fought outside my window, crying and hissing for what seemed like hours. Here *crying and hissing* acts as an adjective modifying the noun *tomcats*.

5. Punctuate each independent clause as a separate sentence. As with comma splices, you can write the independent clauses (and their related phrases and dependent clauses) as separate sentences. Indeed, this is often the easiest way to handle fused sentences. For example:

   I attended the awards banquet even though I was still sick with the flu. As my family watched, the coach presented me with the trophy for most valuable player. Here the subordinate clause attached to the first independent clause *even though I was still sick with the flu* was also moved to the back of the first sentence for the sake of greater readability.

Complete
Additional Exercises
and Practice on
the Handbook
in your MyLab

2 Sentence Inconsistencies

Learning Objectives

1 Recognize and correct faulty parallelism.

2 Use coordination and subordination effectively.

3 Revise mixed sentences to make sentences consistent.

4 Recognize and revise unintended shifts in sentence elements.

Sentences pose difficulties for readers when the grammar is confused or inconsistent. Such problems happen when writers pay attention to what they are saying and not to how they are saying it. Such attention is a natural condition of writing, and careful revision usually takes care of any problems.

2A Parallelism

1
Recognize and correct faulty parallelism.

Parallelism results when two or more grammatically equivalent sentence elements are joined. The sentence elements can be nouns, verbs, phrases, or clauses. (See 2B Coordination and Subordination.) Here is a sentence with parallel elements:

> In a country where college education becomes increasingly everybody's chance, where executives and refrigerator salesmen and farmers play golf together, where a college professor may drive a cab in the summertime to keep his family alive, it becomes harder and harder to guess a person's education, income, and social status by the way he talks. —Paul Roberts

Here is the same sentence with the parallel elements arranged to be more visually accessible:

> In a country
>   {where college education becomes increasingly everybody's chance,
>   {where {executives
>   and {refrigerator salesmen
>   and {farmers play golf together,
>   {where a college professor may drive a cab in the summertime to keep
>   his family alive,
>   it becomes {harder
>   and {harder to guess a person's {education
>   {income,
>   and {social status
>   by the way he talks.

This sentence has parallel clauses (each beginning *where*), parallel subjects (*executives, refrigerator salesmen,* and *farmers*), parallel adverbs (*harder* and *harder*), and parallel direct objects (*education*, *income*, and *social status*). As this sentence illustrates, the principle of parallelism does not require that elements be alike in every way. Some of these nouns have modifiers, for example, and the clauses have different structural patterns.

Parallelism becomes a problem when dissimilar elements are joined in pairs, in series, in comparisons using *than* or *as*, or in comparisons linked by correlative conjunctions. Consider the following examples of faulty parallelism:

> She did not like rude customers or taking orders from her boss. The two elements in the pair are not parallel.

> We were having a hard time deciding what to do in the afternoon: go snorkeling, go fishing, or swim out to the sand bar. The last of the three elements in the series is not parallel.

> Michael decided to complete his degree next semester rather than studying abroad for another year. The two elements compared using *than* are not parallel.

> My sister not only lost the race but also her leg got hurt. The two elements compared by the correlative conjunction *not only...but also* are not parallel. Other correlative conjunctions include *both...and, either...or, neither...nor, whether...or,* and *just as...so.*

Faulty parallelism can be corrected in various ways:

> She did not like *dealing with* rude customers or taking orders from her boss. Words were added to the first element to make it parallel to the second.

> We were having a hard time deciding what to do in the afternoon: go snorkeling, go fishing, or *go swimming.* The last element was rewritten to make it parallel with the others in the series.

> Michael decided to complete his degree next semester rather than *to study* abroad for another year. The verb form of the second element is changed from a participle to an infinitive to make it parallel with the verb form in the first element.

> My sister not only lost the race but also *hurt her leg.* The second element was rewritten to make it parallel with the first element.

Revision of faulty parallelism is usually fairly easy to achieve. What is difficult is recognizing it, and unfortunately there are no tricks to easy recognition. Even experienced writers find that in their own writing they need to make an editing trip through their drafts looking just at their parallel structures. The absence of faulty parallels is a sign of careful writing.

Watch
the Animation on
Parallelism
in your MyLab

2B Coordination and Subordination

Most sentence relationships embody either coordination or subordination. That is, sentence elements are either grammatically equal to other elements (coordination) or grammatically dependent on other parts (subordination). For example, two independent clauses in a sentence are coordinate; but in a sentence containing an

2

Use coordination and subordination effectively.

371

independent clause and a dependent clause, the dependent clause is subordinate (indeed, dependent clauses are also called subordinate clauses).

Coordination

When two or more equivalent sentence elements appear in one sentence, they are coordinate. These elements can be words, phrases, or clauses. Only parallel elements can be coordinated: verbs linked with verbs, nouns with nouns, phrases with phrases, and clauses with clauses. (See 2A Parallelism.) For example:

Broccoli and *related vegetables* contain beta-carotene, a substance that may reduce the risk of heart attack. Two nouns are joined by a coordinating conjunction.

We *ran*, *swam*, and *cycled* every day while we were at the fitness camp. Three parallel verbs are joined in a series with commas and a coordinating conjunction.

American medical devices are equally remarkable, *giving life to those with terminally diseased organs, giving mobility to those crippled with arthritic joints and deadened nerves,* and even, miraculously, *restoring the sense of hearing to those deprived of it.—Atlantic.* The participial (verbal) phrases are joined by commas and a final coordinating conjunction. Also, embedded in the second participial phrase, two coordinate noun phrases are joined by a coordinating conjunction: *arthritic joints and deadened nerves.*

The term "Big Bang" is common usage now with scientists, but it originated as a sarcastic rejection of the theory. Two independent clauses are joined by a comma and a coordinating conjunction.

Subordination

Subordination is an essential aspect of sentence relations. If all sentence elements were grammatically equivalent, the sameness would be tedious. Subordinate elements show where the emphasis lies in sentences and modify elements with independent clauses. A subordinate element—be it a phrase or clause—is dependent for its meaning on the element it modifies. At the same time, it often provides a fuller meaning than could be achieved exclusively through the use of independent elements.

For example:

For walking and jogging, the calorie expenditure is greater for people of greater body weight. The subordinate element is a prepositional phrase, modifying *is greater.*

Increasing both speed and effort in aerobic activities, the exerciser burns more calories. The subordinate element is a verbal phrase, modifying *exerciser.*

Because sedentary people are more likely to burn sugar than fat, they tend to become hungry sooner and to overeat. The subordinate clause modifies the verb *tend.*

People *who exercise on a regular basis* change certain enzyme systems *so that they are more likely to burn fat than sugar.* There are two subordinate clauses, one beginning with *who* and modifying *People,* and one beginning with *so that* and modifying the verb *change.*

Effective writing has both coordination and subordination—coordination that sets equivalent elements side by side, and subordination that makes some elements dependent on others. Both are useful writing tools.

2C Mixed Sentences

In mixed sentences, called faulty predications when they involve the mismatching of subject and predicate, two or more parts of a sentence do not make sense together. Like other inconsistencies, this kind of problem usually occurs when writers concentrate harder on meaning than on grammar.

3
Revise mixed sentences to make sentences consistent.

The following mixed sentences are common in everyday speech and may not seem inconsistent to you. Indeed, in casual speech they are usually accepted. In standard written English, however, they qualify as grammatical errors.

By driving to the movie was how we saw the accident happen. The prepositional phrase *By driving to the movie* is treated as the subject for the verb *was*. Prepositional phrases cannot serve as subjects.

Just because the candidate once had a drinking problem doesn't mean he won't be a good mayor now. The adverb clause *because the candidate once had a drinking problem* is treated as the subject of the verb *doesn't mean*. Adverbs modify verbs and adjectives and cannot function as subjects.

A CAT scan is when medical technicians take a cross-sectional X-ray of the body. The adverb clause *when medical technicians take a cross-sectional X-ray of the body* is treated as a complement of the subject *CAT scan* —another function adverbs cannot serve.

The reason I was late today is because my alarm clock broke. The subject, *reason*, is illogically linked with the predicate, *is because. Reason* suggests an explanation, so the predicate, *is because,* is redundant.

Revise mixed sentences by ensuring that grammatical patterns are used consistently throughout each sentence. For cases of faulty predication, either revise the subject so it can perform the action expressed in the predicate or revise the predicate so it accurately depicts an action performed by the subject. Also avoid using the constructions *is when* and *is where* to explain an idea and *The reason...is because* in your writing.

There are often many ways to revise mixed sentences. In each of the following revisions, the grammatical patterns are consistent and the subjects and predicates fit together logically:

While driving to the movie, we saw the accident happen.

Just because the candidate once had a drinking problem, we can't conclude that he won't be a good mayor.

A CAT scan is a cross-sectional X-ray of the body.

The reason I was late today is that my alarm clock broke.

2D Shifts

Shifts occur when writers lose track of their sentence elements. Shifts occur in a variety of ways:

In person

In music, where left-handed people seem to be talented, the right-handed world puts *you* at a disadvantage. Shift from *people,* third person, to *you,* second person.

In tense

Even though many musicians *are* left-handed, instruments *had been designed for right-handers*. Shift from present tense to past perfect.

In number

A left-handed *violinist* has to pay extra to buy *their* left-handed violin. Shift from singular to plural.

In mood

Every time the *violinist played, she could always know* when her instrument was out of tune. Shift from the indicative mood, *violinist played,* to the subjunctive mood, *she could always know.*

In voice

The sonata *was being practiced* by the violinists in one room while the cellists *played* the concerto in the other room. Shift from the passive voice, *was being practiced,* to active voice, *played.*

In discourse type

She said, "*Your violin is out of tune,*" and that *I was playing the wrong note*. Shift from the direct quotation, *Your violin is out of tune,* to indirect quotation, that *I was playing the wrong note.*

Once you recognize shifts, revise them by ensuring that the same grammatical structures are used consistently throughout the sentence:

In music, where left-handed *people* seem talented, the right-handed world puts *them* at a disadvantage.

Even though many musicians *are* left-handed, instruments *have been designed* for right-handers.

Left-handed *violinists* have to pay extra to buy *their* left-handed violins.

Every time the violinist *played*, she *knew* when her instrument was out of tune.

The violinists *practiced* the sonata in one room while the cellists *played* the concerto in the other room.

She said, "*Your violin is out of tune and you are playing the wrong note.*"

3 Problems with Modification

Learning Objectives

1   Recognize and correct dangling and misplaced modifiers.

2   Distinguish between restrictive and nonrestrictive modifiers.

3   Recognize and revise sentences to correct common errors with adverbs and adjectives.

One part of a sentence can be *modified* by another part. A part that is modified is changed in some way: limited or broadened, perhaps, or described, defined, identified, or explained. Adjectives and adverbs always serve modifying functions, but phrases and subordinate clauses also can be modifiers. This section deals with problems in modification. (See 2B Coordination and Subordination.)

3A Dangling and Misplaced Modifiers

Dangling and misplaced modifiers are words and word groups that, because of their position or the way they are phrased, make the meaning of a sentence unclear and sometimes even ludicrous. These troublesome modifiers are most commonly verbal phrases, prepositional phrases, and adverbs. Here are examples:

1 Recognize and correct dangling and misplaced modifiers.

> *Reaching to pick up the saddle*, the obnoxious horse may shake off the blanket. The dangling verbal phrase appears to relate to *horse*.

> *To extend lead out of the ever-sharp pencil*, the eraser cap is depressed. The dangling verbal phrase implies that *the eraser cap* does something.

> The ever-sharp pencil is designed to be used permanently, *only periodically replacing the lead*. The dangling verbal phrase implies that the pencil replaces the lead.

> Dick *only* had to pay ten dollars for his parking ticket. The misplaced adverb should immediately precede *ten*.

> Theodore caught a giant fish in the very same spot where he had lost the ring *two years later*. The misplaced adverb phrase confusingly appears to modify the last part of the sentence instead of, correctly, the first part.

Errors of this type are difficult for writers to recognize, because, to the writers, they are not ambiguous.

Recognition. Verbal phrases always have implied subjects; in other words, somebody is performing the action. For clarity, that implied subject should be the same as the subject of the sentence or clause. To recognize your own dangling verbal modifiers, make sure that the implied subject of the verbal phrase is the same as the subject of the sentence. In the first example above, the implied subject of *Reaching* is not *the horse*. In the second example, the implied subject of *To extend* is not *the eraser cap*. And in the third example, the implied subject of *replacing* is not *the pencil*. Also check passive voice, because in a passive sentence, the subject is not the doer of the action. In the second example, the dangler can be corrected when the verb, changed from passive to active voice, tells who should depress the eraser (see correction that follows).

Watch
the Animation on
Dangling Modifiers
in your MyLab

Correction. Correcting dangling and misplaced modifiers depends on the type of error. Misplaced modifiers can often be moved to a more appropriate position:

Dick had to pay *only* ten dollars for his parking ticket.

Two years later, Theodore caught a giant fish in the very same spot where he had lost the ring.

Dangling modifiers usually require some rewording:

As you reach to pick up the saddle, the obnoxious horse may shake off the blanket. The dangling verbal phrase is converted to a clause.

To extend lead out of the ever-sharp pencil, *depress the eraser cap.* The main clause is revised so that *you* is the implied subject of *depress* (as it is for *To extend*).

The ever-sharp pencil is designed to be used permanently, *only periodically needing the lead replaced.* The dangling verbal phrase is revised so that the implied subject of *needing* is *pencil.*

3B Restrictive and Nonrestrictive Modifiers

2

Distinguish
between re-
strictive and
nonrestrictive
modifiers.

Some modifiers are essential to a sentence because they *restrict*, or limit, the meaning of the words they modify; others, while adding important information, are not essential to the meaning of a sentence. The first type is called restrictive and the second nonrestrictive. The terms usually refer to subordinate clauses and phrases. Here are examples of restrictive and nonrestrictive modifiers:

Restrictive

People *who plan to visit Europe* should take time to see Belgium. Relative clause modifying and identifying *People.*

The industrialized country *between the Netherlands and France on the North Sea* is constitutionally a kingdom. Prepositional phrases modifying and identifying *country.*

The Kempenland was thinly populated *before coal was discovered there.* Subordinate clause modifying *was populated* and giving meaning to the sentence.

Language and cultural differences have created friction *that has existed for centuries.* Relative clause modifying and identifying *friction.*

Nonrestrictive

Belgium has two major populations: the Flemings, *who live in the north and speak Flemish,* and the Walloons, *who live in the south and speak French.* Two relative clauses, the first modifying *Flemings* and the second modifying *Walloons.*

With Brussels in the middle of the country, both groups inhabit the city. Prepositional phrases, together modifying *inhabit.*

NATO's headquarters is in Brussels, *where it has been since its beginning in 1950.* Subordinate clause modifying *Brussels.*

Covering southeastern Belgium, the sandstone Ardennes Mountains follow the Sambre and Meuse rivers. Participial (verbal) phrase modifying *mountains.*

These examples illustrate several aspects of restrictive and nonrestrictive modifiers:

1. They *modify* a word in the clause or sentence; they therefore function as adjectives or adverbs.
2. They can appear at the beginning, somewhere in the middle, or at the end of a sentence or clause.
3. Most types of subordinate elements can be restrictive and nonrestrictive.
4. Whether a clause or phrase is restrictive or nonrestrictive depends on its function in the sentence.
5. Restrictive elements are not set off with punctuation; nonrestrictive elements are set off with commas (and sometimes dashes).

If you think the distinction between restrictive and nonrestrictive is not worth making, consider the following sentences, the first restrictive and the second nonrestrictive:

People who wear braces on their teeth should not eat caramel apples.

People, who wear braces on their teeth, should not eat caramel apples.

Watch
the Animation on
Commas with
Nonrestrictive
Modifiers
in your MyLab

Set off with commas, the nonrestrictive *who* clause implies that all people wear braces on their teeth and should not eat caramel apples, which is clearly not the case. It does not *restrict*, or limit, the meaning of *people*. In the first sentence, however, the *who* clause does restrict, or limit, the meaning of *people* to only those who wear braces on their teeth. Often, only the writer knows the intended meaning and therefore needs to make the distinction by setting off, or not setting off, the modifier.

Here are a few guidelines that might help you in making this fine distinction:

1. A modifier that modifies a proper noun (one that names a person or thing) is usually nonrestrictive, because the name is sufficient identification. Notice *Flemings* and *Walloons* in the previous example.
2. A *that* clause is almost always restrictive.
3. Adverbial subordinate clauses (those beginning with subordinating conjunctions such as *because* and *when*) are almost always restrictive and usually not set off with commas when they appear at the end of their sentences. If they appear at the beginning of sentences, they are almost always set off with commas.
4. A nonrestrictive modifier at the beginning of a sentence is followed by a comma, one at the end is preceded by a comma, and one in the middle is enclosed with two commas.

3C Adjectives and Adverbs

3

Recognize and
revise sentences
to correct com-
mon errors with
adverbs and
adjectives.

Adjectives and adverbs, often called *modifiers*, describe nouns and verbs (see 9A Parts of Speech). Adjectives modify nouns; that is, they describe, limit, explain, or alter them in some way. By modifying, they *limit* the meaning of the nouns: *red car* is narrower in meaning than *car*, and *fast red car* is narrower than *red car*. Adverbs modify verbs, adjectives, and other adverbs, telling more than the words by themselves would tell: drive *carefully* (adverb modifying a verb), *unexpectedly* early (adverb modifying an adjective), drive *very* carefully (adverb modifying an adverb). Adverbs usually tell how, where, when, and how much.

Adjectives and adverbs occasionally present some problems for writers. Be careful not to use adjectives when adverbs are needed, as in this sentence:

The governor suspected that the legislators were not taking him *serious*. The sentence element receiving modification is the verb *were not taking,* yet the modifier *serious* is an adjective, which can only modify nouns. The correct modifier for this sentence is the adverb *seriously.* (If you are not sure whether a word is an adjective or an adverb, check your dictionary, which should identify parts of speech.)

Another problem in form concerns the *comparative* and *superlative* degrees. The comparative form of adjectives and adverbs shows a greater degree between two things:

Your luggage is *stronger* than mine. Adjective comparing *your luggage* and *mine.*

Your luggage survives airport baggage handling *better* than mine does. Adverb comparing how the two *survive* handling.

The comparative degree is formed by adding *-er* to shorter adjectives and adverbs (*strong, stronger; hard, harder*); longer words are preceded by *more* (*beautiful, more beautiful; seriously, more seriously*). Do not use *-er* with *more* (not *more harder*).

The superlative form shows a greater degree among three or more things:

This is the *strongest* luggage I have ever seen. Adjective comparing the present luggage to all other luggage the writer has seen.

Your luggage survives airport baggage handling *best* of all luggage I've seen. Adverb comparing how all luggage the writer has seen survives handling.

The superlative degree is formed by adding *-est* to shorter adjectives and adverbs (*strong, strongest; hard, hardest*); longer words are preceded by *most* (*beautiful, most beautiful; seriously, most seriously*). Do not use *-est* with *most* (not *most strongest*).

Do not use adjectives and adverbs gratuitously, just to fill space or because you think you ought to. They are effective only when they add meaning to a sentence.

Complete
Additional Exercises
and Practice on
the Handbook
in your MyLab

4 Verbs

Learning Objectives

1   Recognize common verb tenses and forms.

2   Revise sentences to avoid overusing passive voice.

3   Use correct verb forms to express indicative, imperative, and subjunctive moods.

4   Recognize and correct common errors in subject–verb agreement.

Verbs are the central core of a sentence; together with subjects, they make statements. Verbs often tell what the subject is doing:

> The company *agreed* to plead guilty to criminal charges.

> Nearly every miner *can name* a casualty of black lung disease.

Another common function of verbs is to link subjects to complements:

> Logan *is* an isolated county in the corner of the state.

Sometimes the verb tells something about the subject, as the following passive verb does:

> Casualties of mining *cannot be measured* only by injuries.

Through changes in form, verbs can tell the time of the action (past, present, future), the number of the subject (singular or plural), and the person of the subject (first person, *I, we*; second person, *you*; third person, *he, she, it, they*).

4A Tense

The problems that writers sometimes encounter when using verbs in writing result from the fact that verbs, unlike most other words in English, have many forms, and a slight shift in form can alter meaning. Notice how the meanings of the following pairs of sentences change as the verbs change:

1
Recognize common verb tenses and forms.

> The fish *has jumped* into the boat.

> The fish *have jumped* into the boat.

> The concert *starts* at 8:15 p.m.

> The concert *started* at 8:15 p.m.

In the first pair, the meaning changes from one fish to more than one fish jumping into the boat. In the second pair, the first verb implies that the concert has not yet begun; the second, that it had already begun. It is important, therefore, to use the verb form that conveys the intended meaning. Observe how the verb *vanish* changes in the following sentences to indicate differences in time, or *tense*:

Present:	Many agricultural jobs *vanish*.
Past:	Many agricultural jobs *vanished*.
Future:	Many agricultural jobs *will vanish*.
Perfect:	Many agricultural jobs *have vanished*.
Past Perfect:	Many agricultural jobs *had vanished*.
Future Perfect:	Many agricultural jobs *will have vanished*.

To omit an *-ed* ending or to use the wrong helping verb gives readers a false message.

Helping (Auxiliary) Verbs. It is also important to use a form that is a *finite*, or an actual, verb. In the following example, the word that appears to be a verb (italicized) is not a finite verb:

The fish *jumping* into the boat.

The word *jumping* does not have one of the primary functions of verbs—telling the time of the action, called *tense*. The time of the occurrence could have been the past (*the fish were jumping*), present (*the fish are jumping*), or the future (*the fish will be jumping*). We also don't know whether the writer meant one fish or many. The *-ing* form is a *verbal* and requires a helping, or auxiliary, verb to make it finite, or able to tell time: words such as *am, is, are, was, were* (forms of *be*). Other helping verbs are *do* (*Do* you *want* the paper? She *doesn't want* the paper) and *have* (I *haven't seen* the paper; *has* she *seen* it?).

Irregular Verbs. Most verbs change forms in a regular way: *want* in the present becomes *wanted* in the past, *wanting* is used with the auxiliary *be* (i.e., *is wanting*), and *wanted* is used with the auxiliary *have* (i.e., *have wanted*). Many verbs change irregularly, however—internally rather than at the ending. Here are a few of the most common irregular verbs:

Base form	Past tense	Present participle	Past participle
be (is, am, are)	was, were	being	been
come	came	coming	come
do	did	doing	done
drink	drank	drinking	drunk
give	gave	giving	given
go	went	going	gone
grow	grew	growing	grown
lie	laid	lying	lain
see	saw	seeing	seen
take	took	taking	taken
teach	taught	teaching	taught
throw	threw	throwing	thrown
wear	wore	wearing	worn
write	wrote	writing	written

Check your dictionary for the forms of other verbs you suspect may be irregular.

The verb form that is perhaps the most troublesome is the *-s* form in the present tense. This form is used for all singular nouns and the pronouns *he*, *she*, and *it*. (See 4D Subject–Verb Agreement.)

4B Voice

English sentences are usually written in the active voice, in which the subject of the sentence is the doer of the action of the verb:

> Scott misplaced the file folder. *Scott, the subject of the sentence, performed the action, misplaced.*

2

Revise sentences to avoid overusing passive voice.

With the passive voice, the doer of the action is the object of a preposition or is omitted entirely:

> The file folder was misplaced by Scott. *File folder is now the subject of the sentence.*

> The file folder was misplaced. *The person doing the action is not named.*

At best, the passive voice is wordier than the active voice; at worst, it fails to acknowledge who performs the action of the verb. Use the passive voice when you do not know or do not want to name the doer or when you want to keep the subjects consistent within a paragraph.

To avoid the passive voice, look for *by* phrases near the ends of your sentences; if you find any, see if the subject of your sentence performs the action of your verb. If not, revise the sentence so that it does. Another way to find occurrences of the passive voice is to look for forms of *be*: *am, is, are, was, were, been, being*. Not all these verbs will be passive, but if they function as part of an action verb, see if the subject performs the action. If it does not, and if your sentence would be clearer with the subject performing the action, revise to the active voice.

◉
⌐ **Watch** ¬
the Animation on
**Active and
Passive Voice**
in your MyLab

4C Mood

Mood refers to the writer's attitude toward the action of the verb. There are three forms: indicative, imperative, and subjunctive. Verbs in the *indicative mood* are used to make statements, to ask questions, and to declare opinions. For example:

3

Use correct verb forms to express indicative, imperative, and subjunctive moods.

> Not many people today *think* the world *is* flat. Makes a statement.

> *Does* anybody today *think* the world is flat? Asks a question.

> Members of the Flat Earth Society *should reevaluate* their thinking. Declares an opinion.

Verbs in the *imperative mood* issue commands, requests, or directions. Imperative verbs never change form. When the subject of an imperative verb is not explicitly identified, it is understood to be *you*.

> Julia, *stop* teasing your baby brother. Issues command.

> Please *complete* this report by tomorrow morning. Issues request.

> *Turn right* at the light and *drive* for another two blocks. Issues directions.

Verbs in the *subjunctive mood* communicate wishes, make statements contrary to fact, list requirements and demands, and imply skepticism or doubt. They usually appear in clauses introduced by *if*, *that*, *as if*, and *as though*. Use the base form of the verb for the present-tense subjunctive. For the past-tense subjunctive of the verb *be*, use *were* for all subjects.

She wishes that her son's best friend *were* more responsible. Communicates wish.

If the world *were* to end tomorrow, we would not have to pay taxes anymore. Makes statement contrary to fact.

The jury summons requires that your cousin *arrive* punctually at 8:00 a.m. and *sign* in with the court clerk. Lists requirements.

His girlfriend talks as if she *were* a pop music diva. Implies skepticism.

Be sure to select the correct verb forms to express indicative, imperative, and subjunctive moods.

4D Subject–Verb Agreement

4

Recognize and correct common errors in subject–verb agreement.

Clauses are made of subjects and verbs plus their modifiers and other related words. A fundamental principle of usage is that verbs agree with their subjects. In most cases, this principle presents no problem: You say "Birds *have* feathers," not "Birds *has* feathers." But not all sentences are this simple. Before getting into the problem areas, consider first that errors in subject–verb agreement occur only with present-tense verbs and the verb tenses that use present-tense forms of helping verbs (such as *have* and *be*). And, except for the irregular verb *be* (with its forms *am, is, are, was, were*), the problem centers on third-person singular verbs with their *-s* ending. Here is the problem illustrated. Notice that only the verbs in the third-person singular are different. The unfortunate thing is that all nouns are in the third person and, when singular, require this form in the present tense.

	Present		Present Perfect	
	singular	plural	singular	plural
first person	I work	we work	I have worked	we have worked
second person	you work	you work	you have worked	you have worked
third person	he works (she, it)	they work	he has worked (she, it)	they have worked

It is the *-s* form, then, that you need to watch for to avoid errors in subject–verb agreement. Here are some situations that may cause problems.

Intervening Subordinate Element

When a subject and a verb are side by side, they usually do not present a problem. Often, however, writers separate them with subordinate elements, such as clauses, prepositional or verbal phrases, and other elements. The result may be a verb error. The following sentence illustrates this problem:

The realization that life is a series of compromises never occur to some people. The subject is *realization,* a singular noun, and should be followed by the singular verb *occurs.* The corrected sentence would read "The realization that life is a series of compromises never occurs to some people."

Subject Complement

Subject complements follow some verbs and rename the subject, although they are not always in the same number as the subject. Because a singular subject may have a plural complement, and vice versa, confused writers might make the verb agree with the complement instead of the subject. Here's an example:

Watch
the Animation on
**Subject–Verb
Agreement**
in your MyLab

The result of this mistake are guilt, low self-esteem, and depression. The subject is *result,* not *guilt, low self-esteem,* and *depression;* the singular subject should be followed by the singular verb *is.* The corrected sentence would read "The result of this mistake is guilt, low self-esteem, and depression."

Compound Subject

Two or more words may be compounded to make a subject. Whether they are singular or plural depends on their connector. Subjects connected by *and* and *but* are plural, but those connected by *or* and *nor* are singular or plural depending on whether the item closer to the verb is singular or plural. Here are examples:

The young mother and the superior student *are* both candidates for compulsive perfectionism. Two subjects, *mother* and *student,* are joined by *and* and take a plural verb.

Promotions or an employee award *tells* the perfectionist he or she is achieving personal goals. When two subjects, *promotions* and *award,* are joined by *or,* the verb agrees with the nearer one; in this sentence, a singular verb is required.

An employee award or promotions *tell* the perfectionist he or she is achieving personal goals. Here the plural verb, *tell,* agrees with *promotions,* the closer of the two subjects.

Indefinite Pronoun as Subject

Indefinite pronouns are defined and listed under 5C Pronoun Agreement. Although these words often seem plural in meaning, most of them are singular grammatically. When indefinite pronouns are the subjects of sentences or clauses, their verbs are usually singular. Here are examples:

Everyone *has* at some time worried about achieving goals. The singular indefinite pronoun *everyone* takes a singular verb, *has.*

Each car and truck on the highway *was* creeping along on the icy pavement. The singular indefinite pronoun *each* requires a singular verb, *was.*

Neither of us *is* going to worry about being late. The singular indefinite pronoun *neither* takes a singular verb, *is.*

Nevertheless, some of us *are* going to be very late. The indefinite pronoun *some* (like *all, any,* and *none*) is singular or plural depending on context; compare with "Some of the book *is* boring."

Inverted Sentence Order

Inverted sentence order can confuse your natural inclination to subject–verb agreement. Examples of inverted order are questions, plus sentences beginning with *there*. Sentences like these demand closer attention to agreement.

Have the results of the test come back yet? The plural subject, *results,* takes a plural verb, *have.*

There *are* many special services provided just for kids at hotels, ski lodges, and restaurants. The plural subject, *services,* takes a plural verb, *are. There* is never a subject; it only holds the place for the subject in an inverted sentence.

Intervening Relative Clause

Subordinate clauses that begin with the relative pronouns *who, which,* or *that* present special problems in subject–verb agreement. Their verbs must agree with their own subjects, not with a word in another clause. These subordinate clauses demand special attention, because whether the pronouns are singular or plural depends on their antecedents. These sentences illustrate agreement within relative clauses:

Every person who *attends* the baseball game will receive a free cap. *Who,* the subject of *attends,* means "person," a singular noun.

John is one of the few people I know who *care* about frogs. *Who,* the subject of *care,* means "people," a plural noun.

John is the only one of all the people I know who *cares* about frogs. *Who* in this sentence means "one."

Complete
Additional Exercises
and Practice on
the Handbook
in your MyLab

5 Pronouns

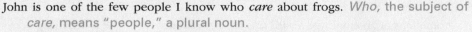

Learning Objectives

1 Recognize and correct common errors with pronoun case.

2 Recognize and correct unclear pronoun reference.

3 Recognize and correct faulty pronoun agreement.

4 Recognize and correct common errors with relative pronouns.

Pronouns can have all the same sentence functions as nouns; the difference is that pronouns do not have the meaning that nouns have. Nouns name things; a noun stands for the thing itself. Pronouns, however, refer only to nouns. Whenever that reference is ambiguous or inconsistent, there is a problem in clarity.

5A Pronoun Case

Case is a grammatical term for the way nouns and pronouns show their relationships to other parts of a sentence. In English, nouns have only two case forms:
the regular form (the one listed in a dictionary, such as *year*) and the possessive
form (used to show ownership or connection, such as *year's*; possessive nouns are
discussed in 8C Apostrophe).

1
Recognize and
correct com-
mon errors with
pronoun case.

   Pronouns, however, retain their case forms. Here are the forms for personal
and relative pronouns:

	Subjective	Objective	Possessive
Personal	I	me	my, mine
	you	you	your, yours
	he	him	his
	she	her	her, hers
	it	it	its
	we	us	our, ours
	they	them	their, theirs
Relative	who	whom	whose
	whoever	whomever	whosever

Notice, first, that possessive pronouns, unlike possessive pronouns, do not take
apostrophes—none of them. Sometimes writers confuse possessive pronouns
with contractions, which do have apostrophes (such as *it's*, meaning *it is* or *it
has*; and *who's*, meaning *who is*; for a further discussion, see 8C Apostrophe).

   Another problem writers sometimes have with pronoun case is using a subjective form when they need the objective or using an objective form when they need
the subjective.

Subjective Case. Use the subjective forms for subjects and for words referring to
subjects, as in these examples:

> Among the patients a nutritionist sees are the grossly overweight people *who* have
> tried all kinds of diets. *Who* is the subject of the verb *have tried* in its own
> clause.

> *They* have a life history of obesity and diets. *They* is the subject of *have*.

> *He* and *the patient* work out a plan for permanent weight control. *He* and *the pa-
> tient* are the compound subjects of *work*.

> The patient understands that the ones who work out the diet plan are *he* and *the
> nutritionist*. *He* and *the nutritionist* refer to *ones*, the subject of the
> clause.

Notice that pronoun case is determined by the function of the pronoun in its own
clause and that compounding (*he and the patient*) has no effect on case.

Objective Case. Use the *objective* forms for objects of all kinds:

"Between *you* and *me*," said the patient to his nutritionist, "I'm ready for something that works." *You* and *me* are objects of the preposition *between*.

An exercise program is usually assigned to the patient for *whom* the diet is prescribed. *Whom* is the object of the preposition *for*.

The nutritionist gives *her* a suitable alternative to couch sitting. *Her* is the indirect object of *gives*.

Modest exercise combined with modest dieting can affect *him or her* dramatically. *Him or her* is the direct object of *can affect*.

Having advised *them* about diet and exercise, the nutritionist instructs dieters about behavioral change. *Them* is the object of the participle *having advised*.

Notice again that the case of a pronoun is determined by its function in its own clause and is not affected by compounding (*you and me*).

Possessive Case. Use the possessive forms to indicate ownership. Possessive pronouns have two forms: adjective forms (*my, your, his, her, its, our, their*) and possessive forms (*mine, yours, his, hers, its, ours, theirs*). The adjective forms appear before nouns or gerunds; the possessive forms replace possessive nouns.

The patient purchased *his* supplements from the drugstore *his* nutritionist recommended. Adjective form before nouns.

His swimming every day produced results faster than he anticipated. Adjective form before gerund.

His was a difficult task to accomplish, but the rewards of weight loss were great. Possessive form replacing possessive noun.

5B Pronoun Reference

2

Recognize and correct unclear pronoun reference.

Personal and relative pronouns (see the list in section 5A Pronoun Case) must refer to specific nouns or antecedents. By themselves they have no meaning. As a result, they can cause problems in clarity for writers. If you were to read, "She teaches technical writing at her local technical college," you would know only that *someone*, a woman, teaches technical writing at the college. But if the sentence were preceded by one like this, "After getting her master's degree, my mother has achieved one of her life goals," the pronoun *she* would have meaning. In this case, *mother* is the antecedent of *she*. The antecedent gives meaning to the pronoun. For this reason, it is essential that pronouns refer unambiguously to their antecedents and that pronouns and antecedents agree.

Ambiguous pronoun reference may occur in various ways:

- More than one possible antecedent.
- Adjective used as intended antecedent.
- Implied antecedent.
- Too great of a separation between antecedent and pronoun.

Here are sentences in which the pronouns do not clearly refer to their antecedents:

The immunologist refused to admit the fraudulence of the data reported by a former colleague in a paper *he* had cosigned. More than one possible antecedent. *He* could refer to *immunologist* or to *colleague.*

In Carolyn Chute's book *The Beans of Egypt, Maine*, she treats poverty with concern and understanding. Adjective used as intended antecedent (possessive nouns function as adjectives). In this case, *Carolyn Chute's* modifies *book* and cannot serve as an antecedent of the pronoun *she.*

It says in the newspaper that the economy will not improve soon. Implied antecedent. There is no antecedent for it.

At Ajax *they* have tires on sale till the end of the month. Implied antecedent. There is no antecedent for *they.*

This only reinforces the public skepticism about the credibility of scientists. Implied antecedent. There is no antecedent for *This.*

One of the primary rules for using humor in advertising is often broken, *which* is that the ad doesn't make fun of the product. Too great a separation between antecedent and pronoun. The antecedent of *which* is *rules,* but its distance from the pronoun makes reference difficult.

Faulty pronoun reference is corrected by clarifying the relationship between the pronoun and its intended antecedent. Observe how the example sentences have been revised:

Watch
the Animation on
**Pronoun Reference
Problems**
in your MyLab

The immunologist refused to admit the fraudulence of the data reported by a former colleague in a paper *the immunologist* had cosigned. *The immunologist* replaces the unclear pronoun *he.*

In her book *The Beans of Egypt, Maine*, Carolyn Chute treats poverty with concern and understanding. The possessive pronoun *her* replaces the possessive noun and refers to the noun subject, *Carolyn Chute.*

The newspaper reports that the economy will not improve soon. The unclear pronoun *it* is replaced by its implied antecedent, *the newspaper.*

Ajax has tires on sale till the end of the month. The unclear pronoun *they* is replaced by *Ajax.*

This *kind of waffling* only reinforces public skepticism about the credibility of scientists. The unclear pronoun *this* is replaced by the adjective *this* modifying the intended antecedent *kind of waffling.*

That the ad doesn't make fun of the product is an often-broken primary rule for using humor in advertising. Parts of the sentence are moved around until they are clear.

Revising unclear pronoun reference is sometimes like working a jigsaw puzzle: finding and adding a missing piece or moving parts around to achieve the best fit. Often, only the writer can make the right connections.

5C Pronoun Agreement

3

Recognize
and correct
faulty pronoun
agreement.

Some pronoun errors result because the pronoun and its antecedent do not agree. In the sentence "When a student is late for this class, they find the door locked," the plural pronoun *they* refers to a singular antecedent, *a student*. There is no agreement in *number*. In this sentence, "When a student is late for this class, you find the door locked," again the pronoun, this time *you*, does not agree with the antecedent. Here the problem is *person*. Pronouns must agree with their antecedents in number, person, and gender. (See the list of pronouns in 5A Pronoun Case.)

Compound Antecedents

Problems sometimes occur with compound antecedents. If the antecedents are joined by *and*, the pronoun is plural; if joined by *or*, the pronoun agrees with the nearer antecedent. Here are examples of correct usage:

> In the pediatric trauma center, the head doctor and head nurse direct *their* medical team. The pronoun *their* refers to both *doctor* and *nurse*.

> The head doctor or the head nurse directs *his or her* team. The pronouns *his or her* refer to the closer antecedent, *nurse* (because the gender of the nurse is not known, the neutral alternatives are used).

> The head doctor or the other doctors give *their* help when it is needed. The pronoun *their* agrees with the closer antecedent, *doctors*.

Watch
the Animation on
**Pronoun–
Antecedent
Agreement**
in your MyLab

Indefinite Pronouns as Antecedents

A particularly troublesome kind of agreement is that between personal or relative pronouns and *indefinite pronouns*. As their name implies, indefinites do not refer to particular people or things; grammatically they are usually singular but are often intended as plural. Here are the common indefinite pronouns:

all	every	none
any	everybody	nothing
anybody	everyone	one
anyone	everything	some
anything	neither	somebody
each	no one	someone
either	nobody	something

Like nouns, these pronouns can serve as antecedents of personal and relative pronouns. But because most of them are grammatically singular, they can be troublesome in sentences. Here are examples of correct usage:

> Everyone in the trauma center has *his or her* specific job to do. **or** *All* the personnel in the trauma center have *their* specific jobs to do. The neutral, though wordy, alternative *his or her* agrees with the singular indefinite *everyone*. The second sentence illustrates the use of plural when gender is unknown.

Each of them does *his or her* job efficiently and competently. **or** *All* of them do *their* jobs efficiently and competently. *Each* is singular, but *all* is either singular or plural, depending on context (compare "*All* literature has *its* place").

Shifts in Person

Agreement errors in *person* are shifts between *I* or *we* (first person), *you* (second person), and *he*, *she*, *it*, and *they* (third person). These errors are probably more often a result of carelessness than of imperfect knowledge. Being more familiar with casual speech than formal writing, writers sometimes shift from *I* to *you*—for example, when only one of them is meant, as in these sentences:

Last summer *I* went on a canoeing trip to northern Manitoba. It was *my* first trip that far north, and it was so peaceful *you* could forget all the problems back home. The person represented by *you* was not present. The writer means *I*.

See also 2D Shifts.

5D Relative Pronouns

Use relative pronouns to introduce clauses that modify nouns or pronouns. Personal relative pronouns refer to people. They include *who, whom, whoever, whomever,* and *whose.* Nonpersonal relative pronouns refer to things. They include *which, whichever, whatever,* and *whose.*

4

Recognize and correct common errors with relative pronouns.

Most college writers know to use *who* when referring to people and *which* or *that* when referring to things, but sometimes carelessness or confusion can lead to errors. Many writers assume that *which* and *that* are interchangeable, when they are not. Use *which* to introduce nonrestrictive clauses and *that* to introduce restrictive clauses (see 3B Restrictive and Nonrestrictive Modifiers). Another problem area concerns the correct use of *who* and *whom.* Use *who* to refer to the subject of the sentence and *whom* to refer to an object of the verb or preposition. Following are examples of common errors:

The lawyer *that* lost the case today went to law school with my sister. Uses impersonal relative pronoun *that.*

Conflict between the two parties led to the lawsuit *that* was finally settled today. The relative pronoun *that* introduces a nonrestrictive clause that modifies *lawsuit.* Nonrestrictive clauses supply extra information to the sentence, not defining information.

The case resulted in a ruling, *which* favored the plaintiff. The relative pronoun *which* introduces a restrictive clause that modifies *ruling.* Restrictive clauses supply defining information.

Later, the lawyer *whom* lost the case spoke with the jurors *who* we had interviewed. The first relative pronoun, *whom,* refers to the subject, *lawyer,* while the second relative pronoun, *who,* refers to the object of the verb *had interviewed.*

Once you recognize relative-pronoun errors, it is usually easy to fix them:

The lawyer *who* lost the case today went to law school with my sister.

Conflict between the two parties led to the lawsuit, *which* was finally settled today.

The case resulted in a ruling *that* favored the plaintiff.

Later, the lawyer *who* lost the case spoke with the jurors *whom* we had interviewed.

Complete
Additional Exercises
and Practice on
the Handbook
in your MyLab

6 Style

Learning Objectives

1   Use editing strategies to achieve conciseness.

2   Use appropriate language that is suitable for your audience and free of sexism and other forms of bias.

Style in writing—like style in clothes, art, or anything else—is individual and develops with use and awareness. But even individual writers vary their style, depending on the situation. At school and work, the preferred style tends to be more formal and objective. It is not stuffy, patronizing, or coldly analytical. It is simply clean, direct, and clear. This Handbook section treats a few of the obstacles to a good writing style.

6A Conciseness

1

Use editing strategies to achieve conciseness.

Nobody wants to read more words than necessary. When you write concisely, therefore, you are considerate of your readers. To achieve conciseness, you do not need to eliminate details and other content; rather, you cut empty words, repetition, and unnecessary details.

In the following passage, all the italicized words could be omitted without altering the meaning.

> *In the final analysis, I feel that* the United States should have converted to the *use of the* metric system *of measurement* a long time ago. *In the present day and age,* the United States is the *one and* only country in the *entire* world except for Borneo and Liberia that has not yet adopted this measurement system.

Repetition of keywords is an effective technique for achieving emphasis and coherence, but pointless repetition serves only to bore the reader.

Follow these guidelines to achieve conciseness in your writing:

1. **Avoid redundancy.** Redundant words and expressions needlessly repeat what has already been said. Delete them when they appear in your writing.

2. **Avoid wordy expressions.** Phrases such as *In the final analysis* and *In the present day and age* in the preceding example add no important information to sentences and should be removed and/or replaced with less-wordy constructions.

3. **Avoid unnecessary intensifiers.** Intensifiers such as *really, very, clearly, quite,* and *of course* usually fail to add meaning to the words they modify and therefore are often unnecessary. Deleting them does not change the meaning of the sentence.

4. **Avoid excess use of prepositional phrases.** The use of too many prepositional phrases within a sentence makes for wordy writing. Always use constructions that require the fewest words.

5. **Avoid negating constructions.** Negating constructions using words such as *no* and *not* often add unneeded words to sentences. Use shorter alternatives when they are available.

6. **Avoid the passive voice.** Passive constructions require more words than active constructions (see 4B Voice). They can also obscure meaning by concealing the sentence's subject. Write in the active voice whenever possible.

Following are more examples of wordy sentences that violate these guidelines:

If the two groups *cooperate together*, there will be *positive benefits* for both. Uses redundancy.

There are some people *who* think the metric system is un-American. Uses wordy expression.

The climb up the mountain was *very* hard on my legs and *really* taxed my lungs and heart. Uses unnecessary modifiers.

On the day of his birth, we walked *to the park down the block from the house of his mother*. Uses too many prepositional phrases.

She *did not like* hospitals. Uses negating construction when a shorter alternative is available.

The door *was closed* by that man over there. Uses passive voice when active voice is preferable.

Corrections to the previous wordy sentences result in concise sentences:

If the two groups cooperate, both will benefit. This correction also replaces the wordy construction *there will be...for both* with a shorter, more forceful alternative.

Some people think the metric system is un-American.

The climb up the mountain was hard on my legs and taxed my lungs and heart.

On his birthday, we walked to the park near his mother's house.

She hated hospitals.

That man over there closed the door.

6B Appropriate Language

2

Use appropriate language that is suitable for your audience and free of sexism and other forms of bias.

Effective writers communicate using appropriate language; that is, language that:

1. Suits its subject and audience.
2. Avoids sexist usage.
3. Avoids bias and stereotype.

Suitability

The style and tone of your writing should be suitable to your subject and audience. Most academic and business contexts require the use of *formal language*. Formal language communicates clearly and directly, with a minimum of stylistic flourish. Its tone is serious, objective, and detached. Formal language avoids slang, pretentious words, and unnecessary jargon. *Informal language*, on the other hand, is particular to the writer's personality and also assumes a closer and more familiar relationship between the writer and the reader. Its tone is casual, subjective, and intimate. Informal language can also employ slang and other words that would be inappropriate in formal language.

As informal language is rarely used within an academic setting, the following examples show errors in the use of formal language:

The director told the board members to *push off*. Uses informal language.

Professor Oyo *dissed* Marta when she arrived late to his class for the third time in a row. Uses slang.

The *aromatic essence* of the gardenia was intoxicating. Uses pretentious words.

The doctor told him to take *salicylate* to ease the symptoms of *viral rhinorrhea*. Uses unnecessary jargon.

Employing formal language correctly, these examples could be revised as follows:

The director told the board members to leave.

Professor Oyo spoke disrespectfully to Marta when she arrived late to his class for the third time in a row.

The scent of the gardenia was intoxicating.

The doctor told him to take aspirin to ease his cold symptoms.

Sexist Usage

Gender-exclusive terms such as *policeman* and *chairman* are offensive to many readers today. Writers who are sensitive to their audience, therefore, avoid such terms, replacing them with expressions such as *police officer* and *chairperson* or *chair*. Most sexist usage in language involves masculine nouns, masculine pronouns, and patronizing terms.

Masculine Nouns. Do not use *man* and its compounds generically. For many people, these words are specific to men and do not account for women as separate and equal people. Here are some examples of masculine nouns and appropriate gender-neutral substitutions:

Masculine Noun	Gender-Neutral Substitution
mailman	mail carrier
businessman	businessperson, executive, manager
fireman	firefighter
man-hours	work hours
mankind	humanity, people
manmade	manufactured, synthetic
salesman	salesperson, sales representative, sales agent
congressman	member of Congress, representative

Using gender-neutral substitutions often entails using a more specific word for a generalized term, which adds more precision to writing.

Masculine Pronouns. Avoid using the masculine pronouns *he*, *him*, and *his* in a generic sense when meaning both male and female. This can pose some challenges, however, because English does not have a generic singular pronoun that can be used instead. Consider the following options:

1. Eliminate the pronoun.

   Every writer has an individual style. Instead of Every writer has his own style.

2. Use plural forms.

   Writers have their own styles. Instead of A writer has his own style.

3. Use *he or she*, *one*, or *you* as alternates only sparingly.

   Each writer has his or her own style. Instead of Each writer has his own style.

   One has an individual writing style. Instead of He has his own individual writing style.

   You have your own writing style. Instead of A writer has his own style.

Patronizing Terms. Avoid terms that cast men or women in gender-exclusive roles or that imply that women are subordinate to men. Here are some examples of biased or stereotypical terms and their gender-neutral substitutions:

Biased/Stereotypical Term	Gender-Neutral Substitution
lady lawyer	lawyer
male nurse	nurse
career girl	professional, attorney, manager
coed	student
housewife	homemaker
stewardess	flight attendant
cleaning lady	housecleaner

Biases and Stereotypes

Biased and stereotypical language can be hurtful and can perpetuate discrimination. Most writers are sensitive to racial and ethnic biases or stereotypes but should also avoid language that shows insensitivity to age, class, religion, and sexual orientation. The accepted terms for identifying groups and group members have changed over the years and continue to change today. Avoid using terms that have fallen into disuse, such as *Indian* or *Oriental*; instead, use accepted terms such as *Native American* or *Asian*.

Complete
Additional Exercises
and Practice on
the Handbook
in your MyLab

7 Punctuation

Learning Objectives

1   Use periods, question marks, and exclamation points correctly to end sentences.

2   Use semicolons correctly to connect independent clauses.

3   Use commas correctly to punctuate sentences.

4   Use colons correctly to punctuate sentences.

5   Use dashes correctly to separate sentence elements.

6   Use quotation marks correctly to set off direct quotations.

7   Use parentheses, brackets, and ellipses correctly to punctuate sentences.

Punctuation is a system of signals telling readers how the parts of written discourse relate to one another. They are similar to road signs that tell the driver what to expect: A sign with an arrow curving left means that the road makes a left curve, a "stop ahead" sign that a stop sign is imminent, a speed-limit sign what the legal speed is, etc. Drivers trust that the signs mean what they say. Readers, too, expect punctuation marks to mean what they say: A period means the end of a sentence, a colon that an explanation will follow, a comma that the sentence is not finished. Punctuation is a way for writers to help readers understand their words in the intended way.

Punctuation corresponds roughly to intonations and other physical signals in speech. When you speak, you use pitch levels, pauses, hand signals, head movements, and facial expressions to make sure your audience understands you. At the end of a sentence, you unconsciously let your voice drop—not just pause, but decidedly drop in pitch. With some questions, your voice rises at the end, as in "Do you want to go?" With other questions, the pitch drops, as in "Do you want to go or not?" You can have brief pauses, or you can lengthen them to increase the drama of what you are saying. You can increase or decrease the sound (volume) of your words. None of these signals are available to writers. To make their situation even more difficult, writers do not have their audience right in front of them to look puzzled or to question them when meaning is unclear. So writers use punctuation.

Ends of sentences are punctuated with periods, question marks, or exclamation points. Semicolons function as "soft" periods, usually marking the end of independent clauses (as periods do) but not of complete thoughts. Commas show relationships within sentences, as do colons, dashes, quotation marks, parentheses, brackets, and ellipsis dots. These marks are explained in the sections that follow. Other marks—those used within words (apostrophes, hyphens, italics, and slashes)—are explained in Section 8, Mechanics and Spelling.

Figure H-1 serves as a quick guide to sentence punctuation. For explanations, refer to the relevant entry.

7A End Punctuation

A period is the normal mark for ending sentences. A question mark ends a sentence that asks a direct question, and an exclamation point ends forceful assertions.

1 Use periods, question marks, and exclamation points correctly to end sentences.

Period

Sentences normally end with a period.

> Studies suggest that eating fish two or three times a week may reduce the risk of heart attack. Statement.

> Eat two or three servings of fish a week. Mild command.

> The patient asked whether eating fish would reduce the risk of heart attack. Indirect question.

Avoid inserting a period before the end of a sentence; the result will be a fragment (see 1A Fragments). Sentences can be long or short; their length does not determine their completion. Both of the following examples are complete sentences.

> Eat fish. Mild command; the subject, *you,* is understood.

> In a two-year study of 1,000 survivors of heart attack, researchers found a 29 percent reduction in mortality among those who regularly ate fish or took a fish-oil supplement. Statement; one sentence.

Question Mark

A sentence that asks a direct question ends in a question mark:

> How does decaffeinated coffee differ from regular coffee?

Do not use a question mark to end an indirect question:

> The customer asked how decaffeinated coffee differs from regular coffee.

With quoted questions, place the question mark inside the final quotation marks:

> The customer asked, "How does decaffeinated coffee differ from regular coffee?"

Watch
the Animation on
End Punctuation
in your MyLab

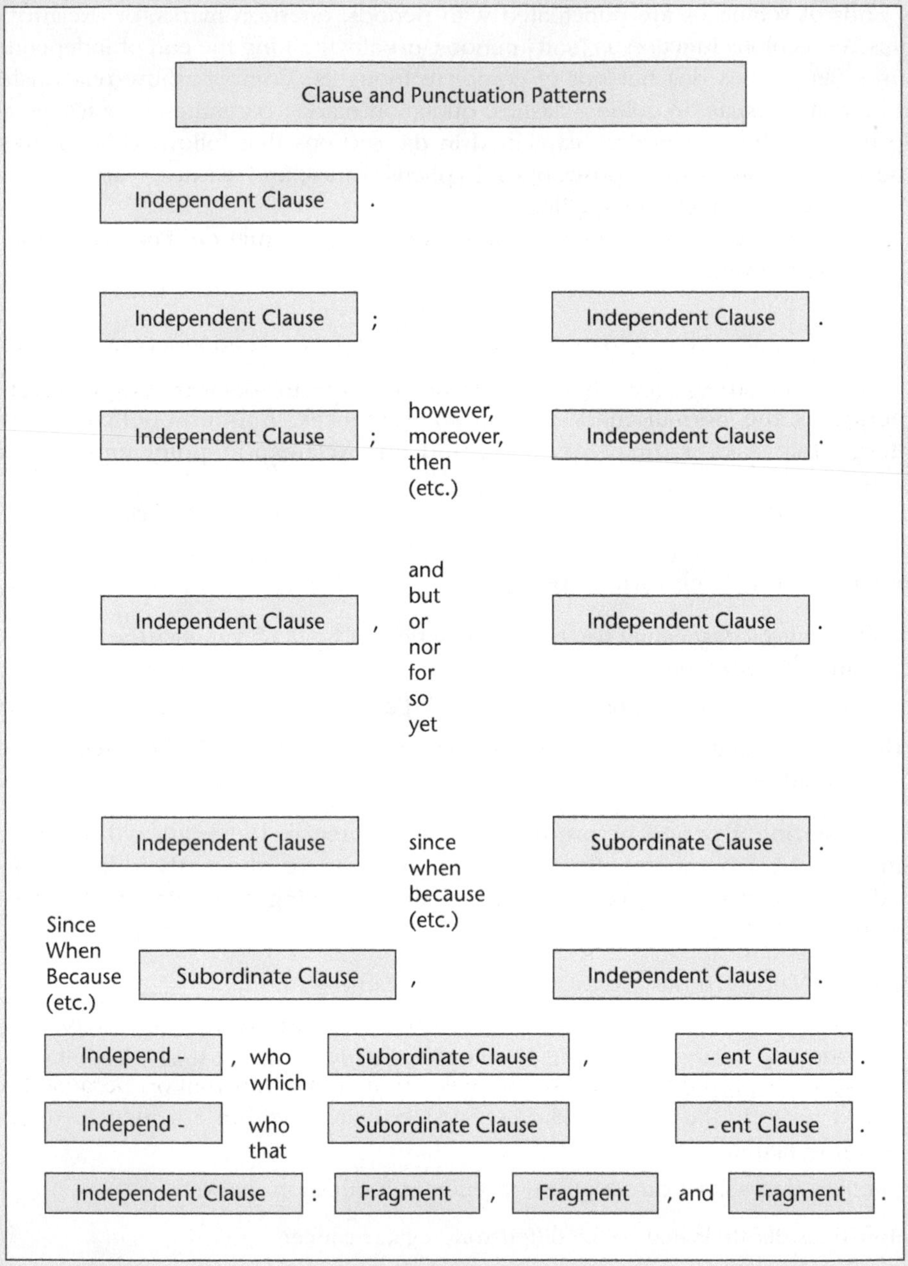

Clause and Punctuation Patterns

| Independent Clause | . |

Independent Clause ; Independent Clause .

Independent Clause ; however, moreover, then (etc.) Independent Clause .

Independent Clause , and but or nor for so yet Independent Clause .

Independent Clause since when because (etc.) Subordinate Clause .

Since When Because (etc.) Subordinate Clause , Independent Clause .

Independ - , who which Subordinate Clause , - ent Clause .

Independ - who that Subordinate Clause - ent Clause .

Independent Clause : Fragment , Fragment , and Fragment .

Figure H-1

Exclamation Point

The exclamation point ends forceful assertions:

Fire!

Shut that door immediately!

Because they give the impression of shouting, exclamation points are rarely needed in formal business and academic writing.

7B Semicolon

The main use for a semicolon is to connect two closely related independent clauses: **2**

> Dengue hemorrhagic fever is a viral infection common to Southeast Asia; it kills about 5,000 children a year.

Use semicolons correctly to connect independent clauses.

Sometimes the second clause contains a transitional adverb (see 1B Comma Splices):

> Dengue has existed in Asia for centuries; *however,* it grew more virulent in the 1950s.

Do not use a comma where a semicolon or period is required; the result is a comma splice (see 1B Comma Splices). In contrast, a semicolon used in place of a comma may result in a type of fragment (see 1A Fragments):

> In populations where people have been stricken by an infectious virus, survivors have antibodies in their bloodstreams; *which prevent or reduce the severity of subsequent infections.* The semicolon makes a fragment of the *which* clause.

Do not confuse the semicolon with the colon (see 7D Colon). While the semicolon connects independent clauses, a colon ordinarily does not. The semicolon is also used to separate items in a series when the items contain internal commas:

> Scientists are researching the effects of staphylococcus bacteria, which cause infections in deep wounds; influenza A virus, which causes respiratory flu; and conjunctivitis bacteria, which have at times caused fatal purpuric fever.

7C Comma

The comma is probably the most troublesome mark of punctuation because it has **3** so many uses. It is a real workhorse for punctuation within a sentence. Its main uses are explained here.

Use commas correctly to punctuate sentences.

Compound Sentences. A comma joins two independent clauses connected with a coordinating conjunction (see 1B Comma Splices):

> Martinique is a tropical island in the West Indies, *and* it attracts flocks of tourists annually.

Do not use the comma between independent clauses without the conjunction, even if the second clause begins with a transitional adverb:

> Faulty: Martinique is a tropical island in the West Indies, it attracts flocks of tourists annually. Two independent clauses with no conjunction; it is a comma splice.

Faulty: Martinique is a tropical island in the West Indies, consequently it attracts flocks of tourists annually. Two independent clauses with transitional adverb; it is a comma splice.

Watch
the Animation on
Commas
in your MyLab

Introductory Sentence Elements. Commas set off a variety of introductory sentence elements, as illustrated here:

When the French colonized Martinique in 1635, they eliminated the native Caribs. Introductory subordinate clause.

Choosing death over subservience, the Caribs leaped into the sea. Introductory participial (verbal) phrase.

Before their death, they warned of a "mountain of fire" on the island. Introductory prepositional phrase.

Subsequently, the island's volcano erupted. Introductory transitional adverb.

Short prepositional phrases sometimes are not set off:

In 1658 the Caribs leaped to their death.

Sometimes, however, a comma must be used after a short prepositional phrase, so that it is not misread:

Before, they had predicted retribution. Comma is required to prevent misreading.

Nonrestrictive and Parenthetical Elements. Words that interrupt the flow of a sentence are set off with commas before and after. If they come at the end of a sentence, they are set off with one comma.

In this class are nonrestrictive modifiers (see 3B Restrictive and Nonrestrictive Modifiers), transitional adverbs (see 1B Comma Splices), and a few other types of interrupters. Here are examples:

This rugged island, *which Columbus discovered in 1502,* exports sugar and rum. Nonrestrictive *which* clause; commas before and after.

A major part of the economy, *however,* is tourism. Interrupting transitional adverb; commas before and after.

Tourists, *attracted to the island by its climate,* enjoy discovering its culture. Interrupting participial (verbal) phrase (see 1A Fragments); commas before and after.

A popular tradition in Martinique is the Carnival, *which occurs just before Lent each year.* Nonrestrictive *which* clause; one comma.

Martinique is an overseas department of France, *a status conferred in 1946.* An absolute, ending the sentence (participial phrase plus the noun it modifies).

Series

Commas separate items in a series:

Martiniquans dance to *steel drums, clarinets, empty bottles, and banjos.* Four nouns.

Dressing in colorful costumes, dancing through the streets, and thoroughly enjoying the celebration, Martiniquans celebrate Carnival with enthusiasm. Three participial (verbal) phrases.

Martinique has a population of over 300,000, its main religion is Roman Catholicism, and its languages are French and Creole. Three independent clauses.

Various sentence elements can make up a series, but the elements joined should be equivalent grammatically (see 2A Parallelism, which discusses faulty parallelism). Common practice calls for a comma before the conjunction joining the last item in the series.

Quotations

Commas set off quoted sentences from the words that introduce them:

"A wise man," says David Hume, "proportions his belief to the evidence."

According to Plato, "Writing will produce forgetfulness" in writers because "they will not need to exercise their memories." The second clause is not set off with a comma.

"*X* on beer casks indicates beer which paid ten shillings duty, and hence it came to mean beer of a given quality," reports *The Dictionary of Phrase and Fable.*

Quotations introduced with *that* and other connectors (such as *because* in the second sentence here) are not set off with commas. Commas at the end of quotations go inside the quotation marks.

Coordinate Adjectives

Commas separate adjectives that equally modify a noun:

The "food pyramid" was designed as a *meaningful, memorable* way to represent the ideal daily diet. Two adjectives modify equally the noun *way.*

When you're not sure about using a comma, try inserting the coordinating conjunction *and* between the two adjectives to see if they are truly coordinate (*meaningful and memorable*). Another test is to reverse the order of the adjectives (*memorable, meaningful*). Do not use a comma between adjectives that are not coordinate or between the last adjective and the noun being modified. (See also 3C Adjectives and Adverbs.)

Addresses and Dates

Use a comma to separate city and state in an address, but do not set off the zip code:

Glen Ridge, New Jersey 07028 *or* Glen Ridge, NJ 07028

In a sentence, a state name is enclosed in commas:

The letter from Glen Ridge, New Jersey, arrived by express mail.

Dates are treated similarly:

January 5, 1886, *but* 5 January 1886

The events of January 5, 1886, are no longer remembered. When other punctuation is not required, the year is followed by a comma.

Commas to Avoid

Some people mistakenly believe that commas should be used wherever they might pause in speech. A comma does mean pause, but not all pauses are marked by commas. Use a comma only when you know you need one. Avoid the following comma uses:

1. To set off restrictive sentence elements:

   People, *who want a balanced diet*, can use the food pyramid as a guide. The restrictive *who* clause is necessary to identify *people* and should not be set off with commas.

2. To separate a subject from its verb and a preposition from its object:

   People who want a balanced diet, can use the food pyramid as a guide. The comma following the *who* clause separates the subject, *people,* from its verb, *can use.*

   The bottom level of the food pyramid contains food from grains, *such as,* bread, cereals, rice, and pasta. The preposition *such as* should not be followed by a comma.

3. To follow a coordinating conjunction (see 1B Comma Splices):

   The food pyramid describes a new approach to a balanced diet. But, the meat and dairy industries opposed it. The coordinating conjunction *but* should not be set off with a comma.

4. To separate two independent clauses (see 1B Comma Splices) not joined with a coordinating conjunction:

   The pyramid shows fewer servings of dairy and meat products, therefore, consumers would buy less of these higher-priced foods. The comma should be replaced with a semicolon (7B).

5. To set off coordinate elements joined with a coordinating conjunction:

   Vegetables and fruits are near the bottom of the pyramid, *and should be eaten several times a day*. The coordinating conjunction *and* joins a second verb, *should be eaten,* not a second independent clause; therefore, no comma is needed.

7D Colon

4

Use colons correctly to punctuate sentences.

The colon is used most often to introduce an explanatory element, often in the form of a list:

The space shuttle *Challenger* lifted off on January 28, 1986, with a seven-member crew: Francis R. Scobee, Michael J. Smith, Ronald E. McNair, Ellison S. Onizuka, Judith A. Resnik, Gregory B. Jarvis, and Christa McAuliffe. The list explains *crew.*

A twelve-member investigating team discovered the cause of the disaster: a leak in one of the shuttle's two solid-fuel booster rockets. *The phrase explains the cause of the disaster.*

Do not use colons interchangeably with semicolons (see 7B Semicolon). Semicolons separate two independent clauses (see 1B Comma Splices); colons ordinarily are followed by a phrase or phrases. Also avoid using colons after verbs and prepositions (see 1A Fragments):

The two causes of the O-ring failure were cold temperatures and design deficiencies. *No colon after were.*

The commission investigating the disaster noted a number of failures in communication, such as one within the National Aeronautics and Space Administration. *No colon after such as.*

Colons have a few other set uses:

Time:	10:15 a.m.
Salutation in a business letter:	Dear Patricia Morton:
Biblical reference:	Genesis 2:3

7E Dash

The dash separates sentence elements with greater emphasis than a comma:

In *The War of the Worlds* (1898), science fiction writer H. G. Wells described an intense beam of light that destroyed objects on contact—the laser.

It is also used to set off a nonrestrictive sentence element (see 3B Restrictive and Nonrestrictive Modifiers) that might be confusing if set off with commas:

A number of medical uses—performing eye surgery, removing tumors, and unclogging coronary arteries—make the laser more than a destructive weapon. *The three explanatory items separated by commas are set off from the rest of the sentence with dashes.*

Like commas that set off nonrestrictive elements within a sentence, dashes often are used in pairs—at the beginning of the interruption and at the end.

A dash is sometimes used in place of a colon when a colon might seem too formal:

Besides its medical uses, the laser serves many other functions—reading price codes, playing compact audio disks, and sending telephone messages.

Use the dash with caution; overuse gives the impression that you aren't familiar with alternative means of punctuation.

5
Use dashes correctly to separate sentence elements.

7F Quotation Marks

6

Use quotation marks correctly to set off direct quotations.

The main use for quotation marks is to set off direct quotations:

> Professor Charlotte Johnson announced, "Interdisciplinary science is combining fields of scientific knowledge to make up new disciplines."

> "Biochemistry," she went on to say, "combines biology and chemistry."

Quotations within quotations are marked with single quotation marks:

> "The term 'interdisciplinary science' thus describes a change in how processes are investigated," she concluded.

Use quotation marks correctly with other punctuation marks. Periods and commas (see 7C Comma) always go inside the end quotation marks; colons and semicolons almost always go outside the quotation. Dashes, question marks, and exclamation points go inside or outside depending on meaning—inside if the mark applies to the quotation and outside if it applies to the surrounding sentence:

> "Do you know the various branches of the physical sciences?" asked Professor Johnson. Question mark goes inside quotation marks because it applies to the quotation.

> Did the professor say, "Histology deals with tissues and cytology with the fine structures of individual cells"? Question mark goes outside quotation marks because it applies to the surrounding sentence, not the quotation.

Do not use quotation marks to set off indirect quotations:

> The professor said that histology and cytology are different branches of study.

Watch
the Animation on
Quotation Marks
in your MyLab

Another use for quotation marks is to enclose titles of works that are not published separately, including short stories, poems, and essays:

> "You Are a Man," by Richard Rodriguez

> "The Incident," by Countee Cullen

Do not enclose titles of your own essays in quotation marks when they are in title position. (See 8D Italics for treatment of titles of works that are published separately.)

Quotation marks are sometimes used to enclose words used in a special sense, but be careful not to abuse this function:

> The "right" way to do a thing is not always the best way.

7

Use parentheses, brackets, and ellipses correctly to punctuate sentences.

7G Other Marks

Parentheses

Parentheses enclose interrupting elements, setting them off from the rest of the sentence or discourse with a greater separation than provided by other enclosing marks such as commas and dashes. They usually add explanatory information that might seem digressive to the topic.

> The Particle Beam Fusion Accelerator *(PBFA II)* is a device designed to produce energy by fusion. Parentheses set off an abbreviation that will henceforth be used in place of the full term.

> The PBFA II stores up to 3.5 million joules of energy. *(One joule is the amount of energy expended by a one-watt device in one second.)* Parentheses set off an explanation framed as a complete sentence.

Parentheses are always used in pairs. They might have internal punctuation (as in the second example), but marks related to the sentence as a whole go outside the parentheses. Parentheses are almost never preceded by a comma. Note the following example:

> During fusion *(joining of two atomic nuclei to form a larger nucleus)*, mass is converted to energy. Parenthetical element is followed by a comma, showing that it relates to *fusion.* If it had been preceded by a comma, it would appear, illogically, to relate to *mass.*

Brackets

Square brackets have limited uses and are not interchangeable with parentheses. Their most common use is to mark insertions in quoted material:

> Describing the Great Depression, Frederick Lewis Allen says, "The total amount of money paid out in wages *[in 1932]* was 60 percent less than in 1929." The words *in 1932* were not part of the original text.

Some writers use brackets to enclose brief parenthetical material within parentheses:

> Jules Verne (*Journey to the Center of the Earth* [1864]) described giant apes and a vast subterranean sea at the core of the earth. The date of publication is parenthetical to the title of the book.

Ellipsis Dots

Ellipsis dots (spaced periods) are used in quotations to indicate where words have been omitted. Three spaced dots mark omissions within a sentence. If the omission comes at the end of your sentence but not at the end of the original sentence, use four spaced periods.

> One of the legacies of the Great Depression, says Frederick Lewis Allen, is that "if individual Americans are in deep trouble,...their government [should] come to their aid." Words following a comma in the original sentence are omitted within the sentence. The brackets enclose an inserted word.

> This idea, adds Allen, "was fiercely contested for years...." Allen's sentence did not end at *years,* where the quoted sentence ends.

Complete
Additional Exercises
and Practice on
the Handbook
in your MyLab

When using ellipsis dots, be careful not to distort the meaning of the original by your selection of what to include and what to omit.

8 Mechanics and Spelling

Learning Objectives

1 Follow conventions for correct capitalization.

2 Follow guidelines for abbreviating names, dates, and other sentence elements.

3 Use apostrophes correctly to indicate possession or contractions.

4 Use hyphens correctly to divide words and form compounds.

5 Use italics correctly for titles and emphasis.

6 Use numbers correctly.

7 Use strategies to correct common spelling errors.

Some "rules" of writing are flexible, allowing choices, but this is not the case with spelling. With the invention of the printing press in the fifteenth century and the publication of dictionaries in the eighteenth century, flexibility in spelling all but vanished. Dictionaries spell almost all their words in exactly the same way as other dictionaries, and readers expect writers to do likewise. We have expectations about the way hyphens are used in compound words, the way apostrophes show possession or contraction, the way suffixes are added to root words, and so on. This section covers the treatment of words: capitalizing, abbreviating, punctuating (apostrophes and hyphens), italics, and spelling.

8A Capitalization

1
Follow conventions for correct capitalization.

The rules for capitalization are relatively fixed. Following are examples of situations calling for capitalization.

Beginning of a sentence

In 1929, the whole credit structure of the American economy was shaken.

Proper names or nouns

With the onset of the *Great Depression, President Hoover* at first tried to organize national optimism. Historical period or event; person.

Bankers on *Wall Street*, manufacturers in *Detroit*, and legislators in *Washington* all had an effect on the economy. Place.

The Great Depression was part of a worldwide collapse, ending only with *World War II*. Historical period or event.

President Hoover set up the *Reconstruction Finance Corporation* to aid banks and businesses. Person; institution.

In 1900, most of the *African Americans* in this country lived in the *South*. Race and nationality; geographical region.

Jell-O, Pepsi, Rice Krispies Trade names.

Aunt Beatrice, Grandmother Dietz, Dad Relationships when they are part of the name; but not *my dad* and *my aunt and uncle.*

Titles

Death at an Early Age, by Jonathan Kozol; *The Dancing Wu Li Masters: An Overview of the New Physics,* by Gary Zukav. Capitalize first and last words, words following colons, and all other words except articles (*a, an,* and *the*) and conjunctions and prepositions of fewer than five letters (*and, but, in, by,* etc.).

Avoid capitalizing common nouns; for example:

For many people, the *winter* of 1902 was bleak. Seasons.

Many people moved *south* to a warmer climate. Compass directions.

My *great-grandparents* were among those who moved. Relationships.

Simon Waterson was a *professor of history* at the time. Titles that are not part of proper names.

8B Abbreviation

While abbreviations are part of the language, not all are acceptable in all circumstances. A general guideline is that they are less common in formal prose than in less-formal circumstances.

2

Follow guidelines for abbreviating names, dates, and other sentence elements.

Titles with proper names

Dr. Paul Gordon	Paul Gordon, Ph.D.
George Grossman, Jr.	

Times and dates

11:15 A.M. *or* 11:15 a.m.	53 B.C.	A.D. 371

Names of organizations and countries

NATO	CIA	NBC

Use *U.S.* as an adjective (*in a U.S. city*) and *United States* as a noun (*a city in the United States*).

Latin abbreviations (write out except in source citations and parenthetical comments)

etc.	and so forth (*et cetera*—applies to things)
i.e.	that is (*id est*)
e.g.	for example (*exempli gratia*)
cf.	compare (*confer*)
et al.	and others (*et alii*—applies to people)
N.B.	note well (*nota bene*)

Abbreviations to be avoided in most prose

The school board not bd. met on Tuesday not Tues. February 3 not Feb.

William not Wm. Townsend was a guest lecturer in the economics not econ. class.

Townsend arrived from Pittsburgh, Pennsylvania, not *PA* or *Penn.* late last night. For letters and envelopes, use the U.S. Postal zip codes, such as PA for *Pennsylvania* and IL for *Illinois.* Note that both letters are capitalized and are not followed by periods.

Consult your dictionary when you have questions about specific abbreviations.

8C Apostrophe

3

Use apostrophes correctly to indicate possession or contractions.

The apostrophe has two main uses in English—to mark possessive nouns and to show contractions—plus a few specialized uses. Avoid all other uses.

Possessive Nouns

Ownership or connection is marked on nouns with apostrophes:

Norton's resume is short and concise. The resume belongs to Norton.

This *week's* newsletter will be a little late. The newsletter of this week.

The *article's* title is confusing. The title of the article.

To make nouns possessive, follow one of these steps:

1. For singular nouns, add *'s* (*nature + 's = nature's; Tess + 's = Tess's*).
2. For plural nouns ending in *s*, add *'* (*strangers + ' = strangers'*).
3. For plural nouns not ending in *s*, add *'s* (*men + 's = men's*).

Do not use apostrophes to make nouns plural. (See 8G Spelling.) And do not use apostrophes with possessive and relative pronouns. (See 5A Pronoun Case and the Contractions section that follows.)

For example:

The *Harris's* are in Florida. Incorrectly uses apostrophe to make the noun *Harris* plural.

The family lost *it's* home in the fire. Incorrectly uses apostrophe with the pronoun *it* to make it possessive.

Watch
the Animation on
Apostrophes
in your MyLab

Contractions

Apostrophes stand in place of omitted letters in contractions:

doesn't	does not
isn't	is not
I'd	I would
you've	you have
it's	it is *or* it has

who's	who is *or* who has
let's	let us
we'll	we will

Because contractions reflect a casual style, they are usually not acceptable in formal writing. Do not confuse the contracted *it is* (*it's*) and *who is* (*who's*) with the possessive pronouns *its* and *whose*. (See 5A Pronoun Case.)

Special Uses

Plurals of letters, numbers, and words used as terms

I am hoping to get all *A*'s this year.

The memo had four misspelled *there*'s. See 8D Italics, which discusses underlining words used as terms.

All the *7*'s are upside down in the 1990s catalog. The plural for years is usually formed without apostrophes.

Omitted letters or numbers

We'll never forget the summer of '78. Restrict to informal writing.

"Be *seein'* ya," Charlie said. Dialect in quoted speech.

8D Hyphens

Hyphens have three main uses: to divide words at the ends of lines, to form compound words, and to connect spelled-out numbers.

4

Use hyphens correctly to divide words and form compounds.

Dividing Words

There are three general rules to remember when using hyphens to divide words at the ends of lines: (1) Always divide between syllables, (2) don't divide one-syllable words, and (3) don't divide words so that only two letters carry over to the second line. Consider the following examples:

After the results came back, the doctor sat me down and explained my *condition*. Correctly divides a word between syllables.

While they could not cure the condition, at least they could alleviate its *symptoms*. Correctly divides a word between syllables.

In the end, after months of waiting and mountains of legal fees, the court *ruled* against him. Incorrectly divides the one-syllable word *ruled*.

Needless to say, when the court ruled against him, he was not *particularly* pleased. Incorrectly divides the word *particularly* so that only the last two letters carry over to the second line.

Forming Compound Words

Knowing when to hyphenate compound words can be tricky. This is because some compound words can be written as single words (for example, *graveyard* or *postmaster*), while others can be written as two separate words (for example, *place kick* or *executive secretary*). Complicating matters further, compound adjectives take hyphens when they precede nouns but not when they follow nouns. Here are some examples of the correct and incorrect use of hyphens:

My *ex-husband* is a *pro-Communist* crackpot. Use hyphens after the prefix *ex-* and any prefix placed before a proper name, in this case, *pro-* before *Communist*. In general, though, most words formed with prefixes are written as one word; for example, *antisocial* or *multicultural*.

The *post-mortem* revealed that her *brother in law* died of natural causes. This sentence contains two hyphenation errors. First, the compound word *post-mortem* should be written as a single word, *postmortem* (see comment on prefixes in the preceding example). Second, the compound noun *brother in law* should be hyphenated as *brother-in-law*.

Twentieth-century fiction is notable for its experimentation. **or** The fiction of the *twentieth century* is notable for its experimentation. In the first sentence, *Twentieth-century* functions as a compound adjective modifying the noun *fiction* and so requires a hyphen. In the second sentence, *twentieth century* functions as a compound noun (specifically an object of the preposition *of*) and does not require a hyphen.

The *secretary treasurer* discouraged the group from making *highly-risky* investments. This sentence contains two hyphenation errors. First, the compound noun *secretary treasurer* requires a hyphen. Second, *-ly* adverbs such as *highly* are written as separate words when they precede adjectives such as *risky*.

Connecting Spelled-Out Numbers

Use hyphens to link compounds of spelled-out numbers and to link numbers to nouns. For example:

twenty-fifth time

nine-page letter

132-page report

six-year-old

35-year-old

Whenever you have a question about dividing words and hyphenating compound words, use your dictionary. Dots usually mark syllables, and hyphens mark hyphenated compounds.

5
Use italics correctly for titles and emphasis.

8E Italics (Underlining)

Italic type slants to the right and is used in printed material in the same way that underlining is used in handwritten or typed copy. It has specialized uses.

Titles of works published independently

The Atlantic Monthly (magazine)

A Farewell to Arms (book)

The Wall Street Journal (newspaper)

Desperate Housewives (television program)

Cats (play)

Ships, aircraft, spacecraft, and trains

Challenger (spacecraft)

Leasat 3 (communications satellite)

San Francisco *Zephyr* (train)

Words, letters, and numbers used as themselves

The process of heat transfer is called *conduction*.

The Latin words *et cetera* mean "and other things."

The letter *e* is the most commonly used vowel.

Many people consider *13* to be an unlucky number.

Emphasis

"I said, '*Did* you buy the tickets?' not '*Would* you buy the tickets?'"

Many people writing with computers use italics instead of underlining. If you are writing a documented paper for class, find out if your teacher approves of italics for titles.

8F Numbers

Numbers can be spelled out or written as numerals. When to employ one style or the other depends on the writing context. In most academic writing in the humanities, and indeed in most writing geared for a general audience, numbers are usually spelled out as discussed next. In the sciences, however, numbers are usually written as numerals.

6

Use numbers correctly.

Unless you are asked to follow different conventions, use the following guidelines to handle numbers in writing:

1. Spell out numbers requiring two words or less, and write numerals for numbers requiring three or more words. In practice, this means you will write out numbers *one* to *ninety-nine* and write numerals for *100* and above.

2. Spell out numbers that begin sentences. For long numbers, this can lead to awkward sentences. In such instances, you should consider revising the sentence to move the number away from the beginning of the sentence so it can be written in numerals.

3. Make exceptions for numbers used in special figures and contexts. In these instances, numbers are usually written as numerals. For example, these might include days and years; pages, chapters, and volumes; acts, scenes, and lines; decimals, fractions, ratios, and percentages; temperatures; addresses; statistics; and amounts of money.

Consider the following examples:

The company mailed *twenty-one* parcels yesterday.

She bought *2,200* acres of ranch land with her lottery winnings.

One hundred and fifty-two cows drowned in the flood.

The Japanese attacked Pearl Harbor on December *7, 1941.*

You will find the answer on page *87* in chapter *5.*

The famous "To be, or not to be" soliloquy appears in act *3,* scene *1* of *Hamlet.*

The temperature reached *105°*F yesterday.

The suspect resided at *221* Dolores Street, apartment *3B.*

The winning margin was *2* to *1.*

With tax, the umbrella cost *$15.73.*

8G Spelling

7

Use strategies to correct common spelling errors.

One of the unfair facts of life is that the ability to spell is not equally distributed: Some people spell easily and some don't. If you're one of the latter, you'll need to put more time into getting your words right. A spellchecker is helpful, because it flags most misspelled words and suggests alternatives. If you are using one of these aids, however, be especially careful to look for misspelled homonyms. Rules of spelling sometimes help, though too many of them are probably a hindrance. Therefore, only the most useful and dependable ones are included here.

Doubling a Final Consonant

When adding a suffix such as *-ing* or *-ed* to a word that ends in a consonant, double the final consonant to keep the internal vowel short; for example, *permit, permitted; stop, stopped.* Double the final consonant when all three of the following are true:

1. The word ends in a consonant preceded by a vowel.

2. The word is one syllable or the stress is on the final syllable.

3. The suffix begins with a vowel.

Here are some other examples:

hop	hopped	begin	beginning
sit	sitting	prefer	preferred
put	putting	occur	occurrence
win	winner	recap	recapped

Words Containing *ie* or *ei*

The familiar rhyme about using *ie* or *ei* is true most of the time—enough times that it is worth remembering: *i* before *e* except after *c* when the sound is long *e*. Thus, words such as these follow the rule:

receive	believe	weight
ceiling	chief	beige
conceited	siege	eight

There are a few common exceptions: *caffeine, either, neither, seize,* and *weird.* Another common word that the rule does not address is *friend* (spelled *i* before *e*, but the sound is not long *e*).

Final *e*

To add an ending to a word that ends in a silent *e*, drop the *e* when the ending begins with a vowel:

believe + able = believable	believe + ed = believed
move + able = movable	move + ment = movement
hope + ing = hoping	hope + ful = hopeful

When the consonant preceding the final *e* is a soft *c* or *g*, the *e* is dropped only when the ending begins with *e* or *i*:

change + ing = changing	change + able = changeable
notice + ing = noticing	notice + able = noticeable
manage + er = manager	manage + ment = management
nice + er = nicer	nice + ly = nicely

Final *y*

To add an ending to a word with a final *y* preceded by a consonant, change the *y* to *i* except when your ending is *-ing*:

happy + ly = happily	study + ing = studying
apply + s = applies	apply + ing = applying
vary + ous = various	vary + ing = varying
try + ed = tried	try + ing = trying

When the final *y* is preceded by a vowel, keep the *y*:

play + ed = played	play + ful = playful
employ + ed = employed	employ + ment = employment

but

say + s = says	say + d = said
pay + ment = payment	pay + d = paid

Never change the *y* when adding an ending to a proper noun: *the Barrys.*

411

Plurals

Plural nouns ordinarily have an *s* ending:

    boy + s = boys   car + s = cars

Words that end in *ch, s, sh, x,* or *z* require *-es*:

    box + es = boxes   church + es = churches

Words ending in *o* are a little more troublesome. If the *o* is preceded by a vowel, add *s*:

    radio + s = radios   video + s = videos

If the *o* is preceded by a consonant, ordinarily add *-es*:

    hero + es = heroes   potato + es = potatoes

A few common words take either *s* or *-es*:

    tornados, tornadoes   zeros, zeroes   volcanos, volcanoes

Some words form their plurals internally or do not have a plural form. Do not add an *s* to these words:

    child, children   deer, deer
    man, men   fish, fish
    mouse, mice   moose, moose

Compound words ordinarily have an *s* at the end of the compound:

    textbook, textbooks   snowshoe, snowshoes
    text edition, text editions   snow goose, snow geese

But when the first word of the compound is the main word, add the *s* to it:

    sisters-in-law   attorneys-general

Whenever you are in doubt about the correct plural ending, check your dictionary.

Homonyms

Watch
the Animation on
**Easily Confused
Words**
in your MyLab

Some of the most troublesome words to spell are homonyms—words that sound alike but are spelled differently. Here is a partial list of the most common ones:

    accept, except   maybe, may be
    affect, effect   of, 've (have)
    already, all ready   passed, past
    cite, sight, site   than, then
    forth, fourth   their, there, they're
    it's, its   to, too, two
    know, no   whose, who's
    lead, led   your, you're

A few other words, not exactly homonyms, are sometimes confused:

breath, breathe	lightning, lightening
choose, chose	loose, lose
clothes, cloths	precede, proceed
dominant, dominate	quiet, quite

Check in your dictionary the meanings of any sound-alike words you are unsure of.

Complete
Additional Exercises
and Practice on
the Handbook
in your MyLab

9 Review of Basic Grammar

Learning Objectives

1 Recognize the nine parts of speech.

2 Identify subjects and predicates in sentences.

3 Recognize objects and complements in sentences.

4 Recognize the six types of phrases.

5 Recognize the primary types of clauses.

6 Identify the five basic sentence patterns.

7 Distinguish simple, compound, complex, and compound-complex sentences.

Grammar is the set of rules used for communicating in a language. Words are the basic units of grammar, which classifies them by their function into the *parts of speech*. In English, grammar determines the form words take and the order in which they can be combined into *phrases*, *clauses*, and *sentences*. Sentences, unlike phrases and clauses, must represent complete thoughts; and to do so, each must contain at least one *subject* and one *predicate*. Sentences can also include *objects* and *complements*.

9A Parts of Speech

This section examines nine parts of speech: verbs, nouns, pronouns, adjectives, adverbs, prepositions, conjunctions, articles, and interjections. Some words can function as more than one part of speech. For example, the word "crow" can function as a noun (The *crow* stole food from our table) and a verb (The fans *crow* insults at the referee). For such words, determine the function the word plays within a sentence before you identify the part of speech it constitutes.

1
Recognize the
nine parts of
speech.

Verbs

Verbs express action (She *ran* for the senate) or a state of being (I *am* sick). Through changes in *form*, verbs can indicate the following: *tense* (present, past, future, etc.); *person* (first person, second person, or third person); *number* (singular or plural); *voice* (active or passive); and *mood* (indicative, imperative, and subjunctive). Other classifications of verbs include *linking verbs, transitive and intransitive verbs, helping verbs,* and *verbals.*

Form. Verbs have five primary forms:

Base	Present + s	Present Participle	Past	Past Participle
ask	asks	asking	asked	asked
climb	climbs	climbing	climbed	climbed
jump	jumps	jumping	jumped	jumped
move	moves	moving	moved	moved
reach	reaches	reaching	reached	reached
vanish	vanishes	vanishing	vanished	vanished
walk	walks	walking	walked	walked

The *base form* is used to indicate present-tense action in the first-person singular (*I*) and plural (*we*), the second person (*you*), and the third-person plural (*they* or a plural noun).

> We *hope* that you *drive* safely.
>
> The hikers *vanish* into the fog.

The *present + s form* is made by adding an *-s* or *-es* to the base form and is used only to indicate present-tense action in the third-person singular (*he, she, it,* or a singular noun).

> She *walks* up the stairs.
>
> The voter *reaches* for the ballot.

The *present participle form* is created by adding *-ing* to the base form. When used as a participle, this form functions as an adjective.

> The *dripping* faucet kept him up all night.

When used as a *gerund,* the form functions as a noun.

> *Dancing* was her favorite activity.

When joined with the verb *be* and helping verbs, the present participle form indicates the ongoing action of the progressive tense.

> He *is studying* at the moment. Present progressive tense.
>
> They *have been listening* to music. Past perfect progressive tense.

The *past form* is made by adding a *-d* or *-ed* to the base form. This form is used to indicate past action.

> The committee *waited* for our answer.
>
> He *moved* with the beat.

Verbs that express past action without adding a *-d* or *-ed* to the base form are known as *irregular verbs* (see the list below).

The *past participle form* is also made by adding a *-d* or *-ed* to the base form. In fact, for regular verbs, the past participle form and the past form are identical. When used as a participle, this form functions as an adjective.

The *wilted* flowers lay on the table.

When joined with the helping verbs *have* and *will*, the past participle form indicates the perfect tenses.

We *have waited* for a long time. Present perfect tense.

She *will have finished* her paper by noon. Future perfect tense.

When joined with the verb *be*, the past participle form is used to indicate *passive voice*.

The guests *were escorted* to their table.

The plan *was approved* unanimously.

Just as they do in the past form, irregular verbs do not add *-d* or *-ed* to make the past participle form. Irregular verbs often change internally to indicate their past and past participle forms. Common irregular verbs and their past and past participle forms include the following:

Base	Past	Past Participle
be (is, am, are)	was, were	been
come	came	come
do	did	done
drink	drank	drunk
eat	ate	eaten
give	gave	given
go	went	gone
grow	grew	grown
see	saw	seen
take	took	taken
throw	threw	thrown
write	wrote	written

Tense. A verb's tense indicates when its action occurred. The *simple tenses* are used the most frequently. They depict action in a straightforward manner in the present, past, and future.

Present	The children *kiss* their grandmother.
Past	The children *kissed* their grandmother.
Future	The children *will kiss* their grandmother.

The *perfect tenses* express action that has been completed by a specific time or action that has already been completed before another action begins.

Present Perfect	The children *have kissed* their grandmother.
Past Perfect	The children *had kissed* their grandmother.
Future Perfect	The children *will have kissed* their grandmother.

The *progressive tenses* express ongoing actions.

Present Progressive	The children *are kissing* their grandmother.
Past Progressive	The children *were kissing* their grandmother.
Future Progressive	The children *will be kissing* their grandmother.
Present Perfect Progressive	The children *have been kissing* their grandmother.
Past Perfect Progressive	The children *had been kissing* their grandmother.
Future Perfect Progressive	The children *will have been kissing* their grandmother.

Person and Number. The relationship between person and number is intertwined, so the two need to be discussed together. The subject's connection to the verb *as a speaker* is expressed through person. In the first person, the subject does the speaking (*I, we*); in the second person, the subject is spoken to (*you*); and in the third person, the subject is spoken about (*he, she, it, they*).

A verb's number can be either singular or plural and is determined by its subject. Singular verbs show the action of an individual subject (*I, you, he, she, it*), while plural verbs show the action of a collective subject (*we, you, they*). The verb form is the same for the singular and the plural in all of the tenses, with the exception of present tense in the third-person singular, which adds an *-s* or *-es* to the base form (see *present + s* form).

	Singular	Plural
first person	*I forgive* the debt.	*We forgive* the debt.
second person	*You forgive* the debt.	(All of) *You forgive* the debt.
third person	*He (she, it) forgives* the debt.	*They forgive* the debt.

Voice. In a sentence written in the *active voice*, the subject is the doer of the verb's action. In a sentence written in the *passive voice*, the subject is not the doer of the verb's action. Instead, the doer of the verb's action is the object of a preposition or is not stated at all. Because the active voice is clearer, more direct, and less wordy than the passive voice, you should strive to write in the active voice whenever possible. Reserve use of the passive voice only for instances in which you do not know or do not want to name the doer of the verb's action.

Susan lost the car keys. Active voice: Here the subject, *Susan,* performs the action of the verb *lost.*

The car keys were lost by Susan. Passive voice: The information communicated in this example is the same as that expressed in the previous example, but now *car keys* have become the subject, and the doer of the verb's action, *Susan,* is the object of the preposition *by.*

The car keys were lost. Passive voice: Here the subject remains *car keys,* but the doer of the verb's action is not stated.

Mood. Mood expresses the writer's attitude toward the action of the verb. There are three forms of mood: indicative, imperative, and subjunctive. Verbs in the *indicative mood* make statements, ask questions, and declare opinions. For example:

He *said* that your argument *is* wrong. Makes a statement.

Did he really *say* that? Asks a question.

He *should rethink* his objection to my argument. Declares an opinion.

Verbs in the *imperative mood* issue commands, requests, or directions. When the subject of an imperative verb is not explicitly identified, it is understood to be *you.*

Don't touch the hot plate. Issues a command.

Class, please *read* the essays tonight. Issues a request.

Turn right at the next intersection. Issues directions.

Verbs in the *subjunctive mood* communicate wishes, make statements contrary to fact, list requirements and demands, and imply skepticism or doubt. They usually appear in clauses introduced by *if, that, as if,* and *as though.* Use the base form of the verb for the present-tense subjunctive. For the past-tense subjunctive of the verb *be,* use *were* for all subjects.

He wishes that he *were* a movie star. Communicates wish.

If I *were* to live for a thousand years, think of all that I would see. Makes statement contrary to fact.

The day care center requires that your sister *sign* a consent form and *provide* proof of immunization for her daughter. Lists requirements.

The lawyer acts as if his client *were* a saint. Implies skepticism.

Linking Verbs. Verbs that link the subject to a subject complement (see 9C Objects and Complements) are called linking verbs. These verbs commonly express states of being rather than action. Common linking verbs include *be, look, sound, taste, smell, feel, grow, appear, seem, become, remain,* and *get.*

I *am* tired.

You *look* thirsty.

Things *sound* grim over there.

She *felt* happy.

Your neighbors *seem* angry.

Helping Verbs. Some verbs require the addition of helping verbs (or auxiliary verbs) to communicate their meaning. The combination of a main verb and a helping verb forms a *verb phrase*. The most frequently used helping verbs are *be*, *do*, and *have*. These three helping verbs can also stand alone as main verbs: I *am* hungry; She *did* her chores; You *have* won. Other helping verbs, however, cannot stand alone as main verbs and can only be used in verb phrases. These helping verbs include *can, could, may, might, should, will,* and *would*. Helping verbs are often required to indicate tense, voice, and mood.

> Mr. Nguyen *will* call you tomorrow. Future tense.
>
> The students *have* completed the test. Present perfect tense.
>
> Next month I *will have been* living here for three years. Future perfect progressive tense.
>
> The report *was* delivered early. Passive voice.
>
> We *can* help you. Indicative mood.
>
> *Did* you leave the door open? Indicative mood.

Transitive and Intransitive Verbs. Transitive verbs express action at objects, which receive that action (see 9C Objects and Complements). Intransitive verbs do not express action at objects.

> She *mailed* the letter to me. Transitive: The direct object *letter* receives the action of the transitive verb *mailed*.
>
> The children *slept* peacefully. Intransitive: The verb *slept* does not express its action at an object—the adverb *peacefully* functions only to modify the verb.

Many verbs can function as both transitive and intransitive verbs.

> The athlete *ate* the roast turkey. Transitive: The direct object *roast turkey* receives the action of the transitive verb *ate*.
>
> The athlete *ate* like a pig. Intransitive: The verb *ate* does not express its action at an object—the adverbial phrase *like a pig* only modifies the verb.

Verbals. Verb forms that function as nouns, adjectives, or adverbs in sentences are known as *verbals*. There are three kinds of verbals: participles, gerunds, and infinitives. *Participles* function as adjectives. The present participle form adds *-ing* to the base form. The past participle form adds a *-d* or *-ed* to the base form of regular verbs (irregular verbs are often conjugated internally).

> The *howling* wolf startled the hunters. The present participle *howling* modifies the subject *wolf*.
>
> She threw the *chipped* vase into the trash. The past participle *chipped* modifies the direct object *vase*.

Gerunds function as nouns and use the present participle form—that is, *-ing* added to the base form of the verb.

> *Fishing* takes patience.
>
> The consequences of *drinking* and *driving* are often tragic.

Infinitives can function as nouns, adjectives, or adverbs. Infinitives begin with the word *to*, followed by the base form of the verb.

Everyone wants *to fall in love.* The infinitive *to fall in love* acts as a direct object and so functions as a noun.

They had nothing *to eat* today. The infinitive *to eat* modifies the noun *nothing* and so acts as an adjective.

You must persevere *to succeed* in life. The infinitive *to succeed* modifies the verb phrase *must persevere* and so acts as an adverb.

Nouns

Watch the Animation on **Parts of Speech** in your MyLab

Nouns include people (ice skater, Malcolm X), places (playground, Grand Canyon), things (bicycle, Empire State Building), and concepts (happiness, liberty). *Common nouns* refer to people, places, things, or concepts that are representative of groups or classes (mechanic, colleges, keys, hardness). *Proper nouns* refer to specific people, places, things, or concepts (President Chirac, Tokyo, the *Titanic*, Marxism). Common nouns may be either concrete or abstract in character. *Concrete nouns* refer to things that have a tangible existence in the world (tears, lawyer, roast beef). *Abstract nouns*, on the other hand, refer to ideas and feelings that do not exist outside of our thoughts or emotions (sadness, justice, hunger). *Count nouns* can be counted and have singular (cat, cookie, bike) and plural forms (cats, cookies, bikes). *Noncount nouns* (or mass nouns) cannot be counted and do not possess plural forms (violence, copper, stability). *Collective nouns* refer to groups; although they are frequently used in the singular, they also possess plural forms (people, family, crowd, party, horde). Nouns may indicate possession by the addition of an apostrophe and -*s* to singular forms (Michael's car, cat's meow) and an apostrophe to the plural forms (dancers' clothes, birds' feathers). Nouns are often preceded by articles (a, an, the) or quantifiers (one, many, some, a few, several). They may also be modified by adjectives (*black* cat), adjective phrases (keys *on the table*), or adjective clauses (car *that was stolen last night*).

Pronouns

Pronouns act as substitutes for nouns. They perform the same functions as nouns, but whereas nouns actually name people, places, things, and concepts, pronouns only stand in for nouns. The noun to which a pronoun refers is known as the pronoun's *antecedent*.

Mrs. Ghatta had a nightmare while *she* slept on the couch. The subject *Mrs. Ghatta* is the antecedent of the pronoun *she.*

While *she* slept on the couch, *Mrs. Ghatta* had a nightmare. The subject *Mrs. Ghatta* remains the antecedent of the pronoun *she* even though the pronoun now precedes the subject in the sentence.

Pronouns are classified by function into the following groups: personal, relative, interrogative, reflexive/intensive, indefinite, and demonstrative. Personal, relative, and interrogative pronouns possess subjective, objective, and possessive case forms.

Personal Pronouns. These replace nouns that name people or things and possess subjective, objective, and possessive case forms.

Subjective	Objective	Possessive
I	me	my, mine
you	you	your, yours
he	him	his
she	her	hers
it	it	its
we	us	our, ours
they	them	their, theirs

The *subjective case form* stands in for nouns that function as subjects or subject complements.

> *They* crossed the street. The pronoun *they* serves as the sentence's subject.

> The fool is *he* who turns his back on wisdom. The pronoun *he* serves as the subject complement.

The *objective case form* stands in for nouns that function as objects of verbs or prepositions.

> Ms. Lin paid *us* in cash. The pronoun *us* serves as an indirect object.

> Their grievances seemed petty to *me*. The pronoun *me* serves as an object of the preposition *to*.

The *possessive case form* shows ownership. This form can function as a possessive adjective (*my, your, his, her, its, our, their*) or as both a possessive adjective and the noun or gerund it modifies (*mine, yours, his, hers, its, ours, theirs*).

> *Your* cat ate *my* canary. The pronouns *Your* and *my* function as adjectives indicating ownership.

> *Theirs* was an unhappy fate. The pronoun *Theirs* functions as both the possessive adjective *their* and the noun *fate*.

Relative Pronouns. These pronouns introduce adjective clauses. Relative pronouns that refer to people possess subjective, objective, and possessive case forms.

Subjective	Objective	Possessive
who	whom	whose
whoever	whomever	whosever

Relative pronouns that do not refer to people (*that, what, whatever, which, whichever, whose*) do not possess subjective, objective, and possessive case forms.

> Ahmed, *who* lives next door, was promoted today. The pronoun *who* is the subject of *lives*.

> She hung up on her boyfriend, *whom* she despised. The pronoun *whom* is the object of *despised*.

We greeted our friends, *whose* home we had watched for the last two weeks. The pronoun *whose* indicates ownership.

They bought a car *that* was within their price range. The pronoun *that* indicates ownership.

Interrogative Pronouns. These pronouns take the same forms as relative pronouns, including subjective, objective, and possessive case forms when they refer to people.

Interrogative pronouns, however, do not introduce adjective clauses. Instead, they introduce questions.

Who lost the argument?

To *whom* did the prize go?

Whose car is that?

What questions did he ask you?

Whatever happened to her?

Reflexive/Intensive Pronouns. Reflexive pronouns refer to subjects or objects introduced earlier in the same clause. Their function is to show action directed by the antecedent at itself. Reflexive pronouns include *myself, yourself, himself, herself, itself, oneself, ourselves, yourselves,* and *themselves.*

She asked me how I managed to keep cutting *myself* while shaving.

Please make *yourself* at home. The unstated subject of this sentence is understood to be *you.*

We tell *ourselves* the same stories over and over again.

The campers washed *themselves* in the river.

Intensive pronouns take the same forms as reflexive pronouns but are used only to emphasize the action of the antecedent, not to show action directed by the antecedent at itself.

She fixed the flat tire by *herself.*

It is surprising the resources one finds inside *oneself.*

Indefinite Pronouns. These pronouns refer to quantities or unspecified people and things. Indefinite pronouns include *a few, a lot, all, another, any, anybody, anyone, anything, anywhere, both, each, either, enough, everybody, everyone, everything, everywhere, few, many, more, most, much, neither, nobody, none, no one, nothing, one, several, some, somebody, someone, something,* and *somewhere.*

Anybody caught shoplifting will be prosecuted.

Few have sacrificed as much as we have.

One good deed deserves *another.*

I have called *everyone* together today to say *a few* words about *something* very important.

Demonstrative Pronouns. These pronouns (*this, that, these, those*) point to antecedents in such a way as to hold them up for special scrutiny or discussion.

> *That* was a spectacular meal.
>
> I will take *these* shoes, please.

Adjectives

Adjectives modify nouns and pronouns. They answer questions such as *How many? What kind? Which?* and *Whose?*

> She bought *five jumbo-sized* platters of appetizers for *tomorrow's* party at *Ken's* house. How many platters? *Five.* What kind of platters? *Jumbo-sized.* Which party? *Tomorrow's.* Whose house? *Ken's.*

Adjectives usually precede the words they modify, but they can follow after words or, as subject complements, even after the verb.

> The ocean, *cool* and *inviting*, lapped at our feet.
>
> The movie was *boring*.

Nouns and pronouns often function as adjectives, in both their subjective case forms and possessive forms. Indeed, a word may function as a noun in one part of a sentence and as an adjective elsewhere in the same sentence.

> *Some* children attend *summer* school; *some* do not. The word *some* functions as an adjective in its first instance and as a noun in its second instance. The word *summer,* frequently used as a noun, functions as an adjective modifying *school.*

Adjectives have positive, comparative, and superlative forms.

> Their house is *big*. Positive form.
>
> Their house is *bigger* than mine. Comparative form.
>
> Theirs is the *biggest* house on the block. Superlative form.

Adverbs

Adverbs modify verbs, adjectives, and other adverbs. They answer questions such as *How? How often? When?* and *Where?*

> *Yesterday*, we *narrowly* won the championship game. How did we win? *Narrowly.* When did we win? *Yesterday.* Both adverbs modify verbs.
>
> Our rivals play *nearby* and had beaten us *frequently*. Where do the rivals play? *Nearby.* How often had they beaten us? *Frequently.* Both adverbs modify verbs.
>
> It was a *desperately* needed victory. The adverb *desperately* modifies the adjective *needed.*
>
> The losing team left the field *very* quietly. The adverb *very* modifies the adverb *quietly.*

Adverbs can come before or after the words they modify. Sometimes, for the sake of rhythm or emphasis, adverbs can be placed at the beginning or end of the sentence.

The detective *slowly* opened the door.

Slowly, the detective opened the door.

The detective opened the door *slowly*.

Adverbs, like adjectives, have positive, comparative, and superlative forms. For adverbs that end in *-ly*, the comparative adds the word *more* to the positive form, while the superlative adds the word *most*.

She sings *beautifully*. Positive form.

She sings *more beautifully* than I do. Comparative form.

She sings *most beautifully* of us all. Superlative form.

Prepositions

Prepositions introduce *prepositional phrases* and show the relationship (place, destination, possession, time, cause, movement, purpose, etc.) between the *object of the preposition*, which is always a noun or pronoun, and another word or group of words. Common prepositions include *about, above, after, around, at, before, behind, below, beneath, between, beyond, by, down, for, from, in, inside, into, like, of, off, on, onto, out, over, past, since, through, to, toward, under, until, up, with,* and *without*.

The police car parked *in* our driveway. Place.

The protestors marched *toward* city hall. Destination.

This is the home *of* a World War II veteran. Possession.

We will arrive *at* 8:00 p.m. Time.

The water is dripping *from* the leak. Cause.

She walked *into* the theater. Movement.

The students studied *for* the final exam. Purpose.

Conjunctions

Conjunctions link one or more words, phrases, or clauses within a sentence. There are three types of conjunctions: coordinating, subordinating, and correlative.

Coordinating Conjunctions. These conjunctions join parallel words, phrases, and clauses (see 2A Parallelism). Coordinating conjunctions include *and, but, for, nor, or, so,* and *yet*.

The pitcher *and* the hitter confronted each other.

She wanted to go to the beach, *but* she had to stay home instead.

You can have orange juice *or* lemonade.

Subordinating Conjunctions. These conjunctions introduce subordinate (dependent) clauses. Subordinating conjunctions include *after, although, as, because, before, even if, even though, if, once, since, so, so that, than, that, unless, until, when, whenever, where, whereas, wherever, whether,* and *while.*

After she won the race, Robin celebrated with her family and friends.

We will not leave *until* Jim returns.

I was on the phone *when* the earthquake struck.

Correlative Conjunctions. Like coordinating conjunctions, correlative conjunctions join parallel words, phrases, and clauses. Correlative conjunctions, however, only occur in pairs. They include *both...and, either...or, just as...so, neither...nor, not only...but also,* and *whether...or.*

She wanted *both* to have a career *and* to start a family.

We will visit *either* the museum *or* the park this afternoon.

Articles

Articles introduce nouns. The word *the* is a *definite article* and it introduces nouns whose specific character is known (*The* cat walked down *the* path). The words *a* and *an* are *indefinite articles* and they introduce nouns whose specific character is not known (*A* cat walked down *a* path). *A* precedes words that begin with consonants; *an* precedes words that begin with vowels or a silent *h* (*an* hour).

Interjections

Interjections are words that express strong feelings, alarm, or surprise. They are common in speech and may be used in personal or informal writing, but are generally inappropriate for formal and academic writing. When they do appear in writing, they typically stand alone as fragments. Common interjections include *boo, cool, oh, oh no, ouch, shhh, uh-oh, wow, yea,* and *yikes.* Profanity is often used as an interjection, particularly in speech, but it is considered offensive in most academic and professional settings.

9B Subjects and Predicates

2

Identify subjects and predicates in sentences.

The *subject* of a sentence is its main topic. The subject is always a noun, pronoun, noun phrase, or noun clause. The *predicate* makes a statement or asks a question about the subject. The predicate must always contain a verb, but it can also contain adjectives, adverbs, nouns, pronouns, and other words.

Subjects

The simple subject is the noun or pronoun that represents the sentence's main topic. It is usually a single word, although proper nouns can run to two or more words (*General George Washington*). The complete subject contains the simple subject and any words or phrases that modify it.

Subject	Predicate
He	slept.
The man	had terrible nightmares that night.
The wearied, defeated prime minister	tossed fitfully in his bed.

Most of us at dinner that evening got sick the next day. The pronoun *Most* is the sentence's simple subject, and *Most of us at dinner that evening* is the complete subject.

Compound subjects are two or more parallel nouns or pronouns linked by commas and coordinating conjunctions or correlative conjunctions.

Mishal, Zanab, and Amir swam out to the sailboat.

Playing to win and playing fair are not mutually exclusive concepts.

Neither you nor I will win the lottery.

Predicates

The simple predicate is the sentence's main verb. The complete predicate contains the simple predicate and any words or phrases that modify it.

The strikers *picketed outside the factory's main gate despite the wind and rain.* The verb *picketed* is the sentence's simple predicate; the simple predicate and all of the words that follow after it represent the complete predicate.

Compound predicates represent two or more main verbs linked by commas and coordinating conjunctions or correlative conjunctions.

We *laughed, ate, and drank* our way through the evening.

He *tiptoed* to the door *and pressed* his ear up against its cold, hard wood.

That afternoon she *not only aced* the exam, *but* she *also submitted* her final paper to her instructor.

9C Objects and Complements

Objects are nouns or pronouns that appear within a sentence's predicate and complete its meaning. *Complements* are nouns or adjectives that rename or describe the sentence's subject or direct object.

3
Recognize objects and complements in sentences.

Objects

There are three types of objects: direct objects, indirect objects, and objects of prepositions.

Direct Objects. These are nouns or pronouns that accept the action of *transitive verbs* (see 9A Parts of Speech). Direct objects answer questions such as *What?* or *Whom?* about their verbs.

She kissed *her children* good night. Kissed whom? *Her children.*

He wrote *the essay* on sustainable growth. Wrote what? *The essay.*

The teacher gave *them* to us. Gave what? *Them.*

Indirect Objects. These are nouns or pronouns for which the action of the transitive verb is performed. Direct objects answer questions such as *For what? To what? For whom?* or *To whom?* about their verbs. Because indirect objects never appear without direct objects, one way to avoid confusing the two is to identify the direct object (DO) first and then the indirect object (IO).

> We mailed *them* the invitations. Mailed what? The invitations (DO). To whom? *Them* (IO).
>
> The county clerk issued *Michael and Caitlin* a marriage license. Issued what? A marriage license (DO). To whom? *Michael and Caitlin* (IO).
>
> Her father gave *their union* his blessing. Gave what? His blessing (DO). To what? *Their union* (IO).

Objects of Prepositions. These are nouns or pronouns that complete the meaning of *prepositional phrases* (see 9A Parts of Speech). When they appear in sentences with direct objects, objects of prepositions convey the same meaning as indirect objects. Objects of prepositions, however, can also appear in sentences that do not contain direct objects.

> We mailed the invitations to *them*.
>
> I left the keys in *the ignition*.
>
> For *the older couple*, the hike would be long and hard.

Complements

There are two types of complements: subject complements and object complements.

Subject Complements. These are nouns or adjectives that follow after a *linking verb* (see 9A Parts of Speech) and rename or describe the subject. Subject complements that are nouns rename their subjects, and those that are adjectives describe their subjects.

> Margaret is *a lawyer*. The subject complement *a lawyer* is a noun.
>
> My grandfather is *ill*. The subject complement *ill* is an adjective.

Object Complements. These are nouns or adjectives that rename or describe the direct object. Object complements that are nouns rename their direct objects, and those that are adjectives describe their direct objects.

> The panel voted Sagiko *the winner*. The object complement *the winner* is a noun.
>
> Many people consider travel *pleasurable*. The object complement *pleasurable* is an adjective.

9D Phrases

4
Recognize the six types of phrases.

A phrase is a group of related words that lack a subject or a predicate or both. A phrase, then, can never express a complete thought as a sentence and independent clause can. Phrases modify words, groups of words, or the entire sentence.

There are six types of phrases: prepositional phrases, participial phrases, gerund phrases, absolute phrases, infinitive phrases, and appositive phrases.

Prepositional Phrases

Prepositional phrases begin with a *preposition* (see 9A Parts of Speech) and contain a noun or pronoun and its modifiers, if any. Prepositional phrases act as adjectives and adverbs.

> The neighbors *across the street* own a speedboat. The prepositional phrase functions as an adjective modifying the noun *neighbors.*

> The satellite burned up *in the upper atmosphere.* The prepositional phrase functions as an adverb modifying the verb *burned up.*

Participial Phrases

Participial phrases contain *present* or *past participles* (see 9A Parts of Speech) and their modifiers or complements. Participial phrases act as adjectives.

> The man *arrested yesterday* was an industrial spy. The participial phrase modifies the noun *man.*

> The dancers *demonstrating the tango right now* are my friends. The participial phrase modifies the noun *dancers.*

Gerund Phrases

Gerund phrases contain *gerunds* (see 9A Parts of Speech) and their modifiers, objects, and complements. Gerund phrases function as nouns and therefore can serve as a subject, direct object, object of the preposition, object complement, and subject complement.

> *Dating over the Internet* has become popular. The gerund phrase serves as the subject.

> The children love *playing computer games.* The gerund phrase serves as the direct object.

> He was exhausted from *running under the hot sun.* The gerund phrase serves as the object of the preposition.

> We wished them luck *climbing the mountain.* The gerund phrase serves as an object complement.

> Her favorite pastime is *knitting wool sweaters.* The gerund phrase serves as the subject complement.

Absolute Phrases

Absolute phrases contain a noun or pronoun, a present or past participle, and any modifiers. Absolute phrases modify an entire sentence, not just one word or group of words within the sentence. Whether they appear at the beginning, middle, or end of a sentence, absolute phrases are always set off with a comma.

> *Its whistle blowing,* the ferry pulled away from the dock.

> The patient, *his body convulsed with fever,* slipped into unconsciousness.

> He stepped on the gas, *his heart racing with adrenaline.*

Infinitive Phrases

Infinitive phrases contain *infinitives* (see 9A Parts of Speech) and their modifiers, objects, or complements. Infinitive phrases function as adjectives, adverbs, and nouns.

He wanted his son *to help him fix the leak.* The infinitive phrase modifies the noun *son* and so acts as an adjective.

She studied *to pass the exam.* The infinitive phrase modifies the verb *studied* and so acts as an adverb.

Before I made a decision, I needed *to think things over thoroughly.* The infinitive phrase acts as a direct object and so functions as a noun.

Appositive Phrases

Appositive phrases are nouns and their modifiers that rename the nouns or pronouns that immediately precede them. They are often set off with commas.

My neighbor, *a doctor,* is a very kind woman.

He has an engineering degree from CalTech, *one of the most prestigious universities in the country.*

9E Clauses

5

Recognize the primary types of clauses.

A clause is a group of words containing both a subject and a predicate. An *independent clause* can function on its own as a sentence.

A *subordinate clause* (dependent clause) cannot function on its own as a sentence and must be linked to an independent clause by a subordinating conjunction or relative pronoun. There are three types of subordinate clauses: adjective clauses, adverb clauses, and noun clauses.

Adjective Clauses

Adjective clauses modify nouns or pronouns in an independent clause or in another subordinate clause. Adjective clauses begin with *relative pronouns* (see 9A Parts of Speech) such as *who, whom, whose, which,* and *that.*

The doctor *who delivered our baby* is from India.

She wrote a letter *that explained how she felt.*

Adverb Clauses

Adverb clauses usually modify verbs in an independent clause or in another subordinate clause, but on occasion they may also modify adjectives and adverbs. Adverb clauses begin with *subordinating conjunctions* (see 9A Parts of Speech) such as *after, although, as, because, before, if, since, so, than, that, unless, until, when, where,* and *while.*

After the movie was over, we strolled through the mall.

They planned to travel the world *until they ran out of money.*

She left the party *when her ex-boyfriend* arrived.

Noun Clauses

Noun clauses serve as a subject, object, or complement. They can begin with relative pronouns or subordinating conjunctions.

> *Where the ship sank* no one knows. The noun clause serves as the subject.

> She asked him *when he would be leaving*. The noun clause serves as the direct object.

> I will not run from *what is coming*. The noun clause serves as the object of the preposition.

> Their complaint was *that the contract had not been fulfilled*. The noun clause serves as the subject complement.

9F Basic Sentence Patterns

A sentence must contain a subject and a predicate. The complexity of predicates, however, means that sentences can follow one of five basic patterns:

6
Identify the five basic sentence patterns.

> Subject + Intransitive verb
>
> Subject + Transitive verb + Direct object
>
> Subject + Linking verb + Subject complement
>
> Subject + Transitive verb + Indirect object + Direct object
>
> Subject + Transitive verb + Direct object + Object complement

These five patterns form the foundation on which all sentences in the English language are written. The following examples show only the simplest uses of these patterns. Because all of the elements that make up these patterns can be modified by other words, phrases, and clauses, these sentence patterns can assume much more complicated forms in everyday writing.

Subject		Predicate	
She		wept.	
The woman who lives next door		personally delivered the letter to me today.	

Subject	Intransitive verb		
We	won.		

Subject	Transitive verb	Direct object	
Our team	defeated	our rivals.	

Subject	Linking verb	Subject complement	
My teammates	were	ecstatic.	

Subject	Transitive verb	Indirect object	Direct object
They	gave	us	the trophy.

Subject	Transitive verb	Direct object	Object complement
Our coach	declared	the game	a milestone.

429

9G Types of Sentences

7

Distinguish
simple, com-
pound, complex,
and compound-
complex
sentences.

Sentences are also classified by the way in which they use *clauses* (see 9E Clauses), into four categories: simple sentences, compound sentences, complex sentences, and compound-complex sentences.

Simple Sentences

A simple sentence is made up of one *independent clause*. The independent clause may contain compound *subjects*, compound *predicates*, and modifying *phrases*, but must not be linked with other clauses.

> Some professional athletes are poor role models for children. Single subject and single predicate.

> Some professional athletes and movie stars are poor role models for children. Compound subject and single predicate.

> Some professional athletes lack social responsibility and are poor role models for children. Single subject and compound predicate.

> Some professional athletes, *their interests focused exclusively on themselves*, lack social responsibility. Single subject, with modifying phrase (in italics) and single predicate.

Compound Sentences

A compound sentence is made up of two or more independent clauses (IC) linked by a semicolon or a comma and a *coordinating conjunction*. Each clause may contain compound subjects, compound predicates, and modifying phrases, but must not be linked with a subordinate clause.

> John was uneasy, but he didn't believe in werewolves. The two independent clauses are linked by a comma and the coordinating conjunction *but*.

> He *checked the lock and stood motionless*; there was someone or something growling on the other side of the door. The two independent clauses are linked with a semicolon.

Complex Sentences

A complex sentence is made up of one independent clause (IC) and one or more *subordinate clauses* (SC). Both the independent and subordinate clause(s) may contain compound subjects, compound predicates, and modifying phrases. Subordinate clauses always begin with *subordinating conjunctions* or *relative pronouns* (see 9A Parts of Speech).

> The lawyer laughed when my wife told the joke. The subordinate clause begins with the subordinating conjunction *when*.

> *I reluctantly* shook the hand of the lawyer who was representing my wife in the divorce. The subordinate clause begins with the relative pronoun *who*.

Compound-Complex Sentences

A compound-complex sentence contains two or more independent clauses (IC) and at least one subordinate clause (SC). The independent clauses must be linked by a semicolon or a comma and a coordinating conjunction. Each clause may contain compound subjects, compound predicates, and modifying phrases.

> They won't believe me until they see you, for you have completely changed. The first independent clause and its subordinate clause are linked to the second independent clause with a comma and the coordinating conjunction *for*.

Complete Additional Exercises and Practice on the Handbook in your MyLab

10 Tips for ESL Writers

Learning Objectives

1 Use definite and indefinite articles correctly.

2 Recognize and correct common verb challenges for ESL writers.

3 Use conventional placement and word order for adjectives and adverbs.

4 Use prepositions properly to show relationships of place and time.

5 Correct common errors with participles.

Many non-native writers of English find it challenging to master the language's complicated grammatical rules. This section offers advice in traditional problem areas for writers of English as a second language (ESL).

10A Articles

Articles introduce nouns, but the rules for determining how they do so are complex. *The* is the *definite article* that introduces nouns whose specific character is known (*The* cat), while *a* and *an* are *indefinite articles* that introduce nouns whose specific character is not known (*A* cat). To use definite and indefinite articles correctly, however, you also need to know whether the noun under consideration is a *count noun*, a *noncount noun*, or a *proper noun*.

1 Use definite and indefinite articles correctly.

Count Nouns

Count nouns can be counted and have singular forms (*cat, cookie, bike*) and plural forms (*cats, cookies, bikes*). Singular count nouns whose specific character is not known take the indefinite articles *a* and *an*; those whose specific character is known take the definite article *the*. Plural count nouns whose specific character is not known—that is, nouns that are referred to in general—do not take articles. Plural count nouns whose specific character is known take the definite article *the*.

> *An aardvark* turned up in my backyard. Singular count noun of unknown specific character—use the appropriate indefinite article *a* or *an*.

The aardvark befriended us. Singular count noun of known specific character—use the definite article *the.*

Aardvarks are interesting animals. Plural count noun of unknown specific character—do not use an article.

The aardvarks moved to our neighbor's backyard. Plural count noun of known specific character—use the definite article *the.*

Noncount Nouns

Noncount nouns (or mass nouns) cannot be counted and do not possess plural forms (*violence, copper, stability*). Noncount nouns whose specific character is not known—that is, nouns that are referred to in general—do not take articles. Noncount nouns whose specific character is known take the definite article *the.*

Peace is universally valued around the world. Noncount noun of unknown specific character—do not use an article.

The peace held while the negotiations dragged on. Noncount noun of known specific character—use the definite article *the.*

Proper Nouns

Proper nouns refer to specific people, places, things, or concepts (President Chirac, Tokyo, the *Titanic*, Marxism). Singular proper nouns generally do not take definite articles, with the exception of the following: noun phrases (*the* Man in the Moon); geographic features (*the* Himalayas); architectural landmarks (*the* Brooklyn Bridge); titles of ships, aircraft, spacecraft, and vehicles (*the Challenger*); titles of political and religious institutions (*the* Senate, *the* Episcopalian Church); titles of political and religious leaders (*the* prime minister, *the* pope); titles of documents (*the* Emancipation Proclamation); and titles of periods and events (*the* Middle Ages, *the* Great Depression). Plural proper nouns take definite articles, with the exception of the titles of companies (General Mills).

President Obama spoke at the commencement. The singular proper noun *President Obama* does not take a definite article.

The president spoke at the commencement. The singular common noun *president* is the title of a political leader and so does take a definite article.

The De Beers are a very wealthy family. The plural proper noun *De Beers* takes a definite article.

De Beers is a very wealthy company. The plural proper noun *De Beers* is the title of a company and so does not take a definite article.

10B Verbs

2

Recognize and correct common verb challenges for ESL writers.

The common verb errors and the basic functions and forms of verbs are discussed elsewhere in this Handbook (see 4 Verbs and 9A Parts of Speech). Challenging areas for ESL writers can include the helping verbs *be, do,* and *have*; modal auxiliaries; phrasal verbs; and gerunds and infinitives.

Helping Verbs *be, do,* and *have*

Helping verbs (or auxiliary verbs) join with main verbs to create verb phrases. The most frequently used helping verbs are *be, do,* and *have,* which can also stand alone as main verbs. How to use these three helping verbs with main verbs can sometimes be confusing.

The Helping Verb *be*. Use the present forms of *be* (*am, is, are*) with the present participle (base form + *-ing*) to make the present progressive tense. Use the past forms of *be* (*was, were*) with the present participle to make the past progressive tense. The other progressive tenses require the addition of the helping verbs *have* and *will* (see the following examples) along with the forms of *be* and the present participle.

> She *is working* at the moment. Present progressive.
>
> I *was calling* overseas when the doorbell rang. Past progressive.
>
> They *will be sailing* tomorrow. Future progressive.
>
> Larry *has been sulking* since last night. Present perfect progressive.
>
> We *had been skiing* for three hours when your brother showed up. Past perfect progressive.
>
> You *will have been barbecuing* chicken all day long before the party is over. Future perfect progressive.

Use the present forms of *be* (*am, is, are*) with the past participle (base form + *-ed*) to create the present tense in the passive voice. Other tenses in the passive voice require the addition of the other helping verbs *will* and *have* along with the forms of *be* and the past participle.

> The car *is stopped* at the light.
>
> In some countries, the local elections *have been rigged* for many years.

The Helping Verb *do*. Use forms of *do* (*do, does, did*) with the base form of the verb to create a verb phrase. Use verb phrases of this sort to add emphasis or to restate a claim that provokes doubt or disbelief. Add the modal auxiliary *not* to make negative claims.

> We *do believe* in the judicial system.
>
> She *does drive* carefully.
>
> I *did mail* the letter to you.
>
> He *does not know* the answer.

The Helping Verb *have*. Use the present forms of *have* (*have, has*) with the past participle (base form + *-ed*) to make the present prefect tense. Use the past forms of *have* (*had*) with the past participle to make the past perfect tense. The future perfect tense requires the addition of the helping verb *will* along with the present form of *have* and the past participle.

> She *has purchased* a new car. Present perfect.
>
> We *had vacationed* at the Grand Canyon before we went to Monument Valley. Past perfect.
>
> They *will have painted* the house by this evening. Future prefect.

Modal Auxiliaries

Modal auxiliaries are helping verbs that cannot stand alone as main verbs. Joined with a main verb, modals express ability, intention, necessity, permission, possibility, or prohibition. Modals include *can, cannot, could, have to, may, might, must, must not, not, should,* and *would*. These modals do not change form, regardless of the main verb's tense or whether the main verb is singular or plural. They only have one form. When joining modals with main verbs, use the base form of the main verb immediately after the modal. Never use more than one modal with one main verb.

> We *can* reach the stars if we try. Expresses ability.
>
> We *cannot* get there tomorrow. Expresses prohibition.
>
> I *have* to wash the dishes. Expresses necessity.
>
> I *might* even clean out the refrigerator. Expresses possibility.
>
> You *should* forget the past. Expresses advisability.
>
> You *would* have a great time in Italy. Expresses probability.

Phrasal Verbs

A phrasal verb is an idiomatic verb phrase that contains a verb and one or two prepositions or adverbs. The meaning of the two- or three-word phrasal verb generally cannot be understood by combining the literal meanings of its words. For example, the phrasal verb *turn down* does not mean "to turn downward" but rather "to reject or refuse." Common phrasal verbs include the following:

act up	run into
break down	stay up
call on	step in
catch on	take off
cut in	throw away
figure out	turn down
hang on	turn on
look into	walk out on
look out for	watch out for

Phrasal verbs are informal and often are inappropriate for academic and professional writing. If you do choose to use them in your writing, be sure you understand their correct meaning.

Gerunds and Infinitives

Gerunds function as nouns and use the present participle form (base form + *-ing*). Infinitives usually function as nouns but can also function as adjectives or adverbs. They begin with the word *to* followed by the base form of the verb. Gerunds and infinitives that follow after main verbs function as objects.

Keep the following guidelines in mind when using gerunds and infinitives with main verbs.

1. **Verbs that do not change meaning whether followed by gerunds or infinitives:**

attempt	like
begin	love
can't stand	omit
continue	prefer
hate	start

In the following examples below, the meaning of the verb *hated* and the gerund *losing* is the same as the verb *hated* and the infinitive *to lose*.

We hated *losing* the game.

We hated *to lose* the game.

2. **Verbs that change meaning when followed by gerunds or infinitives:**

forget	stop
remember	try

In the following examples, notice how the meaning of the first sentence differs from that of the second.

I forgot *practicing* the piano yesterday. Forgot the subject of *practicing* yesterday.

I forgot *to practice* the piano yesterday. Forgot actually *to practice* yesterday.

3. **Verbs that can precede gerunds but not infinitives:**

admit	keep
appreciate	miss
avoid	postpone
cannot help	practice
consider	put off
delay	quit
deny	recall
discuss	resist
enjoy	risk
finish	suggest
imagine	tolerate

In the following examples, the gerund in the first sentence is correct and the infinitive in the second sentence represents an error.

She enjoys *painting* watercolors. Gerunds may be used after the verb *enjoy*.

She enjoys *to paint* watercolors. Infinitives may not be used after the verb *enjoy*.

4. **Verbs that can precede infinitives but not gerunds:**

agree	mean
ask	need
beg	offer
choose	plan
claim	pretend
decide	promise
expect	refuse
fail	venture
have	wait
hope	want
manage	wish

In the following examples, the infinitive in the first sentence is correct and the gerund in the second sentence represents an error.

> They decided *to climb* the mountain. Infinitive may be used after the verb *decide*.

> They decided *climbing* the mountain. Gerund may not be used after the verb *decide*.

10C Adjectives and Adverbs

3

Use conventional placement and word order for adjectives and adverbs.

The correct use of adjectives and adverbs can present challenges for all writers; however, for ESL writers in particular, the placement and word order of these modifiers can be troublesome.

Adjectives

Adjectives modify nouns and pronouns (see 9A Parts of Speech). Other words such as articles and pronouns can also act as adjectives and modify nouns and pronouns. When using multiple adjectives to modify one or more words in the sentence, use the word order listed here:

1. **Article, pronoun, and possessive noun:** *a, an, the, his, my, our, your, a lot, many, some, that, their, those, Steve's, the neighbor's,* etc.

2. **Adjectives indicating number or order:** *one, two, three, one hundred, one thousand, first, second, third, last, final,* etc.

3. **Adjectives indicating judgment, opinion, or evaluation:** *awful, astonishing, beautiful, excellent, evil, good, faithful, ugly, wicked,* etc.

4. **Adjectives indicating size:** *big, diminutive, giant, large, little, long, massive, minuscule, short,* etc.

5. **Adjectives indicating shape:** *boxy, circular, loose, rectangular, round, snug, square, tight, triangular, wide,* etc.

6. **Adjectives indicating condition:** *broken, damaged, fixed, functional, operating, repaired, reconditioned, running, undamaged, whole, working,* etc.

7. **Adjectives indicating age:** *aged, ancient, antique, fresh, immature, mature, new, old, young,* etc.

8. **Adjectives indicating color:** *black, blue, green, mauve, orange, purple, violet, white, yellow,* etc.

9. **Adjectives indicating nationality, ethnicity, and religion:** *African American, Anglo, Arabic, Armenian, Brazilian, Canadian, Chinese, Kenyan, Latin American, Mandarin, Buddhist, Catholic, Hindu, Presbyterian,* etc.

10. **Adjectives indicating material:** *aluminum, birch, copper, cotton, gold, iron, oak, metal, pine, plastic, platinum, polyester, silk, steel, wood,* etc.

11. **Nouns used as adjectives:** *bird* (brain), *dog* (house), *car* (park), *floor* (mat), *mosquito* (net), etc.

12. **The noun being modified.** Examples:

> His last *undamaged birch-bark* canoe sank yesterday.
>
> She found *some beautiful little green turquoise* beads at the flea market.
>
> My grandmother gave *that antique black Chinese silk* dress to my sister as a birthday gift.

Adverbs

Adverbs modify verbs, adjectives, and other adverbs (see 9A Parts of Speech). Adverbs can come before or after the words they modify. Sometimes, for the sake of rhythm or emphasis, adverbs can be placed at the beginning or end of the sentence. Although there is considerable flexibility in where you can place most adverbs, there are also some limitations. Use the following guidelines:

1. **Place adverbs indicating the author's or speaker's *perspective* at the front of the sentence:**

> *Thankfully,* I had recovered from the flu by then.
>
> *Unfortunately,* we won't be able to make your party tonight.

2. **Place adverbs indicating *order* at the front or end of the sentence:**

> *First,* we will consider the results of our fund-raising efforts.
>
> Proposals for overhauling the department will be discussed *last.*

3. **Place adverbs indicating *manner* immediately before the words they modify or at the end of the sentence:**

> They *softly* entered the room.
>
> She answered my questions *sheepishly.*

4. **Place adverbs indicating *time* immediately after any adverbs indicating *manner* or *place* or, if none exist, at the front or end of the sentence:**

> The earth shook *ferociously here yesterday.*
>
> *Tomorrow,* I am leaving for California.
>
> He writes reports *slowly.*

10D Prepositions

Prepositions introduce *prepositional phrases* and show the relationship (place, destination, possession, time, cause, movement, purpose, etc.) between the *object of the preposition*, which is always a noun or pronoun, and another word or group of words. The prepositions used to show place and time can be troublesome for non-native speakers of English.

Place

The prepositions showing place include *in*, *on*, and *at*. Use the preposition *in* to refer to an established physical, geographic, or political space (*in* the garage, *in* Egypt). Use the preposition *on* as a synonym for *on top of* (*on* the coffee table, *on* the roof) and to indicate location on mass transportation, streets, book pages, building floors, and land (*on* the bus, *on* 114th Street, *on* page 177, *on* the eleventh floor, *on* the field). Use the preposition *at* to refer to specific locations, general locations, and addresses (*at* the Museum of Modern Art, *at* my mother's house, *at* the beach, *at* 23349 Westwood Boulevard).

> The Band-Aids are *in* the medicine box.
>
> Her apartment is *on* the fourth floor.
>
> You are welcome to stay *at* my house.

Time

The prepositions showing time also include *in*, *on*, and *at*. Use the preposition *in* to refer to general time of day (except *noon* and *night*), months, seasons, and years (*in* the afternoon, *in* December, *in* spring, *in* 1983). Use the preposition *on* to refer to days of the week and dates (*on* Friday, *on* the 28th, *on* July 4, 1776). Use the preposition *at* to refer to specific time of day and with *night* (*at* 1:15, *at* noon, *at* night).

> I will see her *in* the evening.
>
> We will see them *on* Friday.
>
> He will see you *at* noon.

10E Participles

Present participles (base form of the verb + *-ing*) and *past participles* (base form of the verb + *-d* or *-ed*) can both function as adjectives in sentences. Their meanings are different, however, and they cannot be used interchangeably. In particular, participles that describe feelings and mental states can sometimes be troublesome for ESL writers. These participles include the following:

amazing / amazed	fascinating / fascinated
annoying / annoyed	frightening / frightened
boring / bored	interesting / interested

confusing / confused
depressing / depressed
disappointing / disappointed
exciting / excited
exhausting / exhausted

pleasing / pleased
satisfying / satisfied
surprising / surprised
terrifying / terrified
tiring / tired

To avoid errors with these participles and others, only use present participles to describe nouns and pronouns that *cause* a feeling or mental state. Similarly, only use past participles to describe nouns and pronouns that *experience* a feeling or mental state.

The lecture was *fascinating*. The noun being modified, *lecture,* causes the mental state, so the present participle *fascinating* is required.

We were *fascinated* by the lecture. The pronoun being modified, *We,* experiences the mental state, so the past participle *fascinated* is required.

The news is filled with *depressing* events. The noun being modified, *events,* causes the mental state, so the present participle *depressing* is required.

Julia was *depressed* by events in the news. The noun being modified, *Julia,* experiences the mental state, so the past participle *depressed* is required.

Complete
Additional Exercises
and Practice on
the Handbook
in your MyLab

Index

Page references followed by "f" indicate illustrated figures or photographs; followed by "t" indicates a table.

A

abbreviations, 271, 325, 405-406
Absolute phrases, 427
Abstract nouns, 419
abstracts, 6, 27, 57-58, 179, 276, 333-334
Academic disciplines, 254, 358
Academic journals, 39-40, 270, 318
Academic Search Premier, 57, 88, 115
Academic success, 130, 239
Academic writing, 25, 31, 38, 60, 125, 137, 180, 201, 203-204, 206, 240, 257, 337, 405, 424
   personal essay and, 203-204
accept, except, 412
Active voice, 184-185, 374, 376, 381, 391, 416
Adjective clauses, 419-421, 428
Adjectives, 359-360, 363, 369, 373, 375, 377-378, 387, 399, 408, 413, 418-420, 422-428, 431, 434, 436-438
   comparing, 378
   defined, 375
   parallel, 423-425
   possessive, 387, 419-420, 422, 436
   problems with, 359, 375
   use of, 408, 436
Adverb clauses, 428
Adverbs, 359-360, 366-367, 369-370, 373, 375, 377-378, 398-399, 408, 413, 418-419, 422-424, 427-428, 431, 434, 436-437
   for ESL writers, 359-360, 431, 436
advertisements, 169
Advertising, 5, 107, 365, 387
Advocacy, 103
affect, effect, 412
Aggression, 134, 286
Agreement, 12, 182-183, 193-194, 235, 359-360, 379, 381-384, 388-389
Amazon, 54, 147, 262
Ambiguity, 108-109, 204, 247, 353
American Psychological Association (APA), 161, 241, 307
American Psychological Association (APA) style, 161, 307
analogies, 181
Analogy, 181, 191
Analysis, 89-90, 103, 152, 162, 167-168, 178, 181-182, 352, 390-391
Anecdotes, 67, 73, 147-148, 229-230
Annotated List of Works Cited, 258
Annotation, 53
Antecedents, 384, 386-388, 422
   compound, 388
Anthologies, 261
Anthology, 242, 264, 266-267
APA, 15, 39, 59, 161, 241, 256, 259, 307-349
APA style, 307-349
   for books, 325
Apostrophes, 385, 395, 404, 406-407
Appeals, 124
Appendixes, 255, 323
Applied, 52, 57, 100, 220
   literature, 57, 196
Appositive phrases, 427-428
Argument, 40, 45, 50, 53, 83, 91-93, 96, 98, 109, 122, 125, 127-128, 131, 151, 166, 170, 175, 191, 202, 209, 211, 276, 338, 342, 351, 353, 357, 417, 421
   features of, 209
   inquiry-based, 50, 127
   motives for writing, 202
Argument essay, 166
   purpose of, 166
arguments, 40, 50, 81, 83-84, 96, 112, 132, 144, 167

Articles, 6-7, 14, 25, 27, 31-32, 34, 38-40, 42, 47, 51, 53-58, 61-63, 69, 79, 115-116, 137, 178, 204, 243, 248-249, 256, 268-269, 271-274, 309, 323-324, 326, 330, 332-333, 357, 360, 405, 413, 419, 424, 431-432, 436
Artifacts, 77, 119
Artwork, 243, 282
association, 41, 98, 161, 190, 192, 241, 244, 288, 295, 307, 309
Associations, 64, 89, 220, 222
Assumption, 20, 126, 136-137, 148, 151, 164, 185, 288
Assumptions, 21, 24, 26, 50, 131, 165, 192, 204
   popular, 131
attitude, 81, 193, 381, 417
Audience, 20, 60, 40-41, 70, 74-75, 126, 131, 150, 162, 164, 223, 225, 227-228, 230, 234, 236, 354-355, 357, 390, 392, 394, 409
   for personal essays, 230
Authors, 40, 42, 63, 87, 93, 106, 214, 242, 247-248, 250-252, 257, 259-261, 263-264, 268, 277, 307-309, 311-312, 314, 323-324, 327-328, 332
   authoritative, 40, 309
   credentials of, 42
Auxiliary verbs, 418, 433

B

Background information, 68, 142, 234
Beliefs, 24, 50
Believing, 97, 105, 109-110, 115, 131, 142, 151
Bias, 38, 73, 100, 197, 311, 390, 392
Bibliographies, 40, 56, 59, 116, 119
Blogs, 4, 38, 61, 117, 119, 216
Body paragraphs, 125
Boldface, 319
Books, 1, 7, 9, 14, 32-34, 37, 39-42, 47, 51, 53-56, 59, 62-63, 65, 69, 116, 146, 161, 170, 179, 210, 213, 219, 232, 242, 249-250, 256, 260-264, 267-269, 272, 279-280, 309, 323, 325, 327-328, 351
   online, 14, 33, 37, 39-41, 47, 51, 54-55, 59, 65, 69, 116, 179, 242, 256, 260, 262-263, 268-269, 272, 279-280, 309, 327
Brackets, 158, 270, 327, 334, 394-395, 402-403
Brainstorming, 19
Business, 12, 37, 44, 58, 67, 73, 98, 100, 102, 136-137, 204, 243, 307, 347, 365, 392, 397, 401
   case studies, 243

C

Capitalization, 256, 261, 360, 404
Captions, 322
cartoons, 4
Case, 12, 19, 29, 45, 61, 80, 82, 92, 94, 113, 125, 128, 137, 147-148, 155, 174, 188, 196, 204, 220, 236, 243-244, 247, 249, 251, 253, 261, 263, 271-273, 281, 312, 314-315, 334, 338, 354, 356, 358, 359, 377, 384-390, 404, 406-408, 419-422
   objective, 92, 137, 204, 385-386, 390, 419-421
   possessive, 385-387, 406-407, 419-422
   subjective, 204, 385, 419-422
Case studies, 147-148, 243, 281
Categories, 5, 20, 61, 133, 220, 322, 430
cause and effect, 176
Characters, 6, 146, 196
Charts, 48, 191, 220, 242, 255, 322
Chronicle of Higher Education, 103, 272
Chronological narrative, 231
Chronological order, 324
Chronology, 30, 230-231, 239
citations, 15, 39, 45, 56, 58, 95, 161, 164, 195, 241, 243, 245-246, 255, 263, 266, 268-272, 278, 308, 313, 323, 327, 329-338, 354, 405
Claims, 42, 45, 49, 75, 112, 167, 186, 247, 334, 342,

433
Clauses, 196, 360-361, 365-372, 375-377, 382-384, 389, 394-395, 397-401, 413, 417, 419-421, 423-424, 428-431
   adjective, 367-369, 399, 419-421, 428
   adverb, 366-367, 369, 375, 397-398, 419, 428
   independent, 196, 361, 365-369, 371-372, 394-395, 397-401, 428, 430-431
   noun, 368-369, 372, 377, 383-384, 398-399, 413, 419-420, 423-424, 428-429, 431
Clustering, 220, 222, 239
Clutter, 188
Coherence, 390
collaboration, 9, 228, 312
Collections, 13, 56
Collective nouns, 419
Colons, 195-196, 394-395, 400-402, 405
Color, 5, 104, 115, 167-168, 227-228, 437
Comma splice, 366-368, 397-398
Comma splices, 195-196, 359, 361, 365-369, 397-398, 400-401
Commas, 195-196, 241, 324, 361, 365-366, 368, 372, 377, 394-395, 397-403, 425, 428
Common knowledge exception, 85, 243
communication, 57, 68, 75, 82, 108, 315, 325, 344, 401
Comparative degree, 378
Comparative form, 378, 422-423
comparison, 30, 41, 61, 102, 142, 146, 176, 182, 367
Complements, 360, 379, 383, 413, 417-418, 420, 422, 425-428
Complex sentences, 413, 430-431
Composing, 79, 137, 141, 164, 214, 229
Composition, 57, 76, 203, 263, 351
Compound adjectives, 408
Compound antecedents, 388
Compound predicates, 425, 430-431
Compound sentences, 397, 430
Compound subjects, 385, 425, 430-431
Compound words, 404, 407-408, 412
Compound-complex sentences, 413, 430-431
comprehension, 27
Computers, 18, 409
Conciseness, 360, 390
conclusions, 25, 76, 127, 148, 150, 203
Conjunctions, 187, 256, 361, 364, 366-367, 371, 377, 405, 413, 423-425, 428-430
   coordinating, 256, 366-367, 423-425, 430
   correlative, 371, 423-425
Connecting, 80, 175, 222, 363-364, 408
Content, 6, 43, 61, 72, 91, 101, 119, 170, 232, 258, 318, 322, 390
Contractions, 385, 404, 406-407
contrast, 142, 154, 159, 176, 182, 307, 362, 366-367, 397
Controlling idea, 231
Conversing, 80
Coordinate adjectives, 399
Coordinating conjunctions, 256, 366-367, 423-425
   list of, 366-367
Coordination, 359, 370-373, 375
Correlative conjunctions, 371, 424-425
Count nouns, 419, 431
Creative thinking, 204, 228
Credibility, 42, 203, 342, 387
Criteria, 41, 44
Critical essays, 25
critical thinking, 41, 100, 136, 228, 353
critiques, 186
Culture, 14, 20, 80, 110, 113, 153-154, 166, 280, 320, 349, 351, 398
Cut-and-paste revision, 172, 175
Cyberspace, 45, 60, 75

D

Dangling modifiers, 376
Dashes, 195, 377, 394-395, 401-403

Data, 9, 49, 60, 76, 103, 127, 178, 181, 191, 204, 315, 340, 358, 387
   factual, 181
Databases, 6, 30-34, 40, 44, 53, 56-61, 79, 115-116, 119, 176-177, 256, 269, 271, 274, 276, 333
Date of publication, 39, 55, 268, 270, 307, 324, 403
Definite articles, 432
Definition, 5, 84, 132-133, 166-167, 221, 234
Demonstrative pronouns, 422
Dependent clauses, 368-369, 372
description, 64, 141, 150, 210, 219, 230, 234, 258, 277, 322
Design, 70-71, 73-74, 190, 401
Details, 64-65, 123, 125, 151, 164, 215, 220, 222, 228-231, 240, 243, 252, 324, 390
Dialogue, 78, 80, 104, 106, 122, 124, 137, 142, 198, 354
dictionaries, 178, 404
Dictionary, 14, 265, 378, 380, 385, 399, 406, 408, 412-413
Digital recorders, 68
Direct objects, 371, 425-426
Direct quotations, 105, 394, 402
   using, 394
Discourse, 38, 374, 394, 402
   shifts in, 374
Discover, 2, 10-12, 24, 34, 48, 50, 54, 63, 80-81, 95, 101-102, 117, 134, 140, 151, 162, 163, 173-174, 176, 180, 198, 201, 208, 217-218, 220, 223, 229, 234, 239, 268, 314, 356-357
Documentation, 151, 241
domain name, 42
Doubting, 97, 105, 112
Doubting game, 112
Drafts, 36, 163-164, 171, 231, 354, 371
   first, 36, 163-164, 371
   peer review of, 354

E

Editing, 78, 187, 371, 390
Editorials, 248, 275
Either/or, 74, 108
Ellipses, 394, 402
Ellipsis, 158, 257, 320, 328, 395, 403
E-mail, 42, 44, 59, 64-65, 68-69, 75, 243, 277-278, 280, 309, 315
Emotion, 112, 150, 365
Encyclopedia Britannica, 265
Encyclopedia of Associations, 64
Encyclopedias, 13-14, 39, 178, 266
English as a second language (ESL), 431
   writers, 431
Essays, 6, 8, 23, 25, 38, 55, 76, 126, 148, 165-166, 175-176, 201-203, 205, 209, 214, 216-217, 221, 224, 227-228, 230-234, 238-239, 267, 351, 357, 402, 417
   five-paragraph, 126, 203
Ethos, 203
Evaluation, 96, 99, 102-103, 436
Evidence, 9, 20, 23, 25, 38, 40-42, 50-51, 77, 90, 94, 122, 127, 130-131, 134-136, 149, 162, 171, 173, 177, 230-231, 346, 353, 355-358, 399
Exact language, 84
Examples, 9, 38, 97, 239, 257, 263, 324, 362-366, 371, 375-377, 383-385, 388-389, 391-393, 395, 398, 404, 407-408, 410, 429, 433, 435-437
   series of, 9, 383
Exclamation points, 361, 394-395, 397, 402
Experiences, 24, 67, 70, 95, 97, 99, 101, 105, 129, 137, 144-147, 186, 201-202, 204, 215, 218, 222-223, 228-229, 231-232, 234, 236, 238, 439
Experts, 11, 13, 25, 38, 40, 49, 52, 63-64, 66, 68-69, 87, 95, 117, 131, 166, 234, 244, 344
Explanation, 17, 20, 183, 213, 228, 321, 373, 394, 403
Exploration, 122, 126, 160, 191, 202-204, 230
Exploratory writing, 106, 229
Exploring, 7, 18, 26, 29, 41, 48, 70, 79, 81, 112, 122-123, 129-130, 166, 170, 191, 213, 215, 218, 227, 229, 231, 234, 239, 271, 318
   strategies, 26, 229, 239

F

Facebook, 68, 136, 205, 319, 325
Facts, 19, 38, 45, 49-50, 66, 80-81, 85, 95, 112, 133, 144, 167, 177-179, 229, 234, 243, 351, 410
FALSE, 7, 136, 146, 380

Fastwriting, 27, 80, 113, 218-219, 222, 233, 239
Feedback, 99, 171
fiction, 205, 401, 408
Field notes, 358
Film, 16, 91-93, 158, 275, 282, 310, 336-337, 349
Films, 14, 243, 282, 323
Final draft, 189
First draft, 23, 125, 132, 161-162, 164, 173-174, 229, 232
   developing, 132, 162, 173, 229
   of research essay, 125
   writing, 23, 125, 161-162, 164, 174, 229, 232
First drafts, 164
flexibility, 348, 404, 437
Focused knowledge, 47-48, 50, 59, 132
Foreword, 242, 265
Formal language, 392
forums, 337
   online, 337
Fragments, 174, 220, 359, 361-365, 367, 395, 397-398, 401, 424
Full-text articles, 31, 57-58
Fused sentence, 368-369
Fused sentences, 359, 361, 368-369
Future perfect tense, 415, 433

G

Genre, 25, 216, 239, 322, 351
   examples of, 239
Genres, 224
Gerund phrases, 427
Gerunds, 363, 386, 418, 427, 432, 434-436
Global revision, 164, 172, 179
Google, 13-14, 30-31, 33, 35-36, 40, 53, 55-56, 58, 60-62, 68-69, 76, 114, 117, 176-177, 191, 220, 238, 258, 336-337, 352
Google Groups, 69, 76
Google Scholar, 14, 40, 61-62, 336
Government documents, 32, 39, 116-117, 119, 242, 248, 268
Government publications, 117
Grammar, 164, 192-193, 235, 356, 359-360, 368, 370, 373, 413
   clauses, 360, 368, 370, 413
   for ESL writers, 359-360
   objects and complements, 360, 413
   parts of speech, 360, 413
   phrases, 235, 360, 368, 370, 373, 413
   sentence patterns, 360, 413
   subjects and predicates, 360, 373, 413
Grammar checkers, 192
Graphics, 179
Graphs, 48, 190-191, 322
   line, 322

H

Habits of mind, 101, 204, 351
have, 2, 5-8, 11, 15-16, 19, 21-27, 29-33, 38-42, 45, 47-48, 50, 56-58, 60, 64-68, 70-77, 79-81, 83, 85, 88-92, 95-96, 98-102, 104-118, 121-122, 124-127, 129-132, 134, 138-139, 141-143, 145-147, 150-151, 154-155, 158, 161-162, 163-171, 173-174, 176-177, 179, 181, 183-185, 187-188, 190-193, 195-198, 201-202, 204-205, 207, 209-218, 220, 223-230, 233-234, 236-238, 245-248, 250-255, 259, 269-271, 273, 276, 286, 291, 307, 313-315, 318, 320, 324-326, 340, 342-346, 348, 351-355, 357, 359, 363-364, 366-368, 371, 374-376, 378-380, 382-388, 390, 393-394, 397, 401, 403-404, 406-408, 412, 414-419, 421-424, 431-434, 436
Headings, 33, 318-319
Helping verbs, 363, 380, 382, 414-415, 418, 432-434
   for ESL writers, 432
Hierarchy, 126, 319
Highlighting, 79, 114, 131, 144, 228
   of argument, 131
Home pages, 69
Homonyms, 410, 412-413
Humor, 91, 147, 320, 387
Hyphens, 195, 250, 256, 259, 360, 395, 404, 407-408
Hypothesis, 9, 20-21, 23-24, 133, 135-136, 318-319

I

Illustration, 95, 149, 255-256
illustrations, 78, 190-191, 242, 255
Images, 51, 59, 61, 70, 78, 118-119, 153, 190-191,

214, 216, 220, 226, 240, 280, 287
Imitation, 91, 251, 276
Imperative mood, 381, 417
Incomplete thoughts, 365
Indefinite articles, 424, 431
Indefinite pronouns, 383, 388, 421
   as antecedents, 388
Independent clauses, 196, 361, 365-369, 371-372, 394-395, 397-401, 430-431
   improperly joined, 365
Index, 13, 32-33, 55, 57-60, 69, 104, 117, 327
indexes, 57-59, 178
Indicative mood, 374, 381, 417-418
Indirect objects, 425-426
Indirect quotations, 402
Infinitive phrases, 427-428
Infinitives, 256, 363, 418-419, 428, 432, 434-436
Informal language, 392
Information, 1, 5-6, 9, 13-15, 17-19, 22, 25-27, 29-31, 33-45, 47-51, 53, 56, 58, 60, 64, 66-68, 70-73, 79-81, 84-87, 89-90, 94, 101-102, 104-106, 109, 114-115, 117, 119, 121, 126-127, 131-133, 138, 142, 146-149, 151-152, 158, 160-161, 163, 166-168, 173-175, 177-179, 181, 183, 191, 195, 204-205, 219-220, 229, 233-234, 239, 241, 243-246, 250-252, 254, 256-257, 259-263, 266, 268, 271-272, 276-277, 279, 282-283, 299, 309-311, 314-316, 320-321, 324-327, 334, 338, 351-353, 365, 369, 376, 389, 391, 403, 417
   background, 48, 68, 89, 131, 142, 234
   definitions, 166
   research strategies, 13, 262
Inquiry-based approach, 312
instructor, 7, 9-10, 18, 24, 50-51, 53, 59, 75, 82, 85, 99-101, 122, 138, 143, 161-162, 171, 191-192, 197, 204, 215, 232-233, 241, 254-255, 258, 318, 352, 354-358, 359, 425
Intensifiers, 391
Intensive pronouns, 421
Interjections, 413, 424
Internet, 1, 4, 6, 8, 13, 15, 29-35, 41-42, 45, 59-64, 68-69, 75, 84-85, 100, 114-115, 117-119, 177, 224, 256, 258, 273, 281, 314, 323, 427
   databases online, 31
   discussion groups, 69
   essays on, 6
   keyword searches, 32-35
   Web, 6, 13, 15, 29-30, 32-33, 35, 41-42, 45, 59-62, 64, 68-69, 75, 117, 177, 256, 258, 273
Internet Public Library, 13, 35
Interpreting, 138, 169
Interrogative pronouns, 419, 421
Interrupting elements, 402
Interviews, 20, 30-32, 37, 62-69, 77-78, 119, 126, 130-131, 147, 152, 159, 242, 251, 284, 309, 315, 335, 344
   conducting, 65
   open-ended questions, 66-67
In-text citations, 266, 308, 327, 329-338
   MLA style for, 266
Intransitive verbs, 414, 418
Introduction, 125, 139-140, 175, 190, 242, 262-263, 265, 292, 318, 355-356
Introductions, 27, 139
Invention strategies, 201, 217, 239
Irregular verbs, 380, 415, 418
Issues, 7, 12, 19, 57, 69, 99-100, 103, 179, 235, 331, 349, 381, 417
Italics, 255, 271, 274, 277, 322-323, 325, 360, 395, 402, 404, 407-409, 430

J

Jargon, 24, 26, 38, 355, 359, 392
Journal writing, 96, 229-230
Journalism, 100
journals, 37-40, 44, 57, 164, 268, 270, 318, 331
JSTOR, 57
Judgment, 41, 45, 50, 107, 122, 135, 204, 208, 225, 227, 436

K

Keyword search, 6, 33, 119
Keyword searches, 32-36, 58, 178
knowledge, 5, 11-14, 19, 24, 26-27, 33, 39, 47-48, 50, 53-54, 59-60, 64, 67, 69, 84-86, 95, 100-101, 104, 132, 164, 181, 202, 204, 209, 239,

243-244, 246, 353, 389, 402
integrating, 181

L

Language, 25, 30, 32-33, 62, 73, 84, 87, 93, 106, 132, 134, 147, 161-162, 177, 179-180, 182, 188, 190, 192, 196-197, 204-205, 212-213, 241, 244, 265, 272, 311-312, 331, 353-354, 360, 376, 390, 392, 394, 405, 413, 429, 431
  appropriate, 93, 180, 196, 241, 360, 376, 390, 392, 431
  formal, 106, 190, 192, 204, 354, 390, 392, 405
  informal, 106, 392
  patronizing, 390, 392
  sexist, 196-197, 392
Latin abbreviations, 405
Layout, 254, 308
lead paragraph, 145
Leads, 92, 122, 128, 139, 141-144, 150, 170, 173, 219, 288
Lectures, 119, 243, 283
letter, 37, 55, 233, 243, 271, 275, 310, 323-324, 335, 361, 399, 401, 408-409, 418, 428-429, 433
  business, 37, 243, 401
  to the editor, 243, 275, 310, 335
Letters, 37, 54, 72, 100, 102, 256-257, 261, 309, 315-316, 358, 367, 405-407, 409
Letters to the editor, 257
Libraries, 32-34, 54, 56, 59, 115, 119
  book searches, 59
  online, 33, 54, 59, 115, 119
Library of Congress, 33, 54-55, 118
Library of Congress Subject Headings, 33
Linking verbs, 414, 417
links, 21, 33, 69, 178
Listing, 19, 64, 140, 218, 252, 259, 270, 314, 323
Listing prompts, 218
Lists, 5, 64, 127, 186, 190, 218-219, 229, 249, 259, 310, 337, 361, 382, 417
Literature, 13, 37, 47, 55, 57, 131, 134, 196, 252, 266-267, 356, 358, 389
Literature review, 47, 356
Local revision, 179
Logical structures, 176

M

magazines, 7, 37, 39-40, 57-58, 107, 169, 248, 268, 270-272
main idea, 51, 125, 142, 172-173
  stated, 172
Main ideas, 53
  paragraph, 53
  topic, 53
mapping, 220, 222
maps, 179
Margins and spacing, 254
Meaning, 25, 74, 82, 188, 209, 222, 224-225, 229, 232-234, 250, 338, 364, 368, 372-373, 375-379, 383-386, 390-391, 393-394, 402-403, 418, 425-426, 434-435
  questions for, 224, 229, 232-234
Mechanics, 171, 193, 356, 359-360, 395, 404
Media, 7, 123-124, 239, 279-280
Memoirs, 215
Messages, 69, 83, 218, 401
Metaphor, 95, 102, 181, 213
Metasearch engines, 61-62
minutes, 5, 7-8, 10, 12, 16, 19, 29-30, 35, 67, 71, 75, 79-81, 113, 188, 198, 209, 215, 220-221, 229-230
Misplaced modifiers, 359, 375-376
Mixed sentences, 359, 370, 373
MLA International Bibliography, 57
MLA Style, 94, 195, 241-305, 307, 316
  for books, 261, 267-268
Modal auxiliaries, 432, 434
Modals, 434
Models, 128, 276, 430
Modern Language Association (MLA), 161, 192, 244
Modern Language Association (MLA) style, 161
Modifiers, 359, 363, 371, 375-378, 382, 389, 391, 398, 401, 427-428, 436
  dangling and misplaced, 359, 375-376
  restrictive and nonrestrictive, 359, 375-377, 389, 398, 401
Modifying phrases, 368-369, 430-431
Mood, 25, 359, 374, 381-382, 414, 417-418
  shifts in, 374

Motives, 83, 88, 90, 126, 202, 205
  for writing, 202

N

Names, 13, 25, 40, 42, 66, 115, 117, 195-196, 212, 222, 247-248, 251, 257, 261, 263, 269, 282, 307-309, 312, 314, 324, 327, 377, 404-405
Narration, 78, 227
Narrative, 26, 112-113, 127, 175-176, 204-205, 209, 224, 227-232, 234, 239
Narrative essay, 231-232, 234
  revising, 234
Narrators, 205, 209, 225, 228, 238
National Public Radio, 118
Negating constructions, 391
news stories, 117
newspapers, 37, 39, 57-59, 268, 270-271, 273-274, 358
Noncount nouns, 419, 432
nonfiction, 94, 126, 232
Nonfiction essays, 126
Nonrestrictive clauses, 389
Nonrestrictive modifiers, 359, 375-377, 389, 398, 401
  commas with, 377
Notes, 26, 30, 48, 52, 68, 77, 80, 87, 91, 93-95, 101, 104-106, 109, 111-114, 121, 126, 155, 160-162, 169-170, 177, 193-195, 214, 258, 322-323, 358
  Double-entry, 77, 104-106, 109, 112, 114
  research, 26, 30, 48, 77, 80, 87, 93-94, 104, 109, 114, 121, 126, 160-162, 170, 177, 194, 358
  visual, 48, 214
notetaking, 62, 68, 77, 79-81, 91, 95-97, 103-104, 112, 152, 357
  summarizing in, 91
Noun clauses, 428-429
Noun phrases, 372, 432
Nouns, 308, 363, 370-372, 378, 381-382, 384-389, 392-393, 398, 404-406, 408, 412-413, 418-420, 422, 424-428, 431-432, 434, 436-437, 439
  abstract, 308, 419
  collective, 419
  count, 419, 431-432
  for ESL writers, 431-432, 436
  gender-neutral, 393
  masculine, 392-393
  noncount, 419, 431-432
  plural, 382, 384, 388-389, 393, 406, 412, 419, 431-432, 434
  possessive, 385-387, 406, 419-420, 422, 436
  proper, 308, 404-405, 408, 419, 424, 431-432
novels, 25, 37, 93, 146
Numbers, 54-55, 64, 75, 102, 105-106, 108, 143, 251, 253, 259, 262-263, 266-267, 269-271, 273, 283, 289, 296, 299, 307-308, 311, 315, 319, 323, 325-326, 339, 356, 360, 404, 407-410
  spelled out, 323, 409

O

Object complements, 426
Objections, 188
Objective case, 386, 420
Objectivity, 102, 204
Objects, 10, 77, 207, 209, 220, 360, 371, 386, 401, 413, 417-418, 420-421, 425-428, 434
Objects of prepositions, 425-426
Observation, 20, 76, 135, 152, 205, 217, 223, 229, 358
Online sources, 41, 45, 179, 243, 248, 263, 266, 271, 276
Online text, 260
Op-ed essays, 38
Open-ended questions, 66-67, 71, 73
Openings, 141-143
opinion, 38, 50, 117, 137, 171, 189, 198, 335, 349, 352-353, 381, 417, 436
Order, 13, 32, 41-42, 91, 108, 115, 124, 144, 173, 175, 236, 240, 259, 269-270, 301, 314, 322, 324, 356, 362, 384, 399, 413, 431, 436-437
  space, 108, 259
organization, 41, 43-44, 175, 179, 233, 238, 261-263, 277, 279-280, 283, 298, 318, 326, 355
Outline, 161-162, 210, 354, 356
  time, 162, 210
Outlines, 24, 126, 186, 226

P

Page numbers, 105-106, 108, 251, 253, 259, 262-263, 266-267, 269-271, 283, 307-308, 311, 315, 319, 325, 339, 356
Pamphlets, 243, 248, 283
Paragraph, 53, 94, 97, 125-126, 141, 145, 152-155, 160, 167-168, 173-174, 180, 183-184, 187, 203, 230, 235, 245-247, 251, 254, 273, 299, 316, 319, 323, 356, 381
Paragraphs, 97, 125, 142, 144, 147, 150, 153, 155, 168, 173-174, 183, 235, 257, 316, 319
Parallelism, 359, 370-372, 399, 423
Paraphrases, 105-106, 112, 138
Paraphrasing, 81, 87, 90, 92, 243
Parentheses, 34-35, 108, 185, 244, 251, 270, 310, 312, 324-325, 332, 394-395, 402-403
Parenthetical citation, 83, 153, 155, 244-245, 247-251, 258, 273, 283, 310-314, 319
Parenthetical citations, 161, 195, 241, 243, 246, 313, 323
Participial phrases, 427
Participles, 360, 363, 418, 427, 431, 438-439
  for ESL writers, 360, 431, 438
  past, 363, 418, 427, 438-439
  present, 363, 418, 427, 438-439
Particulars, 11, 18, 203
parts of speech, 360, 378, 413, 419, 425-428, 430, 432, 436-437
Passive, 101, 184-185, 192, 202, 374-376, 379, 381, 391, 414-418, 433
  voice, 184-185, 192, 202, 374-376, 379, 381, 391, 414-418, 433
Passive voice, 184-185, 192, 202, 374-375, 379, 381, 391, 415-418, 433
  use of, 185, 391, 416
Past participle, 363, 380, 414-415, 418, 427, 433, 439
Past participles, 427, 438-439
  for ESL writers, 438
Past perfect tense, 433
Past progressive tense, 433
Past tense, 380
PDF files, 114, 253
Peer review, 40, 354
Periodicals, 32, 40, 95, 256, 268, 270, 323
Periods, 195, 220, 230, 241, 253, 361-362, 365-366, 394-395, 402-403, 406, 432
Personal essays, 201, 203, 205, 209, 214, 216-217, 221, 224, 228, 230-231, 234, 238-239
  examples of, 239
  features of, 205, 209
  questions for, 224, 234
  student essays, 217
Personal pronouns, 420
Photographs, 17, 48, 214, 298, 322
Photography, 16-18, 64, 240
Phrasal verbs, 432, 434
Phrase fragments, 363-364
  prepositional, 363-364
  verbal, 363-364
Phrases, 3, 32, 61, 84, 90, 92, 94, 117, 147, 182, 188-189, 222, 235, 319, 360, 363-364, 368-370, 372-373, 375-376, 381, 383, 391, 398, 401, 413, 418-419, 423-433, 438
  absolute, 398, 427
  appositive, 427-428
  infinitive, 363, 419, 427-428
  modifying, 363-364, 368-369, 372, 375-376, 427, 430-431
  participial, 363, 372, 398, 427
  prepositional, 363-364, 372-373, 375-376, 383, 391, 398, 423, 426-427, 438
plagiarism, 79, 82, 84-85, 90, 151, 245, 248, 256
Plato, 399
Plot, 127
Plural nouns, 406, 412
Plurals, 407, 412
podcasts, 118-119, 217, 239
Point of view, 38, 44, 80, 170, 353
Points, 51, 54, 88, 97, 158, 175, 179, 181, 186, 220, 257, 320, 323, 341, 355-356, 361, 394-395, 397, 402
Popular magazines, 57, 271
Positive form, 422-423
Possessive case, 386, 419-421
Possessive form, 385-386
Possessive nouns, 385-387, 406
Possessive pronouns, 385-386, 407
Possessives, 194

PowerPoint, 48, 101
Predicates, 360, 373, 413, 424-425, 429-431
Preface, 242, 263, 265, 330
prefixes, 408
Premise, 135
Prepositional phrase fragments, 364
Prepositional phrases, 363-364, 373, 375-376, 391, 398, 423, 426-427, 438
   excess use of, 391
Prepositions, 256, 360, 364, 401, 405, 413, 420, 423, 425-426, 431, 434, 438
   for ESL writers, 360, 431, 438
Present participle, 363, 380, 414, 418, 433-434, 439
Present participles, 438-439
Present perfect tense, 415, 418
Present progressive tense, 414, 433
Presentations, 47-49, 101, 354
Pretentious language, 180
Primary sources, 37
prior knowledge, 24, 95
Problems, 52, 83, 85-86, 88-89, 96, 98-99, 109, 132, 139, 147, 162, 163, 171, 191, 193, 196, 198, 271, 359, 370, 375, 378-379, 382, 384, 386-389
   open-ended, 109
Process, 9, 11, 19, 22-23, 26, 75-76, 79-80, 88, 91, 95, 104, 106, 115, 125, 127-128, 132, 135, 150, 161, 164, 176, 181, 191, 198, 203-204, 215, 217-218, 220, 223, 227, 230, 233, 259, 351, 353-356, 409
Product, 1, 47, 98, 107-108, 128, 355, 387
professor, 63-64, 99-100, 102-103, 203, 222, 254-255, 352, 370, 392, 402, 405
Progressive tenses, 416, 433
Prologue, 242, 265
Prompts, 15, 34, 97, 218-221
   fastwriting, 218-219
   listing, 218
   research, 15, 34, 221
   visual, 220
Pronouns, 194, 196-197, 235, 359-360, 362, 381, 383-389, 392-393, 406-407, 413, 419-422, 424-426, 428-430, 436, 439
   case of, 386
   demonstrative, 419, 422
   indefinite, 197, 383-384, 388, 419, 421, 424
   interrogative, 419, 421
   masculine, 392-393
   personal, 235, 383, 385-386, 388-389, 419-420, 424
   possessive, 385-387, 406-407, 419-422, 436
   reflexive/intensive, 419, 421
   relative, 360, 362, 384-386, 388-389, 406, 419-421, 428-430
Proofreading, 192-194, 196
propaganda, 38
Proper nouns, 308, 419, 424, 432
   for ESL writers, 432
Proposals, 437
Prose, 93-94, 137, 153-154, 156, 164-165, 181, 187, 204-205, 215, 220, 225, 227, 232, 356-357, 405-406
Publication dates, 314
Punctuation, 158, 193, 195-196, 250, 308, 359-361, 365-366, 368, 377, 394-397, 399, 401-403
   brackets, 158, 394-395, 402-403
   colons, 195-196, 394-395, 401-402
   commas, 195-196, 361, 365-366, 368, 377, 394-395, 397, 399, 401-403
   dashes, 195, 377, 394-395, 401-403
   ellipsis dots, 395, 403
   exclamation points, 361, 394-395, 397, 402
   guide to, 250, 308, 395
   parentheses, 394-395, 402-403
   periods, 195, 361, 365-366, 394-395, 402-403
   question marks, 361, 394-395, 402
   quotation marks, 195, 360, 394-395, 399, 402
   semicolons, 195-196, 361, 366, 394-395, 397, 401-402
Purpose, 6, 23-26, 41, 50, 64-66, 71, 74, 94, 105, 126, 130, 134, 137-138, 140-141, 144, 148, 151-152, 159-160, 162, 164-167, 172-175, 179, 190, 203, 215, 223, 228-234, 258, 285, 352-353, 423, 438

Q

Quantifiers, 419
Question marks, 43, 361, 394-395, 402
Questioning, 80

Questionnaires, 243, 281
Questions, 1-2, 5-11, 18-24, 26, 29, 45, 47-50, 65-76, 81, 90, 95-97, 101-102, 105-106, 112, 122-123, 125, 127, 129, 131-133, 142, 144, 148, 164-167, 170, 172, 181-182, 198, 202-205, 208-209, 215, 217-218, 220, 222-227, 229, 232-234, 236, 238-239, 309, 354-355, 365, 381, 384, 394-395, 406, 417, 421-422, 425-426, 437
   direct, 73-74, 105-106, 142, 394-395, 425-426
   open-ended, 23, 66-67, 71, 73-74, 81, 97, 112, 122, 172, 203, 354
   researchable, 6, 8, 10, 354
Quotation marks, 34, 83-84, 90, 92-93, 117, 153, 155, 195, 249, 256, 258, 261, 264, 269, 276-277, 281, 283, 313, 319-320, 323, 325, 360, 394-395, 399, 402
Quotations, 79, 105, 107, 112, 153-154, 156-157, 159, 169, 195, 257, 293, 308, 320, 394, 399, 402-403
   block, 157
   indirect, 402
   inserted, 403
   punctuation of, 195
   within quotations, 402

R

Radio programs, 217, 243, 281
Reader-based prose, 164-165, 225
Readers, 17, 19, 23-25, 38, 41, 63, 85, 89, 122, 128-129, 131, 135, 137-138, 140-142, 144-149, 151, 156, 162, 164-165, 170, 175, 177, 179-180, 190-191, 197, 202-203, 216, 223, 228-229, 232, 234, 244-247, 252-254, 257, 269, 288, 314, 316, 326, 355, 358, 368, 370, 380, 390, 392, 394, 404
Reading, 1-2, 24-27, 36, 48, 53, 66-68, 73, 79, 81, 95, 97, 106, 108-109, 112-114, 126, 130, 132, 144, 147, 152, 160, 164-165, 172, 180, 184, 190, 205, 208, 213, 215, 226, 236, 238, 351, 354, 357, 368, 401
reading aloud, 368
reading process, 26
Reading strategies, 24-27
Reading to write, 25
   reading, 25
   reading to write, 25
reasoning, 87, 90, 127, 130, 132, 136, 176, 204, 355, 361
Reasons, 15, 29, 38, 87-88, 92-93, 104, 122, 130-131, 137, 168-170, 184, 190, 203, 213, 338
Recordings, 78, 243, 281
Redundancy, 390-391
Reference librarian, 15, 117
References List, 307, 309, 313-315, 321, 323
reflecting, 204, 228, 233
Reflection, 205, 215, 224-225, 227-228
Reflexive pronouns, 421
Regular verbs, 415, 418
Relative clauses, 376, 384
   modifiers, 376
Relative pronouns, 360, 362, 384-386, 388-389, 406, 420-421, 428-430
remembering, 323, 411
Repetition, 390
Reports, 17, 41, 87, 117, 119, 167, 299, 387, 399, 437
Research, 1-2, 5-27, 29-31, 33-39, 41, 44-45, 47-51, 53-54, 56-57, 59-66, 69-70, 72, 75-78, 79-81, 85, 87-89, 93-94, 103-104, 108-110, 114-118, 121-122, 125-139, 141-144, 146-152, 160-162, 163, 165-168, 170-177, 180-181, 183-185, 188, 190, 192, 194, 198, 204, 221, 229, 234, 241-242, 245, 247, 251, 257, 262, 270, 276, 284, 299, 302, 307, 314, 318, 325, 336, 338, 351-358
   as evidence, 162
Research essay, 2, 10, 17-18, 23, 26, 29, 36, 78, 87, 104, 125, 127, 130, 133, 138, 146, 148-150, 152, 165, 168, 172, 175-176, 185, 190, 242, 284, 338, 351
   citing sources in, 242
   sample, 242
   topics for, 146
Research essays, 25, 76, 148, 166, 176
Research log, 109-110
Research papers, 1, 6, 29, 47, 51, 79, 121, 139, 147, 160, 163, 166, 188, 190, 192, 194, 241, 307, 325, 351-353, 358
Research prompts, 221

for personal essays, 221
Research reports, 17, 41
Research sources, 114
Research techniques, 59
research topic, 1-2, 6-7, 10, 18, 20, 69, 78, 122, 133, 314
Restrictive clauses, 389
Reviews, 37, 186, 337
Revising, 164, 171, 179-180, 190, 192, 228, 233-234, 242, 387, 409
   narrative essay, 234
   steps in, 242
Revision, 73, 151, 163-164, 166, 172, 174-175, 177, 179, 181, 201, 226, 228-229, 232-234, 239, 266, 367-371
   function of, 175
Revision strategies, 201, 233, 239
Rhetoric, 190, 223, 276, 330, 332, 351
   visual, 190
Rhetorical analysis, 352
rhymes, 10
roots, 22, 287
Run-on sentences, 195, 235, 368-369
   comma splice, 368
   correcting, 369
   fused sentence, 368-369

S

Scenes, 228-229, 234, 410
scholarly journals, 38, 57, 270
Scholarly publications, 40
Search engines, 32, 34-36, 58, 60-62, 69, 117-119, 177, 216, 258
Secondary sources, 37, 358
Self-knowledge, 239
Semicolons, 195-196, 314, 361, 366, 394-395, 397, 401-402
sentence, 25, 51, 83, 91, 97, 125, 136, 153, 155-158, 167, 184-185, 187, 194-196, 213, 225, 235, 245-247, 257, 296, 320, 323, 355, 359-379, 381, 383-389, 391, 394-395, 397, 399-400, 402, 408-409, 413, 416, 419-431, 435-437
   topic, 97, 125, 136, 225, 355, 403, 424
Sentence combining, 187
Sentence fragments, 361, 363
   phrase, 361, 363
   subordinate clause, 361
Sentences, 51, 92, 94, 147, 154, 156, 160-161, 163, 166, 184-185, 187, 192-193, 195, 209, 213, 235, 241, 245, 293, 319, 356, 359-366, 368-370, 372-373, 375, 377-379, 381-384, 387-389, 391, 394-395, 397, 399-400, 402, 409, 413, 418, 424-426, 429-431, 438
   complex, 92, 368, 413, 430-431
   compound, 187, 383, 388, 397, 413, 425, 430-431
   compound-complex, 413, 430-431
   mixed, 359, 370, 373
   pronouns in, 388
   run-on, 195, 235, 368-369
   shifts in, 370, 389
   simple, 184, 366, 382, 413, 424-425, 430
   types of, 293, 360, 362, 377, 413, 425-426, 430
   verbs in, 379, 381-382
   wordy, 388, 391
Series, 9, 191, 214, 270, 371-372, 383, 397-399
server name, 42
Setting, 65, 275, 289, 377, 392, 402
Settings, 65, 424
Sexist language, 196-197
   avoiding, 196
Shifts, 99, 186, 359, 370, 374, 389
Short stories, 2, 25, 261, 402
Simple sentences, 430
Skills, 60, 70, 81, 90, 95, 108, 130, 132, 136, 176, 351
Slang, 392
Slashes, 395
Slides, 101, 298
Sociological Abstracts, 57
Software, 33, 35, 61, 65, 78, 114, 192, 215-216, 236, 239
sources, 13-15, 23, 30-32, 35-42, 45, 47, 49, 51, 53-54, 56, 58, 62-63, 67, 79-81, 85, 88-89, 93, 104-106, 114-117, 119, 137, 151-154, 156, 160-162, 166-169, 175, 177, 179-182, 205, 218, 242-244, 248-253, 257-259, 262-263, 266, 271, 276, 280, 307-310, 314, 321, 323-324, 326, 336, 356-358
   evaluating, 41-42, 45, 104
   Internet, 13, 15, 30-32, 35, 41-42, 45, 62-63, 85,

114-115, 117, 119, 177, 258, 314, 323
organizing, 104
Speeches, 119, 243, 283
Spell-checkers, 192
spelling, 171, 192, 213, 235, 359-360, 395, 404, 406, 410
Spirit of inquiry, 351
Splices, 195-196, 359, 361, 365-369, 397-398, 400-401
States, 4, 7, 25, 35, 50-51, 69, 73, 86, 99, 102, 119, 132, 157, 177-179, 186-187, 210-211, 231, 259, 262, 268, 325, 328, 330, 336, 344, 349, 368-369, 390, 405, 417, 438
abbreviations for, 325
Statistics, 19, 38, 131, 147, 178-179, 410
Stereotypes, 394
Stereotypical terms, 393
Stock phrases, 188
Story, 18, 22, 25, 48-49, 78, 80, 92, 95, 97, 113, 127-129, 139-141, 147, 170, 180, 191, 202, 204, 207, 209, 213-215, 217-220, 222, 224-225, 227-232, 234, 239, 284, 327
Stress, 52, 70-71, 74, 229, 294, 348, 354, 356, 410
Structure, 84, 125-131, 143, 164, 172-176, 179, 187, 205, 231-232, 234, 318, 329, 353, 355-357, 404
Student essays, 217
Study, 10, 12, 24, 30, 45, 49, 52, 60, 76, 109, 126, 157, 160, 169, 184-185, 204, 260, 268, 281, 312-315, 319, 321, 323, 352, 358, 359, 371, 395, 402, 411
place, 313, 321, 395
Style, 94, 117, 151, 153, 161, 181, 192, 195, 241-305, 307-349, 357, 359-360, 368, 390, 392-393, 407, 409
Styles, 326, 393
Subject, 2, 5-7, 10-11, 13-14, 16-18, 22, 24, 26-27, 31, 33, 35, 37, 40-41, 54-57, 59, 61, 63-69, 72-73, 81, 88, 95, 101, 115, 117-118, 121-122, 138, 141, 157, 159-160, 162, 166, 176, 178, 184-185, 191, 194-195, 197, 202-205, 220, 223, 230, 233, 239, 251-252, 278-280, 315, 338, 359, 361, 363, 373, 375-376, 379, 381-385, 387, 389, 391-392, 395, 400, 413, 416-422, 424-430, 435
complex, 54, 176, 413, 430
compound, 383, 385, 413, 425, 430
Subject complements, 383, 420, 422, 426
Subject matter, 203, 205
Subject searches, 35
Subjective case, 385, 420, 422
Subjects, 6, 8, 10, 13, 17, 19, 50, 61, 65-66, 68, 71, 117, 179, 202, 239, 360, 370, 373, 375, 379, 381-385, 413, 417, 420-421, 424-426, 430-431
for interviews, 65, 68
indefinite pronoun as, 383
Subject-verb agreement, 359, 379, 381-384
simple, 382
Subjunctive mood, 374, 382, 417
Subordinate clause fragment, 361
Subordinate clauses, 368, 372, 375-377, 384, 428, 430
Subordinating conjunctions, 361, 364, 367, 377, 424, 428-430
Subordination, 359, 370-373, 375
success, 24, 130, 143, 145, 239, 244, 302
suffixes, 313, 404
Summaries, 6, 79, 105-108, 112, 138
summarizing, 81, 91-92, 243, 251
summary, 53, 86-87, 91-92, 97, 105, 112-113, 149-150, 152, 227, 276, 316
Superlative, 378, 422-423
Superlative form, 378, 422-423
supporting details, 125
Surprise, 49, 81, 123, 140, 144, 150-151, 195, 208, 223, 230, 244, 354, 424
Surveys, 30-32, 62, 67, 70-71, 74-75, 99, 243, 281
conducting, 74-75
online, 30-31, 74-75, 243
telephone, 67, 74-75
Symbols, 35, 70, 153
Synonym, 438
Synthesis, 102, 167

T
tables, 190-191, 242, 254-255, 290, 308, 321-322
Telephone surveys, 74
Tense, 220, 295, 359, 374, 379-382, 413-418, 433-434

Tenses, 379, 382, 415-416, 433
Tension, 284, 302
Terms, 13, 25, 31-36, 41, 47, 59, 83-84, 87, 108, 115, 117, 119, 132, 172, 196, 225, 257, 302, 323, 359, 376, 392-394, 407
tests, 186
textbooks, 137, 412
The MLA Handbook, 241
Themes, 153, 209
Thesis, 9, 23-24, 50-51, 105-106, 125-132, 134-137, 140-141, 144, 147-149, 161-162, 164-165, 171-177, 179, 181, 203, 205, 239, 296, 318, 342, 353-357
thesis statement, 51, 161-162
Thesis statements, 134
Thinking, 2, 7, 10, 24, 26, 41, 65, 79-81, 85, 88, 91, 97, 100, 103, 106-107, 109, 112-113, 117, 126-128, 136, 143, 149, 162, 165, 198, 201-204, 208, 213, 218, 220, 222, 224-225, 228, 230, 239, 246, 258, 353, 355, 357, 381
Time, 2-3, 5, 8-9, 13, 15-16, 18-19, 22, 26, 29, 35-36, 38, 40-41, 47-48, 50-51, 53-54, 60, 63, 67-68, 70-72, 75-76, 78, 79-80, 86, 89-90, 92-93, 95-96, 98-99, 101, 107, 113, 121, 124, 126, 135, 144, 156, 162, 163-164, 166-167, 171, 176-177, 187-189, 192, 200, 202, 207, 209-210, 214, 217-218, 220, 224-227, 229-230, 232, 234, 236-239, 266, 274, 285, 287, 291-293, 297-298, 312, 320, 323, 343, 345, 348, 352, 361, 364, 367, 371-372, 374, 376, 379-380, 383, 388, 390, 392, 401, 405, 408, 410-411, 415-416, 423, 431, 434, 437-438
order, 13, 41, 124, 144, 236, 431, 437
prepositions of, 405
Title, 3, 18, 33, 41, 55, 189, 214, 216, 225, 241, 248-250, 253-256, 259-262, 264, 266-270, 274-283, 308, 313, 315-318, 321-322, 324-326, 333-334, 338-339, 402-403, 406, 432
Title page, 241, 255, 261, 267-268, 308, 316-318, 339
Titles, 56, 65, 114, 116, 139, 249, 256, 261, 269, 307-308, 313, 323, 325, 365, 402, 404-405, 408-409, 432
Titles of works, 256, 402, 409
to be, 1, 24, 29-31, 37-38, 41, 44, 53, 60, 66, 73-74, 80-83, 92, 94, 97-98, 106-107, 110, 112-113, 117-118, 123-124, 127, 129-131, 136-137, 140, 143, 154, 157, 164, 169, 175, 179-180, 182, 184-185, 188-190, 192, 201-202, 204, 211-212, 220, 223, 225-226, 228-229, 233, 238, 244-247, 252, 254, 259, 271, 274, 289, 295, 298, 300, 320-321, 326, 342, 352, 354, 362, 370, 374-376, 380-381, 384, 390, 406, 409-410, 416-417, 421
Tone, 141, 144, 203, 212, 354-355, 357, 392
topic, 1-3, 5-13, 15, 17-24, 26, 29, 31, 33-34, 37-42, 44, 47-48, 50, 52-54, 61-70, 73, 75-78, 79, 85, 89, 92-93, 96-97, 105, 113, 115-117, 121-130, 132-138, 141-142, 144-148, 150-152, 162, 163-166, 170, 172, 174, 177, 182, 190, 197, 201, 215, 217-220, 222-225, 227, 229-230, 233, 239, 244, 251, 288, 314, 341, 353, 355-358, 403, 424
topic sentence, 125
Topic sentences, 356
Topics, 2, 6-8, 19, 29-30, 53, 64, 73, 118, 126, 132, 138, 146, 149, 179, 197, 201, 215-216, 219, 223, 227, 229
narrowing, 29
Trade books, 39
transfer, 106, 228, 409
Transitional adverbs, 366-367, 398
Transitions, 174, 235, 260
Transitive verbs, 418, 425
Turning points, 220
Type, 21, 24, 35, 65, 113, 117, 142, 161, 175, 192, 195, 209, 227-228, 255, 259, 289, 299-300, 318, 322, 337, 365, 374-376, 397, 408

U
Underlining, 79, 106, 109, 190, 256, 360, 407-409
Unity, 150, 183
URLs, 307

V
Verb phrases, 363, 418, 433
Verb tenses, 379, 382

Verbal phrases, 363, 375, 383
as fragments, 363
Verbals, 363, 414, 418
Verbs, 185-186, 359-360, 363, 370, 372-373, 378-384, 401, 413-418, 420, 422, 425-426, 428, 432-437
base form, 380, 382, 414-418, 433-434
for ESL writers, 359-360, 432, 436
forms of, 380-382, 417, 432-433
helping, 363, 380, 382, 414-415, 418, 432-434
irregular, 380, 382, 415, 418
linking, 414, 417, 426
phrasal, 432, 434
transitive and intransitive, 414, 418
Videos, 101, 243, 282, 412
Visual prompts, 220
clustering, 220
Visual rhetoric, 190
Visuals, 48
Voice, 78, 87, 93-95, 99, 106, 108, 138, 141, 144, 147, 149, 151, 168, 179-181, 184-185, 192, 202, 207, 212, 216-217, 232, 236, 239, 247, 277, 328, 355, 357, 359, 374-376, 379, 381, 391, 394, 414-418, 433
in sentences, 418
shifts in, 374

W
Web site, 6, 41, 45, 56, 75, 86, 243, 266, 272, 274, 276-278, 309-310, 315, 333, 336
accuracy, 41
source, 6, 45, 243, 266, 272, 274, 276, 315
Web sites, 37, 40, 58, 69, 79, 256
Wikipedia, 4, 6, 13, 266
Words, 3, 9-10, 23, 30-37, 43, 50, 58, 60-61, 68, 82, 86-87, 90, 92-94, 139, 148, 150, 156, 161-162, 170, 172, 182-183, 188-189, 191-192, 194, 196, 202, 204, 213-215, 225, 229, 235, 243, 256, 261, 279, 284-285, 307-308, 316, 319-320, 325, 352, 362-363, 365, 368, 371-372, 375-376, 378-380, 382-383, 385, 390-392, 394-395, 398-399, 402-405, 407-413, 421-429, 434, 436-438
concrete, 365
Wordy expressions, 391
Working knowledge, 11-14, 19, 24, 26-27, 47, 53
Works Cited, 51, 161, 241-242, 244-245, 248-252, 255, 258-259, 261-262, 304, 308
books, 51, 161, 242, 249-250, 261-262
World Wide Web, 32, 35
Writer-based prose, 164
Writers, 10, 27, 31-32, 42, 63, 87, 90-91, 93, 95-96, 106, 125-126, 134, 139, 141, 161-162, 164-165, 192-195, 197, 202, 204, 207, 220, 234, 241, 245, 262-263, 282, 324, 357-358, 359-360, 365, 367, 370-371, 373-375, 378-379, 382-383, 385-386, 389-390, 392-394, 399, 403-404, 431-432, 436, 438
writing, 1-2, 8-9, 15-18, 20, 23, 25-27, 29-31, 37-38, 41, 45, 50, 53, 60, 62-64, 69, 75, 78, 79-82, 85-86, 90-91, 95-97, 104, 106, 109, 112, 114, 121, 123-127, 130, 134-135, 137-141, 144-148, 150-152, 156, 160-162, 163-164, 166-167, 171-172, 174-177, 180-181, 184-185, 187-188, 191-192, 196-198, 199-240, 241, 245-247, 250-251, 265, 268, 277-278, 307-308, 322, 324-325, 351-354, 356-358, 359, 365, 370-371, 373, 379-380, 386, 389-393, 397, 399, 404, 407, 409, 424, 429, 434
essay exam, 9
Writing process, 26, 150, 215, 220, 233
WWW, 13, 15, 51, 60-62, 69, 119, 178-179, 277, 315, 326-327, 329, 332-333, 335-337, 349

Y
Yellow Pages, 63
YouTube, 118, 257, 279, 336